The Idea
of Phenomenology

Northwestern University

STUDIES IN *Phenomenology &*

Existential Philosophy

André de Muralt

Translated by

The Idea
of Phenomenology
Husserlian Exemplarism

GARRY L. BRECKON

NORTHWESTERN UNIVERSITY PRESS

EVANSTON   1974

Originally published by Presses Universitaires de France, Paris, under the title *L'Idée de la Phénoménologie: L'Exemplarisme Husserlien.* Copyright © 1958 by Presses Universitaires de France.

André de Muralt is Professeur ordinaire at the Université de Genève.

Contents

[vii]

Translator's Introduction

IN 1957 A YOUNG SWISS PHILOSOPHER published a careful review of Suzanne Bachelard's translation of Husserl's *Formale und transzendentale Logik* and her commentary on it.[1] While endorsing much of Bachelard's thought, the reviewer—André de Muralt—suggests that for a full understanding of Husserl's phenomenology, it is necessary to depart somewhat farther from the text of his works than Bachelard does. What is needed, he argues, is to gain a phenomenological insight into phenomenology itself by applying the method of intentional analysis to Husserl's philosophy as a whole. Two themes in particular require this treatment: the presuppositions of formal logic and the relationship between transcendental logic and phenomenology. The latter in turn requires getting clear about the status of subjective form. Concluding his critical remarks, de Muralt writes (p. 149): "Eidetic phenomenology is a concrete logic which synthesizes transcendental subjectivism and logical exemplarism in a transcendental logic."

In that review of Bachelard's work de Muralt announced the plan of *The Idea of Phenomenology*, and in its closing statement he concisely formulated a major thesis of the present work.

1. André de Muralt, "Logique transcendantale et phénoménologie eidétique," *Studia Philosophica*, XVII (1957), 140–49—a critical review of the following works: Edmund Husserl, *Logique formelle et logique transcendantale*, translated by Suzanne Bachelard (Paris: Presses Universitaires de France, 1957), and Suzanne Bachelard, *La Logique de Husserl* (Paris: Presses Universitaires de France, 1957). Bachelard's work has been translated into English by Lester E. Embree as *A Study of Husserl's "Formal and Transcendental Logic"* (Evanston, Ill.: Northwestern University Press, 1968).

Since its publication, he has written extensively on diverse topics of philosophical interest; but because *The Idea of Phenomenology* marks this author's first appearance in the English language, a few words of introduction are in order.

André de Muralt does not "do philosophy" in the rather restricted sense this phrase has acquired in the contemporary Anglo-American idiom. What he does might instead be called "philosophical history of philosophical ideas." This distinguishes him from those who do "philosophical history" of ideas from outside the domain of philosophy proper (Hannah Arendt, for example, in the sphere of political and ethical thought) and, on the other hand, from those who do "historical history" of philosophical ideas (Wilhelm Windelband, for example). By philosophical history in general, I mean an account of the "conceptual lineage" of ideas or systems of ideas, a discerning of the relations between ideas with respect to their content and their logical order of precedence, apart from the historical sequence in which they are introduced and developed. De Muralt's ambition is to carry out such "historical" inquiries in the form of a *structural analysis* of philosophy, which he regards as a rigorous philosophical discipline—that is, as a *science*.

To shed some light on the object and method of this science, we must introduce the notion of *de jure* genesis (*genèse de droit*) which de Muralt elaborates in the present work. *De jure* genesis is contrasted with *de facto* genesis. *De facto* genesis consists in the emergence and development of an idea or system of ideas in history and according to a historical sequence. *De jure* genesis, on the other hand, consists in the logically sequential arrangement of ideas or (to shift metaphors) the "topography" of the "logical space" in which an idea or system of ideas has its meaning. The "genetic method" to which de Muralt has recourse is designed to elicit this arrangement and demonstrate its necessary character. He emphasizes that this method amounts to one aspect of intentional analysis as it is expounded in Husserl's works.

De Muralt describes the object of his interest as constants in philosophy or structures which govern philosophical thought. Much of his work has been directed primarily to two abiding philosophical themes: the status of logic and the role it plays in philosophy, and the relation between the real and the ideal—together with themes implied by these. He is especially concerned with the problem of the relationship between consciousness and that of which it is conscious in logical operations. (In-

deed, in 1958, the year this book was published, he also published a work dealing with Kant's conception of consciousness.)
His interests therefore especially qualify him for a study of phenomenology, since this problem can be regarded as the leitmotiv
of Husserl's own thought.

The guiding thesis of *The Idea of Phenomenology* is thus a
"genealogical" thesis, a position regarding the *de jure* primary
categories in which the family of phenomenological concepts
has its logical basis. Corollaries of this thesis describe the logical connections between concepts which have a place in this
lineage.

At the risk of overextending our metaphor, we can say that
this guiding thesis is that the "family tree" of phenomenology
has its roots in two fundamental relational concepts, intentionality and reciprocal exemplarity. The concepts employed in
phenomenology come in pairs connected by these two relations.
Mapping the logical space in which phenomenology moves is
therefore a matter of distinguishing these pairs, explicating the
specific form taken by intentionality or exemplarity as it is
illustrated in each pair, and showing how this form derives from
the primary and most general form of the relation in question.
Ultimately, of course, the problem arises of how these two concepts are themselves related to each other.

Many discussions of phenomenology begin by focusing on
intentionality, but in most of them this concept is seen almost
exclusively in one dimension. That is, intentionality is implicitly
analyzed as simply the relation *of* subjectivity *to* the object. By
contrast, de Muralt proposes and defends an analysis of intentionality as a "two-dimensional" relation occurring on many
levels. The paradigm intentional relation is that *between* subjectivity and the object. It has two aspects, one (the descriptive)
corresponding to the direction from object to subjectivity, the
other (the transcendental) corresponding to the direction from
subjectivity to object. Both aspects of this relation must be taken
into consideration, de Muralt argues, if we are to come to an
understanding of the workings of intentionality. And such an
understanding is the goal of phenomenological investigation.

The method of this investigation is intentional analysis, and
here again we must take into account the two dimensions of
intentionality. Analysis proceeds either from the object to subjectivity or from subjectivity to the object. The first of these
directions is "first for us"; what we have at hand is what is given
in our unreflective historical experience. In particular we have,

for purposes of a "phenomenology of phenomenology," the corpus of Husserl's work and its precursors in science and philosophy.

But what is given in experience? It is in answer to this question that de Muralt introduces the notion of *exemplarity* as the reciprocal relation between the real and the ideal, between the raw fact and the pure idea. We are given science, for example, but the fact of science gains its "scientific-ness" only by virtue of its teleological reference to the idea of science. Conversely, the idea comes into existence and comes to be known (by way of ideation) only by virtue of its being realized by the fact (or, more accurately, by the series of facts which constitute the historical development of science). The relation between idea and fact is therefore an exemplary relation in both directions. The idea is the norm of the factual development of science; it is what the fact would be if the fact were able to be in reality what it is in intention. The fact of historical development is the illustration or current state of exemplification of the idea; it is what there really is of what logically ought to be. Fact and idea are connected in a dialectical process which in the course of time determines both the development of the particular sciences and, by approximation, the content of the idea of science. This is a reciprocal but not univocally reversible relation; the fact is the exemplar of the idea, but not in the same sense as the idea is the exemplar of the fact.

Intentional analysis in its descriptive dimension, then, approaches the real as an index. The fact points intentionally toward subjectivity and teleologically toward the idea. This indicating function of the real defines one last methodological duality. Analysis can proceed from the real fact toward its idea or else toward its constituting consciousness. The former direction is "progressive"; the latter is "retrogressive." The former moves toward the end intended by the fact, while the latter moves toward the origin of the fact.

With this exegetical framework, de Muralt undertakes the analysis of phenomenology. He begins with what might be described as a gloss on Chapters i and ii of Husserl's *Prolegomena to Pure Logic*, which contain in their most pristine and uncluttered form Husserl's reflections on the nature of logic, its normative character, and its relation to science. (In fact, if we accept the interpretation presented here, all of phenomenology can be viewed as an expansion on these reflections!) Formal logic as a discipline is found by Husserl to be a *Wissenschaftslehre*, a theory of science; and logic as the proper object of this discipline is the idea, in the exemplarist sense, of science in general.

From this beginning de Muralt proceeds to a study of the implications of this characterization of logic. Formal logic—the idea of science—in turn has its correlative idea. It, too, serves analysis as the index of a higher discipline: transcendental logic. Once again, the investigation moves from the index to what it indicates, from the science to its logic.

The details of these analyses and the moves between them form the substance of the work. What interests us here is their outcome, the way they shed light on phenomenology as a philosophical discipline. For an *Aufhebung* occurs, once the dualities established by the two fundamental concepts have been elaborated and applied to various derivative distinctions (sense and meaning, sign and signified, whole and part, formal apophantics and formal ontology, etc.): the two aspects of intentionality are shown to be identical and, in their identity, to define eidetic phenomenology as a logic.

This definition of phenomenology is warranted by the concept of subjective form and the role it plays in Husserl's logic. What phenomenology seeks in its search for ideas are the norms which prescribe the real. As formal logic, phenomenology discovers the normative idea of science. But this idea must itself be "normed"; the theoretical nucleus and idealizing presuppositions of formal logic must be grounded in another discipline. It is thus that formal logic motivates the advance to transcendental logic. In its role as the logic of formal logic, transcendental logic yields the subjective correlate of the form "object in general," the form which provides the necessary condition for the possibility of science in general. This subjective form is therefore the normative idea of science in a more ultimate manner than the form elicited by objective formal logic in its apophantic and ontological aspects.

Subjective form is, moreover, its own norm, and it is therefore the ultimate norm of all science and logic. This is so because the concept of subjective form coincides with that of evidence. The subjective form of what there is is the formal or eidetic aspect of the givenness of what there is; and the fundamental and originary mode of givenness is evidence. But if we are to follow Husserl, evidence has no norm outside itself; as reason, it is the ground and guarantee of its own validity. Hence evidence, or subjective form, is the ultimate norm of what there is; it is "the idea" in a definitive and perfect sense.

Rational evidence, however, is also the perfect form of experience; and experience, in the form of the *cogito*, is the act of transcendental subjectivity. It is in this act that the object as well as the subject comes to be constituted. Now, if all this is true, then the "idea of ideas" is also the constitution of the idea. Subjective form is both the idea par excellence and consciousness par excellence. The two dimensions of intentionality coincide at this ideal level, since both are encompassed by the rubric "subjective form." The transcendental subject in its function or *Leistung* not only dictates but *is*, in an ideal sense, the form of the object in general. And this form is the proper object of logic.

Finally, if the goal of eidetic phenomenology is to discover and elucidate the ultimate grounds of what there is, it must be said that phenomenology comes to its fruition in transcendental logic. This will be a concrete logic in both a negative and a positive sense. First, it does not abstract the "analytic" or structural aspect of its object in the manner of objective formal logic. It is a logic of experience, of the living dialectic in which both subject and object come to be constituted and the idea comes to be realized. Second, it is concrete in the sense that its subject is the one absolute concretum, the exercise of intentionality in the *cogito*.

We can summarize the outcome of this line of thought as follows. The *cogito* is the function of the ego in experience. The formal aspect of this function is the constituting of subjective form simultaneously with the constituting of the object in general. The object has the grounds of its validity in the evident character of this constitution, whereas this evidence is self-grounding. The reflective constituting of subjective form is transcendental logic. And since transcendental logic is essentially self-normative, it is tantamount to eidetic phenomenology, the perfect form to which the imperfect, historically conditioned embodiments of phenomenology aspire.

If de Muralt is successful in the present work, then, he has accomplished the undertaking proposed in his review of Bachelard's work. He has shown eidetic phenomenology to be a concrete transcendental (subjective formal) logic in which the thematization of the two dimensions of intentionality—transcendental subjectivism and logical exemplarism—are synthesized.

Properly understood, the title of this volume is uniquely appropriate. It conveys the whole multifaceted theme of the work. This is so in at least three senses. (1) Although this is not as natural in English, the title connotes "the notion of the idea as it occurs in phenomenology." As we have seen, a fundamental theme of the work is the status of the idea in its exemplary relationship with the fact, with what there "really is." (2) "The idea of phenomenology" can also be taken in a loose, colloquial sense to mean the general notion of phenomenology, what it is by nature. This, of course, is the ostensible subject of the work. (3) Most important, the phrase can be taken in the strict exemplarist sense. Accordingly, the book is about ideal phenomenology, the normative idea of phenomenology, the form and end of a certain way of doing philosophy. In short, the book is about the ideal (ideally anticipated) outcome of the return "to the things themselves."

For phenomenology not only intuits ideas, it *is* an idea. Ideal phenomenology is not only an end to be achieved, and therefore something which is not really included in a currently formulated system of philosophy. It is a motif borne within and sustained by the historical development of *de facto* phenomenology (or "phenomenologies," including science and philosophy generally). Thus the *de jure* genetic investigation of phenomenology is a means of eliciting and explicating its "immanent end." The phenomenology of phenomenology yields phenomenology in the form of an idea.

An astonishingly bold claim is made for this idea. This is the claim that phenomenology in its ideal form is the innate end to which all of science, all of logic, and ultimately all knowledge and all of man's striving for knowledge is directed. This is no accident or adventitious privilege on the part of the thought initiated by Husserl. It is rather a consequence of the purpose in which phenomenology originates, the purpose of formulating the structure of the constitution of the world's sense for us (cf. below, p. 5). The teleological end of universal history is identical with the product of transcendental constitution in general, and both are to be reached by us only in an ideal form by way of the eidetic and reflective procedure of phenomenology. The most perfectly and universally exemplary idea is that of consciousness giving itself its own sense by rationally constituting the object in general—in other words, by doing phenomenology in its ideal form as transcendental logic. (One is reminded here of Aristotle's first mover, thought thinking itself—presumably by doing Aristotelian first philosophy.)

In retrospect, then, the book can also be read as a gloss on Appendix IV of Husserl's *Crisis* ("Philosophy as Mankind's Self-

Reflection; the Self-Realization of Reason," which appears as
§ 73 of the German edition), which represents the culmination
of the reflections on science and logic with which phenomenology was historically launched. It would not be stretching de
Muralt's text too far, it seems to me, to consider this Appendix
and the above-mentioned Chapters I and II of the *Prolegomena*
as forming an exemplary pair whose dialectical relationship is
worked out in what de Muralt (following Bachelard) calls *the*
book of Husserl, *Formal and Transcendental Logic.*

Finally, we must clarify our observation that de Muralt does
not "do philosophy." For in *The Idea of Phenomenology* he does
indeed do philosophy, on his own terms, in the form of phenomenology. But he does so expressly in order to gain an understanding of philosophy/phenomenology itself. This understanding eschews criticism; its conceptual apparatus is read out of
Husserl's works, only to be read back into them, transmuted by
the exemplarist point of view. The result is a study of phenomenology with a unique perspective. While this perspective may
be challenged, it cannot be ignored by those interested in phenomenology.

Most studies of Husserl's thought do one or the other of two
things. First, they may view phenomenology one aspect at a
time or one developmental period at a time; the product is a
discrete series of studies more or less unified by a single line of
thought. Second, a particular concept may be singled out and
traced in its development through all of Husserl's work; this pro-
duces studies of Husserl's concept of intuition, of constitution,
of the *cogito,* and so forth. The peculiarity of de Muralt's approach is that it views all of phenomenology under the aspect
of a single category which is held to be its unique unifying factor. The result is an exposition, but it is also in a seductive
way an argument—an argument for the soundness of the exposition and thus for the fundamental status accorded its basic
concepts.

The Idea of Phenomenology cannot fail to leave the reader
with a sense of having participated in a sympathetic and master-
ful criticism of a work of art. Indeed, a modestly proposed corollary of the exemplarist viewpoint is that phenomenology has its
roots in the philosophy art (cf. below, p. 368). With reference
to Plotinus and Husserl, André de Muralt writes that "each of-
fers us a thought with a rare quality of beauty, one by the universality of his mystic vision, the other by the admirable coher-

ence of his logic. In each case unity begets beauty." [2] It is the merit and beauty of *The Idea of Phenomenology* to enhance the beauty of Husserl's thought by exhibiting its unity.

II

The Idea of Phenomenology is a difficult book to read— inevitably so, since it deals with difficult matters in a painstakingly thorough manner. Phenomenological literature is not light reading at best, and the problem is compounded here by the difficulties of moving among three languages and the ways of thinking embodied in them. The original work represents something of a hybrid French and German literary style and a similarly cosmopolitan way of thinking. To eliminate this style altogether would be to alter the sense of the work; to preserve it entire would result in a volume unreadable by native speakers of English. To do either would be unconscionable. Thus I have tried, in the translation, to ameliorate the difficulty of the original, but only where this can be done without misrepresenting its content.

A few observations about the way the book has been rendered in English may smoothe the reader's way somewhat. These observations can be organized under a few general headings. First, however, it should be noted that—unlike some writers in the phenomenological tradition—de Muralt uses unconventional linguistic devices sparingly. The reader will thus do well to take special notice when he does use them.

  1. Only one outright neologism appears in the original of this work, the transitive verb *normer*. I have translated this word with the improvised English cognate "to norm." The word means roughly "to provide or serve as a norm or standard for," but this meaning is elaborated in the course of the work. (The derivative form *normation* also appears and is translated "normation.") The word *terme* as it is used in this text is nearly a neologism, since it acquires a sense quite different from that which it has in ordinary French (which is roughly equivalent to the varied use of "term" in English). The basic sense it takes on here is that of a boundary or limit. The most nearly similar English word is

2. De Muralt, "La Solution husserlienne du débat entre le réalisme et l'idéalisme," *Revue philosophique*, CXLIX (1959), 552.

"terminus," which has therefore been adopted in this translation.

2. The work also contains at least two words that are equivocal in an important way. One is the notorious *sens,* which I have generally rendered as "sense" (see below). The French word is also ordinarily used to denote direction, however, and so the author's conflation of "sense" and *"Richtung"* is quite plausible in French, even though it is not as apparent in English. Another such word is *actuel,* which means both "actual" (by contrast with potential) and "temporally present or current." Where it is clearly indicated by the context which meaning is intended, I have translated the word accordingly. Where this is not clear, and where the author means to play on the ambiguity, I have packed both senses into one phrase (e.g., "presently actual").

3. Many of the more or less technical terms the author uses are open-textured in French in a way which makes them not at all congruent with any English term. Sometimes this open texture contributes to their sense in the work. The most well known of these is the noun *vécu,* which derives from *vivre* and is used in preference to *expérience* in order to designate experience as it is lived (cf. the German *Erlebnis* and *Erfahrung*). I have simply used "experience" to render *vécu,* including the French word in brackets where it seems necessary to do so to make the meaning clear. Another equally important word in this connection is *devenir,* used as a noun. This is the substantive use of the French verb ordinarily translated "become," but it also carries the connotations of growth and development. I have for the most part translated this word as "development," since this most nearly captures the sense in which the author initially and usually uses the word. But the sense of "becoming" should be kept in mind when this word is encountered. Indeed, especially in §§ 56 and 60, *devenir* is sometimes translated as "becoming" in order to fit the context, even at the expense of continuity with other appearances of the word. Finally, we should point out that the word *valeur,* while it is roughly coextensive in meaning with the English "value," takes on a special sense in this book and should not be conceived of as "worth." In such expressions as "value act," value is associated in a general way with the notion of a conferring of meaningfulness or significance of any kind.

4. I have not hesitated to use unusual words that have been introduced in the phenomenological tradition, even when they have not gained universal acceptance. Cases in point are "factical," "irreal," "dator" (for *donatrice, gebend*), and "originary."

The latter warrants special mention. The English "original" has been restricted by common usage to its sense of temporal priority with respect to a class of things of the same kind, and this makes it unsuitable for much of what Husserl and de Muralt want to say. The problem does not arise so critically in French, since that language has three words which translate into English as "original." The word I have rendered as "originary" is *originaire*, which is ordinarily used in compound expressions with the sense of someone or something originating in or from ("originally coming from") something or somewhere (*originaire de . . .*). In short, the stress is on "origin." This is the sense in which I have used "originary," although it gains a special nuance when used in the context of *de jure* genesis.

5. A problem that arises for all translators of philosophical works is that of rendering the various French and German expressions belonging to the family of words connoting meaning in some sense. Here the problem arises especially with regard to *sens* and *signification*. It is impossible to be consistent with the corpus of Husserl scholarship on this point, since this corpus itself is inconsistent. I have chosen to use "sense" for *sens* (which is generally the counterpart of Husserl's *Sinn*) and "meaning" for *signification* (generally the counterpart of Husserl's *Bedeutung*). For the way in which de Muralt formulates the distinction and relation between sense and meaning, see especially p. 17 and p. 130, n. 12, below. The connection between *signifier* and *signification* should also be kept in mind by the reader. Where *signifier* is used in a technical sense, it has been translated "signify." This translation preserves the obvious connection of this notion with that of the sign, but it masks the equally close connection between "signify" and "meaning." These interconnections become especially important in § 5.

6. One uncommon device that the author does use occasionally is unusual hyphenation. When this occurs, it is for one of two reasons. (*a*) It may indicate a conflation of two ideas into one; thus, for example, "idea-norm" and "logic-philosophy." In such cases the hyphen is used to mark the fact that the two notions have been shown to be identical from the exemplarist point of view. (This is also done, in a rather neat way, with the improvised word "idea(liza)tion.") (*b*) It may also be intended to draw attention to the etymology of a word and its implications. As examples of this we have "pre-scribe," "pro-blem," *Auf-fassen*. (In hyphenating "pre-scribe," for example, the author emphasizes the etymological sense of the word—"to write out

beforehand"—by contrast with the so-to-speak "prescriptive" or normative sense in which it is generally taken. Similarly, "problem" brings out the seldom noted origin of the word "problem" in the Greek πρό + βλῆμα, "that which is thrown before you.")[3] In either case, the reader will do well to heed the hyphen.

III

DE MURALT HAS PROVIDED this work with an invaluable scholarly apparatus, including copious references to Husserl's major writings. For the sake of brevity I have used the following abbreviations in these references. (Complete publication data for these and other works appear in the Bibliography at the end of the book.)

CM: *Cartesian Meditations*
Crisis: *The Crisis of European Sciences and Transcendental Phenomenology: An Introduction to Phenomenological Philosophy*
EJ: *Experience and Judgment*
FTL: *Formal and Transcendental Logic*
Ideas: *Ideas: General Introduction to Pure Phenomenology*
Idées: *Idées directrices pour une phénoménologie*
LI: *Logical Investigations*

References to *Idées,* Paul Ricoeur's translation of *Ideas,* are more specifically to Ricoeur's excellent footnotes.

In references to Husserl's works, the page number of the English translation is followed in parentheses by the page number of the German edition listed in the Bibliography. Thus, for example, "*EJ,* p. 88 (83)" refers to page 88 of *Experience and Judgment,* a passage which is to be found in its original form on page 83 of the edition of *Erfahrung und Urteil* published by Claassen Verlag in 1954.

The Bibliography at the end of this volume appears substantially as it did in its original form. For the reader whose interest is whetted by the present work, I have added a list of the author's publications. Many of these explore themes introduced in *The Idea of Phenomenology.* In view of the admittedly inadequate

3. Cf. Johan Huizinga, *Homo Ludens: A Study of the Play Element in Culture* (Boston: Beacon Press, 1950), pp. 115, 148, on this origin and a rather different interpretation of it.

treatment given the epochē in this work, the article "Epochē—Malin génie—Théologie de la toute-puissance divine" (1966) is particularly apposite. Indeed, it is an excellent piece of work in its own right, and one to which de Muralt attaches great importance.

To the extent that was feasible in translation, the author's thorough analytical index to this work has been preserved intact.

IV

CREDIT IS DUE TO the many people who have expedited this work of translation. First mention must go to Karen, my wife, without whose encouragement, assistance, and forbearance the work could not have been done.

Several of my friends and colleagues have helped in various capacities with the preparation of this volume, and they can only be acknowledged collectively. I must expressly thank Joseph Chevalier, however, whose guidance through the complexities of the French language was most helpful. Those at Northwestern University Press who have been associated with the book also deserve recognition, notably Virginia Seidman for her indispensable editorial work.

Ultimately the translator—along with anyone else who might benefit from the translation—is indebted to two men, Professor André de Muralt and Professor James M. Edie. The former provided an outstanding text to work from as well as personal encouragement in his correspondence with me, and it was at the latter's instigation and with his help that I undertook to translate the book.

GARRY L. BRECKON

The Idea
of Phenomenology

(A mon père)

Introduction

§ 1. *The notion of intentionality and the interpretation of phenomenology*

THE NOTION OF INTENTIONALITY as it is used by Husserl is familiar to nearly everyone. After Brentano's descriptive psychology and Sartre's critical remarks concerning knowledge as "assimilation,"[1] we can all define intentionality as the constitutive tendency of transcendental subjectivity toward the object. Intentionality thus appears as the tendency toward a terminus, a teleology. The object appears, correlatively, as the telos, the terminal unity which focuses the constituting consciousness. From this definition we might be led to believe in a Husserlian realism—a realism of consciousness ordered to being, a realism of being as correlate of consciousness. As a matter of fact, the *one-dimensional* notion of intentionality is indefensible in the face of such an interpretation.

  1. *Intentionality does not have just one dimension.* First let us note that we speak of an intentional consciousness and also

1. F. Brentano, *Psychologie vom empirischen Standpunkt* (Leipzig: Duncker & Humblot, 1874); cf. L. Gilson, *La Psychologie descriptive de Franz Brentano* (Paris: Vrin, 1955). J.-P. Sartre, *Situations*, I (Paris: Nouvelle Revue Française, 1947). [The reference to Sartre's work is evidently more specifically to his brief essay of 1939, "Une Idée fondementale de la phénoménologie de Husserl: L'Intentionnalité." This essay is readily available in the helpful edition of *La Transcendance de l'ego* prepared by Sylvie Le Bon (Paris: Vrin, 1966), in which it appears as Appendix V (pp. 109–13).—TRANS.]

of the object as an intentional unity. But consciousness and object cannot be intentional in the same respect. The teleological tendency which connects them is one and the same, even though it is movement and "shifting." [2] But transcendental subjectivity is its origin or point of departure, while the object is its telos or point of arrival.[3] Consequently, intentionality can be considered in two ways: either in the direction from subjectivity to object, from origin to telos, or else in the direction from object to subjectivity, from telos to origin. We propose calling these two dimensions the "transcendental-phenomenological" and the "descriptive-phenomenological." Intentional analysis, being precisely the phenomenologist's investigation along one or the other of these dimensions, also takes these two names.

2. *The object is not the existing object of common sense.* Moreover, the object of which Husserl speaks is an object suspended by the epochē and reduced to its pure sense.[4] Hence it cannot be the object in its material externality, the object whose existence common sense directly affirms. Existence or being is a stratum of meaning in the total objective sense, a being character (*Ideas,* § 103) which, like any other meaningful stratum, needs to be transcendentally constituted. The correlation between consciousness and object is therefore more precisely a correlation between consciousness and objective sense, and transcendental constitution is a sense-giving (*FTL,* p. 10 [9 f.]). The duality we have just noted still obtains, and here too the two dimensions of intentionality—transcendental and descriptive— are to be distinguished.

2. *Verschiebung* (*FTL,* p. 176 [157]). [A list of abbreviations used in citations of Husserl's works is contained in the Translator's Introduction, together with an account of the format used for page references in this translation. See p. xxii.—TRANS.]

3. This is the distinction between *Abzielen* and *Erzielen* (*EJ,* pp. 83 [88], 200 f. [236]; *LI,* p. 563 [II/1, 379]); between *Urstiftung* and *Endstiftung* (*Crisis,* p. 72 [73]); between *Vorform* and *Endform* (*Crisis,* p. 70 [71]); in short, between *Ursprung* and *Telos* in general.

4. We will give no special exposition of the epochē strictly speaking. It is assumed that the reader is familiar with this operation of "neutralization" of the real object, of reduction of real science to its pure sense in and by a historical experience (*FTL,* p. 10 [9]) which consists in living the striving of science from within (*CM,* p. 9 [50]; *Crisis,* pp. 70 f. [72]) in order to participate vitally in its teleology (*Crisis,* pp. 70 f. [72 f.]). On the other hand, we will study in detail the operation of the transcendental reduction properly so called, the reduction to the ego.

3. *Phenomenology is not a description but a logic.* The profound significance of phenomenology is accordingly not that it is to be a realistic description of the real world; instead it is to be a logic, a science of meanings, which has no immediate relation to the real world of common sense but which formulates the structure of the constitution of this world's sense for us. This definition of phenomenology as logic is a necessary consequence of the epochē and of the phenomenological reduction. Phenomenology is a science of senses, as classical logic was a science of second intentions. It studies intentionality which reflects itself, intentionality at the second level (*FTL*, p. 112 [99]), which is constituted in transcendental self-consciousness. In this reflective process, the immediate "naïve" contact with the world seems to be lost—or at least to become less and less immediate.

4. *Phenomenology as logic is likewise structured according to the two dimensions of intentionality.* Now we can understand the constant ambivalence of Husserl's phenomenology. Intentionality, being the reciprocal relation of consciousness and sense, is found again in phenomenology properly so called—the phenomenology of meanings. In its ultimate eidetic form as logic, then, phenomenology is apparently twofold. Formal logic is at once formal *apophantics* and formal *ontology*. It is apophantics insofar as it considers the judgment in its meaning, which is given originarily in the evidence of distinctness. And it is ontology insofar as it considers, within the judgment, the categorial object which is given intuitively in the evidence of clarity (cf. below, § 32). The constitutive criticism of logic is also twofold, depending on whether it is employed in intentionally criticizing the identity (being in itself) of predicative meanings or the a priori truth (in itself) of categorial objectivities (cf. below, §§ 34–38). Finally, transcendental logic itself has two formulations. One, that of *Formal and Transcendental Logic*, moves from formal logic to transcendental logic, from the judgment to transcendental consciousness. The other, that of *Experience and Judgment,* takes an opposite course—from consciousness or prepredicative experience to the universal judgment (cf. below, § 19).

A complete elucidation of the notion of intentionality is therefore needed if we are to give an account of phenomenology in all its multiplicity and richness. The traditionally received one-dimensional conception of intentionality necessarily leads to an interpretation of phenomenology that is too narrow.

§ 2. *Considerations of method*

BUT THIS BRIEF EXPOSITION of Husserlian intentionality takes the form of a conclusion; it is not immediately given as evident. It is the telos of an intentional analysis which undertakes to set it forth in its intuitive character. Husserl provides all the elements necessary for such an analysis, and it is up to us to use them in such a way as to bring out their deeper meaning. Thus the problem of method arises.

Husserl's thought followed a historical itinerary, of course. It sought out its way, and to this end it proceeded by empirical "gropings." Are we to engage in a historical study, a sort of "intellectual biography" of the master? In that case, we would have to investigate all the influences—conscious and unconscious, voluntarily received and passively undergone—which went into the formation of Husserl's thought. This investigation of the historical totality is impossible, in fact and in principle. Instead we must examine Husserl's work itself (especially the work that was published, and hence sanctioned, by Husserl), and we must carry out a rigorous internal criticism with respect to this work.[5] In a word, we have to abandon the idea of a positive historical investigation and deliberately initiate a systematic critique of the meaning of Husserlian phenomenology. Hence we must suspend the historical facticity of Husserl's intellectual life and, following the deepest intention of Husserlian method, work on the pure meaning of the doctrine.

Our method is nevertheless a genetic method. It tries to uncover the "logical" sequence of the notions used by Husserl and bring to light the necessity of their succession. The genesis thus formulated is therefore a *de jure* genesis [*genèse de droit*]. It "brackets" the *de facto* genetic order (i.e., the history), and by reflective analysis it clarifies the originary and perfect notion (entelechy) of intentionality by explicating its secondary and derived forms in their various degrees of originality. By considering, for example, the various intentional pairs, such as sign and

5. In other words, we must extend to those of Husserl's major works which were published during his lifetime the method already fruitfully employed by Mlle. Bachelard in her commentary on *FTL*, *A Study of Husserl's "Formal and Transcendental Logic*," trans. Lester E. Embree (Evanston, Ill.: Northwestern University Press, 1968), p. xxxi.

signified, part and whole, potency and act, factical example and ideal exemplar, our method succeeds little by little in eliciting from its imperfect forms the perfect form of intentionality, which is precisely that of transcendental constitution. It therefore puts into operation the rational method of practical approximation to the idea, which is discussed in *Formal and Transcendental Logic* (p. 7 [6]). This method contrasts with the method of gropings and historical cross-checkings, which is doomed forever to multiplicity. It thereby manifests the intentional unity of Husserl's phenomenology, which is constituted as an idea through its various factual expressions (as well as through its various prefigurations in previous transcendental philosophies)—a unity that is pre-scribed a priori by its purpose of setting forth a radical foundation, a consciousness which constitutes itself, and, correlatively, an ultimate science which norms itself.[6]

As a reflective and teleological method which treats of *de jure* genesis, our method is simply intentional analysis in its descriptive-phenomenological dimension. What the reader will find here is not a historical study but a doctrinal study. It represents the intentional analysis of phenomenology itself; it seeks to set forth the idea of intentionality and, correlatively, the idea of phenomenology. This latter idea, the telos intended by the various formulations that Husserl gave of his own thought, is a logic for the phenomenology of being. And here one of the intentional pairs we mentioned above assumes major importance: factical example and ideal exemplar. Every object in general is the factical example of its idea, which is reciprocally the object's ideal exemplar.[7] Likewise, every science in

6. *Crisis* sharply contrasts the historical method "in the ordinary sense" with the teleological method (p. 70 [71]). Cf., in general, §§ 9, 14, and 15 of *Crisis* on these points of method.
7. To the ideal, then, is opposed the real [*réal*]; to the essence (eidos), the factical. We use the words "real" and "factical" to indicate the character of "lesser reality" which attaches to the empirical object as opposed to the character of "absolute reality" which specifies the idea or essence. Further, the real [*réal*] must be distinguished from the real [*réel*]. The latter word expresses the reality of the psychological life of consciousness, which constitutes the factical or real [*réal*] object as the intentional unity of the constituting consciousness. Cf. below, §§ 6–14, 46–51. [I have used the English "real" throughout to render both *réal* and *réel*. Where the context does not make it clear which "real" is meant, the French word is inserted in brackets.—TRANS.]

general and every *de facto* philosophy is the factical example of phenomenology—which is reciprocally their ideal exemplar. This exemplary quality of phenomenology manifests its normative character and defines its function as a logic.

Hence our intentional inquiry must first of all discover the idea of science (Part I). This investigation will enable us to take up the analytical doctrines of the *Logical Investigations* in the light of phenomenological thought as a whole and thus to define the idea in general in its manifold aspects (limit, signified, whole, as-if, act, exemplar). Then, from the idea of science, the inquiry proceeds to the science of the idea—which is precisely logic (Part II). From this point on, the term "exemplarism" qualifies phenomenology in an essential way. Phenomenology is formulated on a first level as an objective formal logic, the analytic norm and objective form of every *de facto* science, which integrates the entire contribution of classical logic (Part III). However, this form is intentionally normative. That is, its normative character needs to be legitimized and constituted in transcendental subjectivity, like every object in general. The transcendental reduction will bring us, then, to the originary sense-giving by intentionality. Phenomenology will thereby explicitly take on its constitutive and transcendental value. And since intentionality is thematized as an idea in the form of evidence or reason, the phenomenology of intentionality is precisely the transcendental phenomenology of the idea of sense-giving in general—that is, the eidetic phenomenology of consciousness in general. Finally, evidence and reason are the eidetic forms of all constitution in general; they are the subjective forms or synthetic norms of every object in general. Hence they define eidetic phenomenology ultimately as transcendental logic (Part IV and Conclusion). This is the *idea of phenomenology*, the telos of our intentional analysis of Husserlian phenomenology. It defines phenomenology as concrete logic, and it represents the ultimate expression of what we call "Husserlian exemplarism."

WE WISH TO EXPRESS OUR APPRECIATION here to those who have contributed to the appearance of this work: Professors Daniel Christoff, Paul Ricoeur, and Pierre-Maxime Schuhl, as well as all those who have, by their conversation or their books, enabled us to enrich our knowledge of Husserl.

PART I

The Idea of Science

1 / The Discovery of the Idea

§ 3. *Descriptive dialectic of science: the necessity of an invariant*

LET US TAKE ANY SCIENCE AT ALL, considered in its historical facticity. The essential character manifested by the science is its continuous development toward greater exactness and precision. It exhibits a current state of realization and tends toward a more perfect state of realization and completeness. The current state of realization is therefore an essentially relative one for the science, intermediate between a state that is less perfect and one that is more perfect.

The current state of realization, even though it is imperfect, still exhibits a certain (relative) perfection. It is in any case a more complete state than the one which immediately preceded it. The immediately prior state thus tends toward the greater perfection which the current state represents for it. This greater perfection is therefore in a way the terminus [*terme*] or end (Husserl uses the Greek word *telos,* which means terminus or end) toward which the science was tending in its prior state. Furthermore, description grasps the science in a continuous development, so the current state of perfection is not a definitive state of perfection. Hence the current state, too, tends toward a further state of more complete perfection. The state to come, the future moment, represents for the present state a terminus or goal toward which it tends and in relation to which it is defined as a point of departure. There is thus the same relation between the future state (the more perfect completion) of a science and its current state as there is between the current state and the prior state of this same science. Each moment of a science is reciprocally a terminus (telos)—hence a perfection to be reached—and a point of departure for a new striving. The science progresses in this way, from point of departure to telos and from telos to point of departure, realizing an increasing perfection of exactness and precision.

But we are looking for a structure, a stable and necessary element. So far we have only a flowing succession of elements, based one on another in the very rhythm of their development. We would have the solution if, instead of having to be satisfied with establishing descriptively that science progresses by gradually realizing an increasing perfection, we had some reason to say that science realizes the perfect knowledge at which it aims. In other words, the solution is to posit an absolute and definitive perfection toward which a science tends and in which alone it can come to rest as its completion. This perfection at which the science aims is therefore conceived as an idea: the idea of a science which realizes, in conformity with an absolute truth, the knowledge of its own object. We can admit this idea as a working hypothesis or "assumption" and see whether it will be verified (*CM*, p. 8 [49]).

We are saying, then, that science tends toward its perfect realization—which as such is simply the full realization of the idea of genuine science. In fact, genuineness is the terminus at which every activity of reason aims, in whatever way this reason is objectified. And since, by definition, this terminus stands opposed to the reality of the science's development, it can only be ideal (*FTL*, p. 28 [25]). The idea of genuineness or of genuine science is obviously defined here as a final terminus which polarizes the strivings of science. It is not currently or adequately realized. We must therefore either realize it in fact, by actually carrying on the striving of science at the risk of never actually reaching its terminus, or else ideally elicit its essential possibility (*Wesensmöglichkeit*), which emerges in an originary reflective awareness [*prise de conscience*] of the sense of science.[1] This

1. *FTL*, pp. 9 f. (8 f.). It can be seen from this that the notion of idea is close to that of sense (*Sinn*). Actually, *Sinn* is the tendency toward the idea—the sense of science, for example, being precisely to attain this ideal genuineness. Husserl also renders this with the more descriptive expression *Richtung* (direction); cf. *LI*, pp. 550 (II/1, 362), 554 (II/1, 366); *Ideas*, pp. 364 f. (318); *LI*, pp. 588 (II/1, 414), 496 (II/1, 299); *Crisis*, p. 171 (174). The sense of

reflective awareness clarifies the idea of science, though it does not effectively realize it. That is, it elicits in all its ideal purity an idea which is already pre-scribed (*vorgezeichnet*) in the process of its partial realization. This is why the reflective awareness is a clarification (*Klärung*) which has the character of a new sense formation (*neue Sinngestaltung*). And the procedure which ends by formulating the idea on the basis of its partial realization is called "in a word, then: critical discrimination between the genuine and the spurious" (*FTL*, p. 10 [9]).

The idea of perfection is what orients all scientific striving for knowledge; the striving tends toward it as if impelled by a vital instinct.[2] It is the end idea (*Zwecksinn, Zweckidee*) of scientific striving. We have "proof" that this is the case insofar as we know that science proceeds by perfecting itself through a progression in which each moment represents at the time a final result—but a transitory result, since it is destined to become a new basis for progress. More precisely, it is transitory only in its value as terminus and not in its scientific value. New scientific discoveries do not purely and simply negate those which preceded them. They negate them as final and definitive results, but they exploit them and assume their value for knowledge. This is how science gets its character as a constant revision of acquired positions, which is at bottom simply the manifestation of its critical spirit. No discovery is the most exact or most true, and the current state of the science is the one in which we place our confidence (*EJ*, p. 32 [27]; *LI*, pp. 246 f. [I, 256 f.]; cf. *EJ*, p. 261 [313 f.]). The ideal remains ideal, but it is realized ad infinitum through a series of convergent asymptotic approximations.[3] This perpetual development toward a "truer" truth or a "more absolute" absolute, so to speak, expresses the internal dynamism of scientific knowledge and defines its very meaning: the idea of genuine science. It expresses the

science thus manifests the fundamental connection of all the moments of science: ". . . the idea of a unitary science, as a *final idea explicated in evidence* and enabling us to understand that what this mathematics unites, in the manner characteristic of a theoretical technique, belongs together of necessity, by virtue of a congruity of sense having its basis in that clarified idea" (*FTL*, p. 76 [67]).

2. *Crisis*, p. 74 (75). On this vital instinct of growth and preservation, see the notable text of *EJ*, pp. 288–91 (347–52), esp. p. 291 (351). Cf. also *CM*, pp. 66 f. (100 f.); *Crisis*, p. 13 (11).

3. *CM*, p. 12 (53). The word "asymptotic" is, of course, mathematical in origin. Cf. what Husserl says about knowledge in the full sense in *LI*, pp. 61 f. (I, 14).

constructive aspect of science. Science is constructed by the generations of scientists who apply themselves to building it as if to the erection of actual structures (*praktische Gebilde*).[4] Knowledge thereby takes on the specific character of a practical interest in technical realization.[5] By this approach, we will for the first time be able to verify the idea of science which we admitted as a hypothesis.

§ 4. *The idea of science as limit of its progressive realization*

WE CAN VERIFY THIS IDEA by virtue of the fact that every practical realization implies limits, which are precisely the limits of the realizing capacity (*Crisis*, pp. 25 f. [22 f.]). But this capacity increases in the course of mankind's history. Hence, if there is a practical limit to a normal process of realization, this limit recedes with the progress of mankind. The ideal it represents seems to have only a certain "lead" on the current state of its realization. Thus what we have here seems not to be a true limit, since it moves away ad infinitum precisely in keeping with the course of history. If, then, we wish to keep a limit form (*Limes-gestalt*) (*Crisis*, p. 26 [23]), with respect to which the temporal realizations are mere approximations (*bloss ungefähres; Crisis*, p. 25 [22]), this limit must be conceived as an

4. *FTL*, p. 9 (8). This immediately directs our thoughts to knowledge as *activity* [*faire*]. In *EJ* (pp. 200–203) Husserl gives us the most explicit parallel between knowledge and activity. There he describes the structural analogy between the striving of knowledge (*erkennendes Streben*) and realizing activity. He defines knowledge as *Handlung, abzielende Tätigkeit* (*EJ*, p. 202 [238]). Theoretical knowledge is a theoretical *praxis*, the art of theories (*Crisis*, p. 111 [113]; cf. p. 133 [135]). He sees it as a practical *Leistung*, the object of which is *geistige Gebilde* (*Crisis*, pp. 117 f. [120]). This *geistiges Hantieren* (*Crisis*, p. 27 [24]) is motivated by an end idea which as such holds sway over every ideal practical discipline (*CM*, p. 7 [48]). We will encounter this important notion again below.

5. The word "technique" (*technē*) is taken in two senses by Husserl, one favorable and one pejorative. In the favorable sense, technique designates knowledge which is idealized and mathematized but which keeps alive the consciousness of the original sense of knowledge, a sense that roots it in the *Lebenswelt*. In the pejorative sense, technique designates knowledge which forgets this origin, in which case technization takes place.

infinite idea. It is indeed a limit, in the sense that it defines the meaning and structure of science and specifies a terminus or telos of absolute perfection. But it is an infinite limit, since it is not realizable adequately in the present moment but only asymptotically in the course of time. Just as an asymptotic curve meets the coordinate at infinity, so the idea is realized at infinity. That is, an ever closer approximation tends to catch up with the idea without ever completely reaching it. The "lead" which the ideal has over the real is reduced little by little, to be sure. But it subsists ideally and so always remains the motive of an ultimate striving. The rational method of practical approximation to the idea is ideal and infinite.[6] So it evidently amounts to the same thing to say that this limit idea is attainable at infinity or that it is not attainable at all.

Therefore, the limit idea of science is precisely progress, i.e., development; and this development is seen to be thematized in an infinite idea (§ 13, below). The limit idea enables us to transcend the static (finite) character of the real limit. In development itself, the limit idea is the "mobile clue" (*beweglichen Leitfaden; CM,* p. 54 [90]) of which Husserl speaks. All the Husserlian ideas may be understood as limits—limits which are ideal and hence infinite, which limit not really but ideally (ad infinitum). The limit idea is the idealization of the real limit and the objective thematization of its perpetual progress. But if "limit" is taken in the sense of real boundary or limit *point* (*Grenzpunkt*), it obviously cannot be identified with "idea."[7]

§ 5. *The idea of science as signified by its progressive realization*

BUT ONLY THE IDEA OF SCIENCE (or, more precisely, the realization of this idea) is the ultimate terminus of the development of science, its telos in the strict sense. All the stages we can distinguish in the history of a science are intermediate termini or ends (*Zwischenziele; EJ,* p. 201 [237]). They can be

6. ". . . eine rationale Methode praktischer Approximation an diese Idee . . ." (*FTL,* p. 7 [6]).

7. When Husserl rejects the assimilation of idea to limit (*FTL,* p. 62 [54], n. 1), he has in mind the real, finite limit. This static notion of limit excludes by definition the regulative function that Husserl attributes to the idea.

termini despite their intermediacy only because they are wholly oriented toward the full realization of this idea and in a way play the role or take the place of the idea (*stellvertreten*). In fact, their whole sense is to refer (*hinweisen*) to the idea as the essential possibility of their perfection and to make possible its realization by successive approximations. Each stage is therefore a terminus or telos only by reference (*Beziehung*) to the single and unique terminus, the idea; that is, only by participation. All the moments of the realizing development of science are involved in an intentional teleology of which they are only the more or less conscious, more or less cooperating, bearers (*Mitträger, Träger*) (cf. *Crisis*, pp. 70 [71], 71 [72], 74 [75], 340 [275]).

The idea is in fact the motive of realization. It is not, by itself, the concrete realization. In the real world, it is development or history that is responsible for the fate of the idea, that sustains the idea and little by little unfolds it in reality. The progress of science "represents" or takes the place of the idea of genuine science. Hence the extreme importance of each moment of this process of development. It is this process that most clearly manifests the inexorable tendency of science toward its ideal telos and enables us to give science a definition.[8] The moment is what takes the place of the telos in practice, as a substitute or sign.

Now, when a stage actor plays a role, he takes a character's place and substitutes for him. His performance, then, has a *meaning*, a relativity to the character whose role is being played. Hence the character is in a way a model set forth in the actor's performance. The actor tends to come as close as possible to an identification with the character. But what is real is the actor or, more precisely, the actor's performance representing the character. The character remains ideal, a model, and is not itself "plain to see" [*ne "tombe pas sous le sens"*]. What is real is the sign, not the signified. And yet the signified—that is, the idea—is what gives the sign its sense or meaning, by unifying all the actor's movements and words, in short, the many and varied factors that make up his performance. The signified is what makes the sign into a sign. The actor's behavior has sense (i.e.,

---

8. "One's conception of the aims of a science finds expression in its definition. . . . The definitions of a science mirror the stages of that science's development" (*LI*, p. 54 [I, 5]).

coherence and unity) only insofar as it represents and realizes the character. The actor's performance is therefore at the same time a sign and a more or less adequate realization.

This doctrine of sign and meaning carries over to the case of the current moment of a science. Each current moment of science has a meaning; it is a sign expressing a meaning which it bears in itself. For the meaning is in a way included in the sign, since it is possessed by the sign. But it also goes beyond the sign, since it indicates a reference to something else. Meaning is the proper act of reference to the sense; the sign signifies the sense, or at least it signifies the object which gives the sign its sense. (Here we have intentionality in one of its originary modalities.) Meaning is the act of signifying which specifically pertains to one term of this referential relation. Both immanence and transcendence are therefore necessary: immanence of the meaning in the sign, and transcendence of the sense taken in itself. As immanent, the meaning is real; that is, it falls immediately within the sphere of experience. For this reason it is an ultimate descriptive element. It is ultimate because it is the last element that pure phenomenological description can reach before giving way to another method of investigation. Description, which as such can grasp only the real, comes to a stop as soon as it has disclosed, in the reality described, the first term of the meaning relation—the latter being reference to a sense, to an ideal unity which is brought out by intentional analysis (*LI*, p. 400 [II/1, 183]).

In the descriptive historical experience of the realization of science, we perform[9] the meaning of science (*FTL*, p. 8 [8]; *CM*, p. 8 [49]). That is, we aim at the ideal unity intended by the meaning of a certain current moment of science, just as, in

9. [*Opérer*. I have translated this word (where it takes "meaning" or "judgment" as its object) as "perform" because it renders Husserl's *vollziehen*, which most often appears in English as "perform." The reader should be advised, however, that the word does not directly denote the performance of an action but rather the "bringing into being" of the correlate of an action (although these two notions are obviously closely connected). Thus, for example, we "perform" (bring about) the judg*ment*—not the judg*ing*. The performing of a judgment is an operation on the part of subjectivity; in this operation, according to Husserl's logic, we instantiate a class concept which is equivalent to the judgment regarded as an ideal objectivity. Cf. also below, p. 41, where it is said that we can *operate with* such entities as meanings and judgments.—TRANS.]

pronouncing the words of a language, we perform their meaning—that is, we refer to the object they signify. But just as the meaning is not the object (*LI*, p. 287 [II/1, 46]), so the realization of science is not itself science but only *possesses* science. Each moment of science is a partial realization (by participation) of the idea of science. It makes a claim to be more than itself, and this claim implies the idea of science and motivates the positing of this idea (*CM*, p. 9 [50]). The idea grounds the meaning of the real, current science; it is itself motivated by its own partial realization. Here already we see the mutual implication of the transcendental-phenomenological and the descriptive-phenomenological points of view.

Thus, at the same time, science both is and is not. It *is* not what it *has*, since it makes a claim to be what it has. It is (imperfect) and it is not (perfect). It is both actual and potential (cf. the example given in *FTL*, p. 76 [67]). It always includes an element of the ideal or possible, since the idea is always implied in it both actually and potentially (*FTL*, p. 268 [237]) and since each currently actual state implies pre-scribed intentional potentialities. Science therefore involves an element of determination, which is known, and an element of indetermination, which is unknown (except ideally, by anticipation). Contradictions seem to be true. Science has at the same time a structure of determination and of indetermination, a structure of knowledge and of ignorance; it is and it is not. But this is an apparent contradiction, not a real one. For transcendental subjectivity constitutes ideal objectivities in a historical process. The idea is therefore more or less realized. That is, the idea "subsists" in two modes, an actual and a possible mode (cf. *Crisis*, pp. 94 [97], 103 f. [106]). These two modes are in perpetual compenetration; the actual necessarily implies the potential (*CM*, p. 44 [81 f.]). They cannot be contradictory, since they are constituted in the same transcendental subjectivity. Nonbeing, ignorance, and indetermination are modes of being, knowledge, and determination; that is, they are less perfect realizations of the latter states.[10] Being and nonbeing, as well as the other contradictories, are therefore correlative. The negative correlate in each case is the limit idea of the absolute nonrealization of the positive correlate (*FTL*, p. 319 [280]; *EJ*, p. 347 [419]; *Ideen II*, p. 42). Nonbeing

10. *CM*, pp. 58 (93), 116 (145); *FTL*, pp. 121 (108), 127 (113); *EJ*, p. 37 (33 f.); *Ideas*, § 106; *CM*, p. 84 (117).

is ultimately *other-being*, not absolute nothingness. Here already we find an analogy with Plato (*EJ*, pp. 90 f. [97 f.]; cf. Plato, *Sophist*, 256d–259d).

The realization of science is therefore a sign of the idea of science. Thus the problematic of sign and meaning enables us to open up a second way of access to the idea. The nature of the sign is such that consciousness of the sign refers to consciousness of the signified. Hence the sign is a motive of the signified (*LI*, p. 270 [II/1, 25]). Realization motivates the idea; partial realization motivates the perfect (total) realization.

The conclusion of this line of reasoning raises a difficulty, since Husserl himself seems to decide against it. In treating the reference of nongenuine degrees of clarity to the genuine degree of clarity (i.e., the reference of obscurity to clarity), he shows that obscurity refers (*hinweist*) to clarity in the way a color grasped in the mode of imperfect clarity points by itself to the color as it is in itself (*Ideas*, p. 196 [158]). He immediately stipulates that this is by no means a case of the relation of sign to signified. The imperfect realization (here, that of clarity) is not a sign of the perfect realization and hence of the idea. The relationship expressed here by the verb *hinweisen* is not that of a sign to what it signifies, although the same word may designate the latter relationship as well (*LI*, First Investigation, §§ 1–3). Consequently, we would apparently be unwarranted in applying the doctrine of the sign contained in the *Logical Investigations* to the doctrine of science and its historical realization as presented in the *Cartesian Meditations* and the *Crisis*. On this point, then, there would seem to be a hiatus in the evolution of Husserl's thought between the first and the last form of his doctrine.

But this difficulty can be overcome. To be sure, the *Crisis* does not simply elaborate on the ideas in the *Logical Investigations*. Yet it brings no essential modification to phenomenology. The teleology (intentionality) from sign to signified described in the *Logical Investigations* is found again, in its historical form, in the teleology of human reason given by the *Crisis*. Husserl's evolution on this point consists in the move from a static and purely logical point of view to a dynamic, historical point of view, but the same fundamental notion is present in both works. Thus there is a very deep unity throughout Husserl's work, a unity extending to the particulars of his work, beyond and beneath the broad teleological unity that all critics must recognize. This unity among particulars appears in the doctrine of the sign, and it allows us to state the following parallelism: just as the sign refers to what it signifies, as that which gives it its sense and its being, so the currently actual realization of science refers to its ideal possible realization. Current science as a fact is therefore the sign of the end idea of science. And if Husserl dismisses such an interpretation in terms of the sign (in the text cited above), his reason is not hard to find. Husserl's thought, at least in the *Logical Investigations,* takes its origin in a reflection on language (and even on grammar). Now, language is obviously a sign with respect to thought, but it is a sign which has no community of nature with what it signifies. What essential relation is there between the word "horse" and the reality of the horse itself? It is simply a matter of convention. We must come to a clear understanding of the meaning of the word "sign." While we admit that language is a sign, we must also admit that smoke is a sign of fire; there is no smoke without fire. We must further grant that the latter sign is not of the same kind as the conventional sign. In the case of smoke, we have to do with a natural sign, a sign which has an essential and natural community with what it signifies or indicates (*anzeigt*).

If the imperfect realization is the sign of the perfect realization or of the idea, should we take this to mean that it is a sign of the conventional kind or a sign of the natural kind? The answer to this question forces itself on us. It must be a natural sign, since there is an essential community between the perfect realization (the idea) and the imperfect realization which approaches it. The idea is an essence in which its more or less perfect realization participates. This is what justifies the status of realization as a sign with respect to the signified idea. This fundamental essential community grounds the very teleology of the process of realization. Without it there would be no warrant to speak of the tendency of development toward perfect realization of the idea. And hence, if partial realization of the true idea of science were not a natural sign of this idea, we would not be able to affirm the teleology or the intentionality of science. From this it is quite evident that the application of the doctrine of the sign to the doctrine of science is justified and that on this point there is a very close continuity of thought between the *Logical Investigations* and the *Crisis* (and the *Cartesian Meditations* as well). We can therefore state the following principle: the signified gives the sign its sense, but the sign makes the signified known. Or again: the ideal governs the real [*réal*], but the real makes the ideal known. This absolutely universal law of reciprocity holds true in the case of everyday experience of the thing (*Ding*) as well as in the case we are dealing with here. Thus it brings us to the universal principle of the mutual exemplarity of the real and the ideal.

2 / The Dialectic of the Idea and the Real

§ 6. *The dialectic of the idea and the real in science*

IDEAL SCIENCE AND REAL (CURRENT) SCIENCE are reciprocal examples of each other—but in different respects, since they do not both have the same value. The one is absolute, the other relative. The one is ideal, eidetic; the other is real, factical, mundane (*weltlich*). So the two will be examples in different ways. Ideal science (the idea of genuine science) will be, so to speak, the exemplary example, the ideal example of real science. Real science will be the factical example of ideal science. The factical example realizes and thereby illustrates the ideal exemplar, but this very fact implies that the ideal exemplar structures and pre-scribes the factical example.

This doctrine is constant throughout Husserl's phenomenology. It forms the basis for ideation, which uses free variation as its method. In principle, only the individual is a factical example. In itself it is, to be sure, individual; that is to say, it is this or that thing. To discern the individual's type in all its ideal purity, it is necessary to adopt a particular attitude (the phenomenological reduction). This attitude transforms the factical individual into an example illustrating an eidetic generality and introduces it into the dialectic of the real and the idea, i.e., makes the individual a member of this reciprocal relation. The individual is then immediately correlative with the ideal exemplar. The latter is elicited from it and is grasped in and through ideation (idealization), an operation which results in idealizing (ideally seeing) the fact as idea, the factical example as ideal exemplar (*Ideas*, p. 217 [179]; *CM*, p. 70 [104]). Brought to clarity by an exemplary intuition, the factical individual itself becomes an exemplar and is then capable of being formalized ideally as eidos (*FTL*, p. 212 [189]). The eidos is therefore in a way "inferred from" the factical individual after the reduction and the ideation which "delivers its form" (*FTL*, p. 141 [126]), and it expresses in all its ideal purity that which is most formal in the individual. Since this involves the "extraction" [*herausholen*] of an ideality, and hence an ideality that is transcendent with respect to the reality of the concrete individual, we have here an extrinsic form—that is, a *norm* (*Ideas*, p. 401 [354 f.]; cf. pp. 249 [210], 274 [235]). This norm exercises a regulative power over the individual from which it is extracted. The normative character of the eidos, which is a corollary of its transcendent ideality, therefore expresses the formal legislation of the eidos over the fact which tends to realize it. The idea of science prescribes a priori the structure of real science, and the latter concretely realizes this idea in development. But the idea is form or essence (*Ideas*, § 2). This is the heart of Husserlian exemplarism: essence is normative, form is exemplary.

Before being fully elicited, however, the idea or eidos is illustrated in something like an a priori manner (*im voraus*) by and in the individual that realizes it. There is a reciprocity here between the factical example and the ideal exemplar. This exemplification is not flawless; the idea is only "vaguely" present to consciousness at the outset of the investigation (*CM*, pp. 9 [50], 13 [53]). The realization of science is both a revelation of and a screen against the idea of science, just as Galileo hastened and at the same time retarded the progress of science (*Crisis*, p. 52 [53]). Hence it is necessary to get behind the screen, and this is the job of intentional analysis. It is possible, starting with really existing sciences, to infer their end idea. That is, it is possible to reveal their internal teleology by "passing through" the individual sciences in order to attain the perfect formulation of ideal science, which provides a ground for their unity in principle.

This is just what Husserl undertakes to do. For him, particular sciences are so many "points of passage" (*Durchgangspunkte; LI*, p. 231 [I, 235]) for the elaboration of an ideal science or general theory—which will be precisely logic, science of the idea of science (*Wissenschaftslehre*), as it appears especially in *Formal and Transcendental Logic*. The general theory (either of science or of the world, it makes no difference which) is therefore constructed from immediate real data, either the data of everyday experience of the world or those of the historical experience of real sciences—in a word, immediate factical data (*Crisis*, p. 32 [29 f.]). The limit ideas (*Limes-gestalten*) are likewise constructed from real forms which are actually given. More precisely, they are themselves pre-scribed or pre-constituted (*vorgezeichnet*) in the indefinite progress of realization. They are contained in this progress as potential limits describing an infinite horizon of the process of perfecting (*Crisis*, p. 26 [23]). Construction is what objectifies these limit ideas, insofar as the scientist is occupied with determining them, and this construction is simply the idealization of an infinite process of realization.[1] The idea is an infinite (i.e., actually unattainable) pole which is obtained by a sort of ideal extrapolation from a progressive realization. This realization is indefinite, being essentially structured by time (i.e., by the history of consciousness). Idealization of this progress is therefore the only rational means of grasping it scientifically and bringing it into a systematic theory. Thus the idea thematizes the open-infinite horizon of the "and so forth" (*EJ*, p. 357 [433]), expressing the fundamental form "and so forth" (*Grundform des Und-so-weiter; FTL*, p. 188 [167]). This idea of "and so forth" makes it possible to deal with the infinities surrounding the rule-governed series of appearances which converge necessarily in the unity of an appearing object in general (thing or science) (*Ideas*, pp. 418 f. [371]). In sum, this idea is a construct. The "and so forth" is a constructive infinity (*Konstruktive Unendlichkeit;* cf. *FTL*, pp. 188 f. [167]), and, being the world's universal form, it enables us a priori to gain a vantage point over the world constructively.[2]

This idealizing construction or constructive idealization will thus make the potential infinite form of ideal science appear on the basis of actually given forms of factical science. It will manifest both the essence of ideal science and the extrinsic (exemplary, normative) form of real science. Hence what we have is a teleology from the real to the ideal, from factical

---

1. It is insofar as the scientist determines these limit ideas by idealizing the real data that he is a "geometer"—and that for phenomenology the Platonic motto holds: "Let no one enter here who is not a geometer" (*Crisis*, p. 26 [23]).

2. Just as geometry is the idealized system of shapes in the real world and enables us to gain a vantage point on this world by ideal construction. Cf. *Crisis*, pp. 34 f. (32 f.).

science to ideal science; it is a passage from the immediately given, from what is actual and relative, to the ultimate, absolute, ideal telos. This is precisely the order of the genesis of knowledge: from explicit to implicit, from actual to potential. But this may be understood in two ways. First, one may be involved in the effective realization of science. In this case, one is implicitly guided by the idea of science, insofar as one is a bearer of a quasi-blind instinct shared with the "species" of scientists. Or else one may try to thematize this infinite realization at the present time in the form of the *Und-so-weiter* and discern its telos in an ideal anticipation. In short, one may either tend toward the real fullness (*Klarheitsfülle*) of science as such, or else one may objectify its essential possibility (*Wesensmöglich-keit, Eidos*) in an originary sense-giving analysis (*Sinngebung, Besinnung*) and remain thereby within possible experience (*FTL*, p. 9 [8]). The second case amounts to an (immanent) analysis of the implications of the explicit data, an analysis of the potentialities in that of which we are actually conscious. This is the discovery of the internal teleology of science, the intentional analysis of the idea (*CM*, pp. 43–49 [81–86]).

The development of science is therefore, depending on how we look at it, an idealization of real science or a progressive realization of ideal science. And here we have a new way of expressing the reciprocal exemplarity of the idea and the real: it can equally well be said either that the idea is realized or that the real is idealized. The main point is that in any case the idea and the real come together and are grounded in a single perfection. But as long as science continues to progress, the idea that it proposes to itself as an end will remain a transcendent idea. If the idea were ever realized, its transcendence would be absorbed in the immanence of real science. Science would then have reached its telos of perfection, it would have caught up with its ideal pole. Conversely, the idea would have been fully realized in the immanence of the development of real science. The opposition between transcendence and immanence, as well as that between ideal and real, would then lose its meaning. Science would have fully realized its meaning, and it would no longer be only a claim. It would no longer simply *have* a meaning but would *be* this meaning, having reached its ultimate completion in absoluteness and perfection.

But of course we are speaking of the ideal terminus, and we know that this terminus is not realizable in any way, either in the present instant or in the course of the future. We are concerned here with a "mental seeing" [*une vue de l'esprit*]—an ideation of genuine science, of the ideal end which is to be reached through the infinite development of science.

Our inquiry has led us to set forth some main themes of phenomenology. What we have said about science is equally true in all other cases to which phenomenology directs its attention. The same method will always lead to the same result. Perception, judgment, even phenomenology itself (as a problem for itself) will always be studied in the development of their effective realization. But for Husserl every development prescribes an idea or telos which limits the development by orienting it. It would be absurd to follow Heraclitus in admitting a pure succession without a terminus. A telos or end idea is therefore necessary in order to give a structure of coherence and unity to development. Whether this development is taken to be that of successive "appearings" [*des "apparaître"*] of a thing, as the fulfilling approximations to the idea on the part of the real object of perception or the ideal object of the judgment, or as the various prefigurations of the idea of genuine science, every development pre-scribes an idea since its progressive evolution necessarily implies an ideal correlate toward which it tends as its terminus. Conversely, every idea pre-scribes a constitutive process which will realize it by approximations. (This corresponds to the notion of objectivity as index of the system of constituting intentionalities.)

> Denn die Beschränkung auf das erfahrende Bewusstsein war nur exemplarisch gemeint, ebenso wie diejenige auf die "Dinge" der "Welt." *Alles und jedes ist,* so weit wir den Rahmen auch spannen, und in welcher Allgemeinheits- und Besonderheitsstufe wir uns auch bewegen—bis herab zu den niedersten Konkretionen— *wesensmässig vorgezeichnet* (*Ideen I,* p. 330).

> [For the limitation to the empirical consciousness was intended only by way of illustration, as was also the restriction to "things" of the "world." Everything, however far we stretch the framework, and on whatever level of generality and particularity we may also be moving—even down to the lowest concreta—is essentially prefigured (*Ideas,* pp. 375–76).][3]

3. In *Crisis,* Husserl can repeat the same principle: the evolution of science and philosophy pre-scribes an ideal and perfect form of absolute knowledge. The same concern remains, taken in one of its particular modalities. *Ideas* considers more specifically the concrete development of individual transcendental consciousness. This development is temporal, to be sure, but it constitutes an individual

The end idea or ideal end is thus given as a function of unity and meaning, absolutely and universally.[4] Here we have the inner force of Husserlian phenomenology, the force which is expressly worked out in the notion of intentionality. For development tends toward the idea as that which gives it unity and meaning by enabling it to attain its ultimate completion. This teleological tendency is an intentional tendency. Intentionality is teleology,[5] and the idea is an intentional unity. This is what gives this doctrine its remarkable unity; for phenomenology itself is an intentional unity. According to Husserl, phenomenology is an ideal telos. It is the end idea of the entire intellectual history of humanity.

All systems and all previous scientific hypotheses are in fact imperfect realizations of the idea of genuine knowledge, and they pre-scribe this idea as their end and ultimate norm.[6] In general, every imperfect realization and every beginning pre-scribes a direction to the further process of realization and consequently pre-scribes a telos to this process (*EJ*, pp. 80 f. [85]). Every beginning therefore indicates a task to be carried out, every *Ur-stiftung* an *End-stiftung*. And this task is set ideally for all history, from the first step of the knowledge interest until

---

subjective history which does not immediately involve all of humanity. *Crisis* considers the development of intersubjective transcendental consciousness, which goes beyond the limited point of view of the individual and immediately involves the history of human reason as such. Whence its more historical aspect—i.e., more historical in the usual sense of the word. There is another difference between *Ideas* and *Crisis*. The vocabulary is not quite the same in the two works. *Crisis* no longer uses the word "eidos" but replaces it directly with "idea," which is understood as end (telos) and pole. But this terminological difference makes no essential change. The eidos is evidently an idea and a telos. An idea is necessary in order to give development its direction. A development in which everything is done and undone without any ordering to a terminus is absurd, and man could not exist in it (*Crisis*, pp. 6 f. [4 f.]).

4. It is "their unifying principle, as well as their essential aim of research," as Husserl says of the law elaborated by science (*LI*, p. 230 [I, 234]). Cf. *Ideas*, § 86.

5. Intentionality in its purest form breaks down into the "Cartesian" formula: *ego cogito cogitata*. It is the correlation between consciousness and its object, which takes all possible forms: correlation between perception and perceived, between judgment and judged, between idea and realization.

6. *Ideas* (p. 183 [148]) and especially *Crisis* deal with the historical motivation of phenomenology. Cf. *Crisis*, pp. 70 (71), 193 (196), 207 f. (212); *CM*, p. 4 (46).

the task has been completely carried out (*Crisis,* p. 72 [73]). So phenomenology, the fulfillment of the idea launched at the outset of rational humanity by the first experience of wonder (*Crisis,* p. 79 [80]), is a telos and hence an idea which unceasingly transcends itself. To say that phenomenology is the outcome of universal human thought is not to close it off in a complacent self-satisfaction. On the contrary, to say this is to emphasize the essential incompleteness of phenomenology, since it always remains an infinite task (*CM,* p. 87 [119]). The very reality of Husserl's work as it really exists in the whole of his written works is an immediate datum from which the idea of phenomenology is to be elicited—an idea which is only partly realized in Husserl's work itself. Husserl repeatedly dwells on the fact that phenomenology is an infinite task, that he is only drawing up a first draft of it, that he is only at the beginning of the beginning.[7]

We see, then, that the method of investigation which phenomenology uses with regard to various objects elicits a universal structure to which phenomenology itself is subject. Hence this method manifests the profound intention of phenomenology, its *idea,* which we express by the word "exemplarism." In a constructive, dynamic thought like Husserl's, the method creates the spirit. We have already dealt with the essentials of this method by establishing the mutual exemplarity of the real and the ideal in the particular case with which we started, the case of science. Let us return to this theme and generalize it—that is, in a sense, give it its formal logic.

§ 7. *The dialectic of the idea and the real in general*

THIS LAW OF MUTUAL EXEMPLARITY thrusts us squarely into Husserl's logic, at least as it is set forth at the beginning of *Ideas I.*[8] In this important chapter, Husserl delineates the es-

7. *FTL* shows, for example, how formal logic emerges little by little from the earliest works, *Philosophie der Arithmetik* and *Logische Untersuchungen* (*FTL,* § 27). "But here we are only at the beginnings" (*FTL,* p. 182 [161]). "We have expounded phenomenology as a science *in its beginnings*" (*Ideas,* p. 280 [241]—a very interesting text).
8. First Section, First Chapter: "Fact and Essence" (*Tatsache und Wesen*).

sentials of his epistemological thought, along with what might pass (from the noematic point of view) as a "metaphysical" result of his constitutive method.

The fact (*Tatsache, Faktum*) is what immediate experience in the natural attitude gives us. It is defined by its "mundanity" (*Weltlichkeit*), since the framework of the natural attitude is the world and since, from this point of view, being amounts to being-in-the-world (*Ideas*, p. 51 [10]). But natural experience immediately discovers a fact that is going to compel it to break through its own limits: the fact is contingent (*Ideas*, p. 53 [12]). Natural experience posits the fact in an individual form, in a spatiotemporal framework. It follows that this fact could have been situated in another place and another time and that in terms of its circumstances it could have been determined as other than it is. Not only do its external conditions change, but the fact itself changes. This implants contingency and instability in its very being and seems to identify its being with its becoming or development. Certain *de facto* regularities may have occurred, but they show only a factical correlation between external circumstances and the modifications of the fact itself. Laws indicate only an inductively confirmed relation which bears on the extrinsic characteristics of the fact. Hence they by no means determine the essence (*Wesen*) of the thing (*Ideas*, p. 53 [12]). This is why two different orders must be distinguished, the connection of things and the connection of truths. These two orders are a priori given together and inseparably from each other. But this simultaneity by no means purports identity; the thing is not its truth (*LI*, pp. 225 f. [I, 228]). What does this mean?

The radical contingency we revealed above cannot, however, count against another obvious fact. The individual thing changes, as the most immediate experience testifies. But the thing remains itself despite its changes, since we can still talk about it. Hence there is a certain invariance to be reconciled with a perpetual development. Contingency must have a limit, in other words, since a pure contingency is just as absurd as a pure development. Just as development aspires to its telos, contingency aspires to necessity; in each case we have limit ideas before us.[9] This is a necessity to which language itself bears

9. *Ideas*, p. 53 (12). Necessity is the intentional correlate of contingency. This pair, contingency and necessity, brings us back to the pair consisting of fact and eidos. More precisely, contingency expresses the mode of "subsistence" of the fact, while necessity expresses that of the eidos.

witness, and it is by means of language that the science of the truths of things is constructed. If the thing is itself and at the same time in process of developing, then necessarily it does not absolutely coincide with itself. The thing is not absolutely *in itself*. This being the case, it must be relatively in itself.[10]

Here we see relativity introduced into the heart of reality. The thing is relatively itself. It is relative to its in-itself, i.e., to its eidos, which it is not absolutely. Development has its place between two limits: the actual relative and the potential absolute that is to be attained. Development is in sum only the means of mitigating the radical contingency or radical internal fissure in the being of everything; it is the means of tending toward ideal perfection and realizing it, at least approximately. In the present case the development is that of science, and it is to some extent identical with method. The method here, being essentially movement, manifests the radical imperfection of science that is in the course of being worked out, and it provides a means of overcoming actual imperfections in order to reach ultimate theoretical perfection. It expresses the necessity of covering the course marked out from intention to goal, from *Abzielung* to *Erzielung*.[11] Hence knowledge itself is subject to the internal fissure in everything, the fissure which shows up in the distinction between being and development. The very concept of knowledge involves a duality, since knowledge is subject to certain gradations. A certain item of knowledge which is the evidence of a certain thing or state of affairs is relative with respect to absolute and perfect knowledge (which would include, for example, knowledge of all the prior causes, the grounds, and the consequences of a given state of affairs). Knowledge of fact is similarly relative to knowledge of essence and, accordingly, tends toward it (*LI*, pp. 61 f. [I, 14]).

The identity implied by the fact of being a thing is thus replaced by the externality of possession, and the immanence of formal determination is replaced by the transcendence of ex-

10. We can better understand the term "in itself," which Husserl bravely reintroduces, if we depict it in a very concrete form. The thing, in its essential "full bloom," is in itself; it is fully realized and reposes in itself. This idea of "repose in itself" points out that the in-itself is a terminus toward which development of the thing tends, at least so long as it is in process of development [*en devenir*]. The thing is in process of development before it is in itself. Being in process of development and being in itself make up intentionality.

11. "The longueurs of method would lose their sense if to intend meant to succeed" (*LI*, p. 63 [I, 16]).

trinsic (exemplary) formal determination. The in-itself is a
certain transcendence with respect to the thing, which is not
the in-itself but which only possesses it in a partial manner.
Hence the thing is found to participate in its in-itself. (It should
be noted that participation, or *methexis,* implies copossession,
the fact of having something in common with someone.) To
replace being by having in this dialectic that we observed above
is to replace being by participation. That is, to replace being
by having is to substitute for immanent determination a determination by extrinsic denomination according to a transcendent
essence; it is to replace substantial identity by relatedness. To be
sure, it can always be said that the thing is a participation in
its idea or its essence, as it is said that "The daisy is white."
But in an exemplarist view of participation this amounts, formally speaking, to saying that "The daisy has whiteness" and
hence that it "partakes of whiteness." The same truth can be
confirmed with regard to the proposition "Pierre is a man."
(The latter case even has the advantage of being essential and
not accidental, like the case of the daisy.) In a rigorous language, these two notions would be expressed in different judgments, judgments of being and judgments of having (*Ist- und
Hat-urteile*).[12] And Husserl argues that in order to pass from a
judgment of being like "Pierre is a man" to the judgment of
having, "Pierre has humanity," it is necessary to formalize man
as humanity, that is, to perform an idealization (ideation) of
man into the eidos "humanity." Then humanity, fully formalized,
is an independent and absolute notion *in itself,* whose sense
stands by itself. It is pure form or pure idea. It can no longer
be identified in an immanent way with a particular individual.
The only relationships it can maintain with an individual are
those of extrinsic denomination, participation, and normation.
Not being identical with the individual, it is transcendent with
respect to it. The individual cannot *be* this in-itself; it can only
be said to *have* (*metechein*) its in-itself.

For Husserl, this character of participation expresses the
transcendence of the eidos. But it also expresses the infirmity
of the eidos, since Husserl denies any metaphysical reality (of
the Platonic sort) to the essence ideas—their reality consisting
in being possessed by individuals and thereby realized. The

12. *EJ,* § 52 in particular. This doctrine of judgments of being
and judgments of having is closely tied to the theory of nominalization (an important part of phenomenology), one of the modes of
which is substantivation.

individual thing in fact brings the essence into the process of development and in this way bestows a certain concrete existence on it. Here we find essence and individual fact to be in the same situation as science in its development and the idea of science. The eidos therefore proves to be not real but irreal or ideal. The relativity of the thing to its in-itself is after all nothing but the relativity of the real to the ideal. For the in-itself is posited as an idea, as the essence or *quid* of the thing.[13] The essential *quid* of the thing is its idea. And if the thing is not its essence, if it is not its in-itself, the connection between things and their truth is not an identity. What we have seen about color (*Ideas*, pp. 195 f. [158]) holds true for all things universally. Each empirical individual fact refers to its eidos, to the typical and specific structure that is represented by its bundle of essential predicates (*Ideas*, p. 53 [12 f.]). This reference to an essential type is immediate but not explicit. Intentional analysis consists in bringing to explicit actuality what is passively constituted in each individual grasping of a thing.[14] From this point of view, the real fact is evidently given as the means of reaching the eidos.[15] The fact is the substitute for the eidos, its representative in the empirical domain. The fact is the real [*réal*] illustration and individual exemplification of the essence.[16] This value of the individual fact

13. *Ideas*, p. 54 (13). There are two moments to be distinguished. The essence is first of all grasped as the "inner nature" of the thing itself, insofar as the idea or the in-itself (as possessed by the thing) is immanent in the thing. Then the in-itself is elicited in its ideal purity, insofar as possession of the in-itself by the individual thing shows precisely the transcendence of the in-itself with respect to the thing. The essence is thus the a priori, according to *Ideen II*, p. 29.

14. *EJ*, pp. 36 (32), 113 (125), 317 f. (381 f.), 331 f. (398 f.); *Ideas*, p. 396 (349 f.). Type and idea are not, however, one and the same. For the moment it is not important to distinguish between them. Cf. *Crisis*, pp. 25 (22), 30 f. (28 f.); *EJ*, pp. 321 f. (385 f.).

15. A sure means, but not the only one—as the doctrine of free variation shows (*Ideas*, §§ 3–4).

16. The individual fact represents the type. Each object is *Vertreter* of its typical generality (*EJ*, p. 318 [382]) and illustrates (exemplifies) it (*Ideas*, p. 57 [16]). Cf. the "consciousness of example" (*exemplarisches Bewusstsein*) of *Ideas*, p. 56 (16). Cf. also *Ideas*, pp. 217 (179), 226 (188); *FTL*, pp. 41 (36), 184 (163), 192 (170), 198 (176), 212 f. (189); *Crisis*, pp. 41 (40), 114 (116), 129 (132), 235 (239). Husserl also speaks in the same connection of *Veranschaulichung, Verbildlichung, Vergegenwärtigung, Vergegenständlichung*. This must not be taken to mean a direct intuition of the idea but rather an immediate grasp of the factical individual as example of the idea.

as an example can be fully grasped only when the idea has been elicited in all its purity.

It seems at first sight, then, that the immediate relation of fact to eidos establishes an unquestionable continuity between the real world and the ideal world (*Ideas*, pp. 56 [16], 61 [21]). The individual fact breaks through the framework of natural experience and ushers us into the ideal world (*Ideas*, p. 63 [23]). Yet, on the other hand, it must be said that the ideal world is beyond the real world, since it is not contained within the same limits. In this case, however, natural experience cannot reach it. A new method of knowledge is therefore needed, an intuition of essences which grasps essences in all their purity. The relation which immediately unites fact and eidos thus proves to be *fissure;* there is a hiatus between the real and the ideal. There is indeed an analogy, a sort of proportion between the eidetic world and the factical world (*Ideas*, p. 55 [14]). But this analogy expresses a radical community (intuition of essences is still a kind of intuition) at the heart of a diversity that is no less radical. Essence involves no factical element, and eidetic science has nothing to do with the science of facts (*Ideas*, pp. 57 [17], 61 [21], 63 [23]).

However, the fissure is not total. If the eidos admits nothing empirical or factual, this is because it is considered in itself and in its ideal purity. The same is true of eidetic science. In an absolute view of the matter (i.e., in a purely ideal view, from an intrinsic formal or "in-itself" point of view), there is an impassable gulf between the real and the ideal. But this is a *static* view, which is contrary to Husserl's profound way of thinking. He considers the fact in its development, which is to say in a quite concrete manner, since the only way for a thing to be is to become or develop. Hence he considers the fact as progressively realizing the idea. And in this progression of approximations there is necessarily a radical community, a mode of participation, between fact and eidos. But we must guard against misunderstandings if we use the word "participation" here. What we have here is not participation in the form of reflection but rather a constructive participation in the manner of a realizing activity [*faire réalisateur*]. There is an essential analogy between the dynamic relations of fact and eidos and the similarly dynamic relations of the artist's idea and its realization in the work of art; the thing or individual fact more or less realizes its type or idea (*Crisis*, p. 25 [22]). There is no better way than this to point out the *relation to itself* that is set in the heart of reality.

Husserl states more precisely that this is a matter of "oscillation" (*Schwanken*). Development does not always evolve in a necessarily rectilinear fashion; there may also be inhibitions of tendencies (*Hemmung der Tendenzen; EJ*, § 21). So the process may deviate or even regress. But if this happens, it is only a matter of modalizations, which are by definition secondary and which make no change in the structure of the process.

But if the thing as such tends toward its idea, it does so insofar as it is progressively constituted in transcendental (inter)subjectivity. It is to this constitution that a limit idea or a terminus of the realizing process is assigned. According to the Husserlian conception of being, which is *being-for-the-subject*, the idea of the (perfect) constitution of the thing is identical with the idea of the essential fullness of the thing (the eidos). Between this essential fullness and the current state of realization, there is development; and in this development, individual fact and thing essentially remain in the realm of the "approximately" (*ungefähr*). But this necessarily implies that they refer to a measure which is no longer approximate but which represents an absolute. This absolute is clearly the eidos. But as soon as we bring up the notion of measure, we again discover the relation between the real (fact) and the ideal (eidos). There is no measure without something measured, and the eidos turns out to be the measure of the individual thing. Continuity is thus reestablished, but in the reverse direction. Whereas the fact was just seen to refer to the eidos as its essential type, here the eidos measures the fact. Thus it is important to define the points of view from which the fissure appears and from which unity is reestablished.

Only intentional analysis, only an idealizing thought process, can enable us to posit the essence as an idea (cf. *Ideas*, p. 54 [13]). The idea is therefore the result of an idealizing method. It is constituted by such a method, since intentional analysis is at the same time constitutive.[17] But all thinking is directed to

17. Depending on the prevailing interests of the investigator, intentional analysis is either retrogressive or progressive. Only the given is presently actual. We can ask of it what has constituted it and thereby retrace the series of originary subjective *Leistungen* which have contributed to its formation. This is the method of *Nach-erleben*, of *Nach-verstehen*, of *Nach-vollzug* (*FTL*, pp. 9 [8], 10 [9], 57 f. [51], 70 f. [62]; *CM*, p. 10 [51]; *EJ*, p. 49 [48]; *Crisis*, p. 177 [180]). Analysis in this direction is a repetition (*Wiederholung*) of a prior constitution by transcendental subjectivity, and it ends by positing our ego as the constituting principle (*EJ*, p. 49

defining, i.e., to determining its object in its intrinsic formality by exclusion of everything that is not the object. In this way it attains a remarkable analytic purity. But the result of analysis— what is separated out in analysis, according to its most formal and "innermost" notion—is not separate in the order of practical, external realization. Analysis elucidates an idea which is buried in the historical development of the individual fact or the factical science. This means that the idea is not as such presently and actually real; on the contrary, it is potential and is passively (pre)constituted in the development which realizes it. And despite this very precarious status, it guides and teleologically orients this development in a quasi-blind fashion, as if it were a vital instinct. Intentional analysis elicits this idea as eidos or essence (*Wesen*) and defines it intrinsically. At this point the breach we pointed out above can appear. Then, recognizing its teleological function, analysis defines the idea extrinsically as norm of the realizing progress. At this point the dialectical unity is reestablished.

Thus there are three dialectical moments in this investiga- tion: (1) discovery of the essential relativity of fact to eidos; (2) intrinsic (purely analytical) definition of the eidos as ideal essence, pure of all facticity (here the fissure appears); and (3) recognition of the eidos as norm of the factical process of realization (extrinsic, synthetic definition of the fact). In these we have three moments which correspond to the three moments of the Hegelian dialectic: thesis, antithesis, synthesis.

§ 8. *Husserl's Platonism*

IT SEEMS FROM THIS that Husserl returns to a Platonic position on the problem. Didn't Plato show just this mutual exemplarity of fact and eidos? He conceived two worlds, the

---

[48]). We can also ask of the given what it intends or preconstitutes in its meaning. In this way we see in the given an anticipation of the teleological idea. Analysis here explicates and clarifies the potentiali- ties included in what is presently given (*CM*, pp. 45–48 [83–86]). In the first case, what is presently given is an index of prior sub- jective constitutions; in the second, it is a factical example (an- ticipation) of the idea. Cf. below, "General Conclusion."

ideal and the real. These two worlds are radically distinct. Ideal
forms and things constitute two orders of reality that are completely different from each other, to such an extent that ideas
seem to remain forever unknowable to men, and things to the
gods (*Parmenides*, 133b–135c). But this difference by no means
precludes a relation between the two orders. In fact it makes
such a relation necessary, since the one provides the other's
intelligibility. The empirical thing here below has a form. It is
not its form itself; it is its form only relatively. Participation is
by definition a relation which enables each thing to communicate
with the ideas and the ideas to communicate among themselves.
Thus being participates in movement, in rest, in the same, in
the other. Participation makes it possible for the thing both to
be and not to be; to be identical with itself (under the *genos* of
sameness) and other with respect to itself (under the *genos* of
otherness); to be what it actually is and not to be what it ideally
is (the idea or ideal form).[18] Participation respects the diversity
of the two orders of the real (mundane) and the ideal while
maintaining their essential connection. This is why it appears
under two aspects. The ideal is the paradigm of the mundane
reality. As purely ideal (hence separate) paradigm, the form is
present in the empirical individual and is the transcendence
proper to it; as participated in, the form is in a way *possessed*
by the individual. In this way Plato emphasizes the immanence
of the participated-in character, which makes it possible for the
idea to specify the empirical individual in a formal manner. The
pair consisting of presence (*parousia*) and possession (*hexis*)
expresses the nature of the ideas' causality, which is at once
transcendent (formal extrinsic) and immanent (formal intrinsic).[19]

This Platonic doctrine—which involves the same dialectic of
relation, separation, and synthesis as the Husserlian doctrine of
fact and eidos—is certainly not without its difficulties. The most
important of these are already set forth with unequaled lucidity
in the first part of *Parmenides*. Nevertheless, the doctrine of
ideas must be maintained if we want to be able to acquire a
solidly based science of reality. To affirm the reality of ideas

18. To participate is by definition to *be other*; that is, *not to be*.
Every philosophy of participation is dialectical. For such a philoso-
phy, nonbeing is a mode of being and not its absolute contradictory.
Cf. *Sophist*, 237a–259d; see also pp. 18–19, above.

19. Plato takes as an example the just soul, which possesses
justice and has it present in itself (*Sophist*, 247a).

is in fact the only way to secure any permanence in the Heraclitean flux of the world. And since science can only be science
of the universal, hence of the identical and necessary, it necessarily implies ideas. This "logical" necessity of ideas does not
clear up the mysteries of participation, however, and the question remains open. Our goal is not to solve the problem; here
we seek only to determine the relations between Plato and Husserl.

Two points have already been established: Husserl and Plato
each acknowledge a participation of some sort. More precisely,
however, Husserl does not view participation in the idea as a
static replication in the (approximative) manner of a reflection
but rather as a dynamic, constructive realization of the idea. The
fact tends toward the idea, for Husserl, and it reaches it at
infinity. An essential continuity is thereby held to obtain, which
is more complete in two respects than that found in Plato. First,
the *formal* continuity between fact and eidos is more radical in
Husserl, since there is a difference in degree between them but
not a difference in nature (in being). The eidos is the idea of
the fact, but this idea is only the conception of the completed
perfection of the fact. In Plato there is a heterogeneity between
fact and eidos in their very being. We have just seen that the
fact (the empirical fact here below) is a nonbeing for Plato
with respect to the ("really real") being of the idea. Moreover,
Husserl posits a continuity between fact and eidos in the order
of *efficacy:* the fact progressively realizes its idea. Plato affirms
no such dynamism. This is why it may be said that Plato has in
a sense a static conception of participation, since for him the
empirical fact does not tend toward the idea.

We might be tempted to make an exception in the case of
man, whose greatest blessing is to contemplate the world of
ideas. In this privileged case the continuity seems quite similar
to that proposed by Husserl. But the soul is a case apart. The
soul is a fallen idea which is being punished by a sojourn in the
body (i.e., in matter). It can rejoin the world of ideas only by
breaking violently with the real world, and the most effective
break is death. Its continuity with the ideal world thus turns out
to be based on a breach. In any case this continuity of the individual soul with the world of ideas is not a true continuity. The
soul is in principle of the same order as the idea, and it is illusory
to regard it as an empirical fact. It is practically an empirical
fact because it is imprisoned in a body, but this is a state that
violates its nature. The real world here below, far from tending

toward the ideal world, stands opposed to it and is in a way its negation. Matter, the ultimate foundation of the empirical world, is nonbeing. It must be stressed that this is a dualism which Husserl does not recognize or wish to admit. When he states that he wants to avoid all Platonism, we can legitimately infer that he includes Platonic dualism in this denial. He never admits this "cut" in the being of things. His main thesis is that of intentionality, and intentionality regains a teleological (dialectical) unity. The ideal is (so to speak) temporarily or provisionally transcendent; but according to the very sense of the ideal, this transcendence is absorbed little by little in the immanence of realization. At the (infinite) terminus, real and ideal, fact and eidos, must be but one. Even though this identification is seen "with the mind's eye," even though it is an idealization, it is nonetheless true that unity and not dualism forms the basis of Husserl's thought.

But the two masters can be compared in yet another important respect. Participation involves two terms, each of which may be regarded in turn as the point of departure of the relation. This is the mutual exemplarity of fact and eidos. We already know that Husserl's point of departure is always what is immediately and presently given (i.e., the contingent fact revealed by natural experience) and that intentional analysis elicits the idea from this datum. Then the order is reversed, and what was the terminus of the progression (the telos) becomes its principle (*archē*). The idea is pre-scribed in the realizing development, and it pre-scribes this development normatively (a priori). Two points of view are involved here. From the descriptive point of view, the contingent fact is first; it is what provides access to the idea. From the constitutive point of view, the idea is first; it motivates the process of realization. Since the idea is at the origin of a process of constitution, we are actually distinguishing here two genetic points of view. The first, according to which the immediate experience that gives the fact is first, is the descriptive-phenomenological point of view. Since the fact given by experience is a fact which effectively exists in the reality of history, this point of view merges with what we shall call the existence-act point of view. The other, according to which the idea is first as principle of transcendental constitution, is the transcendental-phenomenological point of view. But the idea is the conception of the full realization of the fact, a full realization which plays the role of a priori norm with respect to its partial realization.

This point of view merges with the value-act point of view (cf. below, § 10).

But Plato says essentially the same thing.

The ideas are paradigms "in nature" (*en physei*). That is, they are ideal examples of the empirical world. But in order to reach these paradigmatic ideas, we must start out from empirical examples. To reach the horse in itself, we must begin by knowing the empirical horse. Similarly, the sign must be known before the signified. And further, since the mind that is still mired in matter is ponderous and clumsy, it must be made fit to rise to the ideal world. In order to investigate perfect definitions and exercise the power of defining that is proper to the mind, Plato recommends practicing sample definitions on the humblest subjects. In so doing, he, too, alludes to the two points of view: the descriptive-phenomenological (the order of knowledge) and the transcendental-phenomenological (the order of perfection). The individual fact is then a paradigm of the eidos, which in turn is the ideal and ultimate rule of the fact. Thus there is indeed reciprocity.[20]

But does it follow that Husserl's ideas are the same as Plato's ideas? This raises the question of the metaphysical reality of ideas in Husserl. Now Paul Ricoeur, in his commentaries and notes to the French edition of *Ideas I,* remarks that Husserl's ideas cannot have a metaphysical value (*Idées,* p. 18, n. 5). To be sure; but what does "metaphysical" mean here? Let us first of all dismiss the singularly narrow notion that Husserl gives at the beginning of the *Logical Investigations* (p. 59 [I, 11]). We must look to the Platonic side; to deny a metaphysical reality to ideas is to deny an identification of the Husserlian idea and the Platonic idea.

The Platonic idea is what is most real in the Platonic universe; it is the "really real" (*ontōs on*). Beside it the material world is a mere shadow, a nonbeing. Can the same be said of the Husserlian idea? Apparently not. For if it is true that eidos and fact differ only in degree and not in nature, there must be a

---

20. On the exemplarity of the idea, see in particular *Parmenides,* 132d–133a. In this text, of course, Plato presents this exemplarity more by showing its difficulties (infinite regress) than its advantages. The doctrine nevertheless remains unchanged in principle. On the exemplarity of the fact, see the dialectic of preparatory definitions in *Sophist* (esp. 218d) and *Statesman,* 277d f. (Cf. E. Rodier, *Etudes de philosophie grecque* [Paris: Vrin, 1926], p. 69, n. 3.)

radical community of being and of essence between them. They are both a single essence, but an essence taken in different states of perfection. But even this implies a certain difference in intensity of being. Considered from the descriptive-phenomenological point of view, only the fact is concrete; the eidos is abstract. In the descriptive procedure which ends in positing the idea, the only reality is the point of departure. Only the thing or the individual fact, or science in its current state of realization, falls within the scope of immediate experience, since it alone effectively exists in history. In relation to this reality, the idea appears as an infinite anticipation, with a reality more tenuous than that of the individual fact. It is not realized, and moreover it can be realized only (asymptotically) ad infinitum. Nevertheless, because it anticipates further experience of the individual thing, the idea pre-scribes a priori the course of this experience. It appears as the norm of this experience, as its regulative principle. But this is not enough to confer on it the quasi-physical reality possessed by the Platonic idea. The fundamental ambiguity of the Husserlian idea is that of an ideal principle which regulates a development of subjective constitution and which is pre-scribed by this same development.[21] For the idea always remains, in Husserl's view, a mental configuration (*geistiges Gebilde*). Platonic ideality is, so to speak, "subjectivized" in Husserl, as it is in a number of modern idealists. With this in mind, it can be said that Husserl both rejects Platonism and continues it. He rejects it insofar as he condemns the metaphysical reality of Platonic ideas and the metaphysical dualism to which this thesis necessarily leads. He continues it insofar as he maintains the normation of the real by the (subjectivized) ideal. But here, too, there is a community of nature.

The genetic point of departure of Husserl's procedure is the factual datum, the pregiven (*das Vorgegebene*), the world and objective science. From this the motivating idea is intentionally inferred. This idea is a subjective "extrapolation" and hence the methodical result of an originary constitution. Moreover, it proves to be the norm of the reality from which it was inferred. Everything leads us to think that the real, the point of departure for the procedure, is also a subjective configuration. And this belief is confirmed, since world and science are defined in the

21. We will see in more detail that the idea is both act and potency.

end as the product of constitutive *Leistungen*. Hence the coming
to reflective awareness (*Besinnung*), which is both analysis and
constitution, makes an originary constitution out of what is given
to the philosopher as sedimented "habitus" of tradition. Not
only is the idea subjectivized, but even that which corresponds,
in Plato, to the reality of this world here below.

Husserlian phenomenology cannot therefore absolutely refuse to be qualified as "Platonism." We can easily convince ourselves of this by reading Husserl himself. To be accused of
Platonism is in his opinion a reproach only so long as Platonism
is taken according to the letter of its historical formulation,
implying therefore a realism of ideas and an externality of ideas
with respect to thought (*LI*, p. 350 [II/1, 121]). This point
remains absolutely established and definitive: Husserl's Platonism is a subjectivized Platonism. But this by no means denies to
Platonism a spirit or direction of thought that is infinitely fruitful.[22] Indeed, Husserl often regrets that psychologistic empiricism
has prevented this spirit from developing farther. Empiricism
provoked a wave of almost superstitious fear with regard to whatever even remotely brought to mind an objectification of the
idea or an ideal objectivity. The latter was condemned a priori
in the name of an instinctive and sterile anti-Platonism. In
Husserl's eyes, such an attitude long prevented logicians and
theoreticians of science from recognizing the objectivity of ideal
logical forms (truths, judgments, even elaborated sciences) and
consequently shut them off from a sound critique of knowledge.
Husserl's first objective is accordingly to stem the tide and
unmask this anti-Platonism, which is more emotional than
critical. On the one hand, the fashion was scarcely conducive
to metaphysical speculations in the Platonic style; and, on the
other hand, the reigning empiricism was based on a psychology
which took itself to be the last word of wisdom. On every side the
ideal as object was condemned: either it was simply rejected
under the pretext of anti-Platonism, or it was reduced to psychic
phenomena. Establishing that one can operate (*hantieren,
umgehen*) with ideal objects was the first breach in this logical
anti-Platonism.[23] The problem was to find a middle course

22. A spirit from which modern thought to this day draws all its
vitality, whether it admits this or not. In the case of existentialism,
though, we must add the reappearance of Stoic themes.

23. *FTL*, pp. 81 f. (71 f.), 151 (135), 258 f. (228 f.). It must
not be thought naïvely that because Husserl condemns a certain anti-
Platonism he is necessarily Platonic. It must simply be understood

between the purely empiricist tendency which conjures away ideal objectivity by giving it the same reality as thought (*LI*, p. 350 [II/1, 121 f.]; cf. *FTL*, § 57) and the mystical tendencies which metaphysically hypostatize the idea and in the end discredit it (*Ideas*, p. 56 [16]). Despite Platonic appearances and the disfavor attaching to them, it was necessary to retain the fundamental inspiration of Platonism, regulation of empirical reality by the ideal—or, to use a more Husserlian wording, motivation of the real by the ideal. It is thus the doctrine of transcendental constitution whose defense against psychologistic anti-Platonism is at issue. In *Ideas I*, Husserl is particularly explicit on this point: the problem of transcendental constitution is precisely that of the status of the idea, the status of the ideal intentional unity which is alone capable of motivating and unifying, of regulating and orienting, an indefinite series of appearings.[24] If we want to apply the Husserlian theory of the teleology of history to this case, we might say that the Husserlian idea intentionally removes the historical dross from Plato's original intention and represents the true Platonic idea.

Hence we must radically reject Platonizing realism (*Ideas*, p. 88 [48]) and must define the exact status of the ideal objectivity which seems to oscillate between the subjective and the objective (*FTL*, pp. 81 f. [71 f.]). Finally, it must be admitted that general being (i.e., the idea) is simply the Platonic idea purified of its metaphysical interpretation. The Husserlian idea is the Platonic idea without its metaphysical realism, without its character of real externality (that is, without its real [*réale*] transcendence; only a certain irreal or ideal transcendence in a real immanence is retained). Husserl performs a sort of epochē here. Just as the epochē suspends the external reality and hence the real existence of the objects of judgment (and the judgment itself as regards its truth), so the epochē in this case suspends the real ("spatial") transcendence of the Platonic idea. Only the

---

that if a certain Platonic spirit had been able to persist in spite of the rejection of the historical system, the specific objectivity of the ideal would not have had to struggle so long to gain recognition. As Husserl says, "the purifiable sense and the genuine problem" posed by Platonism were not seen (*FTL*, p. 82 [72]).

24. *Ideas*, pp. 418 f. (371). To be sure, correlation posits as a unity the appearing object rather than the idea. But since the series of "appearings" is infinite, this object is an idea. The fate of Husserlian transcendentalism is therefore bound up with its "Platonism" —as we see from the text of *FTL*, pp. 258 f. (228 f.), and in general from all of *FTL*, § 100.

metaphysical realism of the idea (which is in fact an almost physical realism) is eliminated, while all its other determinations remain. We have seen what is essential in these: the idea, Platonic as well as Husserlian, is essentially a correlate of the individual empirical fact. The law of mutual exemplarity of fact and eidos follows from this. We can scarcely hesitate to accept this view when we read this text:

> Das allgemeine Wesen ist das Eidos, die ἰδέα im platonischen Sinne, aber rein gefasst und frei von allen metaphysischen Interpretationen, also genau so genommen, wie es in der auf solchem Wege entspringenden Ideenschau uns unmittelbar intuitiv zur Gegebenheit kommt (*Erfahrung und Urteil*, p. 411).

> [This general essence is the *eidos*, the *idea* in the Platonic sense, but apprehended in its purity and free from all metaphysical interpretations, therefore taken exactly as it is given to us immediately and intuitively in the vision of the idea which arises in this way (*EJ*, p. 341).]

The Platonic idea is simply purified and grasped in the purity which it has in virtue of being a methodical result of ideation. Since ideation uses an individual example (real or imaginary) as its point of departure, the idea is defined as a dialectical correlate of the fact. The idea should never be conceived as an in-itself, absolutely independent of everything subjective (*EJ*, p. 330 [397]). But, as we have seen, this character of being a dialectical correlate—which is obvious in the Husserlian idea, since its being is a being-constituted—pertains in another form to the Platonic idea. Participation, which is essentially a relation, loses its meaning entirely if idea and fact are not mutually correlated. Allowing for the transposition of Plato's realistic-metaphysical view into Husserl's idealistic-constitutive perspective, we can say that the ideal is in each case, in an exactly analogous way, the *condition of the possibility* of the real (*Idées*, p. 18, n. 5). It remains true that for Platonism as well as for Husserlian phenomenology (although in different senses) the real participates in the ideal (cf. *Crisis*, p. 23 [20]).

3 / The Definition of
Science by the Idea

§ 9. *Description and definition*

SCIENCE IS A HISTORICAL PHENOMENON. Its terminus or
telos is to be grasped from its evolution. The idea of science is
the dialectical correlate of the development of science, it is the
intentional unity at which the indefinite multiplicity of its partial
and successive "appearings" aims. For science aims at a state of
full realization, a state of perfect knowledge of the object. This
aim can be fulfilled only at the end of a long process, of which
we have experienced and will experience only a very limited part.
It thus already appears that genuine science, the idea of science,
assumes that the totality of the steps of approximation to the
idea is realized.[1] Indeed, we know that mere development is not
self-sufficient. If science is considered solely in and according
to its evolution, it appears as the bearer of a sense that is neither
clarified nor justified. Intentional analysis alone can in the end
legitimize its originary sense, by bringing the idea which motivates it clearly to light (*Klärung*).

This is the noematic aspect of the question, which is summed
up in the dialectic of the idea and the real. The noetic (subjective) point of view must also be considered. It will be said
that description grasps the continuous development of science,

1. Thus we encounter for the first time two fundamental and
correlative characters of the Husserlian idea. The idea implies a
totality; but this is an *assumed* totality, i.e., a totality "as if"
(*Quasi-totalität, Als-ob*). This is the element of fiction in phenomenology.

[44]

that description is in fact the immediate experience of this development. But this description by itself remains insufficient; it must transcend itself. A description grasps appearances or "appearings" (*Erscheinungen, Darstellungen*). But just as these "appearings" have meaning only if they are explicitly referred to the thing which appears, so description will remain an incoherent succession of data as long as it does not explicitly refer to the intrinsic determination of the thing described. But what is it that formally expresses the intrinsic determination of a thing, its essence or nature, but the thing's *definition*? Description takes on its meaning only by definition; it is in a way a progressive approach to definition. The same dialectic occurs here between description and definition as occurs between the real and the idea, between factual historical science and ideal science. Description tends toward definition as the real tends toward the ideal.

For Husserl, then, to define a science (or a thing in general) is to determine its idea. Indeed, development is unintelligible by itself. In order to make it intelligible, we must find a necessary structure for it. Since the reality considered in descriptive experience is a development, and since this development must comprise a certain unitary sense, the terminus of this development must be what justifies and legitimizes its sense. It is therefore the telos of the development that defines the development. The telos determines the development's sense and hence its ultimate goal, the end toward which it tends. The definition of science determines the end idea of science (*LI*, p. 54 [I, 5]). Definition by idea is therefore an ideal, ultimate, and necessary definition. But a certain duality immediately enters into this notion of definition, since description can also be regarded as a sort of definition of science inasmuch as it determines the state of science at this or that moment of its development (*LI*, p. 54 [I, 5]). Definition by idea, or ideal definition, appears here as the ideal terminus or telos of an infinite progression of approximations, and description appears as a real definition, a partial realization of the ideal definition. Before being elicited in its perfect purity, the ideal definition will "appear" in partial and imperfect (real) realizations, along with the development of the same science whose ultimate definition it is.

The situation is therefore the same here as in the case of the dialectic of the real and the idea, only now we are on the noetic side. The real definition (description) of science immediately expresses the current stage of science. Since this stage is only a partial realization of the idea of science, the imperfect definition therefore immediately implies the perfect definition—just as the real implies the idea and the actual refers to the potential. This is so because the fact of the current imperfect realization of science implies the possibility of its perfect realization (cf. *LI*, p. 235 [I, 241]; *CM*, §§ 19–20). This is simply the law of development: the current moment, resting on the moments of the past, is the "promissory note" given to the future. The current realization is formulated in the current definition, and the potential realization is formulated in the possible definition. The definition of science by its idea is therefore a possible definition, an ideal definition. It is characterized as such by the gradualness of its process of realization and by the "possible-ness" (potentiality) of its being.[2]

Just as the ideal telos is the only terminus strictly speaking, so the ideal definition is the only definition strictly speaking. Thus we again find the characteristics that are proper to the idea. The idea is a transcendent in-itself, while the thing is relatively its in-itself. Similarly, the definition does not express a perfect coincidence with what it defines but only an intentional coincidence. The definition of science defines science by extrinsic denomination, in an a priori and normative manner. Moreover, the idea defines science as the possible defines the actual. The idea of science is only the possibility of perfectly completed science, and it is therefore necessarily irreal. Hence, to say that the idea of science defines science is to say both that possible science defines real (current) science and that the determination of the possible defines being.

> Die alte ontologische Lehre, dass die Erkenntnis der "Möglich-keiten" der der Wirklichkeiten vorhergehen müsse, ist m.E., woferne sie recht verstanden und in rechter Weise nutzbar gemacht wird, eine grosse Wahrheit (*Ideen I*, p. 194).

> [The old ontological doctrine, that the knowledge of "possibilities" must precede that of actualities is, in my opinion, in so far as it is rightly understood and properly utilized, a really great truth (*Ideas*, p. 232).]

This primacy of the possible over the actual must be understood as a way of expressing the primacy of the idea over the real from the transcendental-phenomenological point of view (*EJ*, p. 353 [427]). Every reality given by experience is subject

2. These are characteristic features of everything ideal. (All these remarks are an explication and commentary on *LI*, p. 54 [I, 5].)

to the conditions of its own possibility, which are the conditions of its originary givenness. Hence science too, as it is given in the experience of its pure sense, is subject to the conditions of its own possibility (*CM*, p. 72 [106]). This is not a matter of purely logical possibility (formal noncontradiction); rather, it is a possibility of transcendental constitution, of motivation of what is currently real by the possible idea.

§ 10. *The idea: act and potency*

THIS BY NO MEANS AMOUNTS to renewing a metaphysical tradition of the possible, however. The possible is the essence or eidos, in Husserl's sense, and this essence is implied in the unfolding of history. Hence it is not without relation to the real. On the contrary, it is a possibility that is motivated by the immediate empirical data which more or less perfectly realize it. Husserl distinguishes between two sorts of possibility. There is, on the one hand, the possibility that is motivated or pre-scribed in the process of effective realization according to an eidetic necessity. On the other hand, there is the *empty* possibility, which has a content [*statut*] of determinations with no foundation in empirical reality (*Ideas*, § 140; cf. *LI*, p. 235 [I, 241]). Thus there is an essential continuity between what is currently and immediately given and its essence (idea, eidos), since the former motivates the latter and since further development confirms this motivation (in the normal case of noninhibition). The current datum anticipates this or that particular determination, which contributes to the eidetic content of the essence and which (taking into account a certain margin of variation[3] expressed by the individual's contingency) must necessarily manifest itself in immediate experience. The current datum makes it possible to expect the appearance of these determinations in advance (*Vor-erwartung*). But this appearance is only partial, since the real in process of development only pre-scribes the

3. This is the "approximately" of approximation to type (*Crisis*, p. 25 [22]), by reason of which the object taken in its temporality is not adequate (identical) to itself taken in its pure essence. Cf. *EJ*, pp. 184 f. (217). Individuation is suppressed by the eidos, and time is the factor of individuation (*EJ*, pp. 173 f. [203]). The eidos is beyond time (*EJ*, p. 261 [313]) and therefore precludes all individuality.

idea of its completion. The possibility motivated by the immediate datum is therefore the totality of the phenomena which this datum announces to our expectation, and it is coextensive with the idea itself.[4] The possible is therefore identical with the idea. The idea is a pure possible which is pre-scribed or passively preconstituted in the real. It is a potentiality included in the actuality that is explicated and thematized by intentional analysis (CM, §§ 19–20). Since the real in question is a development, the potentiality included in its actuality is precisely the potentiality of the phases succeeding (or preceding) the present moment. Descriptive experience immediately grasps the actuality, the present instant of the development of science. This present instant rests on an open horizon of past moments and an open horizon of future moments. The nature of the potentiality is not the same in the two cases, however. The past is known because it is "habitually" sedimented, while the future can be known only anticipatively. We are especially concerned with the latter potentiality, that of the further moments of the development which are implied in the current moment. Grasped in its totality, this potentiality is what is expressed, in the form of an idea, as an objectification of the possible and at the same time as the ideal end of the real development. In this sense the idea-possible precedes the real fact and pre-scribes it a priori.[5]

But a reversal of classical metaphysics is contained in the assertion that the possible determines the real and that, consequently, knowledge of the possible precedes knowledge of the real. For classical metaphysics, act has an absolute primacy over potency. Although in the genetic order it was necessary to "pass through" potency in order to reach act, it is nevertheless true that only act—being the determinate, the exercise of being in its purity—makes it possible to understand potency. In relation to act, potency is a "being in tendency," a being which is not an absolute nonbeing but which does not exist as such. It is genetically prior to act, but, precisely as potency, it is the

4. Here we have a reappearance of the idea as totality.
5. It will be noted that the words "motivation" and "pre-scription" are used in two senses. It can just as well be said that the real development motivates or pre-scribes the idea or else that the idea motivates or pre-scribes the real development. This is the twofold dimension of Husserlian exemplarism: the real makes it possible to reach the idea, and the idea predetermines the real. (We have here the mutual exemplarity of fact and eidos.)

result of a philosophical analysis. For this reason, the greatest
danger the intellect can run is the danger of reifying or hy-
postatizing potency. This would amount to giving it an absolute
reality—or, in other words, to denying it as potency and conceiving it as act. By distinguishing two points of view (the point
of view of nature and the genetic point of view of knowledge),
classical metaphysics established a sort of dialectic of reciprocity
between act and potency, according to which act and potency
alternately have priority. Plato's dialectic of the idea and the
real is a form of this dialectic of act and potency combined with
the dialectic of essence and fact, since the idea is for Plato both
absolute determination and the pure exercise of being.

To the extent that Husserl takes his place in the Platonic
succession, he takes up the heritage of classical metaphysics
and puts into operation this doctrine of act and potency, which
was exploited by Aristotle primarily in the *Metaphysics* (Bk. IX).
But as we might suspect, he takes the same liberty with the
letter of Aristotle as he does with Plato. This "dialectic" of act
and potency is found in Husserl's work, too, but with these two
notions arranged in the reverse order of priority. Classical
metaphysics saw in the act the terminus (telos, end) of
potency and, conversely, built into the notion of potency an
ordering to actuality. Only the act is real or existent; potency
is real only to the extent that it tends toward act and participates
in its reality. Hence what is formulated in metaphysics as the
problem of the act is the problem of final causality.

Husserl turns this doctrine around. For him the possible is
the terminus of the act, and actuality is an ordering to potency.
A certain finality remains, then, but the way Husserl turns the
doctrine around makes this an *ideal* finality. The idea, as a
possibility of being, does not really exist. It is irreal and is
hence an ideal end. The descriptive appearances are saved, and
it may be said superficially that Husserl repeats Aristotle. Husserl sees a teleology between act and potency, a teleology which
Aristotle locates between potency and act. Hence Husserl takes
up Aristotle's vocabulary, but we must not attribute to him an
"Aristotelianism" in the historical sense.

Actually, two points of view overlap here. At first sight it
seems obvious that for Husserl the act of science is its fully
completed state. Current science is in potency with respect to
its own perfect realization, and it tends toward this realization as its telos. Husserl uses the Aristotelian terms *dynamis*

(potency) and *energeia* (act); science evolves by passing from potency to act, "from vague *dynamis* towards its *energeia*." [6] The completed state of science is therefore the act or entelechy of science. When science has reached its telos, when it has absolutely realized its idea, it is *entelechy* strictly speaking—as is shown by the etymology of the word: *en-telos-echein,* the " 'habitual' state of that which has reached its end." But we cannot speak significantly of the teleology of science without implying its progressive realization in the current of history. The Greeks already laid down the idea of genuine absolute knowledge, and this idea is what motivated their strivings for knowledge. This idea, sustained and carried on by generations of scientists, is the entelechy of rational mankind. It is this ideal telos, conceived by the Greeks, which must prove—in the course of the "proof" of its historical realization—whether it is truly the act (entelechy) of cognitive humanity. The highest realization of this ideal—the philosophy inaugurated by the first Greek physicists and brought to its terminus by Husserl—is thus an idea which raises mankind to a new level and which, as it is worked out in the course of a new historicity of human life, constitutes mankind's true entelechy, its full bloom, its *Seligkeit* (*Crisis,* pp. 15 [13], 336 [270 f.]; cf. *Crisis,* p. 340 [275]). It seems at first sight that Husserl has simply taken up the theory of act and potency and that the borrowing of words conceals a more essential borrowing of concepts.

However, we know that the completed state of science, or the idea of science, is an ideal state, since science tends progressively to the realization of its idea. The telos or entelechy of science is therefore ideal. But if it is ideal, it is irreal and hence not actual. For the idea of science is simply the possibility of its perfect realization. Act becomes potency and vice versa. This is a strange conflation, but it is not an arbitrary application of concepts from classical metaphysics to Husserl's phenomenology, since Husserl himself uses these concepts. Hence we must see in what sense he uses them, what modifications he

6. *Crisis,* p. 98 (101). In the quoted passage, Husserl uses this expression in connection with the concept of "transcendental" which he is concerned to set out in its ideal purity. This expression is valid for the elucidation of the structure of all development, as Husserl emphasizes with regard to the object of knowledge in general (*EJ,* p. 29 [24]). Let us note in passing that Husserl draws no distinction between the word *"energeia"* and the word "entelechy." Both are acts in the same respect. This is not the case with Aristotle.

gives them, and to what extent he continues a line of thought that was inaugurated in antiquity.

Act and potency do indeed take on an original sense in Husserl's perspective. Husserl makes them into criteria of value suitable for measuring the relative perfection of ideal science and effective science. Apart from this modification, it can be said from this first point of view that the Husserlian act retains at least one trait in common with the act as conceived by the metaphysics represented here by Aristotle in particular. In each case, act is regarded as determinate perfection. Similarly, potency is regarded in each case as indeterminate (determinable) imperfection. But in classical metaphysics, act and potency essentially have an existential significance. The act is the existent par excellence, that which exercises being; potency is that which is ordered to being but which *is not* in act. Neither potency nor act connotes formal determinations but rather a pure exercise of existing. But for Husserl that which exists (even before having its exact formal determination or its being value) is imperfect science and the imperfect in general, hence the *potency* of absolute perfection and definitive determination; and the act of science (the idea of its perfect realization) is in this respect purely irreal and inactual. It does not exist; it is possible. In other words, the concepts are completely reversed from this second point of view. Potency is act, and act is potency.

It is easy to straighten out the tangle by returning to the distinction between two genetic points of view, the transcendental-phenomenological and the descriptive-phenomenological. The first, as we know, is that of originary transcendental constitution. According to it, the idea is absolutely first, since it is the motivating principle (*archē*) of its factical realization. The idea is fully determined as the norm of the effective historical development. It is the *value* (the exemplary principle) operating in the development. As such, it is the telos at which the development (of science) aims, and this teleology ends intentionally in the entelechy. From this point of view, the idea is act and its realization is potency.

The second point of view is that of the intentional progress from empirical fact to originary idea, beginning with the immediate knowledge we have (by virtue of historical experience) of the fact in its development. But history is real; it is in history that the existence of things (and hence of science) unfolds and is worked out (*entfaltet*). Hence, what is actual here is the fact, the real development. Only imperfect science (tending toward its perfection) exists in the strict sense of "exist." Hence, from this second point of view, the realization is act and the idea is potency.

Let us summarize this important distinction:

From the *value-act* point of view (which coincides with the transcendental-phenomenological point of view of originary constitution), the idea is act (entelechy) and the realization is potency.[7]

From the *existence-act* point of view (which coincides with the descriptive-phenomenological point of view of the intentional discovery of the idea), the realization is act and the idea is potency.[8]

Hence, what is actual from the point of view of existence is, in reality, potency from the point of view of value (ideal perfection). And what is potential (possible) from the existential point of view is act from the point of view of value. The actually existing science is potency of its perfect realization, of the idea of genuine science. Conversely, the idea of science is act with regard to its mode of perfection, since it intuitively represents (*vergegenwärtigt*) the ideal perfection of science. But it is potency, since it is only the possibility of this perfect realization —a possibility that is, to be sure, motivated by the existing imperfect science.

Husserl himself does not draw this distinction. He does formulate the "dialectic" of act and potency, but for him this is simply a matter of formulating the dialectic of the real and the idea. In fact, the latter dialectic makes it possible to combine the two points of view we have distinguished, that of value and that of existence (i.e., of formal determination and of being or, again, of essence and of existence). But this necessarily leads to an exemplarist view of the act (entelechy). We showed above that, for classical metaphysics, act is the explication of the final cause and represents the very principle of existence. In classical metaphysics the end is always a real end, an existent. To make the act into a value is to determine it as a form, to make the end into a form, as we shall see (cf. below, "General

7. Here it is the idea that motivates and pre-scribes its factical realization.

8. Here it is the factical reality, the effective development of history, that motivates and pre-scribes the idea.

Conclusion"). And if we hold to a finality (teleology) of some sort while asserting that the real fact in process of development tends toward its act idea—that is, that what is measured tends toward the principle which measures it—this can be only an ideal finality. It will be the finality of the copy toward its model and hence an exemplarity rather than a finality. Act and potency express the (operational) aspect of being as exercise. The dialectic of fact and eidos remains on the formal level of essence. If the two orders are combined, the formal (essential) aspect—which is the more intelligible—takes precedence. But if we wish to preserve a dynamism, we must direct ourselves to the exemplary (formal extrinsic) side. This is why the perfection which the act exhibits as such becomes a criterion of value (norm). A kind of dynamism is then obtained which is quite similar to that of the artist in the process of realizing his idea.[9]

In sum, it must be said that the development of science involves the two points of view without distinguishing between them. There is no need to distinguish them for the descriptive process that is essential to phenomenology, since science never exists without its greater or lesser degree of perfection. Development itself shows the points of view of existence and of value concretely united and conflated. Intentional analysis therefore does its job by giving an account of this development by means of the dialectic of the real and the idea. It thereby explains the intentional dynamism of the actual existing imperfection, which is wholly drawn toward the possible ideal perfection.

This is why Husserl can say in the end that what legitimizes the current fact of science is its subsumption under the idea of possible science. By this he clearly shows that the possible is what norms the (actual) fact, while we have just defined the idea-norm as act (*FTL*, p. 267 [236]). An analysis is involved here, and every analysis is below (or beyond) the reality analyzed. The concrete mode of realization (development, existence) shows the unity of the principles that are analyzed. Reality is always totality, and the dialectic of eidos and fact is for Husserl the most appropriate way—since it is the most synthetic way—to give an account of reality.

9. Cf. the concrete application of this idea in Mikel Dufrenne, *The Phenomenology of Aesthetic Experience*, trans. Edward S. Casey *et al.* (Evanston, Ill.: Northwestern University Press, 1973). Cf. also below, "General Conclusion."

§ 11. *The idea: idealization of the total development. The phenomenological fiction of the "as if"*

IN THE CASE OF SCIENCE we have an example of phenomenological method which is easily extended by means of a formal generalization to all possible cases. Phenomenology defines a historical being on the basis of its history. But, as everyone knows, history is a succession of facts which can fall within immediate experience, either psychological (internal) or external. However, the development given by experience is and remains unintelligible if no terminus (telos) is fixed for it. The entire problematic of intentional analysis is written here: How is the telos to be determined on the basis of the real and historical development? The development would have to be completed in order for the human mind to be able to perceive its telos and thereby legitimize the direction which, as it seems, historical experience makes it possible to determine. The telos or end of the development will be grasped only when the development is completed.[10] But the development is by definition incomplete.

The only way to get out of this difficulty is the one we demonstrated in the case of science. On the basis of the development, following an exacting analysis of the nexus of relations represented by the phenomenological instant, future development must be anticipated—and at the same stroke its telos must be anticipated. Hence it is necessary to act in a sense *as if* (*als ob*) the development were fully completed and to act *as if* we had *really* arrived at its terminus. In other words, we must apply a method analogous to the mathematical method which consists in supposing the problem to be solved. This is a process which remains purely within the ideal sphere of intentional analysis, a process which consists in ideally going over the course which a real development would have to go over ad infinitum. Rather than accompany the development "descriptively" in the multiplicity of its real phases, analysis lives them intentionally and anticipates what is realized ad infinitum. This ideal anticipation is necessary because the development is infinite. No method of real accomplishment of the development could reveal its telos, since this telos cannot in any case really

10. Cf. H. Bergson, *Creative Evolution,* trans. Arthur Mitchell (New York: Random House, 1944), pp. 116 f.

be reached. The ideal anticipation, the "as if," is therefore an essential necessity. Analysis does not attain fullness of clarity of the end idea with the "as if," but it can at least posit the essential possibility of the end idea with the clarity of anticipation. Instead of a real clarification (*Klärung*), which would be the fulfilling verification of an originary infinite intention, the process of analysis is a purely ideal clarification or a prefiguration (*Vorverbildlichung*) of the idea.[11]

Thus an element of fiction is introduced into intentional inquiry. To act as if the entire development were realized is obviously to "simulate" the realization of its infinite totality. Imagination and fiction are necessary for the elaboration of the idea. They are like revealers of the essence (idea), as Paul Ricoeur has written (*Idées*, p. 24, n. 2[b]). Fiction is in general the vital element of phenomenology and of every eidetic science (*Ideas*, p. 201 [163]).

We must come to a clear understanding of this curious notion of phenomenological fiction. It is not to be confused with the pragmatic-positivist fictionalism,[12] since such a confusion could easily bring ridicule on knowledge of the eidetic kind (*Ideas*, p. 201, n. 1 [163]). (This is the advice of Husserl, who likes to jolt common sense with his paradoxes!) The concept of fiction we are dealing with implies that the idea is a sort of *image* insofar as it is a "reality-as-if," an irreality which is treated as really real (*ontōs on*).[13] By this we are to understand a possibility, in the manner of a "pure and simple conceivability" ("in der Weise der blossen Erdenklichkeit, in einem Sich-denken, als ob es wäre"), a quasi-positional imaginary reality (*phantasiemässige Unwirklichkeit*) grasped in a prefiguring intuition (*vorverbildlichende Anschauung*) (*CM*, § 25). This "conceivability" is a way of intuiting a pure possibility (an eidos), as Husserl writes with regard to perception.[14]

11. We have here the substance of the doctrine of *Besinnung* (cf. *FTL*, pp. 9 f. [8 f.]) and of the *Klärung* of the judgment, which is simply a particular case of *Klärung* in general (cf. *FTL*, pp. 60–62 [53–55]; *CM*, p. 59 [94]).

12. Cf. Hans Vaihinger, *Die Philosophie des Als-ob* (Berlin: Reuther & Reichhard, 1911).

13. Husserl speaks of *Quasi-Wirklichkeit*, *Wirklichkeit-als-ob*, *Phantasie*.

14. *CM*, p. 70 (104). This text is part of the exposition of the doctrine of free variation. It shows the necessary connection between the concepts of irreality, "as-if," pure possibility, mere conceivability by the imagination, and eidos. It appears that the idea (eidos) is an

More precisely, the idea is an "imagination" of the total and completed development. It is the intuitive presentification of the full realization of the development, and since this presentification is by definition not a datum of originary experience (perception), it is necessarily founded on an anticipating activity on the part of the subject. It is idealization, which (according to *Ideas I* and *Cartesian Meditations*) is identified with intuitive presentification, with *blosse Phantasie*, or is at least equivalent to it. The positing of the idea loses none of its value if it is the result of an ideal anticipation of the idea's fulfillment. On the contrary, by a mere change of attitude—the change from the real attitude to the ideal attitude of intentional analysis (the epochē)—the intuitive presentification is equivalent to the originary presence of the datum of experience (*Ideas*, p. 391 [345]). The *Als-ob* of ideal experience is equivalent to the real of effective experience. This must be understood in a purely ideal sense, since the *Als-ob* of the idea expresses the possibility of the full completion of the real fact in process of development. "Imagination" of this kind can be only anticipation, and it therefore gives, not the current reality of the content of the idea, but the possibility of this content. Ideal anticipation can be only the thematization of the possible development (*CM*, p. 59 [94]). For this reason it gives no actual existence. The idea is not positional, as is the fact of empirical perception; it is quasi-positional, since it posits a pure possible. It is important to understand the quasi-positional character of the idea, which will also enable us to understand its character as an image.

The idea is quasi-positional only with respect to the fact of which it is the idea. This fact is presently given in descriptive experience, and it is given first from the descriptive-phenomenological point of view. It is thus the existent, with respect to which the idea (the essence) is an ideal possibility. But this phenomenological point of view merges with the existence-act point of view, as we saw above; and only from the latter point of view can we identify idea with image as being the possible motivated by the existing actual. As such the idea may be regarded as the result of an anticipation based on the partial real experience of the idea's content, implying a spontaneous activity

image, a mere imaginative thought, a mere possibility devoid of any facticity or any existential character. This is more than is needed to establish the identity between the idea and the quasi-reality which duplicates the real world. (This is one interpretation of *CM*, § 25; another is given below, p. 57, n. 15.)

of the ego to make up for the deficiencies of this experience. From the transcendental-phenomenological point of view, the idea is fully act. As such it is the object of a genuine and specific ideal experience. From this second point of view it no longer makes sense to identify idea with image.

Hence only the descriptive-phenomenological point of view allows us to substitute the distinction between real and imaginary, between *Wirklichkeit* and *Phantasie,* for the distinction between fact and eidos. We should instead call the former another aspect of the same distinction. The correlation between fact and idea (development and its telos) actually goes back to an essential split in consciousness. On the one side there is the sphere of the actually present, of what is immediately given in the real immanence of descriptive experience. On the other side there is the sphere of the possible, of the idea (based on the immediate datum) as the irreal transcendence of the actually present experience. In fact we find here not a heterogeneity of nature but only a difference in degree of the same reality. We always have the idea before us, either as being actually realized or as remaining a pure possibility. Actuality and potentiality are simply *modes* of the idea, hence of consciousness and reason. The ideal-objective categories of reason (that is to say, reason itself) are concealed (*verborgen*) in its cognitive operations [*Leistungen*] and, as such, are applied to the world of sensible experience. But this same reason can also manifest itself in a way that is absolutely devoid of any application to sensible data. This is the pure exercise of reason, which is manifested in mathematics and in all the eidetic sciences generally (the ideal sciences, philosophy and logic) (cf. *Crisis,* pp. 94 [97], 103 f. [106], 52 [53]). But these two modes of the idea or of reason respectively describe a sphere of reality (*Wirklichkeit*) and a sphere of irreality or quasi-reality (*Quasi-Wirklichkeit, Wirklichkeit-als-ob*), the one real and the other imaginary. We know that *Wirklichkeit-als-ob* is identical with *Phantasie,* that the idea is identical with the *phantasiemässige Unwirklichkeit;* and we know the exact conditions of this identity.[15]

15. This radical bifurcation of consciousness between fact and eidos, between the actual and the possible, is warranted by *CM,* § 25 and by *Ideas,* § 114. Each of these sections alludes (that of *CM* implicitly and that of *Ideas* explicitly) to the doctrine of neutralization. Neutralization is said to modify, by a mere change of sign (or of quality, in the words of *LI*), the value of conscious experiences [*vécus*] without affecting their material basis (*Bestand*). But

Neither imagination nor fiction is arbitrary, however. On the contrary, they are motivated by their point of departure. The possible is an anticipation based on the actual, hence it is not merely suspended in the void (although, in *CM*, p. 70 [104], Husserl uses the expression "suspended in the void of pure conceivability"). The irreal, the *Als-ob*, is the thematization of the possibility of further development of the real, based on its past and current development. The expression "imagination" is therefore ambiguous (*CM*, p. 59 [94]). The imaginary in Husserl's sense of the word is not arbitrary but motivated. It is not a mere mental creation, as, for example, the image of a centaur would be, but a possible essence which pre-scribes the progressive development of its own realization. Only in this way can we understand how Husserl can say that the idea (essence) at the same time both is and is not an image or fiction (*Ideas*, § 23).

In order to explicate this equivalence of the possible with the really given, let us return to the development of science. This development is a realization which is always partial but which

neutralization is sometimes conflated with imagination (*FTL*, p. 206 [183]), and thus neutralized experience, or experience *"als ob,"* is identified with experience in imagination. If we take into account that imagination gives rise to a new universal concept of "possible" (according to *CM*, p. 58 [94]), it can be said that neutralization is an operation which makes the actual possible—that is, which brackets the existential value of the actual. On the other hand, however, neutralization is sometimes radically distinguished from imagination (*Ideas*, § 111; cf. *LI*, Fifth Investigation, § 40). But this distinction is hard to conceive (as Husserl himself admits), since imagination is at least a type of neutralization. Moreover, according to what we have just seen, neutralization is a type of epoché which suspends the being value of what is neutralized by making it a mere possible. If neutralization is an imagination of sorts, it follows that the epoché is related to imagination. The epoché, like imagination-neutralization, brackets the external existence of the object without losing any of its determinations. Under the reduction, the object comes to be non-positional rather than positional, or at least its positional aspect comes to be ideal rather than real. The object is reduced to its meaning, i.e., to its pure essence (a mere possible). It can therefore be seen that the radical bifurcation of consciousness of which *Ideas* speaks in § 114, between noema and neutralized noema (counter-noema, *Gegennoema*) can be considered as the universal and a priori distinction between fact and eidos; for the idea is in a way the fact itself, at least as to its formal determinations, "abstracting" from its real positionality. It is the essence of the fact, the essential possibility of the fact, by which we are to understand in the strict sense the condition of the fact's possibility—and therefore its a priori norm or ideal exemplary principle.

tends toward its definitive perfection. However, since descriptive experience is necessarily located in a temporal moment, it can grasp only the actuality of this development and not its possible ideal terminus. In order to grasp the terminus, we must conceive the development as completed in its totality; we must act as if it were completed. The intuitive presentification of the essential connection between development and telos is in a way substituted for the originary presence of the telos. That is, the presentification substitutes the idealized development (the idea) in its totality for the entire real development. In fact it is impossible to conceive the development as total and real, since it is in itself infinite. The only way to grasp the telos of the development is therefore through its idealization. But the notion of equivalence implies two terms of the same value put into relation; we would have to put the ideated total development and the real total development in relation to each other, which is impossible. There is no equivalence in the strictly theoretical sense. There is instead a practical equivalence, in the sense that the realization of the idea is practically equivalent to the idea itself insofar as there is a teleological tendency of the first toward the second.

Another way of expressing the fundamental thesis of phenomenology is to be seen here. Reality can never be adequately grasped in its *Selbst;* from the mere fact that it is only development, it is necessarily infinite. All knowledge consists in approaching it asymptotically. The error is to posit a real [*réelle*] absolute knowledge. A possible absolute knowledge must be posited, which, as possible, motivates an infinity of steps of approximation and which for this reason will never be actually realized. An absolutely completed knowledge must be renounced, but we need not renounce approaching it. Here we have the whole dynamism of science expressed by the term "teleology." Far from an agnostic resignation, this doctrine of the idea as fiction has behind it a voluntary decision to break through the transcendence of the telos (whether this is the idea of the object or the idea of science) and disclose (*entfalten*) its essential possibility (*Wesensmöglichkeit*) by and in an approximation ad infinitum.

It is nevertheless the case that since knowledge never reaches its telos, since it is always and by definition inadequate to its intention (its claim or "pretension"), there remains for this reason an opening for a sort of mythical view. Such a view at least "preserves appearances" by permitting the knowing subject (who cannot receive absolute satisfaction) to have a practical satisfaction equivalent to that which he would have if his theoretical interest were perfectly satisfied (in the case of a science having reached the ideal telos of its development).[16]

The *Als-ob* of fiction cannot be the result of a real process, then, since the only real process is one of going along with the development in order to arrive, as it were, at the terminus of

16. Phenomenology "deciphers" the world and thereby gives it a sense having the advantage of coherence and simplicity. Perhaps, since fiction is characteristic of phenomenology and "vital" to it, the world might have another sense; but it is not "morally credible," as Descartes says, that such a clear and captivating reading of the world's cipher should be false. "If, for instance, anyone wishing to read a letter written in Latin characters that are not placed in their proper order, takes it into his head to read B wherever he finds A and C wherever he finds B, thus substituting for each letter the one following it in the alphabet, and if he in this way finds that there are certain Latin words composed of these, he will not doubt that the true meaning of the writing is contained in these words, though he may discover this by conjecture, and although it is possible that the writer did not arrange the letters in this order of succession, but on some other, and thus concealed another meaning in it: for this is so unlikely to occur, especially when the cipher contains many words, that it seems incredible" (R. Descartes, *The Principles of Philosophy*, § 205, in *The Philosophical Works of Descartes*, trans. E. S. Haldane and G. R. T. Ross [Cambridge, Eng.: At the University Press, 1911], p. 301). Thus for Descartes a greater probability is sufficient, i.e., an appearance of explanation, or at least of the explanation of the more or less imagined possibility of things. "Touching the things which our senses do not perceive, it is sufficient to explain what the possibilities are about the nature of their existence, though perhaps they are not what we describe them to be (and this is all that Aristotle has tried to do). . . . I believe that I have done all that is required of me if the causes I have assigned are such that they correspond to all the phenomena manifested by nature, without inquiring whether it is by their means or by others that they are produced. [Note here that Descartes implicitly hints at a sort of exemplarity of the fact with respect to the essence, of the existing actual with respect to the possible.] And it will be sufficient for the usages of life to know such causes, for medicine and mechanics and in general all these arts to which the knowledge of physics subserves, have for their end merely the application of certain sensible bodies to one another, so that by the operation of natural causes certain sensible effects are produced; and one will be able to accomplish this quite as well by considering the succession of certain causes thus imagined, although false, as if they were true, since this succession is supposed to be similar so far as sensible effects are concerned" (*ibid.*, § 204, p. 300). In the latter passage we find the practical equivalence of the imagined, the doctrine of the "*als-ob*."

development at the same time as the development itself. Experience *Als-ob* or intuitive presentification is a pure act of thought, an idealization or ideation; it is an intuitive presentification which is the fundamental act of intentional analysis, the ideal method of anticipatory intellectual intuition. In the first (descriptive) attitude, this intuition regards the development as pure flow. But being dissatisfied, it immediately seeks a necessary, permanent, and stable element in terms of which the development can be defined. According to the very terms of the problem thus posed, the definition can only be a definition by extrinsic denomination. But the development itself, anticipated in its totality, is obviously the stable element that is sought, all the more so because it makes it possible to determine exactly the end of the process. The whole makes it possible to define the part, but this whole—not being actually realized—is ideally anticipated in the form of a pure essence, an eidos or idea. The development is therefore defined by the idealization of its own totality. This is what is meant by our conclusion that the development is defined by the idea. Only in this way does the development take on meaning. When the totality of the development can be visualized as if it were completed, its ideal terminus is anticipated at the same time, and its meaning and unity are revealed. The idea thus issues immediately from the development as the immediate and determinate idealization of a whole that is not immediate and not determinate. And this applies to all cases of development in search of their definition—the development of the constitution of the thing as well as the teleological development of science.

In general it is enough to have the part in order to anticipate the whole and thereby to give an account of the part. It is enough, for example, to perceive a single conscious experience "perceptively" in order to see sketched before oneself the possibility of intuitively continuing the glance to the future series of experiences, as far as this series may extend. This is a possibility, an irreality, since only the first experience (because it is effectively realized) is real. Hence the same principle is always applied: on the basis of what is currently realized, the realizable (the potential or possible) is "extrapolated." For history, this will be the guiding idea of history; for the sciences in their current state, it will be the idea of genuine science. This idea is in each case the idealization of the total development. It is therefore an intuitive (ideating) grasp of this totality, produced in the infinite form of the intuitive grasp of an absence of limits in a process. This is what Husserl is saying in an admirable passage in *Ideas I*, where he shows how the idea is the means of thematizing an infinite flow of experiences (*Ideas*, pp. 239 f. [201 f.]).

§ 12. *The theory of wholes and parts applied to the dialectic of the idea*

IF THE IDEA IS THE WHOLE, and if the more or less perfect realization of the idea is a part, this brings us to the problematic of wholes and parts. This doctrine was elaborated for the first time in the *Logical Investigations*, in the series of logical-analytical studies in which the study of sign and meaning also figured (*LI*, Third Investigation). It seems subsequently to have been relegated to a rank of secondary importance. Neither *Ideas I* nor *Formal and Transcendental Logic* alludes to it.[17] *Experience and Judgment* takes up the theme again, being naturally led to it by the theory of perception and explication of the object (*EJ*, §§ 30–32). Nevertheless, Husserl seems not to have attributed major importance to this doctrine, in any case not in the properly phenomenological domain of the intentional analysis of the idea. Indeed, he himself never explicitly brought the problematic of wholes and parts together with that of the real and the idea, as he did, for example, the "dialectic" of act and potency. However, just as we saw the fruitful use of the doctrine of the sign in the dialectic of the real and the idea, so we shall see the theory of wholes and parts shed a new light on the doctrine of the idea. Thus for the second time we see the logical-analytical teaching of the *Logical Investigations* extended into themes which are properly phenomenological and constitutive (cf. above, § 5).

Among parts, Husserl draws a distinction between those which are *independent* and those which are *dependent*. The former are those which can be conceived separately and which therefore have a sense that is self-sufficient. The latter, on the other hand, cannot be conceived separately but only together with other elements which in a way play the role of support

17. Except in a roundabout manner, in connection with the concrete and the abstract (*Ideas*, § 15).

for them. Thus, for example, the trees in the boulevard are independent parts (*Stücke*), and the color of an object is a dependent part (*Moment*). This difference in the very being of parts is expressed—and is immediately constituted—in the experience that grasps them (*EJ*, p. 142 [163]). Husserl illustrates this assertion with an example. He takes the perception of a footed ashtray which is red in color. Perception first grasps the confused totality of the ashtray and the parts that make it up. Perceptual explication then discerns the various parts; depending on the order that the glance follows, it distinguishes first the ashtray itself and then its foot, for example. The perception of the first part of the ashtray (in our example, the cupped part) is accompanied by a characteristic phenomenon which may be called "consciousness of remainder." The first part in effect calls for the second part (the foot), thereby implying a surplus (*Überschuss*) which completes it (*EJ*, p. 143 [164]). Thus, perception of the first part tends to go beyond itself to perception of the second part, the two perceptions finally constituting the whole of the ashtray. This consciousness of remainder is what makes it apparent that we have to do with an independent part (*Stück*). It is not produced in the explication of a dependent part (*Moment*); at least the manner in which the "remainder" is present to consciousness in the second case is quite different. The example of color is particularly appropriate for making Husserl's thinking understood. Perception of the ashtray's red color does not leave room for a further explicative perception of a second part which would complete this first perception (*EJ*, pp. 143 f. [165]). That is, the whole ashtray is red, whereas the whole ashtray is not its foot.[18] However, the ashtray is not its red color either. The latter is therefore a (dependent) moment of the ashtray; it can be grasped by itself only in an abstraction. In the present case the entire ashtray is the *concrete* and the color is the *abstract*. Indeed, the goal of abstraction is to make a part that is inseparable from its whole into an object on its own account, an object that is capable of being intuited by itself (*LI*, p. 429 [II/1, 219]). This necessarily implies that the dependent part (*Moment*) does not subsist on its own account but is only "distinguished" in a "special" way by abstraction.

18. Thus is founded the doctrine of judgments of being and judgments of having, which we have already encountered (above, § 7).

In the case of independent parts, the "remainder" is added to the part that is already present to consciousness; the various parts are consequently added together. In the case of dependent parts, the "remainder" and the original part interpenetrate inseparably; the parts in this case, since they are not external to one another, cannot be added together. They are parts of the whole in a more immediate way than independent parts, which can be separated from the whole.[19] In this sense they are *properties* or qualities (*Eigenschaften*) of the whole (*EJ*, pp. 145 f. [167 f.]).

This doctrine easily carries over to the case which concerns us. The imperfect realization of science tends toward the perfect realization, toward the idea of science. This means that each current stage transcends itself and requires to be continued in a new stage, in such a way as finally to reach the telos or end idea itself. Science is thus engaged in a continual movement toward a *plus ultra* (*EJ*, p. 82 [87]), just as the perception of the ashtray discerned a first part and then a second in immediate continuity. The "claim" set forth by science (*CM*, p. 9 [50]) is therefore the analogue of this consciousness of remainder (*Überschuss*) which turns up in the explication of independent parts. The progress of science is never completed; the idea is more or less closely approached, and hence there is always a "remainder" for which a fulfillment may be claimed. And this fulfillment is also effected by the addition of successive steps, which, like independent parts, are "external" to one another. Moreover, explication discerns parts in the object, but it does so with a view to explicitly realizing the whole. If there is consciousness of remainder in explication, then, this is because there is a whole which polarizes the explication. This whole is therefore in a way the intentional telos or end idea of explicative perception. Similarly, in the case of science, there is a claim because there is an end idea to be realized. We know that this end idea is the ideal perfect realization of science and that it polarizes the multiplicity of its development.

It is therefore legitimate to see in the idea of science the completed *whole* of science, just as the object is the whole of its successively explicated parts. Conversely, the imperfect realization of science is a *part* of ideal science. But we must not rush into a hasty assimilation of the concepts we are dealing with. It

19. On this point *EJ* (p. 143 [165]) refers to *LI* (p. 475 [II/1, 276]).

must first be emphasized that the whole of perfectly completed science is not a currently realized whole. It can be currently grasped only in the form of an idea, hence as an irreality. Further, we must ask whether the imperfect realization of science is to be regarded as an independent or a dependent part in relation to its idea. According to what we have established, it seems that it is an independent part, since we have compared the consciousness of remainder in explicative perception of *Stücke* with the claim of science.

Nevertheless, it is clearly impossible to make the realization of the idea of science (i.e., currently actual science) into an independent part of the idea of science. The whole sense of current science is to be a proximate realization of ideal science. All its strivings are oriented toward the ultimate telos which ideal science represents. Moreover, each stage is a bearer of this sense and transmits it to the following stage. The realization of science, whatever its degree of approximation to the idea, is nothing in itself or for itself. It does not subsist by itself, since by itself it is mere relativity. It depends—in its definition, in its sense, and in its "existence"—on the in-itself which the idea represents. Therefore, the realization of the idea is in this sense a dependent part or *Moment* of the idea. Like every dependent part, it can subsist only through something else; and this "something else" in the case at hand is its in-itself. Here again we find the doctrine of extrinsic determination of fact by eidos. The fact is not, in itself, its essence. It does not even have its essence in itself in an absolute way, but only relatively, by participation. The fact can only be relative; the eidos (idea) alone is absolute. It appears from this that the fact is necessarily dependent on the idea.[20]

Conceiving the realization of the idea as moment of the idea thus confirms what we said earlier concerning the idealization-idea of the total development. The realization is a moment of the idea because it is intrinsically part of the idea (an integral part) and plays a role in constituting it. We know that development pre-scribes and motivates the idea. But this idea, this "more" which is pre-scribed in the development, is still not

20. *LI*, pp. 446 f. (II/1, 240). Cf. an analogous line of thought in M. Merleau-Ponty, *Phenomenology of Perception*, trans. Colin Smith (New York: Humanities Press, 1962), p. 455; *Sense and Non-Sense*, trans. Hubert L. Dreyfus and Patricia Allen Dreyfus (Evanston, Ill.: Northwestern University Press, 1964), pp. 9–25.

actual. Even as pre-scribed or claimed, it is only possible.[21] Intentional analysis has only to elicit it in all purity. Thus, saying that the realization of the idea is a moment of the idea is equivalent to saying that the idea is the idealization of the total development. There is the same equivalence here as when we said that it amounts to the same thing to say that current science is idealized or that ideal science is realized. The same intentionality is involved in both cases, according as it is considered in the direction from fact to eidos or from eidos to fact. Let us add, as a last consequence of this discussion, that if the realization is a dependent part of the idea, it is a property of the idea. The very essence of ideal science or of the idea in general requires that it should be realized. This is precisely transcendental constitution.

The doctrine of wholes and parts therefore finds useful application here, but not without a nuance. The more or less perfect realization of science is a part which belongs to both categories, *Stück* and *Moment,* as they are distinguished by Husserl. It partakes of the *Stück* insofar as the whole toward which it tends is not a currently realized whole (as is the ashtray in the example cited above) and, consequently, insofar as it tends toward this whole in a perpetual self-surpassing which is motivated by a claim (consciousness of remainder) to fulfillment. It partakes of the *Moment* insofar as the ideal whole toward which it tends is the intentional telos which gives it its own sense and content. Hence we must make use of a twofold analogy, which corresponds to the two dimensions of exemplarity, in order to formulate perfectly the partial character of the realization of the idea of science. The idea is thus the necessary thematization of a totality which is an infinite totality.

The conclusion we mean to establish is, in sum, that only the idea is concrete, since it alone is an independent essence. Or, again: what is concrete is ideal, since only the idea can intuitively represent the infinite and absolute totality. Everything that is not ideal remains by definition abstract and relative (*Ideas,* p. 76 [36]). Thus, for example, only when the totality of relativities brought to light by the experience of the object has been explicated will we have an intuition of the object in

21. This is really what Husserl is pointing out when he explains that the second part of a whole which is to be explicated is "apprehensible" (*erfassbar*) in possible (further) explication. Only the first part is actually apprehended; from this point of view, the second part is only potentially apprehended (*EJ,* p. 143 [164]).

its full concreteness (*EJ*, p. 363 [441]). Idealization is thus the only means of attaining concreteness. It enables us to reach, by anticipation of the infinite goal, a "closed" (*geschlossen*) concretum; whereas the real development moves indefinitely in approximation to this idea and necessarily remains an abstractum (*EJ*, p. 364 [442]). Similarly, the isolated experience is not truly concrete but is rather abstract. Only the infinite idea of the flow of experience is concrete (cf. *Ideas*, p. 240 [202]). The notions of concreteness and totality are therefore in necessary connection. Only the totality is concrete; and, being by essence infinite, the totality is grasped in the form of an idea, i.e., of a thematization of an absence of limits. Concreteness and totality are two characteristic marks of the idea. In short, only the flow of conscious experiences is concrete—that is, the intentional life of the ego, transcendental subjectivity (*CM*, pp. 37 f. [76], 84 [117]). The only concretum in the absolute sense is the synthetic unity of the intentional life of consciousness, including all its noetic acts and all their noematic correlates.

Conversely, every realization of the idea (whether this be the idea of the infinite flow of consciousness, the idea of science, that of the object, etc.), being necessarily partial, is abstract in relation to the (idealized) totality. Even as realization it cannot be dissociated from or subsist independently of the idea which it realizes. This is an apparently paradoxical result, since the idea is defined as irreality. It would seem, therefore, that irreality is the concrete and reality is the abstract. Here again we find an aspect of the reversal brought about by Husserl: the absolute primacy of the possible over the actual (value-act point of view). If the idea gives a sense to its own realization, this realization is necessarily dependent on the idea. And the independent is the concrete; it is the self-sufficient whole. Thus we keep coming back to the dialectic of the idea and the real.

It is legitimate to think that from a descriptive-phenomenological point of view it is the part that is concrete and the whole that is abstract. The part (the realization of the idea) is what descriptive experience gives as currently actual and existing; hence the part is what is concrete from this point of view. The current reality of science is what is manifested in the first place in historical experience, until intentional analysis discovers that this current reality is only a claim to absolute (ideal) reality, that this factical concreteness is a presumption (*Präsumption*) of absolute concreteness, and that only what is claimed or presumed is, as Plato said, really real (*ontōs on*). Thus the "parting of the waters" is effected as follows: on the side of the idea are the concrete, the absolute, the independent, the for-itself (in-itself); on the side of the realization are the abstract, the relative, the dependent, the "through-another" (participation). With the former we have the whole, with the latter the part.

§ 13. The definition of the idea

HOWEVER, a contradiction seems to arise here. The idea is what defines the development, hence the idea is a determining and defining factor for this development. But in order for it to be able to play this role, the idea must be in itself a *definition*,[22] an absolute determination. To define is to determine the innermost nature of a thing, and this essence is in some way an absolute, an in-itself, with respect to the thing. The idea that defines the development would have to imply an absolute determination, which seems to connote finitude. It seems that the idea must be finite.

But the idea is infinite, since it is the anticipatory objectification of an indefinite series of potential phenomena which have their places in the development. Thus Husserl speaks of the truth, the evidence, the *Selbst* of the thing or of phenomenology, etc., as infinite ideas (*unendliche Ideen*) and as ideas open to infinity (*offenendlose oder unendlich-offene Ideen*). This open infinity is that of "and so forth"; that is, it is the thematization of an absence of limits in a process.[23] And if we note further

22. [The reader should note that "*-tion*" forms in French translate ambiguously as either "-tion" or "-ness" (and sometimes "-ing" as well) in English. Accordingly, *définition* connotes both "definition" and "definiteness"; *détermination*, both "determination" and "determinateness." The author's exposition—although not his argument —trades on this ambiguity. Rather than try to mark these distinctions in English, thereby making the text almost unreadable, I have as a rule used the "-tion" form exclusively.—TRANS.]

23. Cf. *EJ*, p. 342 (413); *Ideas*, p. 239 (201). Truth is an idea (*LI*, p. 148 [I, 128]), "an *idea*, lying at infinity" (*FTL*, p. 277 [245]). Evidence and its correlate, pure and genuine truth, "are given as ideas lodged in the striving for knowledge, for fulfillment of one's meaning intention. By immersing ourselves in such a striving, we can extract those ideas from it" (*CM*, p. 12 [52]); truth is "an infinitely distant 'pole'" (*Crisis*, p. 42 [42]). Cf. also, on evidence,

that this infinity, which is specifically attributed to the idea, is that of a potentiality to be actualized in an indefinite progression of asymptotic approximations, then we see that this infinity of the idea above all brings to it an essential indetermination, an indefiniteness (or "indefinition"). For the potential is the actualizable, the determinable, or the realizable. The idea is therefore essentially inactuality (potentiality), indetermination, irrealization (idealization). This infinity therefore appears impossible to thematize. How, then, can it define a development?

In fact, the objection poses the question poorly. We cannot deny that Husserl uses the formula "infinite idea," but we must investigate the meanings of the expressions he uses. What does Husserl mean, then, when he speaks of the infinite idea? He cannot be denying an absolute determination to the idea. The idea is a determination, and it is therefore definite. It can be indefinite or potential only from the descriptive-phenomenological (existence-act) point of view. From the transcendental-phenomenological (value-act) point of view the idea is determined, since it is the in-itself strictly speaking. Nothing in it remains open to infinity, since it thematizes the total development ideally-anticipatively.[24] Only the development, insofar as it is incomplete, is an always open horizon. Development may well be infinite in all its forms (theoretical history, individual constituting consciousness, etc.), but this does not prevent its totality in itself from being a finite notion. But this totality is not effectively realized. It is visualized as an idea, i.e., thematized in

---

FTL, p. 125 (111); on the *Selbst* of the thing, i.e., its originary givenness, cf. *EJ*, pp. 287 (346), 294 (355), 297 (358); on phenomenology, cf. *CM*, p. 88 (120) and all those passages in which Husserl asserts that phenomenology is an infinite task. Since everything is eidetically pre-scribed (*Ideas*, p. 376 [330]), everything—absolutely everything—has its correlative idea, which is its ideal state of perfection: the world, the judgment, perception, clarity, distinctness, etc. So, likewise, Plato—in order to avoid rendering human knowledge unintelligible—had to acknowledge a form-idea for everything; cf. *Parmenides*, 130d–e, 135b–c.

24. *Ideas*, p. 397 (351). This text provides an excellent illustration of the constant imbrication of the two points of view. The idea is the perfect realization of the thing (or of science). It pre-scribes a system of realization which, as realization strictly speaking, is infinite but which is perfectly definite in its eidetic type. We must therefore distinguish between the infinity of the process of realization and the idea objectifying this infinity (in the univocal form of the "and so forth"; cf. *Ideas*, pp. 418 f. [371]). This is the means of avoiding contradiction.

the ideal form of "and so forth" (cf. above, p. 68, n. 23; *FTL*, pp. 188 f. [167]; *EJ*, pp. 217 f. [257 f.]). The idea is therefore really a notion that is absolutely determined in itself (*Ideas*, pp. 397 f. [351]; cf. *Ideas*, pp. 417 f. [370 f.], 375 [330]). The very infinity of the development, its essential indefiniteness, necessarily entails the corresponding finitude or definiteness of the idea. In other words, the part necessarily implies the whole. The part motivates the whole; the realization motivates the idea.[25]

The idea is therefore always totality and definition (transcendental point of view of constitution), and it is always partialness and indetermination (descriptive point of view of progressive partial realization of the idea). It is finite as notion, infinite as to its content. Its "objective existence" is finite, its objective content is infinite; its ideal *Objektivität* is definite, its *Gegenständlichkeit* is indefinite (*Ideas*, p. 240 [202]; cf. below, § 22).

Two different meanings are telescoped in the expression "infinite idea," then. Language can obviously use the abridged expression with a view to terminological simplification, as long as it does not give rise to confusion and we remain conscious of its original meaning.

§ 14.   *The idea: eidetic axiom*

IF THE IDEA IS A FINITE NOTION, it can define development; the idea of science defines science. But the science that is defined is a development, a multiplicity of acts of knowledge. The one therefore defines the many. And since the one defines by measuring, this is a case of exemplarist definition or definition by extrinsic denomination. The development is defined by the idea, by virtue of participating in this idea in the dynamic

25. Here again we find the idea as totality. For example, to investigate the object as it is in itself is precisely to investigate the systematic totality of possible experiences of this object—i.e., the idea of a complete synthesis of the possible concordant experiences of this object (cf. *FTL*, p. 247 [218]; *Ideas*, p. 239 [201]). The regional idea "thing" is constituted only when all the relativities of experience have been (ideally) explicated (*EJ*, p. 363 [441]). The atemporality of the intelligible object is an omnitemporality (*EJ*, p. 261 [313]). Cf. *Ideen II*, p. 35.

mode of realization. The development of historical science is a definite multiplicity (*eine definite Mannigfaltigkeit*). And so we naturally come to the theory of multiplicities (*Mannigfaltig-keitslehre*), which Husserl worked out particularly in his logical works, the *Logical Investigations, Formal and Transcendental Logic,* and *Ideas I.* This theory of multiplicity was influenced by the mathematical ideal of deductive science, and by geometry in particular. Husserl saw in geometry the adumbration of the ideal of rational absolute knowledge which deductively traces an ideal multiplicity back to a small number of a priori principles. Geometry, of course, uses a finite system of fundamental axioms in order to define all the ideally possible geometric forms. These axioms contain in themselves a priori all the essential determinations of all possible shapes, which are then deductively made explicit. Only the ultimate individualization escapes this a priori formal legislation, since what the axiom does is determine in advance a general framework (an eidetic rule) within which the effective realization of shapes can vary freely without going beyond its bounds.[26] The more the number of axioms is minimized and the greater their fecundity (i.e., the more shapes the axioms comprise as possible idealities), the more rational is geometry and the more rigorously defined is the possible multiplicity (*Ideas,* p. 62 [22]). It follows from this that the axiomatic system by itself constitutes a priori the entire science of the ideally possible domain in question (in this case, the domain of geometric shapes). Deduction only "reveals" what is implicitly contained in the axiomatic system, "what in itself already exists in truth" (*Crisis,* p. 22 [19]). The progress of deductive science neither invents nor discovers anything that is not already contained a priori in the axiomatic principle. It simply makes explicit what is implicit, and the type of

26. For example, the essential determinations of the triangle in general hold true for each triangle in particular, whether it be isosceles, equilateral, or right. It can be seen that the type (exemplar) "triangle in general" is obtained (or can be obtained) by means of a free variation of particular concrete triangles. The type "triangle in general" is an idea irreally transcending particular triangles, since in itself it is not a real triangle but an eidos which ideally represents—by an extrinsic and therefore normative formality—the universal conditions of the possibility of particular triangles. Here we see the origin of certain Husserlian doctrines: free variation, the exemplary character of the transcendence of irreal inclusion (*Transzendenz irreellen Beschlossenseins*), the formal a priori (exemplary) legislation of the idea (eidos), etc.

knowledge to which it gives rise is strictly analytic. Truth under these circumstances is not defined as synthetic adequation to the thing but solely as analytic consequence from a priori principles. What follows from the axiom is true, and what is inconsistent with the axiom is false. Truth is thus only a purely ideal truth of consistency or inconsistency (*Ideas*, p. 204 [167 f.]).

It is clear from this what repercussions such a conception of truth is going to have for formal logic regarded in its normative function. The system of axioms quite obviously plays the role of a norm with regard to the analytic consequences of the axioms, since it extrinsically determines (a priori) the truth or falsity of these consequences. Hence the system of axioms has the value of a *measure*, the value of an exemplary unity for the many which is deduced from it.

It is understandable, then, that there emerged the idea of a science of nature conceived on the model of geometry. This idea began to be realized with modern physics, which has seen its rationality grow in proportion to its mathematization. But with physics we still have only a particular case. There is no reason not to extend this ideal by a process of formal generalization to knowledge in general. Husserl states that this is what modern thought has done, with its usual boldness and originality (*Crisis*, p. 22 [20]).

A striking parallel presents itself to us. Just as the closed and definite system of axioms defines the ideal multiplicity of all possible mathematical shapes, so the idea—which is also a closed and finite notion—defines the infinite development of science. In each case we have a unitary a priori which defines a many. The idea of science thus plays the role of an axiom. Grasped in the immediate evidence of idea(liza)tion, it serves as a foundation for the entire process of its realization; it orients and measures this process. It is therefore an eidetic state of affairs, since it ideally represents the fully completed state of science. And this ideal and perfect state governs a priori the current and imperfect development of science as a true eidetic axiom (axiomatic state of affairs).[27]

However, Husserl acknowledges a radical difference between

27. Cf. *Ideas*, p. 62 (22), the definition of the essence of eidetic science. All the intermediate stages of such a science have an eidetic value by virtue of their subsumption under an eidos-axiom, i.e., by the deductive formulation of their implication in the a priori axiomatic principle.

geometry and science as we have studied it. To be sure, each is defined by an idea, a finite eidetic axiom. But the sense of "defined" is different in the two cases. The definition of geometry by its system of axioms is the definition of the geometric *object*, the multiplicity of which is implicitly contained in the axiomatic state of affairs. The system of geometric axioms defines a many which is perfectly homogeneous with the system itself; the possible shapes are deduced from their principle in an analytic manner. And they can be deduced because they are already included a priori in their a priori system of definition. In other words, we have here a static point of view, according to which consequences are deduced from their principle as the explicit is deduced from the implicit. Geometry is entirely an eidetic science—that is, an ideal science. There is perfect homogeneity between principles and consequences.

Can the same be said for the science we are considering? We started from the description of its development. Hence, what we were considering is a factical existent reality, given in and by history. But this development exhibits a tendency; it shows itself to be the realization of an idea. We may, then, legitimately propose the definition of science by its end idea. But in doing so we implicitly maintain a certain duality between the idea (the ideal end) and its realization. There is a hiatus of sorts between factical science (in progressive realization) and ideal science (which is the ideal terminus of its completion); the one is not the other. It will no doubt be said that this duality tends to be absorbed in unity. But this "absorption" is located at infinity. It is an ideal and therefore unrealizable telos. The duality therefore necessarily remains. Factical science, tending toward its own ideal perfection, always remains in tendency toward its idea. Hence we have a necessarily *dynamic* point of view, that of realization of the idea by development, which contrasts with the static point of view of deduction. Even if the idea is analogous to an axiom, definition of science by its idea is not the definition of science's object but of its own development as science. This development is, to be sure, a "consequence" of the idea, since it is motivated a priori by it. But it is not deduced from its idea as the analytic consequences of a geometric axiom are deduced from the axiom. This is so, in the first place, because for us the idea is "inferred" (*herausholen*) from the development. (This alone enables us to assert, in the second place, that the idea pre-scribes the development.) The inference here is of such a kind that the idea is the idea(liza)tion of the total development. Science in process of development tends to become equal to the idea of science. In realizing this idea, it therefore passes from less to more, from potency to act, from nonbeing to being. Hence it is really the idea that manifests or clarifies (*erhellt*) itself in the historical development. But this explication is of a nature quite different from the explication of the consequences of the geometric axiom. The latter consequences are in themselves already in act, as to existence, in their principle. From this point of view they do not have to pass from potency to act, since their entire existence is an ideal (or mathematical) existence and is therefore defined by the system of axioms. They nevertheless have to pass from implicit to explicit, i.e., in a sense, from potency to act from the point of view of intelligibility.[28] This explication is therefore a purely

28. This point of view of intelligibility is in fact conflated with that of expression in language, since the whole point here is to discover whether the ideal existence of the mathematical object is identical with its being intelligible. If this is the case, the passing from implicit to explicit which makes manifest the virtualities included in the geometric axom is a passing from ideal virtuality to expression in language or, in other words, from intelligible act (the consequences are within the principle, in themselves and in their truth) to express act (formulas, theorems, and even the most material form of *Dokumentierung*, the book, etc.). But this "expression" by means of language is necessarily located in time and in history. To express the consequences of the axiomatic principle in language amounts to conferring a certain reality on them (where "real" is understood in contrast to "ideal"), a reality that is *ipso facto* necessarily historical. This means that the formulation of the consequences analytically contained in the principle (and indeed in the expression) will be a *realization,* just as development is a realization of the idea. Here we find a more univocal parallel between the mathematical ideal of deduction and the definition of the development of science by its idea. And it must be admitted that the conception of the idea as idealization of the total development inclines toward this position, since it has as a consequence precisely the establishment of a univocal continuity between realization and idea. However, we must recognize that Husserl rejects this parallel. In the text of *Ideas* (pp. 62 f. [22]), where Husserl describes the ideal of exact eidetic (mathematical) science, he takes pains to stipulate in a footnote that "it is apparent that this mathematical ideal cannot be valid in general, and so not for phenomenology" ("es zeigt sich, dass dieses mathematische Ideal nicht überall gültig sein kann, so nicht für die Phänomenologie"; *Ideen I*, p. 22). [The footnote in question is omitted from the English translation.—TRANS.] So despite all the similarities between mathematical-deductive sciences and eidetic-phenomenological sciences, there is a fundamental dif-

ideal and analytic process. But the development of science cannot be a purely ideal process, since it is precisely a matter of realization of the idea in historical fact. Here there is no *ideal explication of intelligibility;* there is *factual realization.* The development of science is a real multiplicity ideally defined by the idea of science, whereas the many defined by the geometric axiom is a purely ideal many. The mathematical multiplicity is homogeneous with its principle, since it is merely the explication of this principle in terms of intelligibility; we do not leave the ideal domain by passing from one to the other. The multiplicity of the factical development of science is not homogeneous with its idea. It is the realization of this idea. With it we leave the ideal domain to emerge in the domain of fact. The relation between fact and idea is therefore not analytic but synthetic. This amounts to saying that the multiplicity of the development of science is not contained analytically in the axiom-idea but is the synthetic realization of the axiom-idea.

The parallel we have drawn still obtains, though, as long as it is not regarded as a perfect parallel. The basis of our argumentation on this subject is as follows. *De facto* science is not ideal science. The first cannot be deduced from the second. If it could, it would follow that ideal science (the idea) is first from the descriptive-phenomenological point of view. The axiom is absolutely first for geometry, and so geometry does not distinguish between a genetic (phenomenological) order and an order of perfection (a transcendental order). But according to good Husserlian doctrine, the idea is not first descriptively-phenomenologically. On the contrary, the idea is the telos (final terminus) of intentional investigation. What first comes within the purview of intelligence (*das Nächstliegende und zunächst sich Darbietende*) is the fact, the constituted. What is first is descriptive experience, not the idea(liza)tion. It is in this sense that we are to understand what Husserl says when he contends that phenomenology is not a deductive science. The intentional method involves two directions and therefore two points of

___

ference between them. Primarily, there is an inversion of point of view—deduction proceeding exclusively from the ideal principle to its analytic consequences (formulated in expressions) and the intentional method proceeding from fact to idea. Of course the intentional method is also inverted insofar as the idea motivates the fact. Despite this, however, there remains a difference in the direction taken by the two procedures.

departure or "firsts." [29] The deductive method involves only a single direction, that of explication of consequences which are included a priori in the principle. The deductive method employs a procedure of mediate visualization in order to attain a full and unique mastery of its domain. The phenomenological method is meant to be descriptive, hence purely intuitive and always immediate. It excludes any nonintuitive procedure, and, precisely as eidetic, it is meant to be descriptive and hence intuitive (*Ideas*, p. 190 [153]; cf. *Ideas*, §§ 71, 74–75). Geometry and phenomenology are both eidetic sciences; but the deductive method is a deduction of essences, while the phenomenological method is a direct intuition of essences. For phenomenology, any operation other than intuition has only the value of a methodical expedient that is essentially provisional (*Ideas*, pp. 190 [152], 210 [173]).

29. This duality characterizes Husserlian method and sets it in contrast with deductive method. It corresponds to the distinction between two sharply distinguished orders, which we have already encountered in the form of the transcendental-phenomenological and the descriptive-phenomenological points of view (§§ 8 and 10)—or, more precisely, the genetic order of transcendental constitution (which implies priority in point of perfection on the part of the originary, i.e., ultimately on the part of transcendental subjectivity) and the genetic order of phenomenological description. The descriptive-phenomenological order is well represented by *Crisis* (and, in another manner, by *FTL*), while the transcendental-phenomenological order is best represented by *Ideas* and *CM*. Once again it is simply a question of two possible directions of intentional analysis which are distinguished by whether analysis goes from constituted to constituting or from constituting to constituted, from noema to noesis or from noesis to noema, from the object to consciousness (of this object) or from consciousness (of the object) to the object.

PART II

Logic: Science of the Idea of Science

1 / The Genuinely Logical
Sense of Part I

THE PRECEDING INQUIRY has the value of a factical example. What has been established by intentional analysis of the development of science is equally valid for the idea in general, which thus turns out to be alternatively act and potency, reality and fiction, whole and part. Let us keep our initial point of view, however. The idea of science defines science and at the same time polarizes its theoretical striving. It is form and end, eidos and telos; that is to say, it is ideal and a priori form. It will be well to study this form of science in and for itself. For after we have determined the idea of science, we must turn to the study of this same idea taken in itself. After the idea of science, we will take up the science of the idea (cf. Plato, *Parmenides*, 134b).

But just as the idea norms the development of its own realization, so logic—science of the idea of science—norms effective science. In this way, Husserl immediately places his study of logic under the aspect of exemplarity. This normative logic will have two levels, however. It is concerned first with retrieving the autonomy of the logical domain, and it is in this way that strictly objective formal logic is immediately founded. Further, the autonomy of the logical domain is guaranteed only by a return to logical reason, i.e., to transcendental constitution. Logic, the science of the idea of science, thus opens up a new direction of investigation—one which properly belongs to transcendental logic and which leads to the thematization of the transcendental ego, the final subjective form and absolute foundation. The exemplarity of logic will thus be either objective or subjective, and logic will be either objective formal logic or subjective formal (transcendental) logic. These two logical formalities or normations are, moreover, intentionally continuous. The normative function of objective formal logic leads teleologically to the essential self-normation (in itself) of transcendental logic. The goal of the following pages is to trace the general framework of the Husserlian logical problematic, which will enable us better to understand the subsequent detailed studies.

§ 15. *The outcome in traditional logic*

LET US NOTE THAT, if we are dealing here with logic, we are for the moment dealing only with logic taken in its traditional sense, the "study of science" or *Wissenschaftslehre.* Logic in this sense has as its proper object what is formal in science, independently of any *de facto* material realization and hence of any particular object, in conformity with the purest requirements of objective formal universality. Thus we seem to end up with logic in its most traditional sense.

What does this mean? Does Husserl's entire effort consist, in the last analysis, in justifying traditional logic? Does Husserl content himself with entering into a tradition that he has neither criticized nor reconstituted? No, indeed. Here again we find a characteristic feature of Husserl's thought. Husserl knows that he forms part of a closely interdependent human community. Hence he knows that he cannot completely disregard its efforts, its labors, even its theoretical results. This is an evident truth, which the philosopher of transcendental intersubjectivity, the philosopher who devotes himself to bringing to light the historical teleology of human reason and who acknowledges the history of human reason as the primary field of philosophical experience, would be unlikely to deny. Thus he knows that logic already existed before him and that it had even reached a certain theoretical perfection parallel to that of mathematical science (which is, as it were, its twin sister) (*LI*, p. 179 [I, 170]). Formal logic is "already there"—not as an ideal realization, to be sure, but as a partial realization which prefigures in its immanent structure the end idea of the logical interest (cf. *FTL*, pp. 75 f. [66 f.]). It is therefore possible to elicit its intentional sense and anticipate its ideal realization.

In this way Husserl submits traditional logic to the same

intentional analysis that enabled him to discover the idea of
science as the principle of its real structure (*FTL*, p. 75 [66]).
In doing so, he rejoins the logical tradition which descends from
Plato in its original form. Put in theoretical form and "crys-
tallized" by Aristotle (*FTL*, p. 7 [7]), this logic came down
through the centuries virtually intact. Husserl knows it at first
hand, as is shown by the numerous references and quotations
which appear, especially in *Experience and Judgment*. He retains it as having, in his view, the greatest value in the entire
classical heritage. For it is with this logic that the interest in
genuine knowledge is born, the interest which shapes all of
European thought and motivates all its attempts to seek an
ultimate apodictic foundation. Let us not forget that what is
born with the foundation of dialectic by Plato is science itself
and not simply logic, as a hasty reading of Plato and Husserl
might lead one to believe.[1] But despite its relative perfection,
this logic is only the rough draft of the most comprehensive
logic, the logic that is alone completely explicated, which is to
be Husserlian logic.

Thus, just as science taken in its historical development
tends toward a progressive idealization, logic too shows a teleological tendency toward an absolute and definitive logic. But
there is a continuity between science and logic, the latter being
the idea of science. Hence it is not by accident or by a stretching of phenomenological method that we end with logic after an
intentional analysis of real science. But it should be noted that
we *end* with logic; we do not accept it as an a priori presupposition. In this sense, our previous inquiry legitimizes and
justifies traditional logic and gives logic its genuine sense by
tracing it back to its origin. But it immediately appears from
this that our inquiry also goes beyond traditional logic.

Traditional logic is given as a theory of science, as an a
priori study of the possibility of science. As such, it is precisely
the form of science; i.e., it is any science, considered formally-
generally.[2] But this form of science can be regarded in different

1. That is, science taken in its strictest and most formal sense
as that which makes a science into a science—i.e., its object and its
theoretical structure, or its matter and form. "Science in a new sense
arises in the first instance from *Plato's establishing of logic . . .*"
(*FTL*, p. 1 [1]). Cf. *FTL*, p. 143 (128).

2. Cf. the following passage from *FTL*, p. 108 (96): "If our
activities embody such an interest, we stand within the horizon of a
science; and in the case of a formally universal consideration, we

ways. (1) It can be regarded as presupposing real science and the exemplary criticism of real science, taken as exemplary point of departure and leading to the idea of science (*FTL*, pp. 28 [25], 130 [115]). In this case, logic refers in its very sense to the effective science whose form or idea it studies. To be sure, we end with an a priori, i.e., a pure possibility. But this is a possibility that is motivated and (pre)constituted in real science. (2) It can be considered simply as a priori, as an absolute which is given as such, as if it did not have to give an account of its rights. This is the tendency that has shaped traditional logic, to the extent of giving it the illusion of being an absolute which no longer has to be justified but which imposes itself necessarily. Here too we have an a priori, but an a priori that is separated from the originary sources of its own meaning. Such a logic tends to harden progressively, since it develops only in isolation—independently on the one hand of any "historical" experience of science, which alone could intentionally motivate it, and on the other hand of any real experience, capable of justifying its constitutive concepts. Hence it leaves itself open to the accusation of arbitrariness which strikes at all theories *von oben her*.

Philosophizing *von oben her* is, for Husserl, equivalent to philosophizing in the way that dogmatism in general does: by taking for granted precisely what is in question (cf. *FTL*, p. 228 [203]). In the matter of evidence and truth, for instance, a theory *von oben her* will from the first attribute to certain particular experiences the privilege of being evident and hence immediately true. Thus internal experience, the perception of the ego by itself, may enjoy this privilege. This is the fault with which Husserl reproaches Cartesian transcendental realism and the psychological empiricism which follows this realism—for which evidence or the feeling of evidence becomes a veritable epistemological gimmick (*FTL*, p. 162 [145]; *Ideas*, p. 400 [354]). Yet if we go beyond this narrow point of view, in which evidence is reduced to a mere internal experience, we do not thereby abandon the idea that evidence "must" be an absolute grasp of being or that there "must" be an absolute experience without which no knowledge would be possible (*FTL*, p. 280 [247 f.]; *EJ*, p. 18 [9 f.]). Similarly, logic is a dogmatic a priori

stand within *logic*. . . ." Correlatively, the object in general is any object, considered logically (formally-generally); cf. *FTL*, p. 110 (98).

if it lays down the idea of science with no concern for finding out whether it is a possibility motivated or pre-scribed by fact. It is necessary to return to the fact and clarify the essence that it involves. What is needed, of course, is a genetic means of gaining access to the idea; for the idea taken in itself preexists ideally (*EJ*, p. 260 [312]). A logic *von oben her* consists in according an immediate and evident absolute knowledge to the knowing subject and according an immediate absolute normative power to logic. To philosophize *von oben her* is therefore to hypostatize the second moment of the dialectic while ignoring its factical exemplary origins (cf. above, § 7).

§ 16. *The outcome in traditional logic implies transcendental logic*

BUT THE VARIOUS MOMENTS OF THE DIALECTIC cannot be isolated. The dialectic is synthetic, and each of its stages taken by itself is unintelligible. The idea is therefore inseparable from the fact which pre-scribes and passively preconstitutes it.

If with the idea of science we arrive at logic, then, we are not condemning logic to being merely a terminus of the approximative advance toward the idea. We are simply showing that logic requires this approximative advance as its intentional motivation. For logic, too, is a foundation, insofar as it intentionally explicates transcendental subjectivity.

Now we realize that from the first lines of our study we have been situated within a logic strictly speaking—not traditional logic, to be sure, but phenomenological logic. Husserl is concerned to take up whatever is valid in the philosophical tradition. But something is valid only insofar as it is intuitively legitimized in a recourse to originary experience. The ultimate legitimizing recourse in phenomenology is to intuition, i.e., direct intuition in immediate originary experience, as far as possible; or else to justification by deduction, i.e., by mediate visualization rooted in primary experience.[3] This principle is

3. "Deduction" is to be understood as deduction of the mathematical sort, which is an "extended" intuition or, in other words, an explication of intuition itself; in short, it is a mediate but essentially intuitive visualization. The idea, too, is an intuition in the form of the "and so forth." This is by no means a matter of demonstrative inference, which Husserl would vigorously reject. Cf. the phrase

absolutely universal, and it holds for every object in general, real as well as irreal. In more everyday terms, it holds for the real thing as well as for the concept. This is the *principle of principles:* intuition alone (the *Selbstgebung* of the object) is a source of legitimacy.[4]

But the intentional analysis of science which leads to logic is precisely this "dator intuition" of logic. Traditional logic, taken as the legacy of classical thought, cannot enjoy a transcendental understanding since it is not explicitly grounded in its intentional origins. It is not rooted in the originary (historical) experience of the real science which it is to norm. It is a pure a priori possibility, which appears as unmotivated and irrational. By turning back toward experience and criticizing logic in an intentional reflection on science and, conversely, by explicating the real development of science and its teleological tendency toward the idea in a constitutive progressive anticipation, we intuitively legitimize traditional logic. And by the same stroke we extend traditional logic, breaking it out of a framework that has become too narrow. Formal logic is broadened into a transcendental logic. This is the logical significance of Part I, above. Traditional logic is henceforth *transcendentally understood, taken up,* and at the same stroke *surpassed* by phenomenological logic.

This transcendental understanding is the result of the intuitive motivation or constitutive justification of logic. It is a particular application of the principle of principles. Logical theory is transcendentally understood when its derivation from

---

"the same countersensical *type* of procedure (by way of inferences)" (*FTL*, p. 280 [247]).

4. *Ideas*, pp. 92 (52), 392 (346); *LI*, pp. 235 (I, 241), 237 f. (I, 244 f.). This obviously entails a broadening of the concepts of intuition and evidence (and, correlatively, the concept of the object, since to each type of objectivity there corresponds a type of evidence; *EJ*, p. 21 [12]); cf. *Ideas*, p. 55 (14); *FTL*, pp. 40 f. (36), 45 (40), 81 (71), 155 (139). But this broadening changes nothing in principle; cf. *Ideas*, p. 379 (333), *FTL*, p. 158 (142), among other texts. The principle also applies to the method, which is legitimized only at the moment when its intentional operation (*Leistung*) is clarified, that is, when its intentional telos (idea) is grasped with evidence in the appropriate eidetic intuition (cf. *FTL*, p. 187 [166]; *Ideas*, p. 381 [335]). It follows from the necessities discussed here that no objectivity is legitimized or has validity for me (*Geltung für mich*) unless it is grounded in an originary constitution in transcendental consciousness, i.e., in a transcendental system of constitutive intentionality (*FTL*, p. 235 [208]).

experience has been explicated. It is motivated in the first place by the progressive reality of science in process of development. However, this motivation is not the only one that pertains to logic. The recourse to experience of which we spoke is a transcendental motivation of logic from the point of view of the ideal completion of science. We must consider yet another motivation, one which has to do with the objective content of logical configurations. Hence we have, on the one side, the motivation of logic as theoretical structure, i.e., as noetic *Leistung* strictly speaking. On the other side we have the motivation of categorial concepts (categorial objectivities pertaining to logical science) and of their relativity to the *Lebenswelt*. These are two motivations which will extend formal apophantics and formal ontology, respectively, the latter comprising two correlative and equivalent thematics which ultimately go back to transcendental subjectivity. Logic, then, has no special privilege which would warrant giving it a dignity superior to that of any other object. It too must be referred to transcendental subjectivity as the only ultimate and absolute source of all meaning for us (*FTL*, p. 15 [13 f.]).

Analysis of the development of real science thus reaches the grounds of this science's logical validity (*logische Geltung*) in two respects. It does so, first, insofar as it leads to the pure *Wissenschaftslehre* and, second, insofar as it manifests the exploding of the traditional conception of formal logic and shows how logic or pure analytics must be complemented by a logic that is synthetic, transcendental, and constitutive—a logic of which analytic logic is itself the cornerstone. Thus it is clear how the outcome of the Husserlian approach to formal logic by no means amounts to taking up traditional logic as it is and how this outcome is at the same time a surpassing of formal logic. Traditional logic is grounded and taken up, but it is also surpassed and broadened. Part I has therefore already brought into play the subjective thematic of logic, by showing that the logical domain is actually much larger than traditional logic suspected (*EJ*, pp. 12 f. [3]).

2 / The Surpassing of Traditional Logic

LOGIC IS THE SCIENCE OF SCIENCE, the science of what is formal in science. But what makes a science into a science comprises two elements, one purely formal, the other material or objective. In other words, in order for a science to merit the name, it must on the one hand have a certain *theoretical structure*, it must be a certain formation of cognitions; and on the other hand it must be precisely knowledge of an *object*. Hence two elements constitute a science, its formal theoretical structure and its object.

This assertion is the basis of the fundamental division of logic into formal apophantics and formal ontology, and it leads to the transcendental extension of logic, since formal ontology— as an a priori theory of the object—needs to be extended into a thematic of evidence. But formal structure and object are in close interdependence; their correlation is in a way a mutual determination. However, this seems to make logic as we see it here impossible.

§ 17. *Difficulty and possibility of a formal logic of the object (formal ontology)*

FOR ALTHOUGH LOGIC is the science of science, it is not the science of each and every science taken in its irreducible concreteness. It is not a unique method of every science, since every science—being the science of this or that object—has its own mode. Each object has its own mode of appearing and of

[86]

being known, which, correlatively, pre-scribes a theoretical form proper to the science. It seems impossible to conceive a universal logical science, a science which is the universal science of science both as to its form and its object. At best it seems possible to construct a logic which examines only the universal theoretical structure of science in general. This must be possible, because all the sciences, regarded from a sufficiently formal point of view, possess the same systematic structure. They all use the judgment and syllogistic reasoning for their expression. This is why traditional logic is concerned with this apophantic aspect in particular.

The objection is valid, however, only if the object is regarded in its full concreteness, in its originary and individual material fullness, in its *Selbst*. From this point of view the individualization of the object does indeed render it irreducible to anything else. But a more extended analysis immediately shows that, despite their material irreducibility, objects group themselves in certain *regions*, and that the concept of a region determines a priori and synthetically every object included in it. Moreover, these regions themselves show a certain objective universal structure, i.e., a universal form of the object in general, which determines a priori the essential characteristics of every object in general.[1]

Of course, the operation which enables us to rise from the individual and material concreteness to the corresponding region is not the same as the operation which enables us to rise to the highest category of the object. The first yields a material essence —a true essence, that is, since only material essences are true essences. The second yields a purely formal essence or, more precisely, a mere objective essential form which can belong to any material essence, as well as to any individual object, as its pure essential form. We are not to see a univocal progression here, as if we were proceeding from the individual to the material essence and from this to the formal essence in a series of continuous stages. Reflection proceeds just as well from the individual directly to the formal essence, to the highest eidetic form. If there were a continuous progression here, we would have a superordination of genera and species; we would have generalization, not formalization.[2] Husserl therefore begins by

1. This is the distinction between material ontologies and formal ontologies by means of material essences and formal essences; cf. *Ideas*, § 10.

2. On this question see *Ideas*, § 13.

distinguishing these two operations. He sees generalization as an operation which always keeps a close contact with the pre-given world. By reason of this presupposition, and despite its universality, generalization retains a quasi-empirical and material character. Formalization, on the other hand, is an operation which does not keep any link whatever with any pregiven world but ends instead solely with the universal (empty formal) form of a possible world, i.e., of a possible object in general (ideation by free variation).

It seems that this position is provisional, however, and that Husserl ends by conflating generalization and formalization as two formalizations which differ only in degree. This is only a terminological difficulty, arising from the fact that Husserl's logical vocabulary is for the most part borrowed from traditional logic (genus and species) and transposed into an original exemplarist "platonizing" perspective. In this line of thought, generalization appears to consist in eliciting one element which is common to a multiplicity of individuals, an element which does not enjoy a perfect actuality but is, on the contrary, in potency with respect to its own specific differences. Traditional logic in effect united genus and matter (*genus sumitur a materia*). Formalization, on the other hand, consists in eliciting an element which is also common to a multiplicity of individuals, but one involving no imperfection, one that is completely actual. The latter element is independent of the lower terms which fall under it. In the first case we have an operation which elicits a form that is imperfect relative to its abstract determinations; in the second we have an operation which elicits a completely actual form that is in no way relative to other forms, either higher or lower. If the genus is regarded in what we are calling an exemplarist perspective, we can see that it can be accorded the full actuality of a form. The genus regarded in this way is not relative to its individual concretizations (which are its specific differences) but is quite independent of them (the second moment of the dialectic). Here the relations that obtain between the genus and lower realities are no longer relations of generic subsumption but of participation. Essence—even material essence—can therefore plausibly be qualified as genus (*Ideas*, §§ 1–17, esp. pp. 66 [26], 71 [31]).

Formal and Transcendental Logic sheds an interesting light on this point by distinguishing between the contingent a priori and the necessary a priori. The notion of form can be taken in two different senses, either as form "in principle" or as "contingent" form relative to a domain of possible empirical realities. Thus "sound in general" is a contingent a priori. It comprises a material (hyletic) core which, since it is regarded as a priori, has a formal value. We have here the material essence as it appears in *Ideas*, the only true essence—as opposed to the pure form or the formal a priori, which pertains to every material essence or contingent a priori and which is the object in general or the category of *being* (*Wesen*) (*FTL*, p. 29 [25 f.]).

But logic is concerned only with pure forms: pure form of science and pure form of the object. Formal object therefore includes two dimensions. The first is the formal *apophantic* dimension, which thematizes the pure form of science as such. The other is the formal *ontological* dimension, which thematizes the pure form of the object as such, the object in general. A formal logic of the object thus proves to be possible.

In fact, in virtue of the intentional correlation of science and its object, the exemplary criticism of science is necessarily accompanied by the exemplary criticism of its object. The object need not be made completely explicit when the logical interest bears on science itself (its theoretical structure) above all else, but the implication of the second criticism by the first nevertheless needs to be elucidated. For just as a certain real object corresponds to a certain real science (as the object of nature corresponds to physics), so the clarified object corresponds to clarified genuine science. And to the *ideal science* (of the conditions of the possibility of any genuine science) there necessarily corresponds the *ideal object* (i.e., the ideal condition of the possibility of any object). This perfect correlation between science and object is "for the time being" suspended as an effect of the reduction, or is at least suspended in its real form, since it always remains in an ideal form (reduced science keeping its meaning as science, and intentionality therefore being no longer intentionality directly to the object but rather intentionality to the idea of science, which implies the idea of the object). Hence the reduction suspends the real-empirical manifestation of the correlation between science and object only the better to recover this correlation in its ideal form at the level of the idea of science and of the object in general.

However, the exemplary criticism of the object takes a different form from the exemplary criticism of science. It takes the form of an *ideation by free variation*. This ideation is a process which is exactly correlative (on the side of the object) to intentional analysis (on the side of science).

The point of variation is to proceed from a given object, as real or imaginary point of departure, to the invariant eidetic structure that is revealed as the essential form of the object.[3] If the formalization is completely pure, we have access immediately to the object in general (i.e., to the essential form of every object in general). Hence it is a matter of proceeding to the originary object (*Urgegenstand*) (*Ideas*, p. 66 [26]), which can be regarded in two quite different ways. It can be regarded logically, in which case the originary object is regarded as the absolute substrate of every logical derivation. This is the object in general properly so called, the something in general, the pure empty form of every object in general. By virtue of its "emptiness," this object = X.[4] It can, on the other hand, be regarded empirically. In this case it is conceived either as the primary object of experience—the substrate of empirical determinations, the sensible and individual object[5]—or else as the total substrate of all real determinations, i.e., as nature or the world.[6] In any case, in whichever way the originary object is regarded and in whatever region it is considered, we readily see that it always appears as substrate of determinations— either sensible empirical determinations or syntactic ontological

3. This is ideation, whose procedure is imaginative variation (*Ideas*, § 4) and whose terminus is *Wesenserschaaung* or *Ideenschau* —ideal, eidetic, or intellectual intuition, the intuitive grasp of an essence or pure *Wesen* on the basis of an empirical fact. This real-empirical fact is also a factical example; it undergoes a free variation of imagination. As such, it is the substrate of ideation or of variation. Cf. *FTL*, p. 41 (36): "objects as examples, to serve as substrates for 'ideations'" (exemplarische Substrate für Ideationen). (In this text Husserl is speaking of the intentional analysis of science and seems to be comparing the exemplary criticism of science with the exemplary criticism of the object.) Ideation is therefore an *"insight into the essence,"* an *"intuitive representation* of the essence in adequate Ideation" (*LI*, p. 238 [I, 244]).

4. "Something completely indeterminate from the point of view of logic" [Das logisch gänzlich unbestimmtes Etwas] (*EJ*, p. 139 [160]). Cf. *Ideas*, pp. 74 (34), 70 (30), 129 (90), 159 f. (125), and § 131. The object in general or mere "Something (= X)" is also defined as the pure individual which logical derivations require (*Ideas*, pp. 76 [36], 88 f. [48]).

5. *EJ*, p. 139 (159); *Ideen II*, p. 17. As such, the originary empirical object falls under the category of individual *schlechthin* or absolute object, which is simply its own formalization as object in general (*Ideen II*, p. 34).

6. "*Das All-seiende,*" "*das All-etwas*" (*EJ*, pp. 137 f. [157]); "*Die Allnatur,*" "*das Universum der Körper*" (*EJ*, p. 139 [159]).

determinations. We hereby reach the essence or formal concept of the object in general. The object in general is "intuitable"; it is capable of being grasped in an experience. Since intuition grasps it with its determinations and properties, the object in general is "explicable"; its determinations can be "explicated" as determinations belonging to this substrate object (*EJ*, p. 250 [299]). Conversely, the object in general involves the form of substantivity, the "substrate form of being"—which clearly demonstrates that it is a pure determinable (*EJ*, p. 222 [263]; *Ideas*, p. 365 [320]). These are the essential characteristics of this pure eidetic form which belongs to every object. This "oberste Formbegriff Gegenstand überhaupt oder das in leerster Allgemeinheit gedachtes Etwas überhaupt" ("highest form-concept 'object in general,' 'something in general' conceived with the emptiest generality") delimits a formal ontological domain, a domain in which all the derivatives of this concept appear as fundamental concepts (*FTL*, p. 77 f. [68]; translation altered).

Thus it is logic that gives rise to free variation or ideation, since the object in general is the proper object of formal ontology. By eliciting the formal structure of every object in general, ideation enables us to determine the ideal object of ideal science. Logic is a *Wissenschaftslehre*, an a priori formal study of science as such; and it is an a priori formal study of the object, a formal ontology—that is, an *apriorische Gegenstandslehre* (*FTL*, p. 78 [68]). Traditional logic is thereby broadened into a dialectic whose principal theme is the possibility of science in general and of being in general (*FTL*, p. 223 [198]). *Logic is broadened into philosophy*, since it becomes in a way a science of being and no longer stops, as traditional logic does, at being a science of beings of reason. For the moment we are saying this at the one-sided level of objective logic. But obviously, transcendental logic will be with even greater right a philosophy. For the introduction of the object into logical considerations amounts to the introduction of intentionality into traditional logic. That is, it introduces a two-sidedness into a science which has hitherto been exclusively one-sided. Formal logic cannot be merely apophantics; it is formal ontology as well. And the extension of the latter is what will open the way to transcendental logic.

Any objectivity at all—whether real or ideal—concretizes the formal structures which are explicated in terms of the object in general. But this possibility of application does not imply any appearance or any empirical character. Rather, the object in general is determined a priori; it has no links which would make it depend on any empirical object whatever. This is why the object in general is capable of entering into the domain of formal logic. It does not pertain specifically to any particular science; no particular science has the object in general as its proper object, although every object necessarily participates in its structure. It is the *object in general of science in general,* or of pure logic. In this way, at the purely eidetic level, a logic can be conceived which is absolutely independent of any particular science even though it studies the formal theoretical structure involved in each science. Such a logic is, moreover, free of any relation to an empirical material object, although it determines a priori the formal objective (*gegenständlich*) structure belonging to every possible object. The logic of science and the logic of the object, formal apophantics and formal ontology, can now take their places together within a single science or, more exactly, within the two objective-analytic dimensions of a single science. Here we can appreciate the importance of raising logic beyond any reference to a pregiven world, which traditional logic did not do. Traditional logic cannot be formal-ontological, since the sciences that it studies are always particular sciences having particular individualized material objects. The only common formal element remaining under these circumstances is the theoretical formal structure, and logic can only be apophantic (*FTL,* § 12).

In this way Husserl attains the great ambition of the Platonic dialectic. This dialectic, being the study of science in general and of being in general, is also in a way an apophantic and ontological logic. Logic at its origin already had a broader extension than Aristotle's crystallization left to it. Dialectic was science of being and science of science. That is, as we have seen from Husserlian logic, it was science of the science of being (*FTL,* pp. 223 [198], 1 [1]). For Plato, dialectic is philosophy itself, a purely a priori philosophy which does not admit any science or any "real" world as a necessary presupposition. The grasp of "really real reality" (*ontōs on*) unfolds ideally within the framework of the dialectical method. Since thought is inseparable from its object, the universal and highest science can only be the science of thought and its object; for dialectical thought is a thought which discovers and posits being, and constitutive intentionality is already implied in this positing. Let us not forget the mathematical origins of Platonic speculation. Dialectic, like mathematics, is a knowledge which "discloses" the ideal *Dasein* of preexistent essences. Knowledge is knowledge of being; that which fully is, is fully an object (cf. *EJ*, p. 260 [312] and Plato, *Republic*, 477a). This is also why the investigation of participation in Plato proceeds immediately from a reflection on language, i.e., on knowledge. What is true is that without which there could be no logical thought.[7]

In Plato, however, apophantic logic and ontological logic are identified. This is a result of his theory of ideas, which identifies thought and being. In Husserl, on the contrary, formal apophantics and formal ontology are correlative; and it is the phenomenological reduction that makes it possible to affirm the possibility of a formal logic of the object. The attitude of the phenomenological reduction does not consider any of the particular sciences, since its effect is precisely to suspend these sciences as to the existential reality of their objects and hence as to their truth value. A definition of science by its object cannot be obtained directly. We must get free of empirical facticity and gain access to the level of purest formality, since only the idea of the object, the essential form of the object in general, can be the adequate intentional correlate of the idea of science or the form of science in general. From this point of view, the intentionality which obtains between science and its object takes the form of fulfillment. Science fully knows its object, and, conversely, the object is fully known by science. This must be understood as an ideal anticipation. At the terminus of the teleological process, science will be fully realized. Or, to put this in the formal a priori mode that is proper to logic: the idea of science is the ideal knowledge of the object. Ideal science (logic) is the ideal knowledge of the ideal object (the object in general). Only at the level of pure formality can logic be both apophantics and ontology.

§ 18. *The twofold logical thematic: a glance at its two possible distortions*

IF LOGIC is the science of the object in general, a pure formal logic will then be twofold: science of science (formal

---

7. *Platon: Oeuvres Complètes*, trans. August Diès (Paris: Société d'édition "Les Belles Lettres," 1963), Vol. 8, pt. 3, p. 285. [The reference is to a passage in the editor's "Notice" to *Sophist.—*TRANS.]

theoretical structure) and science of the object in general. In short, it will be science of the science of the object in general. Here the phenomenological point of view appears. Husserl has already gone beyond traditional logic from the formal point of view, to be sure, but he does so especially from the transcendental point of view. For to say that logic is the science of the science of the object is to bring in intentionality in two respects. First, logic has a correlative object which is science itself; and second, the science that is thematized by logic also has its own object. Hence we have one objectivity on top of another, both of them indices of constituting intentionalities in univocal continuity (*Verschiebung der Intentionalitäten*). Science is a *Leistung* of consciousness, and hence its theoretical constitution must be studied. The object, too, is an index of constituting intentionality and refers to originary experience; if there are only objects *of* knowledge, there are also objects only *for* knowledge. Knowledge—and, more fundamentally, consciousness—is what constitutes the object (or at least the sense of the object). Therefore, theoretical reason is what constitutes both science as object and the object of science. The objective thematic of logic therefore necessarily carries over into a subjective thematic. Formal logic is completed and grounded in a transcendental logic. This is the second extension of traditional logic that we mentioned: the transcendental grounding of logic in the strongest and strictest sense (cf. above, § 16).

Logic therefore pursues a twofold interest. In the first place, it is to establish a pure formal science of science; in the second, it is to give an account transcendentally of science, i.e., provide a transcendental understanding of science. To this end it must proceed to the foundations of science in constitutive intentionality, to the ego's own transcendental consciousness. These are the two thematics of logic, the objective and the subjective, as Husserl outlined their broad features in the introduction to *Formal and Transcendental Logic* (§§ 8–10). Needless to say, this conception of logic is absolutely novel and peculiar to Husserl. The goal that Husserl sets himself is to show the transcendental motivation of traditional logic and consequently the intentional (pre)constitution of transcendental logic in traditional logic. The main reproach that Husserl addresses to traditional logic is that it was unable to see the original dimension that was opened to its investigation. This is the reproach of one-sidedness (*Einseitigkeit*) addressed to the formal logic of

Aristotle and the tradition.[8] When traditional logic turned to subjective questions, it usually took them to pertain to a real subjective thematic; hence it abandoned to psychology the task of providing a constitutive grounding for logic. In any case, logic failed in its task. It failed on the one hand by being satisfied with a purely objective analytic-logical view and on the other hand by letting psychology take precedence, i.e., by confining itself to being simply an application of a real [*réale*] science. These two orientations of logic clearly show the two dangers that lie in wait for the twofold logical problematic. If the objective-analytic aspect alone is considered, there is a tendency to move toward a definition of formal logic as exclusively norma-tive (technicism). And if we appeal to psychology for the sub-jective thematic of logic, we distort the profound transcendental sense of logic (psychologism). We must, then, look briefly at these two outgrowths of logic. They are not unrelated to each other.

Logic, even when it is restricted to a purely objective the-matic, is an objective science of the (subjective) cognitive operation. As such, it cannot fail to come in contact with a particular objective science—psychology, the objective science of the subjectivity of man (and animals). Since psychology is a science of the subjective, it was quite natural that an objective logic should turn its subjective problematic over to it (*FTL*, p. 38 [33]). Furthermore, the normative preoccupation of logic was also conducive to bringing out the subjective aspect of logic, since logic proposed laws that were meant to govern the subjective operations of knowledge. The normative preoccupa-tion thus concealed the ideal objectivity of logical configura-

8. On the other hand, Husserl recognizes that this one-sidedness is natural and even rooted in essential grounds (*FTL*, p. 8 [7]). In any case, this one-sidedness is necessary in objective logic. It es-sentially determines the objective character of traditional logic (*FTL*, p. 10 [9]), and it is open to criticism only if it tends to be absolute and to close all access to transcendental logic. The latter alone can prevent an entire "part" of logic from remaining in complete ir-rationality (*FTL*, pp. 16 f. [15]). Ancient philosophy also remains one-sided (*Crisis*, p. 176 [179]). One-sidedness is, in short, a super-ficiality, since it characterizes a science which contents itself with what appears—the *constituted*—without regarding it as an *index* of the *constituting*. Cf. the "life of the plane" and "life of depth" (*Flächenleben* and *Tiefenleben*) discussed in *Crisis*, § 32.

tions.[9] In this way the entire criticism of knowledge was in the end turned over to psychology simply on the basis of the evident fact that every science—being knowledge of an object by a subject—is a subjective configuration. Experience and judgment, along with their correlative objects, thus came to be regarded as themes of this psychology which set itself up as criticism of knowledge. However, no psychology was sufficient to this task, since psychology is a real science, which, like every other science, is necessarily motivated by transcendental subjectivity (*FTL,* pp. 38 f. [34 f.]). The main defect of this psychologistic conception of the criticism of knowledge is its assumption that an objective science of the subjective can in the final analysis ground knowledge, whereas, as objective science, it is itself a subjective *Leistung.* Only a subjective science of the subjective —being an intentional explication of transcendental subjectivity —can perform this ultimate and definitive function. This science is transcendental phenomenology, universal science of the noetic *quomodo* of the pregiven world (*Crisis,* pp. 146 f. [149] and § 34c).

But psychology's claim to success in a task which exceeds its means had unfortunate results. Not only did logic lose its supremacy, which was so strongly affirmed in Plato's dialectic, but it lost its autonomy as well. From the queen of the sciences it became a mere application of psychology. Furthermore, so far as the thesis of intentionality is true, logic lost the sense of the specific character of its object. Because the objectivity proper to logic—the categorial objectivity—necessarily derives from a judgment, and because the judgment (*Urteil*) originates in judication (*Urteilen*), psychological logic was not long in confusing judgment and judication, noema and noesis, thereby destroying intentionality itself. The ideal objectivity of logical configurations was completely lost, partly in order to avoid a dreaded return of alleged Platonizing realism. The confusion which no one would make in mathematics (confusing collecting with the collection, for example) was committed in logic and in the criticism of knowledge.[10] Instead of seeing its formal

9. *FTL,* p. 45 (40). This is a quite paradoxical result, one which nicely points out the ambiguity of the normative function of logic. Insofar as it sets down pure concepts and ideal laws, logic is exclusively objective-analytic. Insofar as these laws *in actu exercito* govern a subjective process of knowledge, logic is subjective.

10. *FTL,* pp. 81 f. (71 f.). Cf. above, § 8, on Husserlian Platonism. Let us recall here simply that it is necessary to affirm the reality

continuity with mathematical analysis, logic was driven more and more into a psychologistic empiricism in which judgments themselves, as categorial configurations, arise from subjective internal experience.[11]

It should be noted that the first outgrowth, the conception of logic as exclusively normative, is not irremediable, as the second one is. In fact, traditional logic, although remaining exclusively in an objective thematic, is not necessarily closed to a subjective thematic. Formal logic is susceptible to a transcendental extension. This is why it is legitimate to carry on its striving by working out its intentional tendencies.

Husserl denies that logic is solely formal-analytic logic and is thus one objective science among others. But he also rejects the view that it is only an art or technology designed to govern the objective results of science. He regards logic as the highest function of the transcendental theoretical interest (*FTL*, p. 16 [14 f.]). This shows that he means to go beyond formal logic while assuming it as an integral part of his subjective logic. In order to begin to understand the transition from formal to transcendental logic, it will be worthwhile to show how Husserl effected this surpassing with regard to the normative character of traditional logic.

The problem of logic as technology or *Kunstlehre* is what first preoccupied Husserl. This is quite understandable, since this is the most manifest aspect of logic, being the aspect in which logic is exercised (as normative). Hence this is also the aspect which the tradition has most thoroughly worked out. The principle of a *Leistung* is to be grasped only by starting from this *Leistung* itself. An index is needed to point reflection to the constituting intentionality. It is the normative, "artificial,"

---

of logical objectivities while avoiding the Platonic metaphysical hypostasis as well as the materialistic empiricism of the psychologistic point of view.

11. In *FTL*, § 57, Husserl gives a brief and excellent exposition of logical psychologism. The principle of this doctrine is that nothing is foreign to the psychic, from which it follows that all logical data are "real [*réel*] events" in the sphere of the psychic. The main tenet of the psychologism he condemns is described thus: "Our main concern here is the equating of judgment formations (and, of course, of all similar formations produced by acts of reason in general) with phenomena of internal experience" (*FTL*, p. 154 [138]; translation altered)—which amounts to a reduction of logic to psychology and, correlatively, a reduction of the logical ideal objectivity to a psychic reality, which is precisely that of thought.

"exemplary" aspect that is most manifest in logic. And so it is from this aspect that Husserl sets out. To begin with, he proposes a definition of logic as normative-technological science (*LI*, p. 72 [I, 28]). Logic determines to what extent a science meets the conditions which formally constitute a genuine science (*LI*, pp. 70 f. [I, 26 f.]). When this logical norm becomes an end in itself, logic becomes, strictly speaking, an art which as such proposes to the particular sciences an end to be realized.[12] However, this definition of logic can be only provisional; for this norm is precisely the idea of science, and Husserl will thus be able to go beyond the exclusively normative aspect of logic. As we know, the idea of science is the essence of science; and hence it is the object of a corresponding knowledge.

Before speaking of a normative logic, then, we must acknowledge a purely *theoretical* logic, a pure science of the idea of science. Every practical science presupposes a theoretical science in this way (*LI*, Prolegomena, chap. 2). But the pure science of the idea of science, or *Wissenschaftslehre*, is an a priori eidetic discipline. As such it *is* a science, not a technology; but it *has* a normative-technological function. Logic *is* not normative but *becomes* normative-practical (*FTL*, p. 31 [28]). Husserl thus distinguishes, within the practical-normative discipline that is logic, a theoretical nucleus which is self-sufficient and which may consequently be detached from logic taken as a normative discipline. The normative laws of logic are therefore derived from the purely theoretical truths of this same logic (*LI*, pp. 87 f. [I, 47–49]). The role which logic as theoretical plays as foundation of its own normative function warrants calling it "nomological." A science is nomological when it studies a law in itself (*nomos, logos*); that is, a law independent of its function, independent of its exercise as law (apart from all normation). It is by definition a *possible* science, and it requires completion in a normative discipline as its function or proper exercise. Before being in *act* of normation, before being actually normative, it must therefore be a pure and theoretical science.

Thus logic studies the essential possibility of genuine science, and this enables it to guide a priori the current development of the particular sciences (*FTL*, p. 13 [11]). More precisely,

12. *LI*, pp. 71 f. (I, 27). Note that this "finality" is immediately posited, not as real, but as ideal, since the principle of measure, the norm itself, is found to be the telos. Ideal finality is precisely *exemplarity*.

Husserl characterizes theoretical sciences as nomological insofar as they contain "their unifying principle as well as their essential goal of research" in their laws (*LI*, p. 230 [I, 234]). Such a science studies the point of view of *theory;* that is, it studies the unity in principle of a domain of knowledge which possesses its system of clarifying principles in a fundamental law (*LI*, p. 230 [I, 233 f.]). Husserl is thus led to define nomological science as a deductive science, a science for which there are no truths which do not derive deductively from a fundamental law (*FTL*, p. 96 [84]). This is another way of formulating the normative function of nomological science.

However, the normative function we are considering here is strictly limited to formal logic as analytic and objective. This does not mean that transcendental logic is not normative or formal, but its normation takes on an originary constitutive mode. This is why Husserl is anxious to have us understand that analytic formal logic is not essentially normative but that one of its functions is normative. As a matter of fact, the normation on the part of transcendental logic is precisely transcendental constitution. This normation is not simply a function of transcendental logic, but rather its very nature (cf. below, "General Conclusion").

Formal logic as exclusively normative therefore amounts to a hypertrophy of the objective thematic. Logic thus regarded is meant to be "critical," but in a practical manner.[13] This claim to be critical is analogous to that of the psychology which claims to give logic its definitive grounding. In the latter case a subjective thematic, because it was conceived in the real [*réal*] mode, was reduced to a thematic that was psychological and hence still objective. Here an objective thematic, also conceived in the real mode, is reduced to a thematic that is "artistic" and therefore subjective-real (since doing or making is subjective). We have here two thematics, each of which would be absolute and definitive to the detriment of the only absolute thematic, the transcendental. Each is directed to a subjective-real thematic which cannot go beyond the framework of the natural attitude.[14]

13. This is logic as "dogmatism" knew it (*Crisis,* p. 92 [94 f.]).
14. This subjective-real is the uncriticized empirical. Like the natural world which subtends it, it has claims to absoluteness unless it is "converted" to subjective-relative (i.e., relative to transcendental consciousness). Cf. *Crisis,* § 34.

§ 19. *Transcendental logic: phenomenology of science and phenomenology of logic*

WE HAVE JUST SEEN an aspect of the criticism of genuineness (*Kritik der Echtheit; FTL,* p. 96 [84]) applied to objective logic with the intention of exorcising its two fundamental outgrowths. Husserlian logic thus begins with a criticism of traditional logic. Here there appears an ambiguity which can only complicate the picture we wish to present. It seems that transcendental logic is a criticism both of science and of logic.

Logic is indeed a *Wissenschaftslehre,* which seeks to determine the "in principle" pertaining to science and to construct a purely ideal science of science. Here again we find the exemplarist schema of the phenomenological method. Logic considers the sciences as they are progressively realized, as adumbrations or embryonic forms of genuine and perfect science. The logical interest is therefore to take these embryonic sciences into consideration as data, as a field of exemplary investigations, and to elicit in full perfection what is in a latent state in the existing adumbrations (*FTL,* p. 130 [115]). The existing sciences imply a reference to genuine ideal science as their very meaning. Intentional analysis thus elicits the idea in an ideal anticipation on the basis of its partial realization; it proceeds from factical example to ideal exemplar. Hence it is structured on the schema of exemplarity or participation or, more precisely, on the two dimensions of exemplarity, depending on whether we consider the advance of thought moving from ideal exemplar to factical example (transcendental-phenomenological point of view, in itself) or from factical example to ideal exemplar (descriptive-phenomenological point of view, for us). Our present study obviously takes the second point of view. Logic elucidates the ideal exemplar—genuine science and its formal conditions—on the basis of the current realization of science, which plays the role of factical example. Considering what is given in the historical experience of existing sciences as a field of exemplary experiences, logic undertakes an exemplary criticism (in other words, a criticism of genuineness) with respect to them (*FTL,* pp. 28 f. [25], 10 [9]).

However, *Wissenschaftslehre* in general had already come to light before Husserl began his undertaking. It had already experienced the beginning of its realization. It is already there, and historical experience gives evidence of it.[15] Traditional logic is not perfect, to be sure; but, as it is at least a beginning of realization of the idea of logic, it includes a certain share of perfection. Husserl takes it up and applies his intentional method to it. What we have seen in the case of science in general is transposed and confirmed in the case of logic.

Intentional reflection also finds an exemplary field in the logical adumbrations it finds, just as it did in the embryonic forms of science. On the basis of these factical examples, it elicits the ideal exemplar; on the basis of traditional logic, it intentionally elicits transcendental logic. Hence the problem at hand is to show how Husserl's phenomenological logic is the intentional telos toward which traditional logic obscurely tended. Here again we find a familiar theme. The situation here is exactly the same as when Husserl showed phenomenology to be the intentional terminus toward which all prior transcendental philosophy tended (cf. *Crisis*, pp. 70 [71], 193 [196], 207 [212]). In both cases there is a transition from an embryonic form to a perfect form, from a potential form to a fully actualized form, from potency-*dynamis* to act-entelechy. Traditional logic is thus the potential form of a more perfect logic. Transcendental logic —or, more precisely, phenomenological logic, including a purely objective-analytic "part" and a purely subjective-synthetic "part" —is the actuality or entelechy of the logical interest that was launched in the history of human reason with the first steps of Greek science. Consequently, two stages are to be distinguished, since Husserl's object is first of all to elucidate the intentional sense of objective-analytic logic as such. In the first place, formal logic itself is to be clarified. Analysis thus enables us to distinguish three superimposed strata. Husserl gives this first intentional analysis of formal logic in *Formal and Transcendental Logic*.[16] But there is no break in continuity; Husserl is trying to elicit a genuine formal logic, and transcendental logic extends this newly clarified formal logic. This transcendental extension amounts to a new intentional analysis, or rather an extension of the intentional analysis of objective logic. After having intentionally elucidated genuine formal logic, we must intentionally elucidate transcendental logic. This "interlocking" of intentional

15. *FTL*, pp. 75 f. (66 f.). Historical experience finds a logic— or, more precisely, theoretical configurations—which are, as it were, "at hand." Cf. *FTL*, p. 10 (9).

16. It results in the tripartite division of logic (*dreifältige Schichtung der Logik*). Cf. *FTL*, Part I(a).

analyses occurs with no collision, as if it were a matter of one and the same analysis. We are led by formal ontology and the study of ultimate substrata to the study of experience and of evidence—that is, to the constituting intentionality of the ego.

By showing this teleological outcome, Husserl at the same time justifies and motivates transcendental logic by traditional logic and traditional logic by transcendental logic. This occurs in two different senses, which are determined by the two dimensions of intentional analysis. He motivates transcendental logic as the intentional telos of traditional logic; and, conversely, traditional logic is motivated as the factical example is motivated, in the last analysis, by the ideal exemplar, as the embryonic form is justified by the full-blown form.

Hence if Husserlian logic is strictly speaking a *Wissenschaftslehre*—i.e., in virtue of intentional analysis, a genuine phenomenology of science—it must also be said that it is an intentional elucidation of formal logic and therefore a phenomenology of formal logic.[17] Husserlian logic is essentially both one and the other. This logic is indeed intended to be a phenomenology of science—a clarification of its meaning and an elucidation of its pure idea. But it has been preceded in this investigation by traditional logic, which represents a first approach to the goal toward which phenomenological logic tends. It is therefore to be expected that Husserlian logic would integrate this first logic. On the one hand, it does so by maintaining traditional logic within its proper limits and consequently retaining what is valid in it. On the other hand, it does so by taking it as point of departure for a constitutive exemplary criticism which is intended to elucidate the latent intentional sense of its immanent structures and to show its necessary outcome in a transcendental logic. From this second point of view, the phenomenology of traditional logic is an essential and integral part of Husserlian phenomenological logic, since the exemplary criticism of the fact is an integral part of the eidetic sci-

17. *FTL*, pp. 10 f. (9). This is a turn from logic as theory to logical reason (*FTL*, p. 267 [236]), i.e., the grounding of logic as ideal-objective configuration in transcendental subjectivity. It is to be noted that the intentional analysis of formal logic is twofold, since formal logic itself is both formal apophantics and formal ontology. Husserl first subjects traditional logic to criticism, a logic which is essentially apophantic in orientation (*FTL*, § 47). He is thereby led to the tripartite division of formal logic (*dreifältige Schichtung*). Second, in order to arrive at a perfect conception of formal ontology, Husserl intentionally criticizes formal mathematics (*FTL*, § 24).

ence of the ideal exemplar. In other words, the phenomenology of traditional logic is an essential *moment* of logic as phenomenology of science. Logic remains a *Wissenschaftslehre* directed toward science itself. In its concrete striving for realization, however, it makes use of and criticizes the entire previous contribution of traditional logic while ridding this logic of the impurities that have made it deviate from its first intention.[18]

It is possible, however, to conceive a transcendental logic which gives no intentional analysis of traditional logic. In this case we must show what may be called with Husserl the *genealogy* of logic, beginning with perception or originary experience. Thus, there are two possibilities for phenomenological logic. Either we begin with traditional logic, which is already something of a realization of the idea of logic; and by an intentional analysis of its immanent structure, we are led to a transcendental logic (passing through a genuine formal logic) and we ground all logic on originary experience and transcendental subjectivity. Or else we begin immediately with this originary experience (i.e., with subjectivity) and show how logic is "born" on the basis of primary perception. These are two possibilities for logic, following the two dimensions of intentionality: either from logic to experience (i.e., from constituted object to constituting consciousness) or else from experience to logic (i.e., from constituting consciousness to constituted object). On the one side we have the reflective-constitutive method; on the other, the progressive-constitutive. These two possibilities are illustrated by Husserl in an admirably thought-provoking way in two logical works, *Formal and Transcendental Logic* and *Experience and Judgment,* which are intended to establish the same logic but which are nevertheless quite different. The former work represents the line of advance from formal logic to experience. It follows the retrogressive-constitutive method, which proceeds from constituted to constituting; and it corresponds to the descriptive-phenomenological point of view. The second work represents the line of advance from experience to logic. It follows the progressive-constitutive method,

18. We are here considering the relation of traditional (historical) formal logic to complete Husserlian logic. It will be necessary to broaden the issue and ultimately consider the relation between logic in general and transcendental phenomenology. It will then appear that the phenomenology of logic is the eidos of the phenomenology of science or, in other words, that transcendental logic is eidetic phenomenology. Cf. below, "General Conclusion."

which proceeds from constituting to constituted; and it therefore corresponds to the transcendental-phenomenological point
of view. It is the constitution of logic by transcendental subjectivity, on the basis of experience. The mind takes this latter
line of advance easily. *Formal and Transcendental Logic* is, on
the other hand, more arduous to read than *Experience and
Judgment;* but we also feel that the former work is more typical.[19] Of all Husserl's works, *Formal and Transcendental Logic*
is the most representative. It is the work that gives the most
adequate idea of phenomenology and its difficulties. Together
with the *Cartesian Meditations,* it gives the most complete exposition of phenomenology. Moreover, it has the advantage over
the *Cartesian Meditations* of more clearly manifesting Husserl's
deepest intention. With the *Cartesian Meditations* we feel the
philosophical influence of Cartesian method. In *Formal and Transcendental Logic* we become aware of Husserl's ambition to
give a total philosophy that is at once *logical, critical,* and *constitutive—*in a word, *transcendental.* Phenomenology in its
deepest sense is a *logic,* a logic based on a criticism of science,
advancing through a formal logic of being and of knowledge
and ending in a constitutive logic of being. It advances from a
logical criticism to an objective-analytic philosophy, then to a
subjective-synthetic philosophy. This philosophical logic—which
is a science of both being and knowledge, hence a science of
intentionality—is a dialectic. Phenomenology is thus philosophy
to the extent that it "Platonizes," that is, to the extent that it
affirms as a primary principle the mutual exemplarity (hence
the intentionality) of consciousness and that of which it is
conscious. This "exemplarist" style, or rather this intentional
style in its exemplarist form, is formulated especially in *For
mal and Transcendental Logic* and in the *Crisis.* These two
works best represent the descriptive-phenomenological point of
view in Husserl's work, that is, the method of proceeding from
fact (factical example) to ideal exemplar. In *Formal and
Transcendental Logic* we proceed from the "fact" of clarified
formal logic to the "idea" of transcendental logic, from a particular ideal objectivity (formal logic) to what originarily con-

19. This is *the* book of Husserl for S. Bachelard, as it is for us.
See Bachelard, *A Study of Husserl's "Formal and Transcendental
Logic,"* trans. Lester E. Embree (Evanston, Ill.: Northwestern Uni-
versity Press, 1968), p. xxx.

stitutes it—namely, transcendental consciousness.[20] An analogous line of thought is followed in the *Crisis* from the *de facto* sciences to transcendental phenomenology, i.e., from objective sciences to transcendental subjectivity. Husserl's other works— as, for example, *Ideas I* and the *Cartesian Meditations*—have a Cartesian style, as we noted. They begin immediately from pure transcendental experience, from the transcendental consciousness of the ego. Their approach is the progressive-constitutive line of advance from constituting consciousness to constituted objectivity.[21] *Experience and Judgment* shares these same characteristics. Its approach is likewise more Cartesian than that of *Formal and Transcendental Logic*, since it goes from originary consciousness (which is in fact simply assumed) to constituted logic. Such a point of view therefore leaves no place for a phenomenology of traditional logic, since formal logic is reached as the telos of the line of advance and hence as perfectly completed telos rather than as imperfect point of departure for an intentional analysis. The phenomenology of traditional logic is, on the other hand, the point of departure in *Formal and Transcendental Logic*. In other words, from the descriptive-phenomenological point of view, the phenomenology of science is at the same time the phenomenology of traditional logic. Transcendental logic is both phenomenology of science and phenomenology of formal logic. But from the transcendental-phenomenological point of view, transcendental logic is only a genealogy of formal logic, without an exemplary criticism of traditional logic.

20. The exemplary reciprocity remains, since transcendental logic (i.e., the idea of logic) motivates traditional logic and formal logic. In any case, the constituted necessarily implies the constituting (consciousness), and the constituting is necessarily objectified in the constituted.

21. The transcendental-phenomenological dimension of intentionality is therefore what determines the Cartesian character of works such as *Ideas* and *Cartesian Meditations*. We should by no means see a historical reason here but rather a doctrinal reason. If we were to adhere strictly to a historical account of things, we would have to say that it is because Husserl held a series of lectures during February, 1929, in the Descartes Auditorium of the Sorbonne that phenomenology took on a Cartesian complexion. But didn't Husserl himself say that phenomenology takes root in Cartesian thinking? This could scarcely have been a mere courtesy toward his French listeners!

§ 20. *Logic: genuine science and philosophy*

WE MUST GO INTO MORE DETAIL concerning some of the last points we touched on. We saw that objective logic, insofar as it develops into a formal logic of the object or of being (*apriorische Gegenstandslehre*), is a "philosophy." However, even though objective logic is first for us, it is not the ultimate logic (*FTL,* p. 271 [239]); and thus formal ontology (or philosophy) is extended in a constitutive ontology (or philosophy). We saw just now that transcendental logic is a phenomenology of logic and hence, since logic is simply an exemplary criticism of science, a phenomenology of science. But this criticism is not self-sufficient if it does not concern itself with the *object* of science. In other words, logic must take intentionality into account. This amounts to saying that the logic of science, as phenomenology of science, is also a logic of the object or a logic of being. We saw the difficulties of this logic, we saw how to overcome them, and finally we saw how to gain access to this object of logic. But since formal logic is extended in transcendental logic, the logic of the object also has a constitutive dimension and becomes a transcendental philosophy of being. The latter therefore leads us to the ultimate foundation of all objectivity, to transcendental subjectivity.

Only transcendental logic includes a properly phenomenological study of science, since it includes a constitutive study of science. That is, only transcendental logic accords to intentionality its true constitutive character. Hence it alone is an ultimate science, inasmuch as it is constitutive. Intentionality, which was necessarily subjacent in objective-analytic logic, has so far led only to positing the necessity of the correlative objective term without explicating its intentional motivation from the subjective-synthetic point of view. But now intentionality immediately takes on its essential dynamic dimension. The intentionality of science is a constituting intentionality, and it refers the objective unity to the multiplicity of its noetic constitution—that is, to experience. Experience is the most originary and most elementary *Leistung* of transcendental subjectivity. Transcendental logic is thus an intentional analysis of experience and an explication of the transcendental consciousness which motivates experience.

And precisely qua constitutive study of the object itself, logic is necessarily a philosophy of the object or a *transcendental philosophy of being,* since all being is only insofar as it is constituted by the originary *Leistung* of subjectivity.[22] In its full development, transcendental logic is a transcendental phenomenology, a philosophy that is at once logical, critical, and constitutive (*FTL,* p. 13 [11 f.]). Phenomenological logic pursues a genuine philosophical interest by intentionally explicating the immanent sense of the structures of science and logic, since it leads to the originary constitution of its correlative object (*FTL,* pp. 74 f. [65 f.]). Logic is therefore identical with philosophy. This is an ultimate consequence of the thesis of intentionality, which cannot be repeated too often. Science being necessarily science of the object, the science of science is both science of science and science of the object—the latter being understood either in the dimension of the objective-analytic thematic or in that of the subjective-synthetic thematic. Logic-philosophy is not only an intentional motivation of logic as theory but is also an originary constitution of being in general in every conceivable sense. Transcendental phenomenology is thus the ultimate justification of ideally completed science as a theoretical structure, as well as the ideal justification of the "objective" content of the constitutive concepts of this science. This is the dual motivation we mentioned.[23] Being science of science and science of the object in complete universality, phenomenology perfectly realizes the ideal of the Platonic dialectic—as Husserl likes to emphasize (*FTL,* p. 223 [198]).

What must be understood, finally, is that phenomenology is the ultimate science because it is the originary constitutive science. It is constitutive, and hence it constitutes itself. The originary *Leistung* which motivates every other objectivity is an intentional life. And this intentional life of subjectivity is *absolute being* insofar as it constitutes itself while constituting

22. Cf. the important texts of *FTL,* pp. 232 f. (205 f.) and § 103.
23. Cf. above, § 16, and *FTL,* p. 271 (239). Transcendental phenomenology as constitutive philosophy of being is therefore, according to Husserl, a sort of "formal ontology." It retains the latter's character as a priori science of the object in general, and hence as ideal norm, but gives it a new and strictly constitutive coloring. Being the science of the intentional constitution of every object in any sense whatever, it is a transcendental ontology, an ultimate and absolute philosophy. Cf. *FTL,* pp. 272 (240), 13 (11 f.).

other beings.[24] Philosophy-phenomenology is therefore its own norm; it is what ideally realizes the "endless striving for self-normation" which shapes human reason from its birth.[25] It refers only to itself, since it reaches the foundation of foundations, the presupposition of all presuppositions, the transcendental ego. This presupposition alone is presupposed legitimately. For it alone is to be genuinely criticized, it alone is to be by itself genuine and permanent self-criticism (since it is nothing but the transcendental consciousness of the ego by itself)—the transcendental ego being a primordial fact, the originary basis of my own world, and the only absolute presupposition, the presupposition which gives other presuppositions their sense (*FTL*, pp. 237 [209 f.], 276 f. [244]; *Crisis*, p. 78 [79 f.]; *CM*, p. 21 [61]). This ego is the adequate object of a philosophy, the first of philosophies, *first philosophy* or absolute knowledge, which grounds all metaphysics and all philosophy which would present itself truly as science (*Ideas*, pp. 45 f. [8]). All the prejudices of the naïve-natural world are indices of this fundamental presupposition and need to be intentionally justified in it. So far as they are grounded and criticized in and by it, these prejudices enter as objects into an apodictic and absolutely grounded science which fully realizes the idea of philosophy. Only in this way do the prejudices of the natural world lose their pejorative character by being grounded by intentional reference on the fundamental prejudice. Since as ultimate norm it judges itself, this fundamental prejudice—the transcendental ego—is the source of its own validity and can be called a presupposition or prejudice only in a positive sense—i.e., in the sense that it is a necessary foundation, set down a priori. The transcendental criticism which it performs with regard to itself thus guarantees that the ego realizes the ideal of presuppositionlessness [*Vorurteilslosigkeit*] which genuine science requires. This is the radicalism of self-constitution by itself, by and in transcendental self-consciousness. The transcendental ego is therefore this originary *Leistung* of self-giving of sense. Thus it is clearly impossible to rise beyond the ego in a transcendental philosophy. The foundation of all phenomenology is a transcendental subjectivity, but this must not be taken as a

24. "Absolute being is being in the form of an intentional life—which, whatever else it may have present to its consciousness, is at the same time consciousness of itself" (*FTL*, p. 273 [241]; translation altered).

25. *Crisis*, p. 15 (13) [translation altered].

"being" in the static sense of the word. Rather, it is a *Leistung,* an activity, a pure act, a subsisting vital dynamism, an intentional life that is fully autarchic and self-constitutive (*FTL,* pp. 276 f. [244]; cf. below, § 53).

This *Vorurteilslosigkeit* is grounded and explicated in transcendental self-consciousness, which is nothing but the constitutive criticism of the ego by itself. Correlatively, this self-consciousness is expressed by the reference to itself (*Rückbeziehung zu sich selbst*) of transcendental phenomenology, the science of the ego. Phenomenology, as science of the transcendental foundation, as constitutive science of the *Lebenswelt,* of science and of logic-philosophy, is really the highest science. It is the science which no longer has above it any other norm, governing it a priori, but is instead its own a priori. This autonomy manifests the absoluteness and genuineness of phenomenology.[26] In phenomenology, the process of reflective regress resolves into a transcendental self-normation or pure constitutive act of self-criticism. Transcendental subjectivity is also the ultimate foundation, the first presupposition, which is no longer relative to anything other than itself. It resolves the reflective search for the ultimate foundation in transcendental self-consciousness, the pure act of self-giving of sense and pure self-constitutive spontaneity. Phenomenology as well as subjectivity thus has the possibility of turning back upon itself; this is the *Selbstnormierung* (self-normation) of the former and the *Selbstbesinnung* (self-giving of sense) of the latter. And this possibility heads off the danger of any *processus ad infinitum* (or, more precisely, an infinite regress) in the search for the last foundation. The iterative process is not eliminated; but the infinite regress which seems to result from it is, as it were, neutralized by this possibility of self-constitution (*FTL,* pp. 267 f. [236], 273 [241]). It can be said metaphorically that the search for the foundation, instead of rising even higher toward a more originary element,

26. The entire life of consciousness is dominated by a single universal constitutive a priori. Insofar as it is a universal intentional analysis of this life of consciousness, phenomenology cannot fail to lead to this universal a priori, which, according to what we have said, is the transcendental ego itself, the transcendental presupposition as spontaneous and originary source of itself (*FTL,* p. 246 [217 f.]). This ego is a "prelogical" concrete universal a priori which "norms" (by constitutive normation) all of objective logic and therefore all the objective a prioris of this logic. The ego is a subjective a priori; it is "prelogical" in that formal logic is a constituted "objectivity" (*Crisis,* p. 141 [144]).

is "stabilized" by closing in upon itself and "moving in a circle." The metaphor of the circle thus replaces that of the ladder. The dynamic movement of constitution is not interrupted, but it is, so to speak, mastered or dominated (*beherrscht*, as Husserl says with reference to the universal a priori). Transcendental constitution shows itself to be infinite. It is an idea; and, like every idea, it is an a priori system of determination of an infinite multiplicity, the a priori definition of a multiplicity (cf. above, § 14). The metaphor of the circle is not chosen arbitrarily, and Husserl himself uses it to illustrate his intentional method. Just as the fact is grounded in the idea, so also, in the intentional search for the foundation, traditional (formal) logic is grounded in transcendental logic and objectivity is grounded in transcendental subjectivity. But every objectivity and every being (*Seiendes*) whatever must put forth its claims to validity. If relative science is grounded in absolute science and the object is grounded in constituting subjectivity, phenomenology and subjectivity must also somehow be grounded. But phenomenology and subjectivity are absolute and ultimate. They must therefore be grounded in themselves. This means that they must transcendentally constitute themselves, either by *Selbstnormierung* (in the case of the ultimate science) or by *Selbstbesinnung* (in the case of the ultimate subjective foundation) (cf. below, § 53).

But traditional (formal) logic and the object play the role of *fact* with respect to transcendental phenomenology and subjectivity. Hence the latter pair plays the role of *idea*. The reflexive relativity of fact to idea undergoes an essential iterative process (*FTL*, p. 52 [46]), since the fact is never fully grounded by the idea or, more precisely, since the idea itself is infinite and represents the infinite totality of the fact. The idea itself therefore needs to be grounded. And since it is "absolute," it can be grounded only in itself; it refers infinitely to itself, it is infinite. But if, by referring infinitely to itself, it "neutralizes" the regress in this movement of reflective search for the ultimate foundation, it is also correct to say that in turning back upon itself it is fundamentally motivated by an inverse relativity to the fact (i.e., to the totality of the fact). This is the case because the idea is nothing but this totality of the fact and because this totality itself can be only ideal.

Thus once again we find mutual exemplarity at the end of our advance. The fact refers to the idea as its ultimate eidetic foundation. Traditional (formal) logic refers to transcendental logic, and the object refers to transcendental subjectivity. But if the relative is grounded in the absolute, the absolute can be grounded only in itself. The infinite regress is thus "mastered" in the circular return upon itself. Transcendental phenomenology and transcendental subjectivity are absolute and ultimate; they motivate themselves by a sort of self-constitution. In other words, the idea is motivated by a reference to itself. But the idea is only the (ideal) totality of the fact. Hence it is motivated ultimately by the fact conceived ideally, i.e., in an ideating (anticipating) and originary intuition of itself. Similarly, phenomenology is the "total" logic-philosophy—that is, logic and philosophy as traditionally conceived, in their ideal synthetic completion; and transcendental subjectivity is the infinite totality of the conditions of every object. Being motivated by themselves, they refer only to the historical "fact" of which they are part and of which they represent the ideal conception.

In this way the infinite regress closes in upon itself rather than continues. Instead of being lost in a ceaselessly recurring duality of grounded and grounding, intentionality is epitomized in the dialectical unity of the transcendental reciprocity between consciousness and object.[27] The exemplarity of fact and eidos, instead of crystallizing in an irreducible duality (the second moment of the dialectic), on the contrary shows the unity and constitutive reciprocity of fact and eidos. The circle as an image of reciprocity shows the dialectical unity of the two intentional poles without concealing their duality. It is an adequate symbol of the dialectic (cf. *Crisis*, p. 58 [59]).

Everything, even transcendental subjectivity itself, is thus relative to transcendental subjectivity. Conversely, transcendental subjectivity is relative to everything because it originarily constitutes all being in any sense whatever (*FTL*, p. 273 [271]). The same is true of phenomenology with respect to science. Every science is relative to it, and, conversely, it grounds all the sciences and guarantees their unity in principle. In this way Husserl can foreshadow the end of his critical efforts: the unity of the sciences is grounded in the unity of being, which is constituted in a univocal manner by transcendental subjectivity (*FTL*, p. 4 [4], 272 [240]).

Thus we see that transcendental logic or phenomenology is

27. A reciprocity which can also be called "bipolar" (*FTL*, p. 262 [232]). According to this passage, then, intentionality cannot have one dimension only; it must have, rather, a polar reciprocity—as we have been arguing. Intentionality is a correlation; it is the "universal a priori of correlation" discussed in *Crisis*, § 46.

not a new logic. Nor is it a second logic that is, so to speak, set above the first (viz., formal logic) (*FTL*, p. 291 [256]). On the contrary, it is the subjective and transcendental dimension—and hence the natural extension—of formal logic. It is a radical criticism of formal logic, an intentional and constitutive criticism. The phenomenology of logical reason is thus a synthetic criticism of this particular ideal object, logic, a criticism which extends the analytic "first criticism" of formal logic (*FTL*, pp. 170 f. [152 f.], 182 [162]). It is a noetic reflection on logic, i.e., a reflection which explicates the essential constitutive relativity of logic to the noetic multiplicity of its intentional *Leistungen* [*EJ*, p. 295 [356 f.]).

By tracing the formal-analytic logical configurations back to their motivating origin in experience and in the end making them particular objectifications of the originary spontaneity of transcendental subjectivity, transcendental logic manifests a tendency which has long shaped logic and which has unfortunately most often taken the form of logical psychologism. It introduces a pure subjective preoccupation (subjective-subjective, we might say, as opposed to the objective thematic of psychology). It broadens the analytic domain of formal logic with a synthetic thematic, and it avoids logical psychologism by a sort of transcendental psychology (cf. *Crisis*, Pt. III B, esp. pp. 257 f. [261 f.]). In a word, it brings into being a *concrete logic.* Transcendental logic neither conflicts with nor suppresses the formal logic inherited from the tradition. To assert the need for a concrete transcendental extension of a discipline that was hitherto purely analytic and abstract is not to substitute the first for the second. On the contrary, it is to "radicalize" the second by the first, to implant it in its originary source.

This occupation with concreteness makes it possible to reintroduce in transcendental logic some concerns of the material (*sachhaltig*) order which a purely formal and analytic logic, even in its ontological dimension, would be unable to admit. By showing the transcendental constitution of the theoretical configurations of formal logic, transcendental logic exhibits a schema of intentional constitution which is valid for all objectivity and all being in general, a schema which therefore extends to all the material ontological disciplines and grounds them. Transcendental logic thereby grounds the possibility of other constitutive "logics," of ontological domains other than that of pure formal logic. But for this reason, transcendental logic—because it formulates the universal structure of intentional constitution and ties this structure immediately and fundamentally to transcendental subjectivity—plays the role of highest constitutive logic with respect to these particular constitutive logics. That is, transcendental logic plays the role of *universal constitutive norm* (cf. above, p. 107, n. 23, and p. 109, n. 26). As the proper science of transcendental subjectivity, it formulates the structures belonging to the constitutive originary spontaneity of this subjectivity (the structures of intentionality) in a completely originary and primary mode—hence in a mode that is exemplary and normative for all possible particularizations of this universal structure (cf. below, § 51 and "General Conclusion"). As such it is truly the "formal" logic and ontology of the absolute science, of transcendental phenomenology. It is a genuine *subjective formal logic*. More exactly, transcendental phenomenology is its own logic with respect to itself. Here what we just saw concerning the self-normation of transcendental phenomenology finds immediate application. Science possesses a logic, and formal logic likewise possesses a correlative "logic" which is its own transcendental criticism. Here too there is a distinction between science and logic, between formal logic and transcendental logic. Logic norms science, but it is not science; transcendental logic norms formal logic, but it is not formal logic. In the present case, transcendental phenomenology norms itself; the logic of phenomenology is phenomenology itself. In this way the reflective search for the ultimate norm is also resolved by a constitutive self-normation. This is how we are to understand Husserl when (in the conclusion of *Formal and Transcendental Logic*) he speaks of the highest logic as the logic of absolute science or the logic of transcendental-phenomenological philosophy (*FTL*, p. 291 [256]).

Far from being a second logic, then, transcendental logic is absolutely first. It is the foundation of traditional formal logic. Transcendental logic is therefore first from the transcendental-phenomenological point of view and last from the descriptive-phenomenological point of view. This is why it appears in *Formal and Transcendental Logic* as an implication that is pre-constituted in traditional logic; and this is why it is fully formulated only at the end of this work, whereas in *Experience and Judgment* the thinking unfolds in a climate that is transcendental from the first.[28] These two logical attitudes are by no means contradictory. On the contrary, they are dialectically one.

28. Cf. *EJ*, pp. 67 f. (71 f.), a very important text for the transcendental interpretation of Husserl's works.

PART III

Formal Logic

OUR FIRST TASK NOW is to set out formal logic in its full purity and formulate its constitutive strata. Husserl is anxious to establish a sound formal logic before putting forth his transcendental logic.

This formal logic does not consider the object in its concrete existence. Nor, consequently, does it consider science in its synthetic correlation (adequation) with existing reality. Husserlian formal logic is a logic of essences, and, like traditional logic, it is purely analytic. But by virtue of its object it contains the promise of being surpassed in transcendental logic.

It is a tortuous path, however, that leads us to formal logic in the formulation Husserl gives it. It passes through historical experience—that is, through *language*—in order to get to *meaning*. When we have elicited and defined what meaning is, we will have reached the proper domain of formal logic. To do this, let us take up where we left off.

§ 21. *The historical experience of traditional logic: language and meaning*

PHENOMENOLOGICAL LOGIC as it appears in *Experience and Judgment* takes its departure from transcendental subjectivity and its originary expression as experience. This approach thus seems more originary than that of *Formal and Transcendental Logic*, which begins with an analysis of traditional logic, a categorial objectivity that is already constituted. However, the logic of the latter work also rests on an originary and immediate evidence. Here, too, the approach is radical and originary, but it explicates logical intentionality in a different dimension from *Experience and Judgment*. We have either a logic which passes from the prepredicative domain to the predicative domain or a logic which passes from the predicative domain to the prepredicative world. The line of advance is either from experience to logic or from logic to experience, from fact to idea or from idea to fact.

Although *Experience and Judgment* and *Formal Transcendental Logic* represent the two possible dimensions of intentionality, then, there is no reason why the logic of the former should be more originary than that of the latter. Each is originary in the Husserlian sense of this word, i.e., each is intuitive and evident. One is derived from the originary experience of the world (perception), while the other is derived from the originary experience of science—that is, in the present case, the originary experience of traditional logic. So here we again come across the historical experience that was brought into play above, in Part I.

We saw that this experience has great importance for the intentional analysis of science. It grasps development as the development of science reduced in the phenomenological epochē. This experience is what "originarily" gives us the sciences as they currently are and logic as it is currently realized. More exactly, it gives us the adumbrations of genuine science and logic. But it obviously cannot give the sciences or logic in the very *act* of scientific or logical knowledge. This act is strictly individual and consequently incommunicable. It is the personal affair of each scientist and each philosopher to know and to reach the truth (*CM*, p. 2 [44]). In this sense, the truth is not communicable. Insofar as it is grasped and experienced, it is an incommunicable, ineffable act. But what is communicable and hence capable of coming within historical experience is the *expression* of this act of grasping the truth. This expression is by extension called "science" or "knowledge" in its oral or written form (documentation). This is what is, strictly speaking, communicable, by virtue of its possessing a certain objective content [*teneur*]. But what we have here is simply *language* (the language of science and the language of logic). Husserl affirms, then, that logic must begin with an inquiry into language (*LI*, pp. 248 f. [II/1, 1 f.]; *FTL*, §§ 2–5, 15, 16a). The experience that enables us to get logic going from the descriptive-phenomenological point of view is therefore the experience of language. Thus there are two kinds of originary experience which correspond to the two dimensions of intentionality: the originary experience of the world and the originary experience of language.[1] And language is what gives historical experience the stable and permanent object that it requires.

When in a purely personal and genuine act (hence in an originary experience) I grasp noetically that "this tree is green," my act is, to be sure, individual and incommunicable. But at least it seems that its noematic correlate, "this tree is green," is endowed with a certain objectivity, that it at least has a certain objective validity. Further, the act may not stop at this stage but may instead continue to develop. It may grasp, for example, that this green is a dark green—and so on. The act is therefore, like every noesis, an infinite movement. At each moment of its

---

1. These correspond, respectively, to the evidence of clarity and the evidence of distinctness; cf. below, § 38.

development, however, it involves a certain objective correlate which is stable and permanent. For "I have seen what I have seen." This assertion of a purely analytic necessity may seem to be an irreducible self-evident truth, a mere self-identity or tautology. Even if what I have seen turns out to be false, or at least otherwise now than when I saw it, it still remains that this assertion, taken strictly by itself, must be true. In other words, the identity of what I have seen amounts to an objective validity and enables what I have seen to become an acquisition to which I "can always return." [2] The whole difficulty is to find out where and how this stable and permanent correlate is grounded. And here we seem to be in an inextricable predicament.

On the one hand, the act of knowing is ineffable. It is pure act, and as such it needs to be continued in a further development. On the other hand, the object or the thing itself is also incommunicable. For the green of this tree that I presently grasp is no longer the green that I grasp immediately afterward. From neither the noetic act nor the object, the *Gegenstand,* can we derive this stable objective content which we need in order to justify our knowledge. The knowledge we have is in fact knowledge of a flowing object (*Gegenstand*) or, more exactly, of this object at a certain moment of its development. It is given to me by an act which is determined but which is already past. In other words, there is no longer anything that corresponds to my current knowledge which stays in my mind—neither the object, which has changed meanwhile, nor the noetic act, which has passed. The stable objective content I am seeking therefore seems incapable of being justified. Nevertheless, it must necessarily exist; otherwise, there could no longer be language, and no expression would be possible. Here language testifies to the ideal objectivity of our knowledge and enables us to motivate it.

There is a difficulty here which is precisely the difficulty that sets apart the upholders of philosophical idealism and those of realism (cf. below, "General Conclusion"). Only a phenomenology, a science of meaning essences, can reconcile the two sides of the question by situating itself, as it were, beneath (or beyond) this secular quarrel. In outline, idealism holds that knowledge takes its objective content from the very act of knowledge. Realism holds, on the contrary, that knowledge takes its

2. Cf. *FTL,* § 74: "Idealities of And-so-forth" ("*Die Idealitäten des Undsoweiter*"). Husserl himself gives a typical example in *EJ,* p. 261 (313 f.). Cf. also *FTL,* pp. 185 f. (164).

objective content from the thing that is known. But this alternative between act of knowledge and thing, between subjectivist idealism and dogmatic realism, is too coarse.

For phenomenology in general it is not a question of choosing between realism and idealism in the usual sense of these two words, i.e., between the ego and the thing. For the "orthodox" phenomenology of Husserl it is not even a question of choosing between the two points of view of intentionality, between the primacy of constitution (the constitutive a priori) and that of progressive realization of the fact. A choice of this kind would in a way hypostatize one of the terms of intentionality. Intentionality is necessarily synthetic. We must therefore choose both the ego and the thing and show their correlation, their constitutive simultaneity. Thus there is a middle way in the question we are concerned with here. We keep the absolute incommunicability of the pure noetic act and of the thing which it tries to grasp. But we also maintain the objectivity of knowledge. And for this we orient ourselves on the side of *meanings*. Let us take up the example we were discussing a moment ago.

I grasp the truth "this tree is green" in a personal act. Both act and thing are ineffable, since they enjoy no permanent stability. But the correlate of the act in question remains as correlate of this act itself, even if the act continues to develop further; for this correlate possesses a sense, it is a meaning. It can be said that in a way the act, which is absolutely incommunicable, "sediments" in the meaning "this tree is green." From this sedimentation we can go back to the originary act, since, even if the latter has passed, its correlate or meaning always persists. This clearly shows that the meaning as such is not an act or an operation of the intellect. "This tree is green" is a meaning which takes the form of a judgment, but it is not a judication. It is, on the contrary, an *ideal objectivity*. It is an objectivity because it possesses a certain content, a certain stable consistency; it is ideal because its objectivity is not that of a real empirical reality. Being stable, being an ideal objectivity, the meaning is an *acquisition*, and it is *identifiable ad infinitum*.

§ 22. *The objectivity of the meaning:* Objektivität *and* Gegenständlichkeit

THIS POSSIBILITY OF IDENTIFICATION implies that the meaning as such is numerically and qualitatively one. It is because the meaning is perfectly identical that it is identifiable, that it is usable in an objectively identical way by everyone (*FTL*, pp. 162 f. [145]). It possesses for everyone an objective validity (*eine objektive Gültigkeit*) which makes it a *habitus* or permanent acquisition.[3] After my noetic act "this tree is green," I possess as its correlative meaning the noema "this tree is green" (independently of any question of synthetic adequation, since experience does not stop with possession of the meaning noema). This meaning represents for me an acquisition of knowledge which has the value it has and which remains what it is. It is identical, and I can always return to it in order to take it as the point of departure for a new theoretical inquiry, for example, or simply with the goal of verifying it again in the evidence of originary experience. I can therefore make use of it, I can "operate" with this objectivity "as if" it were a material object (cf. *FTL*, pp. 81 f. [71 f.]; and above, § 8). Thus it appears as independent of the noetic acts in which it is constituted. The noetic act comes and goes, or at least it continues in a new act which is an extension of the present act. The noetic act is not identifiable, but it is *repeatable*. This implies that two noetic

3. The word "*habitus*," like so many others (adequation, intentionality, *dynamis*, entelechy, exemplar, supposition) is borrowed from Scholastic terminology and hence from the classical tradition. *Habitus* is the translation of the Greek word *hexis*, which Plato used to designate the possession by the thing of the idea in which it participates (*Sophist*, 247a). The *habitus* is therefore a stable disposition which perfects and specifies its subject. In Plato the idea specifies a reality. Similarly, the Husserlian *habitus* sediments in the ego and makes it a personal ego with an abiding style, since the *habitus* persists and endures—which is the classical conception of the Greek *hexis* (*CM*, pp. 66 f. [100 f.]). In a similar manner, all knowledge is "stabilized" in a knowledge acquisition, an "acquisition which remains in continual objective validity" ("*ein bleibender Erwerb fortgeltender objektiver Geltung*") or an "ideal cognitional result" ("*ein ideales Erkenntnisergebnis*"; *FTL*, p. 170 [152]). Every act in general becomes a *habitus*, and its active acceptance becomes habitual: "*die aktuelle Geltung verwandelt sich in eine habituelle*" (*FTL*, p. 117 [104]).

acts can be qualitatively identical but that, since they are two distinct acts, they can never be numerically identical (cf. *FTL*, p. 185 [164]). But the correlate of these two acts which are numerically distinct and qualitatively identical is the meaning which is both qualitatively and numerically identical. These are the two essential marks which define the "possibility of identification" (*Identifizier-barkeit*). Being independent of noetic acts (the various noetic experiences in which they are constituted), meanings transcend these acts, as Husserl says (*FTL*, pp. 34 [30], 40 f. [36], 117 [104], 184–87 [163–65]). This cannot of course be a real transcendence. Sense-giving (*Sinngebung*) is an operation of transcendental consciousness. It constitutes the unitary sense of a noetic manifold by referring it intentionally-synthetically to one sense, to one unique and identical meaning. More exactly, it constitutes this unitary sense by making the various partial meanings of the partial noetic experiences converge in one unique and identical meaning. The noetic manifold is real [*réelle*]. The unitary meaning, which surpasses it and toward which it tends intentionally insofar as it is polarized by the meaning, is therefore an irreal or ideal transcendence that still remains within the immanence proper to transcendental subjectivity. Here we come to a major thesis of Husserl, the thesis of the *ideal transcendence of intentional unities* (idea, eidos, essence, meaning). All of Husserl's work would have to be cited to illustrate this thesis (especially *Ideas*, Sections III and IV; *FTL*, § 62).

Every objectivity, without exception, is an intentional unity, which means that it is an ideal transcendence with respect to the various noetic experiences in which it appears and is constituted. Hence what we have here is a new way of expressing Husserlian exemplarism, since the object, by virtue of giving the noetic experiences their sense, is the constitutive unity of this multiplicity of noetic experiences. This is true, as we know, for every object—for the object of perception and the categorial object of the judgment as well as for science, logic, and phenomenology. It is true for every being, since every being is constituted in transcendental subjectivity. Every object is an ideal unity pole with respect to the multiple flow of its corresponding constitutive noeses (cf. *FTL*, p. 134 [119]). Furthermore, this transcendence is a reduced transcendence situated in the reduced and therefore ideal world of the phenomenological epochē. There is therefore no possible way to compare this ideal transcendence with a God by any dialectical artifice. The real world and God himself (who is only a real-polar transcendence of this world)[4] are both reduced and are only guiding threads for intentional analysis (cf. *FTL*, p. 268 [237]). Reduced transcendence is precisely meaning. The latter is thus an objectivity of a special kind, an irreal or ideal objectivity which irreally transcends the immanence of the various noetic experiences. It is not an objectivity in the real-empirical sense (as, for instance, that of this tree or this table). It is instead a new objectivity, which forces us to broaden the traditional concept of the object and, by a necessary correlation, the traditional concept of experience (cf. *FTL*, pp. 40 f. [36], 45 [40], 81 [71], 155 f. [139 f.]; *Ideas*, § 3). The meaning is therefore an ideal objectivity which stands opposed to the subjective manifold of real noetic experiences as well as to the real objectivity of the thing. This is the middle way which phenomenology takes between the two irreducible absolutes represented by traditional idealism and realism. We can easily see that this is the way of intentionality. Confronting both the immanence of absolute idealism and the transcendence of dogmatic realism, it represents the *immanent transcendence* of the idea constituted in and by the development of the fact.

In Husserl's terminology, this ideal objectivity is called *ideale Objektivität*, by contrast with the *Gegenständlichkeit* of the thing or material object.[5] However, Husserl often uses the expression *Gegenständlichkeit* to denote an ideal objectivity, for instance the judgment corresponding to judication. In fact he speaks of categorial or irreal *Gegenständlichkeiten*, which are simply the correlative noemata of judications (nominalized propositions, *Sachverhalte*). However, he never uses the term *Objektivität* in place of the term *Gegenständlichkeit*. We may draw the following conclusion from this fact. *Objecktivität* is the word meant to express the "reality" (the irreality) of ideal objectivities (meanings, noemata of judications and of perceptions). It expresses their "existential" being, their ideal existence strictly speaking. *Gegenständlichkeit* is the word that enables us to indicate the relativity of such an ideal objectivity (*Objektivität*) to an

4. Cf. *Ideas*, p. 174 (139 f.). This leaves no possibility for pious good intentions of constructing "phenomenological theodicy" by, for example, bringing into play the monistic (totalizing) thesis of phenomenology and the intentionality toward ideal transcendence. Of course we are here staying within Husserlian orthodoxy.

5. Thus Husserl always speaks of the *ideale Objektivität* of logical configurations; cf. *FTL*, pp. 35 (31), 81 (71).

external reality (*Gegenstand*). But simply because ideal *Objekti-vität* pertains to meanings, which as such have a sense, i.e., an intentional relativity to an object (*Gegenstand*), it often happens that Husserl, in order to designate immediately the "existential" irreality of meaning, uses the word that expresses the relativity of meaning to what is meant. And since the entire being of the meaning is to intentionally imply a sense (a reference to an object), it follows that the word *Gegenständlichkeit* can be used in place of *Objektivität*, but not the reverse. (As a matter of fact, we are saying this in terms of *Formal and Transcendental Logic* in particular. The whole doctrine of the object in Husserl is more complicated, although the terminology remains clear cut.)

The notion of *das Objekt* represents in general every "toward which" [*vis-à-vis*] of consciousness. Since the *Gegenstand*—which is, more specifically, the external object of the world—is a "toward which" of consciousness, it too is an *Objekt*. It is a type of object, just that type whose objectivity appears in a system of successive adumbrations which manifest its transcend-ence and externality (its mundanity). Furthermore, when the *Gegenstand* itself (in its own "itself") is an idea, it too enjoys an ideal existence. It is then an irreal *Gegenständlichkeit* and possesses an *Ideal-Objektivität* (a mathematical "existence"), like the logical configurations (*logische Gebilde*). But, as an idea, it is then—like these configurations—the result of a founded act; whereas the *gegenständlich* correlate of a percep-tion is the result of a simple act. Ideally speaking, then, *Gegen-ständlichkeit* is an ideal *Objektivität* insofar as it represents an object in its completed "itself," i.e., an ideal telos. It is necessary to distinguish further between two sorts of objectivity. On the one hand we have *Gegenständlichkeit,* which necessarily indi-cates a relativity to a *Gegenstand* or external object, even if this *Gegenständlichkeit* proves to be irreal on account of the ideality of the "itself" of its object and thus becomes identical with an *Ideal-Objektivität*. On the other hand we have *Objektivität,* which as such can represent only ideal objects (judgments, categorial objects, mathematical numbers, etc.)

We have the following list, then. Ideal *Objektivität* repre-sents ideal objects, either mathematical or logical objects or else *Gegenstände* conceived ideally in their *Selbst. Gegenständ-lichkeit* indicates a relativity to the external object of the world, to the thing. In any case, by virtue of the intentional teleology between the real and the eidos (between fact and idea), every objectivity (whether *Gegenständlichkeit* in the first sense or ideal

Objektivität) partakes of the essential form of the object in general or *Gegenstand überhaupt*—which can also be called the *Objekt überhaupt*, since with it we are on the level of the purest ideality.[6]

After having determined the objectivity belonging to the meaning, we understand how it is this *Ideal-Objektivität* that gives the meaning a permanent and stable, identifiable, and communicable being. Because of this possibility of identification and communication, it can become an acquisition. The ideal objectivity of meanings is therefore expressed immediately and "naturally" in language. Language is in fact the bearer of meanings, and by way of language we arrive at meanings. The experience of language is therefore more precisely the experience of meanings.

Let us note, however, that if the meaning is a stable and identical objectivity, it is an intentional unity. As such it is constituted in a multiplicity of noetic experiences, each of which corresponds to a moment of the thing that is meant. Taken in itself, then, the meaning finds no adequate correlate (either noetic or *gegenständlich*) in any of the experiences in which it is constituted or in any moment of the corresponding thing. One might be tempted to say that the correlate is simply the totality of the constitutive experiences. But this totality is infinite and cannot be a definite correlate for the meaning, since the very notion of adequation implies determination and definition. The same holds for the moments of the thing which are correlative to each experience. Only their totality could be the adequate *gegenständlich* correlate of the meaning, if this totality were not infinite. But the "itself" (*Selbst*) of the thing, and in it the very existence of the thing, is an infinite idea. Therefore, if the existence of the thing is given by an infinite experience, and if, by reason of this infinity, the meaning cannot find in this existence an adequate correlate, it follows that the meaning does not

6. Here are some places where the doctrine of the object can be found: *Ideas*, §§ 35, 37, 90, 91, 131; *FTL*, §§ 8, 11, 26b, 57, 58, 61–63; *Crisis*, §§ 29, 34, 37. This is only a very incomplete list. The problem of the object in Husserl is coextensive with that of intentionality, and the entire corpus of Husserl's works would have to be cited. It should be emphasized that *FTL*, of all Husserl's works, seems to us to be the one in which the distinctions discussed here are most clearly observed. In *Crisis*, on the contrary, these distinctions are less closely observed, and the word *Objekt* tends to replace the word *Gegenstand*.

of itself imply the existence of the object meant. It is not as such *positional*. The meaning as such is the meaning of a reality divested of its real [*réelle*] existence; it is an *essence without existence*. This pure essence is either the essence of the object taken in its full totality or else the essence of a certain moment of the object, since the meaning can be either meaning of the thing in its totality or meaning of some moment of the thing. The meaning of the object is either partial or total.[7] In either case we have a singular essence, a *Wesensbestand* of a certain thing or state of affairs. The meaning does, therefore, represent a sense which refers to the thing itself, but this relation is not "finite." It is, on the contrary, infinite, because the originary experience of what is meant is itself infinite; hence the meaning does not imply the existence of what is meant. This infinite relativity is therefore an ideal relativity, and it gives the meaning its immediate eidetic value. It shows that the intentional telos of the meaning is an eidos, an idea, an essence deprived of real [both *réelle* and *réale*] existence. This is also why phenomenology, which is a science of meanings, is often rightly said to be a *science of essences*.[8]

7. These relations of part and whole are, however, relative. The meaning of a certain moment of the object, which is partial with respect to the total meaning of the object taken in its entirety, is also an intentional unity constituted in a corresponding noetic and noematic diversity. Consequently, the partial meaning is also the unity of a manifold, just as the total meaning is the intentional unity of the multiplicity of the total experience. In other words, the partial meaning is the intentional telos of subordinate meanings which play the role of parts with respect to it—and so on ad infinitum. Transcendental constitution is an infinite idea which brings us, from one reduction to another, to the primary transcendental reduction, the self-constitution of transcendental subjectivity, the originary intentional *Leistung*. Everything constituted is the one corresponding to the many of its constitution. The infinite regress can be escaped, as we saw, only by a return of consciousness upon itself performed in the originary purity of transcendental consciousness. In order to escape the dialectical duality of constituted and constitution, we must necessarily posit as a first element a pure act of constitution, a constitution of constitution, a pure *Leistung* or pure act.

8. M. Merleau-Ponty uses these words to define phenomenology: "Phenomenology is the study of essences; and according to it, all problems amount to finding definitions of essences: the essence of perception, or the essence of consciousness, for example" (*The Phenomenology of Perception*, trans. Colin Smith [New York: Humanities Press, 1962], p. vii). Phenomenology sees the essence considered apart from existence as only a first stage, however. It

These essences as such, taken in themselves, can only be true. More precisely, the question of truth as synthetic adequation to reality does not arise at their level. However, if we hold that the transcendent thing is not given immediately, but by successive adumbrations, we must also say that meanings are given immediately with evidence. As such, they are "true." But truth in this sense is only the analytic establishment of their "ideal existence," not truth by synthetic adequation. Husserl is thus led to distinguish between the experience of the transcendent spatial thing and the experience of the immediate lived experience [*l'expérience du vécu immédiat*]. One is mediate and transcendent, the other is immediate and evident. This distinction between immanent and transcendent perception leads him to the distinction between being as consciousness, as lived experience, and being as thing. Taken up and explicated, this is qualified as an ultimate, originary, and absolute distinction. It is the distinction between objects which are senses and those which are not, between categorial or irreal objectivities and objects *schlechthin* (pure and simple). In short, it is the distinction between *meaning* and *thing*.[9] With the thing, we enter the domain of the evidence of clarity or synthetic verifying evidence. With the meaning, we remain at the level of the evidence of distinctness, the evidence of articulated meanings (cf. below,

---

"puts essence back into existence." But this ontological tendency, at least as it appears in Husserlian phenomenology, is an infinite approximation.

9. We find here another aspect of the distinction we have drawn between *Objektivität* and *Gegenständlichkeit*. On the distinction between being as consciousness and being as reality, cf. *Ideas*, §§ 42, 44, 46. This distinction, which leads to that between *Gegenstände* and *Sinne,* is an absolute and ultimate distinction. It divides the intentional life of consciousness in an exemplary manner (cf. *EJ*, p. 269 [325] and all of § 65). *FTL* also exhibits this distinction (p. 132 [117 f.])—again described as ultimate—between meanings and objects. In other words, every *Ideal-Objektivität* of any degree must be founded originarily on a *Gegenständlichkeit*. Every compound act fundamentally implies a simple act. The *Ideal-Objektivität*, defined as a "vermeinte Gegenständlichkeit als vermeinte," necessarily implies a "vermeinte Gegenständlichkeit schlechthin" (i.e., a *Gegenständlichkeit* in the sense we gave this word above), since it is obviously an objectivity for us only if it is thought in some way. Cf. also, in *LI* (Second Investigation), the distinction between *Begriff* and *Begriffsgegenstand*. This distinction, too, is absolute (*LI*, p. 431 [II/1, 222]). Husserl also mentions the danger of infinite regress, which is just what motivates an ultimate and "absolute" distinction.

§ 32). But it must be kept in mind that meanings or essences are directly expressed in language. The proper place of essences, of the ideal existence of meanings, is language itself. For language in itself abstracts from the factical existence of things and grasps only meanings. This is the point of Merleau-Ponty's excellent phrase, "the separated essences are those of language." [10] In other words, a thought which moves solely on the level of language is necessarily in the attitude of the phenomenological reduction; it is set squarely in the eidetic world of meanings or pure experiences. This is why the *Logical Investigations*, which begin with an extremely close analysis of language and its functions, develops a logic that is in a truly phenomenological spirit even though it makes no reference to any phenomenological reduction. It should be clear that this is necessary from the point of view of language. *The reduction is implicitly carried out*—simply performed and not yet made explicit—as soon as language is considered on its own account.[11]

§ 23. *Toward the formal logic of the judgment*

THESE FEW REFLECTIONS put us in a position to understand the first direction that Husserl's logical inquiry is going to take. We have said that the method of intentional analysis (always regarded in one of its dimensions) takes its point of departure in a historical experience of "already" existing realities. If this is so, what happens in the case of logic?

The intentional analysis of logic finds forms which are already more or less elaborated, a logical structure (*geistiges Gebilde*) which is more or less perfect. But is this *geistiges Gebilde*, the ideality belonging to logical configurations, what is grasped in the first place? No indeed; instead, we grasp its expression in language, a quasi-corporeal expression. And by language we mean every form of expression, oral as well as literary, but reserving priority for oral expression.

But language is not the intentional terminus of the investi-

---

10. *The Phenomenology of Perception*, p. xv.

11. *Ideas*, p. 189 (151); *EJ*, pp. 57 f. (58 f.). Cf. S. Bachelard, *A Study of Husserl's "Formal and Transcendental Logic*," trans. Lester E. Embree (Evanston, Ill.: Northwestern University Press, 1968), p. xxxi.

gation. It is a sign, and it refers to its signified. The latter is what we are ultimately aiming at, it is the telos (*Endabsehen*) of the logical inquiry. The logical interest is directed to the meanings that language manifests and finally toward logical reason itself. Language nevertheless plays a role that is scarcely negligible, and by itself it shows a certain intentionality. This is easily understandable, since language is a sign or thematic index. Perhaps this will bring to mind our reflections on the realization of the idea as sign of the idea (cf. above, § 5; and cf. *FTL*, p. 27 [24]).

Language involves a certain materiality, in virtue of which it gives a "corporeality" to meanings and makes it possible for them to be "located" in the world. When language is considered as a sign or thematic index, this "material" aspect of language is ignored. Or rather the logical interest passes through this aspect in order to reach meaning essences (cf. *FTL*, p. 22 [20]). However, when language is considered as an adequate sign of meaning (in virtue of the universal coincidence of thought and language; cf. *FTL*, p. 24 [22]), the logical investigation which tries to abstract from this aspect cannot absolutely detach itself from it. It can use language only for its own ends, not for the sake of language itself. Meaning is not external to the words of language but is with them and in them (*FTL*, p. 22 [20]). In short, logic wants to go beyond the sign in order to reach the pure signified; but since it moves solely on the level of language or separated essences, outside any synthetic adequation to reality, it can objectify what is signified only by expressing it in the sign (cf. above, p. 74, n. 28). This is why a logic which begins in a historical experience is a science based on an experience of language and of meanings at the same time. The logic of the *Logical Investigations* is a logic of language as well as a logic of meanings. This explains the analytic and tautological character of this first logic. This logic can only explicate the peculiar ambiguity of the problem of meaning and language, their interdependence and their interlacing (*LI*, pp. 248–98 [II/1, 1–61]).

The logical investigation must therefore be sufficiently fine and sharply focused to leave one of the aspects of this indissoluble correlation in the background. Having in view the meaning as such, it "lives" in the meaning without explicitly performing the act of expression which is essentially conjoined with it. In this way logic reaches the purely eidetic world of meanings and finds its proper domain. More accurately, it reaches the eidetic world of pure *senses,* since our present attitude keeps us at a distance from the "expressive" stratum to which the meaning as something signified belongs.[12]

The historical experience of logic is therefore subtle and complex. We have so far simply stated its principal characteristics: that of unfolding in the attitude of the phenomenological reduction and that of grasping the progressive realizing of science independently of its synthetic adequation to suspended reality. What we have seen concerning language enables us to go into more detail. The attitude of reduction that is necessary to the historical experience of science amounts to considering the sciences in their "external" expression. This expression, being objective and identifiable, is what comes within the scope of historical experience and hence of intentional analysis. Historical experience is once again the point of departure for intentional analysis. It grasps in the first place the "expressions" or the language of science and logic respectively, their *Aussagegebilde.* But it brings out only their "inner aspect," their meanings or pure senses. Hence it "goes through" language in order to explicate the intentionality proper to meaning. The historical experience of traditional logic is therefore an originary experience of the language of this logic and hence of its meanings, of its genuine sense. Considered in its function as expressive sign, then, language remains in the background, implicitly operative and necessary.

But the experience in question is the experience proper to a theoretical study of science (*Wissenschaftslehre*). What we reach is therefore logical interconnections of meanings—scientific theories viewed in themselves, in their meaning, and not in their synthetic relation to factical reality. This study of science examines in particular the form and theoretical structure taken by the scientific interest. And this form is, in a privileged way, that of the judgment (*FTL,* p. 26 [23]). The transcendental criticism of logic, the phenomenology of logic which leads Hus-

12. *Ideas,* p. 346 (304). Language is the place of meanings, but these meanings are acts of meaning [*actes de signifier*] and are therefore expressions of a sense. This new distinction, which seems to be of little importance, is in fact simply the application of the correlation between noesis and noema to meaning. The act of meaning is the noesis to which the sense (noema) intentionally corresponds. An objective logic therefore deals with senses, and the logic of consequence is in fact a *Sinneslehre,* a "pure systematische Theorie der Region der Sinne" (*FTL,* p. 137 [121 f.]).

serl to introduce his transcendental logic, takes a study of judgments as pure meanings as its point of departure. And it is by this approach that the legacy of traditional logic can be integrated into phenomenology. Husserl takes up this legacy in the form of a pure formal apophantics. If we keep in mind that, by virtue of the reduction already implicitly operated by language, the meaning is a pure essence, independent of the factical real existence of what is meant (i.e., implying no concern for truth or synthetic adequation to reality), we see that the proper and specific object of formal apophantics is the judgment considered in itself, the *apophansis* or proposition in its purest formality, from the purely analytic point of view of internal consistency. This is what Husserl calls the *distinct judgment* (the judgment at the level of the evidence of distinctness). And, as Husserl indicates, we are to take "evidence of distinctness" to mean the mere compossibility of meanings among themselves, without regard for a verifying adequation to the thing, i.e., a meaningful articulation of predicative senses (*FTL,* p. 62 [55]). Here again we notice the purely formal and analytic aspect of traditional logic, which is thus found to be taken up in a pure formal logic, a pure apophantics, a pure analytics of judgment meanings, the first objective dimension of a more fundamental and more comprehensive logic.

2 / The Morphology of Meanings (*Reine Formenlehre der Bedeutungen*) or Pure A Priori Grammar

BUT THE QUESTION IMMEDIATELY ARISES as to when the judicative operation is truly genuine and explicit. When can the judgment be said to be a judgment strictly speaking? This brings us to the question of the form of the judgment.

A judgment is necessarily a certain interconnection of meanings, even if these meanings are not meanings of a determinate material objectivity. Even if the material core has been "cut away" from the meaning of a determinate objectivity, it is still true that the judgment is always an interconnection of meanings of the object in general. These purely formal meanings signify the various modes of an absolutely indeterminate something (*Etwas*) in the form of either substantivity or adjectivity (absolute or relative). A pure study of the judgment under the exclusive aspect of its form therefore amounts to a pure study of meaning forms, *eine reine Formenlehre der Bedeutungen*—that is, a pure study of the various possibilities of conjoining the fundamental cores of meaning (*Kerngebilde*) (*FTL*, pp. 49 f. [43 f.]). Even if it unfolds on the purely formal (*formal-leer*) plane, such a study obviously is by no means allowed to be arbitrary. On the contrary, it establishes a necessary order or hierarchy among the various possible forms. And it thereby ends by positing a first form, an originary form, which by virtue of its primacy will play the role of a formal principle in which every other (derived) form will partake more or less, in a closer or more remote manner. This will be an extrinsic formal principle, since the derived forms will be extrinsically denominated by it and since it represents their transcendent eidos. This means that it will be an exemplary principle, since the derived forms of judgment will be measured by it insofar as they partake in it. We therefore reach a fundamental form or "proto-form" (*Ur-form*) which is simply that of the fully explicated categorical judgment "*S* is *p*," that is, the simple and necessary categorial structure of every possible judgment (*FTL*, p. 51 [45]).

§ 24. *The simple morphological elements of the judgment*

THIS ORIGINARY JUDGMENT is a connection of the meanings *S* and *p*, which, from the purely formal point of view that we are adopting here, are only pure formalizations of ultimate syntactic matters. Husserl distinguishes within the proposition (the *syntagma* or autonomous functional unity) between the syntactic form and the syntactic matter. In a simple judgment, the syntactic form will be the *categorein,* the simple categorical form "*S* is *p*"; the syntactic matter will be the two terms ("tree" and "green," for instance). Considered in itself, this ultimate syntactic matter constitutes a pure matter, a purely material core (*Kerngebilde*) divested of all syntactic form (the form of predicative function, of subject, of object, of attribute, of demonstrative, etc.) (*FTL*, Appendix I, pp. 294 f. [259 f.]). Nonetheless, it can be analyzed further, and Husserl distinguishes within it a core form (*Kernform*) and a core matter (*Kernstoff*). The first appears when two syntactical matters of the same species are compared, e.g., the syntactic matter "paper" and the syntactic matter "man." Despite the difference of their respective meanings, an identical character in the two syntactic matters cannot fail to stand out—an identical character which immediately proves to be an essential and formal generality. It is in fact the form of substantivity that appears here in a sort of originary "visualization." Exactly the same holds for the form of adjectivity. A comparison between two syntactic matters such as "round" and "white" makes the form of adjectivity appear. The situation here is more complicated, though, since certain adjectives include degrees (comparatives and superlatives). That is, they involve a relative determination (such as "similar," "larger," etc.). The form of adjectivity must admit two species, then, one absolute and the other relative. All syntactic matters necessarily occur in one or the other of these meaning forms, which are nonsyntactic forms of meaning (*FTL*, p. 308 [271]; cf. *LI*, p. 516 [II/1, 325]).

The core matter (*Kernstoff*) appears when we compare two syntactic matters which stand in one or the other of two relations to each other. First, it appears when one is the nominalization of the other. To take the case of a proposition as an example, "this tree is green" is nominalized as "the greenness of this tree." Second, it appears when one is the result of the substantivation of the other. To take the case of a substantivized adjective, we have "red" and "redness" or "similar" and "similarity." In either case we have two syntactic matters which differ in nonsyntactic form but which have a radical community through their objective content. This fundamental identical element is precisely the nonsyntactic matter of meaning (*FTL*, pp. 309 f. [272]).

Nonsyntactic matter and nonsyntactic form together make up syntactic matter. In Husserl's words, they constitute a fully determinate substantive or adjective (absolute or relative), a *Kerngebilde*. With this configuration we penetrate the deep structure of predication—and even, by analysis of the nonsyntactic elements, the ultimate and fundamental structure of meanings.[1] Nonsyntactic matter and form are abstracta which as such are not self-sufficient. For this reason they are closely and necessarily interdependent. They make up dependent parts of the ultimate meaning, which is the syntactic matter.[2] For neither nonsyntactic form nor nonsyntactic matter by itself has meaning without the other. Nonsyntactic form defines in a certain way the mode, the function, and the place which nonsyntactic matter takes in an articulated proposition (*syntagma*). It defines the "how" of the matter's meaning.

Nonsyntactic matter by itself is therefore a matter with no

---

1. "The fully determined substantive, adjective, and relative are syntactic matters" ("Voll bestimmtes Substantiv, Adjektiv, Relativum sind syntaktische Stoffe"; *FTL*, p. 309 [272], translation altered). We might even translate *"voll bestimmtes Substantiv"* as "substantive with fulfilled determination." This is indeed a question of fulfillment, since there is a unity of form and matter—a new unity, distinct from and deeper than the unity of syntactic form and matter (*FTL*, p. 309 [271]).

2. This is the "ultimate material substrate" or "core of every syntactic configuration." Cf. *Ideas*, p. 74 (34).

meaning form. It is the last element, the matter in the ultimate sense (*FTL*, p. 310 [273]; cf. *LI*, p. 640 [II/1, 483]). It can be reached only by analysis, so it has meaning only as an element or as the end of an analysis and not in itself. Even analysis can say nothing about it, since it has no meaning. The most analysis can say is that nonsyntactic matter is a pure indeterminate. Taken as such and in itself, it is on the hither side of all knowledge and *a fortiori* of all language. Not that it does not exist; on the contrary, it ultimately grounds everything else that makes an appearance logically. But it is inaccessible to us. It can be grasped only as long as it is informed by elementary nonsyntactic meaning forms, which are the *Kernformen*. The latter alone make it possible for nonsyntactic matter to take on a meaning, since they activate the potential for meaning that is contained in the matter. Nonsyntactic matter is really the nonsyntactic matter of a meaning when it appears informed by a nonsyntactic meaning form (adjectival or substantival form).[3]

On the other hand, though, nonsyntactic form is empty, and its formal meaning will be empty as long as it does not inform a nonsyntactic matter of meaning. Nonsyntactic matter is thus the condition *sine qua non* for the nonsyntactic form to have a material core that is meant according to this or that formal mode, that is, for the nonsyntactic form to be able to play its role as nonsyntactic meaning form. It must therefore be said that the nonsyntactic form as such has a meaning as form but that it has no meaning as object. Only the unitary composite of nonsyntactic matter and meaning form has meaning. Syntactic matter is the ultimate and fundamental meaning; nonsyntactic matter and nonsyntactic form are its abstract elements.

However, when we speak of the two components S and p of the originary form of the judgment, we should not think of them simply as the substantival and adjectival forms. On the contrary, a formalization of the material core or syntactic matter (comprising its nonsyntactic matter and form) is involved here. Husserl by no means sees in S and p an abstractive consideration of nonsyntactic form independent of its corresponding nonsyntactic matter. Matter and form are inseparable here; we

3. With this notion of pure nonsyntactic matter, Husserl in his own way takes up a Kantian position. This matter plays the same role in phenomenology as the thing in itself plays in the Kantian system: ungraspable, indeterminate so long as it is not informed by a category of meaning, but nevertheless necessary.

cannot speak of one without thereby necessarily implying the other. Here as elsewhere, matter and form are correlative and mutually imply each other. We might even say here *more than* elsewhere, since, as we have seen, neither nonsyntactic matter nor form has meaning without the other. We can think of one without the other only in an abstractive manner. We cannot attribute an act of meaning to either of them, so we cannot express ourselves without implying their synthesis at the time we do so. In a proposition I can distinguish the syntactic form from its matter without destroying the sense of the matter. Matter without syntactical form retains a meaning; "tree" and "green" remain syntactic matters of meaning. But if by an ultimate abstractive effort I separate the nonsyntactic matter from its nonsyntactic form, the former loses all meaning. I cannot speak of the nonsyntactic matter without thereby attributing a nonsyntactic meaning form to it. As soon as I speak, I imply that I am speaking of something. More profoundly, as soon as I think, I am thinking of something, and this implies that my thought has a meaning.

In other words, an elementary form (*Kernform*) is filled by an indeterminate elementary matter (*Kernstoff*). This filling of *Kernform* by *Kernstoff* is just what legitimizes the formalization of the material core (*Kerngebilde*) constituted by their conjunction. Let us take a filled *S*, a determinate syntactic (matter of) meaning: "tree." We have here the conjunction of a nonsyntactic meaning form (substantivity) and a nonsyntactic matter of meaning. When I wish to express what the nonsyntactic matter of "tree" is, I cannot; it is on the hither side of language, of all meaning and intelligibility. I can say only: this matter is "tree." But in saying this, I imply a nonsyntactic meaning form. That is, I perform a meaning, I inform a nonmeaningful matter. I can speak of substantivity, on the other hand. I can even define it, since it is pure form or pure determination. Although it possesses no objective determination (meaning), substantivity possesses the character—considered formally—of a substrate of determinations, the character of subject. But what about the matter? What is "tree" without its substantive form? It is due to this nonsyntactic meaning form that we can gain access to the syntactic level of meaning, of expression, of language, and hence to the level of the explicit judgment. It is in language, in the judgment, that "tree" is substantive. In reality it may be mode, part, attribute, or determination of an infinite substrate reality.[4] Once again we come across the important phenomenological thesis that meaning is on the level of language, that the intelligibility of the world is that of its meaning, which is immediately expressed in language.

With the notion of *Kernstoff*, then, Husserl reaches the limits of philosophical analysis. The nonsyntactic matter is a "beyond," or rather a "beneath," which we must posit but which we cannot determine in itself as to its nature. By adding the *Kernform*, Husserl provides all the elements which enter into the composition of the judgment. We now know the essential conditions with which the judgment must comply if it is to come within the purview of formal logic. Judgments must be considered from a purely formal point of view; that is, their meaning must be reduced to that of a mere "something in general" (*Etwas*). But this formalization does not amount simply to a formulation of the pure nonsyntactic meaning form. To formalize the term "tree" is not to keep only its form, "substantivity." Formalization as it is seen here does assume this nonsyntactic form, but it also formalizes the nonsyntactic matter implied in "tree" as mere *Etwas*. As such, the nonsyntactic matter which is inexpressible in its material indeterminacy becomes expressible and intelligible in formalization, in the form of "object-about-which in general" (*Gegenstand-vorüber*). This is what is gained by the logical operation. Here we find again a logical law that we have already encountered: just as the attitude of the phenomenological reduction leaves no place for the object of science in its concrete materiality and recovers this object explicitly only in the absolutely pure form of the object in general, so here a nonsyntactic pure matter of meaning—which is inexpressible

4. It will be, according to Husserl, a determination of the absolute and ultimate substrate—which is the world or *Allnatur* (*EJ*, § 29). The nonsyntactic matter, by reason of its fundamental indeterminacy, is not incompatible with any nonsyntactic meaning form. Thus a single nonsyntactic matter can take many nonsyntactic forms, as shown by the example Husserl gives in *FTL*, p. 309 (272) (*Ähnlichkeit, ähnlich* and *rot, Röte*). Cf. also *LI*, p. 516 (II/1, 325). In an ultimate and universal way it can be said that the world itself in its totality, or the *Allnatur*, is an in(de)finite matter which assumes an infinity of meaning forms (nonsyntactic and syntactic). This explains from another perspective the intuitionist-monist tendency of phenomenology: a single intuitive grasp of a single, unique, and synthetic reality.

and hence unintelligible—becomes expressible and intelligible after having undergone formalization. S and p are therefore really both material cores, each having its nonsyntactic matter and form.

But let us inquire further into the matter. Here, as in the attitude of the phenomenological reduction of science, it is a question of formalizing the matter—in practice, the object without its form—and bringing it to the level of universality of the form. The nonsyntactic meaning form by itself is much more general and has a much greater extension than the nonsyntactic matter. Isn't the substantive form, for example, capable of extending to every nonsyntactic matter, either directly or indirectly (by nominalization)? By formalizing this nonsyntactic matter, a pure indeterminate "something" is obtained which is the adequate and immediate correlate of the nonsyntactic form of substantivity. Form and matter (substantivity and "something in general," to stay with the same example) now have the same extension, the same universality. Hence we have here the same problem which arose with respect to the correlation between formal apophantics and formal ontology. Here, too, it is a matter of raising one term of the correlation to the universality which the other term possesses by nature. Furthermore, the following parallel may be proposed: apophantics is to the nonsyntactic meaning form as formal ontology is to the nonsyntactic matter of meaning. The problem of the logic of the object is always the point at issue (cf. above, § 17, and below, p. 201).

It can be said more simply that analytic formalization consists in conceiving the syntactic matters (*Kerngebilde*) of judgments as mere "somethings," in such a way that only the essential form of the object in general becomes determinative in a formal study of the judgment—or, more exactly, the syntactic form, comprising nonsyntactic form and formalized nonsyntactic matter, becomes determinative (*FTL*, pp. 202 [179], 72 [63]).

Thus by virtue of formalization we gain access to the simple element or elementary meaning which formal logic demands.[5]

5. Husserlian analysis is extended quite far in this investigation of the simple element of meanings. *LI* studies the correlation of meanings with their objects in order to find whether there is an adequate and immediate correlation between meaning and object and hence a distinction of the correlations between a simple meaning and a compound object, between a compound meaning and a

In the order of effective realization, in fact, an object pure and simple (*schlechthin*), a nominalized proposition, or a substantivized adjective can be a subject. A purely formal point of view does not allow us to distinguish whence the syntactic form S comes, whether it comes from a nominalized proposition or from an adjective functioning as subject. When I have before me in formalized fashion the material core of the syntactic meaning S, I obviously cannot distinguish whether this term comes from "tree" or from the nominalization of "Pierre is good" as "Pierre who is good" (cf. *FTL,* § 82). A purely formal thematic is not concerned with the relativities involved in the various formalized cores. Moreover, it does not have to be concerned with them. It attends only to the possession of an elementary and simple meaning. Indeed, only an elementary and simple meaning can enter into the composition of the originary form of the judgment, since the originary judgment itself must be the originary connection of simple meanings. But every objectivity, however complex, can be expressed in a simple meaning if it is formalized. So, in a formal study, S and p represent an object or predicate in general, considered logically, i.e., generally. This is why this ultimate pure form is best expressed by the term "something in general" (*Etwas überhaupt*), which necessarily represents a simple element of meaning.[6]

But if formalization enables the morphology of meanings (*reine Formenlehre der Bedeutungen*) to gain access to simple meanings which are capable of entering into the originary form of the judgment, it seems useless to refer to the (real-factical)

---

simple object, and between a simple meaning and a simple object (*LI,* Fourth Investigation, §§ 1–3). This leads to a study of definition (*LI,* p. 498 [II/1, 301]). Then Husserl examines independent (autonomous, concrete) meanings or categoremata and dependent (nonautonomous, abstract) meanings or syncategoremata. He goes so far as to include among the latter the syllables of words, whose meaning value he studies (§ 5). Next follows a study of defective (*lückenhaft*) and abbreviated expressions (exclamations, orders, etc.) (§ 6).

6. In the retrogressive investigation of the simple meaning, Husserl shows the necessity of ending with a primary element. And the fact that there is an elementary simple meaning is guaranteed by the indubitable sense of the *Etwas* in general (*LI,* p. 494 [II/1, 296]). This text not only guarantees the existence of simple meanings but above all posits *one* simple meaning, that of "something in general."

point of departure of formalization. And this reference would indeed be useless in a logic which is meant to be only an objective formal logic. But formal logic is extended in a transcendental logic, a logic of motivating experience, of transcendental subjectivity. This new logic takes its point of departure in formal logic qua logic of the object or formal ontology. This means that it takes its point of departure in a logic in which the preoccupation with the (formalized) material core assumes a certain importance. Thus we will see that Husserl establishes transcendental logic by tracing the pure form of the object in general back to the particular object—that is, by going through a course that is the reverse of formalization.[7] This logic traces the object in general back to its first source, the individual object. It moves from the universal to the particular. By this singular object the preoccupation with evidence and thus the preoccupation with constitutive intentionality are introduced.[8]

Hence, only from a genuinely phenomenological point of view, according to which it must at every point be possible to proceed to origins in motivating experience, can such a preoccupation with the point of departure for the formalization of the substrate S have importance, in order to prevent us from falling into the ever seductive illusion of the sufficiency of an analytic and purely formal logic. The necessary surpassing toward a transcendental dimension therefore already appears clearly in the very heart of formal logic, in this issue of the substrate.

§ 25. *The laws of meaning of the judgment*

BUT IF THE ORIGINARY FORM of the judgment "S is p" is actually composed of simple and absolute meanings—that is, if S and p actually represent the forms of subject and predicate in general—then we can formulate the fundamental laws of

7. "Die Materialisierung dieser Form" (*LI*, p. 511 (II/1, 319).
8. The problem of evidence concerns every objectivity in general. But it gives rise to a truly original thematic only in the case of experience (perception). Every objectivity other than the datum of perception is a founded and secondary act. For example, the idea, too, is given with evidence in intentional analysis (ideation), but on the basis of the real-factical. The experience of the latter is therefore primary.

meaning of the judgment.[9] That is, we can lay down the conditions of the possibility of a judgment having meaning.

If we are to set forth any judgment at all, we must respect the specificity and the order of the terms composing the judgment as they are formulated in all their purity in the form of the judgment in general. In the concretization of the universal form, only subjects can figure in the place of S—that is, only material cores (syntactic matters) in substantive form, and not predicates. Conversely, only predicates can figure in the place of p—that is, material cores (syntactic matters) in adjectival form, and not subjects. The fundamental law of meaning of the judgment is therefore this: every judgment must respect the originary form of the judgment "S is p"; it must concretize S by a subject and p by a predicate in order to assure its own meaning (*LI*, p. 511 [II/1, 319]). If the judgment does not respect this a priori norm,[10] which governs and measures every judgment meaning in a universal and formal way (in an extrinsic-formal or exemplary way), if it transposes S and p in concretizing the originary form, then it results in a non-sense (*Un-sinn*). The concrete material cores can of course be varied at will, on condition that the necessary order imposed by the originary form is respected. As long as we remain within categories of meaning determined by the fundamental law of meaning, we can end with ridiculous judgments at worst, depending on the variations; but we cannot end with judgments deprived of the originary sense of the judgment. The sense of a valid judgment (i.e., of a meaningful judgment) must be explicitly performable (*vollziehbar*) as a unitary judgment sense (*LI*, p. 512 [II/1, 319]). A judgment that is consistent with the law of meaning necessarily has a sense and, moreover, a *single* sense. The *apriorisches Bedeutungsgesetz* is what normatively determines and guarantees the possibility and unity of this sense. We must therefore say, explicating the law of meaning given above, that there is judgment meaning when there is unity of sense. When the judgment infringes the fundamental law of meaning, on the other hand, it destroys the unity of sense and falls into *non-sense*—i.e., a collection of words, each of which by itself has a sense separately but the conjunction of which has no sense. If, for example, I form the judgment "red

9. The "*apriorisches Bedeutungsgesetz*" (*LI*, p. 513 [II/1, 321]).
10. *LI*, p. 524 (II/1, 336). Cf. also the expression "*festes Mass*," "fixed standards."

is the earth" as an illustration of the originary form "S is p,"
I infringe the fundamental law of meaning of the judgment.
I do not respect the diversity of the meaning categories in this
particular interconnection of meanings, in this particularization
of the originary form of the judgment. Instead, I invert the
formal order dictated by the law, and I set forth a non-sense.
Obviously, for this to be the case, "red" must be taken in its
proper adjectival value and not, as the grammatical formulation seems to indicate, as a substantivation of the adjective
"red." Even if "red" is taken as a substantive, though, the
presence of a subject ("the earth") in the place where a predicate
is required results in a non-sense.[11] On the other hand, if I
illustrate the originary form "S is p" in another fashion, by
constituting the judgment "the circle is square," I have in no
way infringed the pure law of meaning of the judgment. In
this case I have a judgment with real meaning but with *counter-
sense* (*Wider-sinn*).

Of course, in each case I have incompatibility (*Unver-
träglichkeit*) between the terms brought together. In the first
case, however, this incompatibility expresses a complete absence
of meaning or an absolute non-sense. There is no meaning, no
unity of sense. There is not even a judgment, since there is no
possibility of meaning in the form of unitary judgment. In the
second case, this incompatibility involves only a contradiction
of the individual meanings that are brought together, a counter-
sense, an inconsistency of terms with regard to their value as
meanings of objects. Counter-sense, although it excludes the
possibility of a synthetic verification by adequation to reality,
nevertheless comprises a unitary meaning. That is, it represents a judgment having judgment meaning, since it respects
the formal law of meaning of the judgment. There is a meaning, a meaning "exists" (in the sense of "mathematical" exist-

11. The example given here is not perfect in its French form
[or in its English form—Trans.], although it is pertinent. The German language allows more clarity on this point. In German it is
possible to resort to typographical devices to indicate that "red"
functions as an adjective and not as a substantivized predicate.
Thus, in the sentence in question, "red" would appear (ungrammati-
cally) in the form "das rote"; whereas the substantival form would
be recognized in German by its initial capital letter. In any case,
substantivation involves a morphological transformation of the
word: *rot, das Röte*. (This is the point of the footnote to the example "this careless is green," in *LI*, p. 512 [II/1, 319].) [The footnote
in question does not appear in the English translation.—Trans.]

ence, *Ideal-Objektivität*); but the correlative object (*Gegenstand*) does not exist. This is why we remain on a purely analytic level with the judgment meaning. In the case of nonsense, there is neither a meaning nor (*a fortiori*) a correlative object (*LI*, pp. 517 [II/1, 327], 493 f. [II/1, 294 f.]). A proposition devoid of unitary sense is as such beneath all concordance or contradiction. It does not look to the object, even the possible object; and it does not yield a sense, strictly speaking. It is not a whole, since it has no unitary sense. It is not even a judgment. As Husserl says, we cannot even "obtain it as possible." On the contrary, the judgment that is self-contradictory "has harmony, in the unity of a 'sense'; but contradiction and harmony . . . are mutually exclusive opposites, and it is obvious that they already presuppose a unity of this 'sense.' " [12]

Now we see what the morphology of meanings investigates: the condition of the possibility of judgments having meaning. It expresses this condition in the pure formal law of meaning of the judgment. Only this law makes it possible to set forth a judgment which has meaning, and it alone guarantees the meaning of the judgment. It alone makes it possible to avoid meaninglessness in judgments (*Un-sinn*). It expresses the extrinsic, exemplary formality of the originary form "S is p." Since this is the case, it norms all possible forms of judgments. It explicates the specificity and the order of the categories of meaning; whatever comes under a certain substantival meaning form cannot be filled by a meaning of adjectival form, and vice versa. Hence it is not a question of inquiring after the conditions of the true judgment or even the laws which govern the compossibility of meanings among themselves. In other words, the pure theory of meaning forms is not occupied with any interest in possible or actual truth or in the objective validity of the meanings themselves (*LI*, p. 493 [II/1, 294]; *FTL*, p. 50 [44]). This theory deals only with the meaning value, strictly speaking, of meanings—i.e., the meaning as such—and, more specifically, with the meaning value of the judgment, the meaning as such of the judgment.[13] This meaning of the judgment is bound in a purely analytic way to the necessary and a priori forms of the various possible connections of the meanings S and p. And, as we shall see, these necessary forms are derived constructively from the absolute exemplary originary form "S is

12. Cf. the way this doctrine is worked out in *FTL*, § 89.
13. *FTL* speaks of *reine Formenlehre der Urteile* (§ 13).

p" (*LI*, p. 518 [II/1, 329]). The proper theme of the morphology of meanings (*reine Formenlehre der Bedeutungen*) is therefore the mere possibility of judgments as judgments, regardless of their truth or falsity (*FTL*, pp. 49 f. [43 f.]). It determines the conditions of meaning of a judgment, i.e., the mere conditions of unity of sense (*LI*, p. 493 [II/1, 295]). Its laws are grounded solely in the categories of meaning (*Bedeutungskategorien*), and they form the first part of the formal apophantic laws. In this sense they are to be contrasted with the formal ontological laws, which are grounded in the objective categories (*gegenständliche Kategorien*).[14] Taking into consideration only the categories of meaning and not the objective categories, the morphology of meanings considers meanings only as *pure senses*, as senses qua senses, and not as meaning objects. In Husserl's words, it considers the *vermeinte Gegenständlichkeiten als solche, als vermeinten*, the *Vorstellungen von Vorstellungen*, and not the *vermeinte Gegenständlichkeiten schlechthin*, the *schlichte Vorstellungen* (cf. *FTL*, p. 132 [117]; *LI*, p. 517 [II/1, 327]).[15] From this they acquire their purely analytic character, which excludes the laws of possible truth (i.e., of possible synthetic adequation). Further, the morphology of meanings is not meant to avoid the possibility of counter-sense but only of non-sense. Only those expressions which have no sense are excluded from its proper thematic. These expressions are not judgments, they do not even enter into the logical domain; they simply have no logical value.[16]

The laws which govern this pure domain of the meaning of the judgment are therefore not true *logical* laws, in the pregnant sense of the word. They ignore the conditions of the truth of the judgment; in a way, they abstract from the knowledge interest of logic. The very sense of logic implies an interest

14. *LI*, p. 493 (II/1, 294). Cf. *LI*, Prolegomena, § 67; *Ideas*, § 10; *FTL*, §§ 27, 38.

15. [In the vocabulary of the respective English translations, these terms translate as "supposed objectivities as such, as supposed"; "ideas of ideas"; "supposed objectivities pure and simple"; "plain ideas."—TRANS.]

16. *FTL*, pp. 70 f. (62). There are two sorts of expressions having no sense: (1) a collection of words which does not even have the appearance of a judgment: "a man and is," "a round or" (*LI*, p. 517 [II/1, 326]; cf. *Idées*, p. 41, n. 2); (2) a collection of words which has at least the appearance of a judgment but which infringes the formal law of meaning of the judgment (such as the example given above).

in the object. And insofar as the logic of pure meanings concerns itself only with the meaning as such and not with the meaning as meaning of the object, it "brackets" the interest in knowledge of the object which determines its genuinely logical sense and manifests its intentionality.[17] However, the laws of meaning cannot completely be denied a certain logical validity, since they determine in the most universal and formal manner the conditions which bring it about that a judgment exists as a judgment having meaning. What we have here are logical laws in a very broad sense, since the very notion of logical law implies a certain intentionality to the object meant (*LI*, p. 522 [II/1, 333]). These laws can also be regarded as genuine laws of formal logic in the traditional sense, since they take no account of determinate material objectivity (*Gegenständlichkeit*) and since they are situated at a purely "abstract" level. Moreover, it is thus that Husserl brings them into the framework of logic itself; the laws of meaning of the judgment are logical in that they govern and guarantee the unity of sense of the judgment formally considered (*LI*, p. 494 [II/1, 295]).

After what we have said, we can also see how the morphology of meanings can be called *pure a priori grammar*. By determining the universal formal conditions on which there is meaningful judgment, the morphology determines the universal laws of the *ideal language* of which all national idioms amount to participating particularizations. Grammar is thus raised to the level of a philosophical study of language in general and, even further, to the level of a formal study of the conditions of thought. It yields the primary and ideal structure of the expression of human thought in general, the ideal type of human language. This ideal structure (*ideales Gerüst*) is an exemplary measure, an a priori norm, which describes the proper sphere of the "grammatical" (*das Grammatische selbst*)—that is, of

---

17. *LI*, p. 493 (II/1, 294 f.). This is also why the *reine Formenlehre der Bedeutungen* is only a first phase of Husserlian logic. Just as phenomenology, by way of the reduction, manifests pure essences and then puts them back into existence (cf. above, p. 126, n. 8), so the intentionality to the object—which is characteristic of genuine logic and is "bracketed" by the *reine Formenlehre der Bedeutungen*—regains its primary position in completed formal apophantics (in an analytic-ontological mode) and is made fully manifest in transcendental logic (in a synthetic-constitutive form). Cf. *FTL*, §§ 52, 54(a), 54(b). Formal logic is really the logic of possible truth.

the formal law of meanings.[18] This ideal language is an *idea* which all possible expressions of human thought approach asymptotically. Grammar, too, manifests an exemplary-intentional structure in which the telos is both a norm and an ideal goal (*LI*, pp. 524–26 [II/1, 336–39]). This is the dignity peculiar to grammar, and it is also what imposes the need to integrate it into a complete and concrete logic.

§ 26. *The total system of possible meaning forms*

HOWEVER, IT IS NOT ENOUGH for the morphology of meanings to determine the first originary form of the judgment. Pure a priori grammar is intended to explore all possible forms of language. Language exhibits a plurality of logical or categorial forms—affirmative propositions, negative, universal, singular, particular, hypothetical, causal, conjunctive, disjunctive, etc.—all of which are grounded in the ideal being of meanings (cf. *LI*, p. 526 [II/1, 339]). All these forms are therefore necessarily rooted in the fundamental law of meaning of the judgment, and they necessarily represent a (second) realization of the originary form "S is *p*." They must therefore derive —in a manner which remains to be made clear—from this originary form, which is the first source and exemplary realization of the fundamental law.

In fact, Husserl even attempts a sort of a priori deduction of the meaning forms (cf. *LI*, p. 520 [II/1, 331]; *FTL*, p. 76 [67]). This deduction, carried to its end, would have to realize the ideal of a priori determination of all possible meaning forms by way of a system of laws capable of standing a priori over this infinite class of forms (*Ideas*, p. 372 [327]). It must be understood that every originary form is a universal genus with respect to derived forms.[19] The notion of genus must obvi-

18. "The grammatical" is what grounds "the logical." It must not be said that *grammar* grounds *logic*, since this would be to fall back into a factual (empirical-real) point of view. Cf. *FTL*, pp. 70 f. (62).

19. In fact there is only one absolutely primary form, the affirmative form. Only the categorical judgment is the originary predicative form (*LI*, p. 640 [II/1, 482]; *EJ*, p. 292 [353]). The negative judgment is therefore not an originary form. Negation is a mode of positing and can therefore be traced to an originary posting (*EJ*, p. 293 [353]; *Ideas*, p. 301 [260]); nonbeing is a mode

ously be taken here in the phenomenological exemplarist perspective (cf. above, p. 88). A genus as such is never realized; it is the result of a real [*réale*] abstraction. The genus of which Husserl speaks is an ideal form, an ideal objectivity which is "realized" in an ideal or "mathematical" existence and which as such motivates and pre-scribes the derived forms of the subordinate judgments. The Husserlian genus is a genus in the sense in which Plato's idea is a genus, as we have seen. Subsumption of derived judgment forms under the originary form "S is p" must be understood as a hierarchical (teleological) ordering according to their participation in this first form.[20] Thus, for example, "Sp is q" participates ideally in the originary form in the sense that it reproduces the formal structure of the originary form but not its ideal purity (simplicity). The same holds for the form "Spq is r," the form "$Spqr$ is v," and so on. On the other hand, we find the originary form "S is p" again in the secondary forms such as "if S is p," "but S is p," "because S is p"—but here we find it modified. A complete morphology of meanings must therefore establish a general descriptive classification of all possible meaningful judgment forms and must connect them in an exemplary fashion with the originary form "S is p" (cf. *FTL*, pp. 49 f. [43 f.]). Completed in this way, it will be truly an apophantic morphology, a morphology of apophantic propositions or syntaxes (cf. *Ideas*, § 134).

It should be kept in mind that the form "S is p" is a "genus" or exemplary eidos in two respects: both in the sense that other judgment forms are derived from it and in the sense that other forms modify it. Hence it is a genus from two points of view, that of derivation (*Abwandlung, Ableitung*) and that of modalization. It may seem at first that these two points of view are the same. Modalization and derivation always necessarily involve the same originary form. But in derivation, the originary

---

of being (*FTL*, pp. 121 [108], 127 [113]; *CM*, p. 58 [93]). The negative judgment is a fixation of "existent nonbeing" (*EJ*, pp. 292 f. [353]), since nonbeing is an intentional object like any other (*LI*, p. 587 [II/1, 412]).

20. It is because the Husserlian genus (*Gattung*) is a fully actualized eidos, because it is fully act (from the transcendental-phenomenological point of view of the value act), i.e., an idea as entelechy, as we have seen, that Husserl can even conceive of a "deduction" of the possible meaning forms. This is so because deduction has an essentially exemplary mode. Is this not a key part of the mathematical method?

form takes on new (material) elements which are integrated in its own structure. For example, in the form "Sp is q" the form S is "augmented" by the predicate (attribute) p, which comes from the prior and hence originary judgment "S is p." Thus it is the very structure of the originary form that is changed. In modalization, on the other hand, the structure itself is not changed. Instead, an "index" accrues to it which modifies its doxic (positional) value. For example, from being categorical the originary form becomes hypothetical: "If S is p." In fact, then, we have two changes that are specifically different.[21]

It is possible to construct both the infinite series of modalizations and the infinite series of logical derivations of the originary form "S is p." All that is needed for the first is to set up the complete series of doxic modalities of the judgment and apply them to the originary form. Second, it is easily seen how the entire system of derived forms can be deduced from the originary form. We need only continue ad infinitum the operation which enabled us to pass from the originary form to its first derivation, from "S is p" to "Sp is q." Finally, if we observe that derivation and modalization are most often mixed, we can see that the a priori derivation of the possible judgment forms yields the whole series of fundamental forms (*Grundformen*) to which modalization will then be applied in addition. Modalization is therefore (as its name suggests) a second operation with respect to derivation, since derivation is what gives modalization the forms which play the role of originary forms with regard to it.

Let us turn to the originary form "S is p." This form is originary in two respects: with respect to possible derivations ("Sp is q," etc.) and with respect to possible doxic modalizations ("If S is p," etc.). Now, take the first derivation "Sp is q." This is itself an originary form in two respects: with respect to its own possible derivations ("Spq is r") and with respect to its possible modalizations ("If Sp is q").

Thus each derivation from the originary form is itself an originary form with respect to the derived forms and modalizations which arise from it. Each form is thus the end of a first derivation and the point of departure of a second derivation. And so on ad infinitum, at least for the descending phase. But we must necessarily go back to a first originary form, which

21. This distinction is based on a text in *Ideas*, pp. 372 f. (327). Cf. *FTL*, pp. 72 f. (63 f.).

is precisely "*S is p*"—the originary doxic positing.[22] Only this form is absolutely first and exemplary. All its derivatives are second; they are only factical examples, which can nevertheless —by reason of their closer proximity to the originary exemplar "*S is p*"—in turn play the role of exemplar with respect to other derivatives which are more remote from the originary form. Thus "*Sp is q*" is originary with respect to "*Spq is r*" and with respect to "If *Sp is q*." This example shows that modalization is necessarily second with respect to derivation, as we said.

We have already encountered this relativity within exemplarity—a relativity which must nevertheless be grounded in an irrelativity, in an absolute exemplarity—in the descriptive dialectic of science. Every form is originary with respect to its derivations and second with respect to a prior form of which it is itself a derivation. Every second is a first with respect to a third, and second with respect to a first. Every modality of being or of positionality is in its turn being or positionality in the primary sense (*schlechthin*) (cf. *Ideas*, §§ 104–5). A *processus ad infinitum* results from this which can be thematized as a complete unity only in the form of an idea. The essential relativity of every present moment to the prior moment which prescribes it and to the coming moment which it pre-scribes determines an ideal teleology that is delimited ad infinitum.

If this *processus ad infinitum* requires a primary form or first exemplar, and if the infinite series of possible forms of meaningful judgments requires that a primary form be posited, this form must be an idea. The originary judgment "*S is p*" is in fact an infinite idea which is never realized as such but which every particular form of judgment presupposes and partially realizes. Here too we have the exemplarist schema of the idea and its realization. Hence this ideal originary form is the starting point from which the series of all judgments having a possible meaning—which is an infinite series but is nevertheless "closed" on itself—can be constructed. The primary and determinative concept of this series is the originary judgment "*S is p*," i.e., the *apophansis* considered in its originary realization (*FTL*, p. 51 [45]; cf. p. 54 [48]). Apophantic morphology is therefore a science delimiting an infinite class of possible forms by way of a finite system of a priori laws. It realizes a type of definite multiplicity, as does the development of the realization of the idea. Hence the morphology of meanings, too,

---

22. "*Doxische Ursetzung*," *Ideas*, p. 372 (327).

is an idea to be progressively realized. And insofar as it describes a domain that is infinite but ideally "definite" (*definite Mannigfaltigkeit*), it is capable of taking on a deductive form.

This construction ad infinitum may once again seem to be trivial or arbitrary,[23] since it merely repeats one identical operation ad infinitum. But we should recognize that it is justified only with respect to the use to which Husserl intends to put it in the domain of knowledge proper. As long as he remains in purely formal logic, in fact, he shows only the possibility in principle of constructing the complete series of meaningful judgments. Consequently, he does not show, at least not explicitly, the very concrete service to which he will put it. This part of logic, which, because it is quite fundamental, is still elementary, must be understood in terms of the intuitionist ambition of phenomenology: to grasp the totality of reality in a single view. This ambition already emerges in the doctrine of the idea as idealization of the total development. Reality in its infinity is the single, unique object. It will therefore be the unique substrate of the predicative determinations expressed in the total science, since science, or knowledge strictly speaking, is formulated only in the judgment. The infinite reality will be grasped scientifically and "intuitively" only in a unique infinite judgment, whose subject will be the infinite reality and whose predicate will be the totality of its determinations. But the construction of meaning forms ends in one form, which is situated at the infinite end of the investigation: "*Spqrstu . . . is z.*" This infinite form is what enables us to formulate scientifically the exhaustive knowledge of reality in its infinite totality. Finally, if we were to perform nominalization, we could modify this infinite predication into an infinite intuition of a substrate S endowed with the infinity of its attributes: *Spqrstu . . . z.* Science thus terminates in a single categorial intuition of a nominalized infinite judgment. An ideal and actually unrealizable termination, this is the hidden aspiration of the entire human knowledge interest.

This is obviously an application of the *reine Formenlehre der Bedeutungen*. As such it cannot enter into the formal analytic thematic, since, qua application, it necessarily involves an objective reference and an objective validity. But from this ap-

23. Cf. S. Bachelard, *A Study of Husserl's "Formal and Transcendental Logic,"* trans. Lester E. Embree (Evanston, Ill.: Northwestern University Press, 1968), p. 6.

plication it is apparent that the ideal and total science can realize its idea only if an instrument is given to it, an instrument that is adequate and fully criticized. In order for science to be incarnated in a unitary and infinite predicative system, a formal study must determine a priori the meaning forms in which it is to be embodied.

Derivation and modalization are operations which modify the originary form. But to each fundamental form of modification there corresponds a fundamental form of *operation*. The morphology of meanings is what establishes this necessary correlation. It must formulate the nature and laws of these operations, the laws being correlative with the laws of meaning. In the case of modalization, the matter is simple; the operation consists simply in changing the doxic value of the corresponding form of derivation. Derivation is a more complex matter. The operation at the origin of derivation is *nominalization,* transformation of a predicate into an attribute (*FTL,* pp. 52 [46], 313 [275]; *Ideas,* p. 337 [295]). In effect this amounts to reduction of the judgment to one of its terms, the subject, augmented by its sedimented predicate. "S is p" is nominalized as Sp. The proposition becomes a positum or "position" (*Satz*). The judgment becomes an object of (categorial) intuition, but it thereby becomes a subject for a new judgment. The parallel with the laws of meaning holds true; just as each meaning form is the originary form for the new form which derives from it, so each operation of nominalization of a judgment furnishes the subject of the further judgment. The predication goes on. "Sp is q." Performing nominalization, we will thus have Spq, then "Spq is r," and so on. The operation of derivation can therefore be continued ad infinitum, and the fundamental law which governs it is precisely the *law of iteration.* This law of iteration is what definitively guarantees the possibility of constructing the infinite series of meaning forms (*FTL,* pp. 52 [46], 313 [275]). The relativity on the part of exemplary-originary forms finds its parallel here in this essential iterability of the constructive operation of new forms. However, if in a sense the operation goes on ad infinitum, there must necessarily be a primary operation, just as there is a primary form. And from what we have seen, it appears that this primary form will be "Sp is q"—as the first derivation of the originary form "S is p."

Looking at this matter more closely, we must go beyond the originary form which the morphology of meanings lays down as the absolute norm. This form itself is the product of a previous primary operation, that of determination of the subject S by the predicate p (*FTL*, p. 52 [46]). By way of the guiding concept of operation (cf. the section title of *FTL*, § 13c), the morphology itself shows how it must be surpassed by an operational thematic. It needs to be transcended in a transcendental endeavor. If the originary form of the meaningful judgment "S is p" is already the result of an operation, on what does this operation bear? It cannot bear on a judgment strictly speaking, an explicit judgment. Instead, it must bear on the *experience* of the substrate of this judgment, on the experience of the object and its determinations, which, when experienced, sediment and are expressed in the judicative subject and predicates.

In sum, we have a formal logic to which Husserl seems to deny a genuine logical value because it has no interest in truth or adequation to the thing and because it does not take into account the objective validity of meanings, hence of *Gegenständlichkeiten*. We can see how the world of experience already shows through in this elementary logic as substructure and as necessary foundation. Nevertheless, it is also apparent that the morphology of meanings, and hence formal logic, does not admit a consideration of originary experience or, consequently, of the originary individual object—the first, the fully "material" and not formalized term of the judgment. Formal logic does not admit such a consideration any more than it occupied itself just now with the application of pure meaning forms to a material domain. Knowledge of the object—of the totality of the object and therefore, finally, of the world, of being itself: this is the ultimate goal or telos of Husserl's logical endeavor. Logic in its purest and emptiest formality (and the *reine Formenlehre der Bedeutungen* as morphology of pure meanings is the most formal part of logic) therefore appears as provisional, as essentially relative to a foundation which is still more originary and which consequently has a universality that is more radical, although different in nature.

3 / The Second Level
of Formal Logic

THE QUESTION WE POSED when we took up the morphology of meanings was this: when is the judicative meaning genuine and explicit? But obviously, two elements contribute to the constitution of an explicit judgment, the form and the mode of givenness. With the *reine Formenlehre der Bedeutungen* we have seen the former. But the morphology of meanings as we have seen it from the express texts of the *Logical Investigations* and *Formal and Transcendental Logic* is not a sufficient answer to our question (*LI*, Fourth Investigation; *FTL*, §§ 13, 22). It gives us the formal law of meaning (i.e., the formal and fundamental condition for a predicative connection of meanings to be meaningful); it determines the a priori of meanings which guarantees the unity of sense of a judicative proposition. Further, it establishes a priori the essential possibility for a logic of constructing ideally all possible meaning forms, and by virtue of the law of operational iteration it guarantees the a priori universe of possible formal interconnections of meanings. These two results retain a permanent validity: every judgment is necessarily subject to the law of meaning; furthermore, the infinite series of meaning forms is a priori possible. Putting these two assertions in conjunction yields the result that every judgment is essentially possible insofar as it is derived from the originary form.

Thus we see that the morphology of meanings, by establishing the laws which are a priori valid for the entire sphere of judgments, forms the foundation of formal logic in its entirety. Indeed, all the logical disciplines which Husserl distinguishes are based upon it.[1] As we have seen, however, the morphology of meanings—despite its character as universal foundation of formal logic—is in a sense not yet a logic strictly speaking. If Husserl nevertheless grants this discipline a logical character, he is fully aware that it is not self-sufficient and that only a close connection with a higher logical discipline can legitimize its logical character. The *reine Formenlehre der Bedeutungen* is a logic only if it is explicitly taken up into the genuinely logical disciplines.

A new logical discipline is therefore necessary. This is the logic of consequence (*Konsequenzlogik*) or logic of noncontradiction (*Logik der Widerspruchslosigkeit*), which Husserl calls a higher degree of the formal logic of judgments and the science of possible forms of true judgments (*FTL*, pp. 52 f. [46]). The universality of the morphology of meanings is a universality of indeterminacy which must be "narrowed" and made determinate in a higher logic. But just as the determination of matter by form constitutes a single autonomous being, and this information is what gives matter its proper quality of being determinate, so the morphology in its universality is not yet logic. It will be a logic only when it is taken up by a higher logical discipline, with which it will then form a single science (*FTL*, p. 137 [122]). But even this is not yet enough.

§ 27. *The evidence of distinctness of the judgment*

THE MORPHOLOGY OF MEANINGS yields the fundamental law of meaning of every judgment in general. It thereby guarantees the *possibility* of every meaningful judgment. This does not yet give us, strictly speaking, the explicit judgment, it does not yet give us any originary "experience" of the explicit judgment. The a priori guarantee of the essential possibility of a meaning form needs to be actualized. A possible form, if it is truly possible, must be capable of being actually given in an originary self-givenness (*Selbstgegebenheit*). This the morphology, as

1. The *reine Formenlehre der Bedeutungen* contains the form of distinct judgments insofar as these judgments, as explicit, conform to the fundamental law of meaning of the judgment (cf. *FTL*, p. 63 [56]). Every formal logical discipline is therefore based on it, and, conversely, it is implied in every formal logical discipline (*FTL*, p. 137 [122]).

we have seen it up to now, does not yet provide us. In fact, the morphology remains on a level that is completely universal and empty. The judgment in general, or rather the condition in general of the possibility of the judgment's meaning, is what it gives us. But what is a judgment?

In the judgment, the knowing-judging subject deals only with objectivities in categorial forms. It is not possible for him to be concerned with other objectivities (*FTL*, p. 146 [130]). These objectivities are those given in originary experience, which have then entered into a judicative process of "fixing." According to Husserl's own words, the judgment "fixes" (*feststellt*) the objectivity given in experience in the same state in which it is given and at the moment at which it is originarily given.[2] A "fixative" of some sort is therefore necessary, and this is the role that categorial formation (*kategoriale Formung*) plays. The originary objectivity takes a certain categorial or syntactic form depending on the function it fulfills in the predicative judgment.[3] The judgment is therefore the categorial-syntactic fixing of the originary objectivity, and the predicative judgment in particular is constituted by a relation of categorial objectivities that are fixed in this way. This relation is a connection which insures the meaningful unity of the categorial whole (insofar as this whole conforms to the formal law of meaning). Despite the plurality of categorial objectivities entering into composition in the judgment (there are at least two of these), a unity of meaning (a unitary meaning) is constituted. The judgment is therefore a meaning, i.e., an ideal objectivity or *Ideal-Objektivität*.[4]

2. This is the consistent doctrine of *EJ;* cf. § 13, esp. Part II, pp. 197 f. (231 f.).

3. These categorial (syntactic) forms belong to a particular typical exemplar; they are concretized (materialized) modes of the object in general. Cf. *FTL*, pp. 113 f. (101).

4. Husserl expressly characterizes the judgment as *ideale Gegenständlichkeit* (*FTL*, p. 60 [53]). Cf. the phrase: "with regard to the objects taken at first only as distinct judgments" (*FTL*, p. 65 [57]). We are acquainted with the *ideale Objektivität der Urteilsgebilde* (*FTL*, p. 81 [71]). In the theory of the judgment, the judgment is the *ideal-identisches* constituted in the noetico-noematic multiplicity of the life of consciousness (*FTL*, pp. 261 f. [231 f.]). The broader concept of the judgment coincides with that of *kategoriale (doxische) Gegenständlichkeit überhaupt* (*FTL*, p. 313 [275]). In general the judgment is, like every constituted objectivity, an ideal transcendent with respect to the multiplicity constituting it (*FTL*, pp. 165 f. [148]).

But now the following question, which pertains to every object, arises: what is the originary experience that constitutes this object of a new type? Judgments in their genetic constitution do indeed refer to the originary object of experience (perception). This experience is the originary experience of the individual objectivity, and it guarantees the originary character of the perceived object. But it is obviously situated on a level other than the level with which we are concerned. For if we accept the individual object as a genuine objectivity, and if we also consider perception to be the only originary and constitutive experience, this does not mean that we reject every other type of objectivity. Even if every objectivity ultimately refers to the object of originary experience, every objectivity nevertheless has its own originary givenness; every object must be constituted in its own evidence. Consequently, if we recognize in the judgment an ideal objectivity of a new kind, we must also acknowledge an experience or constitutive evidence which is its originary manifestation.[5]

This originary evidence of the explicit judgment is what Husserl calls the evidence of distinctness (*Evidenz der Deutlichkeit*). It is in this evidence that the judgment is manifested in its own "itself" as categorial (syntactic) objectivity, whereas the morphology of meanings only guarantees a priori the possibility of its ideal existence but does not effectively give it to us. The evidence of distinctness is the evidence in which the judgment is given originarily and as it is—that is, as it is syntactically constituted in and by the operation of the judging subject. This evidence or originary experience is simply the actual syntactic construction of the judgment by the judging subject. The explicit distinct judgment is given and is mani-

---

This is why it can be given identically in different subjective modes (*FTL*, pp. 56 [49], 319–21 [280 f.]). In the specific case of the distinct judgment, it is a question of a distinct mode of givenness of a *Gegenstand für sich* (*FTL*, p. 65 [58]). Cf. in *EJ*, p. 16 (7): "*das Urteil . . . als eine Art objektives Gebilde*"; and p. 23 (16), where the judgment is said to be "not a real [*reelles*] moment of cognitive activity" but an "identical moment of the repetitions. In a word, it is not immanent in a real [*reell*] or individual sense but in an irreal, supertemporal sense." Cf. *EJ*, pp. 62 (64), 198 (233), 207 (244), 216 (256), 237 f. (282 f.).

5. "*Aber jede Art von Gegenständen hat ihre Art der Selbstgebung = Evidenz*" (*EJ*, p. 20 [12]). Cf. *FTL*, pp. 41 (36), 45 (40), 81 (71), 155 f. (139), 161 (144); *Ideas*, § 3; and, in general, the doctrine of eidetic intuition (ideation).

fested, then, in an explicit and distinct judication, which is called "evidence of distinctness" to mark the essential fact that it is the constitutive experience that is intentionally correlative with the distinct judgment. Just as the distinct judgment is the explicit judgment or the judgment strictly speaking, so the evidence of distinctness is the actual judging.[6]

Evidence in general, and the truth which emerges in it, is obtained by adequation to the thing itself. The empty anticipation of the intention is fulfilled, and the ultimate terminus of this fulfillment coincides with the full manifestation or originary presence of the thing. This is the completely universal schema of evidence as Husserl gives it. The schema is differentiated in a manner determined by the objectivities to which it is applied. In the case of the judgment, we have a specific objectivity, as we know; it is an ideal objectivity, a pure meaning. It is, further, a meaning that is articulated according to the verbal articulations of language, and this articulation must result in a unitary meaning. The evidence of distinctness is therefore not to be confused with the evidence of a real object of perception. It occurs at the level of meaning. Neither is it the evidence pertaining to the idea or eidos; it is not ideation. It is analogous to the latter evidence, however, since it, too, is an ideal evidence. But ideation is an immediate and intuitive grasp of a simple eidetic meaning. In the case of the judgment, we have a complex but unitary meaning—an *apophansis,* a judgment considered as an ideal object. The evidence of distinctness is still a genuine evidence, however. It reproduces the universal schema of evidence in general, the fulfillment of an anticipation by progressive synthetic coincidence. In order to understand its mechanism, we must consider the subjective manner in which the judgment can be given.

The subjective modes of givenness of the judgment can be extremely diverse. In fact there seems to be a possible infinity of them. I can "become aware" ["*prendre conscience*"] of a judgment first in a confused and vague manner. When I vaguely hear someone talking near me, I listen inattentively and vaguely perceive an articulation of words which remain

---

6. *FTL*, pp. 59 f. (52 f.). Notice that Husserl writes in these pages that the evidence of distinctness is the originary "appearing" of the judgment but is not yet a thematic consideration of the judgment. The distinct judgment is only constituted; it is not thematized on its own account, as we will find it to be in the apophantic critical attitude.

an empty noise for me as long as I do not give it my attention. Similarly, when I inattentively read a book, I perceive at least visually a succession of words, but these also remain a "dead letter" (as in the case of speech) as long as I make no effort to grasp their unity. In general, I confusedly perceive judgments in someone else's language (written or spoken) if I do not pay attention to what is said or written. But I can also perceive a confused judgment in myself, as, for example the sudden irruption of a memory (*Einfall, Er-innerung*) or the sudden appearance (*Auftauchen*) of a predicative belief to which I have previously given assent and which returns to me confusedly today. This confused manner of givenness involves no explicit act of judgment on my part. The process unfolds in an entirely passive, confused, and inarticulate way (*FTL*, p. 56 [49] and App. II, § 3). The language of another person, the words themselves, may be precisely articulated in themselves, but their meaning "says nothing" to me; in no way do I perform the explicit act of predicative meaning. I do not judge, strictly speaking. In the case of the language of others or the reading of a book, I grasp aurally or visually a unity of the sign. Hence there is in fact a certain perception. So too, in the case of the *Einfall* or the *Auftauchen* of a past meaning, there is an internal perception. But this is the perception of a sign as a thing pure and simple, not as a sign of a meaning. I do not accompany this perception with a parallel act of genuine thinking (*Denken*), and the verbal articulation of the sign is not accompanied by the "thought" articulation of the meaning. I do not perform the synthetic passing from sign to signified. The judgment as such therefore remains confused. It is given to me at a "prepredicative" level as a confused sensory experience. I perceive something and am aware that it is a judgment, but I do not grasp it explicitly as a judgment (*FTL*, pp. 56 [50], 59 [52]).

The *judgment* as such is nevertheless *given* to me. If it is not "tried out" as an explicit judgment, this stems from the passive and imperfect mode of reception on my part. The signs —the words of others, the words of the book, the *Auftauchen* of the judgment in my memory—are indeed anticipations of the signified. The sign refers to the signified and indicates it "in advance." Language possesses a power of indication, which is simply its own intentionality. It is therefore a priori possible to actualize this intentionality, i.e., to pass synthetically from sign to signified, from the indication to what is indicated. In this way a synthesis of identification is realized which fulfills the empty indication of language (the empty consciousness) and "makes distinct" the meaning confusedly intended in the judgment which was perceived before. This synthetic process is explicit judging.[7] The word prefigures the signified, but the word is not fully experienced as sign so long as the meaning to which it refers is not explicitly performed. In other words, an act of meaning must fulfill the word's indicating anticipation in order for the word to appear as sign of the meaning and in order for the meaning itself thus to appear explicitly. There is therefore a synthetic fulfillment here which is characteristic of a genuine evidence. The evidence here is of a specific kind, which is not that of the originary experience of the individual object but which nevertheless requires an originary activity of the ego, a synthetic fulfillment of an empty indication. Just as the evidence of perception is the synthetic fulfillment of an objective anticipation (meaning) by the thing itself, so, here, evidence is a progressive synthetic fulfillment of an empty indication. The anticipation of language as such is fulfilled by a correlative originary "signifying." At the end of this operation, the word or sign has taken on all its meaning. It is no longer an empty indication or an empty consciousness but a fulfilled verbal intention, a genuine meaning which is originarily given in the evidence of a progressive fulfillment.[8] This is the case for each word separately, of course, but it is also the case for the judgment itself or a series of judgments (for example, a conversation or an entire book). Each word is a sign by itself, and hence it refers to its meaning. But a collection of words is also a unitary, though complex, meaning.

Two things are therefore to be distinguished. First, there is the originary perception of a sign; the sign that is the judgment as spoken or written is a judgment which is not explicit, which is intentionally indicated by a verbal articulation appearing to me perceptually in an explicit manner. Second, there is the explicit and distinct judgment, i.e., the final result of the fulfillment by a subsequent act of meaning, a second understanding (*Nachverstehen*), of the verbal indication that is articulated but empty (*FTL*, p. 58 [51]). In passing from empty

7. *FTL*, p. 56 (49 f.). The sign is fulfilled by its meaning. Sign and signified form an autonomous objective unity (*FTL*, pp. 322 f. [283]).

8. *FTL*, pp. 57 (50), 177–79 (158 f.). Husserl sees this as a particular case of the general law of fulfillment of every empty consciousness; cf. *FTL*, p. 57 (50 f.).

indication to fulfilled indication—from sign to signified, from language perceived as such to the explicitly performed judgment that is "lived" in its meaning—I perform the specific synthesis which consists in affirming that what I now possess as a distinct and explicit meaning is identical with what was given to me before in a vague and confused form. In particular, I syntactically construct a categorial meaning, a predicative judgment, which had previously appeared to me as a vague, empty anticipation.[9] This constructive syntactic synthesis of progressive fulfillment of a verbal anticipation (written or spoken language) is nothing but genuine judication in the evidence of distinctness. With it we have, following the confused modes of givenness of the judgment, its distinct mode of givenness.

§ 28.   Nach-verstehen *and reflective analysis*

WE MUST NOTE, however, that the notion of an originary judgment can be taken in another sense. In the present case we do indeed have a judgment that is originary and as such primary. We have seen that this judgment is bound up with a previous judicative process and that it reappears in consciousness in various modes. Its originary character consists in the fact that by an original reflective understanding (*Nach-verstehen, Nach-urteilen, nachträgliche Auseinanderlegung*) it revivifies at the present time a judgment previously posited by myself or by others. This judgment is first grasped apperceptively in a confused and inexplicit manner. The distinct judgment is originary insofar as it is the result of a process of making distinct (*Verdeutlichung*) the meaning that was previously intended. However, instead of conceiving an originary judgment as bound up with one or a series of prior judgments which are more or less "blurred" and which appear in consciousness in improper (*uneigentlich, nicht-ursprünglich*) forms, we can also conceive a judgment which is immediately bound up with the fundamental perceptual experience. This judgment, too, is originary, but in another sense, because it is immediately founded on an originary perception and implies no previous predicative

9. *FTL*, pp. 59 f. (52), 337 (295). The originary givenness of the distinct judgment coincides with the originary syntactic construction of this categorial objectivity.

element. It is primary and "pure" in a way; it is originary productive activity through and through (*durch und durch*). Hence there is no reproductive activity, no revivification or *Nach-verstehen* involved in it. It appears in the normal course of experience and knowledge, and this is how *Experience and Judgment* presents it. This judgment possesses a sort of absoluteness; whereas, with respect to it, the originary judgment in the former sense has a relativity, insofar as it revalidates previous propositions. Nevertheless, in each case—insofar as there is evidence, i.e., evident syntactic construction of a predicative meaning—there is judgment that is originary in just this sense (*FTL*, pp. 324 f. [285]).

However, as Husserl writes, the first case is the more frequent. Very seldom is an experience or cognition originary through and through—as *Experience and Judgment* shows, for example. This is the normal case, the *norm case*, and hence the *ideal case*. In fact, the process of distinct judication is for the most part bound up with earlier propositions which have already been formulated but whose distinctness and clarity are slightly "blurred" or "faded." This is why experience is most often secondary for us, while in itself it is primary. We recover primary experience from judgments which are perceived confusedly, and *Nach-verstehen* or reflective analysis is for us a more natural procedure than the ideal way of immediate experience.

Thus we find the two dimensions of intentionality again at the level of the judgment. The originary modes of the judgment distinguished by Husserl correspond to the two over-all ways of looking at intentionality—the descriptive-phenomenological and the transcendental-phenomenological—according to whether we consider the judgment as given in the first place in the perception of the confused judgment and then "made distinct" (i.e., as "to be verified," *zu bewährendes*) in experience or, on the contrary, as founded immediately on originary perception. Thus intentional transcendental criticism has two contrary modes, retrogressive and progressive. That is, criticism is either a "secondary" process (but one which is originary in its "secondariness," since it is a secondary understanding or reconstitution of what is given in descriptive and immediate historical experience), or else it is an immediate process, an originary constitution on the basis of the primary *Leistung* of the life of consciousness. The phenomenologist thus operates either directly or reflectively (*Crisis*, p. 177 [180]). This is once again the distinction between logics that appears in *Formal and Transcendental Logic* and *Experience and Judgment*. The theme of *Nach-verstehen* is in fact much more frequent in the former work than in the latter, because the former is descriptive-phenomenological and the latter is transcendental-phenomenological. *Formal and Transcendental Logic* takes its point of departure in a science and a logic which are already constituted. Historical experience has before it ("in hand") objectivities which are already constituted, and it finds itself before a world that is "already there" (language). The primary phenomenological attitude here is therefore that of description of the existent. But intentional inquiry returns to the idea, i.e., to originary experience. This "return" is reconstitution or *Nach-verstehen*. Description discovers a motivating intentionality and emerges in the transcendental point of view. Let us take up this problematic, then, as it is given in *Formal and Transcendental Logic*.

Husserl begins with the simple experience of language. A proposition is given to me confusedly; it may be a judgment which I hear, a judgment which "returns" to me (*Einfall*), etc. I will at first merely apply myself to understanding it. But I will have understood its sense when I have reconstituted the proposition by performing its meaning. This understanding is second with respect to the perception of the judgment, and it is second also with respect to the primary understanding which accompanied the originary constitution of this proposition— whence the word *Nach-verstehen*. Dialogue and reading similarly involve a reflective understanding (*Nach-verstehen*) insofar as I myself again perform the meanings of the spoken or written discourse. A *Nach-sprechen* is also to be distinguished here, insofar as I perform more precisely the verbal articulations of discourse. *Nach-sprechen,* in virtue of the mutual imbrication of language and meaning, is accompanied by a *Nach-verstehen;* and only when this is the case is there truly dialogue or reading. This reflective understanding engenders distinctness (*Deutlichkeit*).[10] In practice, *Nach-verstehen* (*Nach-sprechen,* *Nach-urteilen*) tends to become a *Mit-urteilen* (*Mit-verstehen*). But this coincidence is an idea, since there is always a temporal

10. *FTL*, p. 71 (62); *Ideas*, p. 350 (308). The complete process of *Verdeutlichung* thus comprises the following stages: (*Hören-Lesen*)—*Nachsprechen* and *Nachverstehen*—*deutlich verstehen*, i.e., *logisches Verständnis*.

lag between *Hören* and *Verstehen*, between the perceiving of the confused judgment and the explicit performing of the meaning.

We cannot admire too much the precision and pertinence of these analyses, which are elaborated particularly in *Formal and Transcendental Logic*. As we might foresee, these analyses are not fruitless; for it must be apparent that the schema of *Nach-verstehen* is precisely that of reflective intentional analysis (descriptive-phenomenological point of view). Science and logic are given to us. As such, they remain unintelligible for us until we have reconstituted their originary sense in an experience which is "second" and relative with respect to their givenness in historical experience. I am not the sole author of the science which I criticize. I myself can merely continue it and thus insert myself in its progressive noetic movement; or else I can submit it to a reflective intentional analysis and thus investigate its motivation and its claims to transcendental validity. I cannot, therefore, constitute it originarily in the full sense of the word but can only reconstitute it in the originariness of transcendental consciousness. In this way I can reflectively understand it (*nach-verstehen*). Husserl says this explicitly of science and logic (cf. *FTL*, pp. 9–11 [8 f.]). Once science and logic are explicated (*auseinandergelegt*), I understand them reflectively (*nach-verstehe*) and possess their distinct meaning.

Notice the parallel here with the experience of language. A confused discourse must first be brought to a certain verbal articulateness, which then makes possible the passage to distinctness. But this "articulation" of discourse corresponds point by point to the intentional explication (*Auseinanderlegung*) of science and logic. (Science as it enters into historical experience is the language of knowledge strictly speaking, as we know.) Reading, too, if it is to have meaning, must "articulate" meanings. In this case it will be the reading of a distinct meaning. In general, then, all reflective intentional analysis is a reconstitution (*Nach-vollzug*) of past historical constitutions (*Leistungen*) which have resulted in an objectivity that is thenceforth given as "already there" (*EJ*, p. 49 [48]; cf. *EJ*, § 11; *FTL*, Pt. II, Ch. 4; *Crisis*, pp. 103 f. [105 f.]). The entire phenomenological enterprise is a *Nach-verstehen* of the sense of the world and of the object in general; in descriptive phenomenology, the phenomenologist simply "lives experience" [*vivre du vécu*]. Only in this reflective attitude can the expression "live an experience" make sense. However, intentional analysis is not only reflective. There is a dimension of analysis which goes from the constituted to the constituting; we must also take into consideration the correlative dimension, which shows the ideal telos of constitution. Thus *Nach-verstehen*, which rises to transcendental subjectivity, is transcended in a transcendental understanding of the teleological noema of consciousness. Here too we find the analogy with language. *Nach-verstehen* consists in explicitly performing the linguistic meaning. But the latter is in turn the meaning of an object, and *Nach-verstehen* is transcended in a constitutive experience of the object—which is thus the unique ideal telos of the intentionality of language.

We see now to what extent it is correct to say that Husserl's logic begins with a study of language. The schema of the experience of language turns out to be that of intentional analysis. This is to be expected, since we know that the relativity of sign to signified (i.e., to meaning) is a form of intentionality. Language is the sign of the sense (cf. above, § 5). There are therefore two sources of philosophical knowledge: experience strictly speaking, which is experience of the world or of the object in general; and the experience of language, which can take many forms (direct, as in the informative use of language, or critical, as in the "historical" experience of factually given sciences).

§ 29. *The distinct judgment: proper theme of apophantic analysis. Difficulty of the relationship between the evidence of distinctness and the logic of consequence* (Konsequenzlogik)

THE PRECEDING ANALYSIS is a phenomenological description of the evidence of distinctness of the judgment. Its results can be summarized as follows: the evidence of distinctness is the originary givenness of the distinct judgment, and this givenness is the actual syntactic construction of the predicative objectivity by explication and synthetic identification of a categorial meaning intended in a confused judgment. The evidence of distinctness therefore gives in an originary way one of the possible predicative meaning forms which are guaranteed a priori by the morphology of meanings. It must therefore respect the formal law of meanings. In this respect the evidence of distinctness of the judgment itself enters into the

morphology of meanings insofar as the latter determines beforehand and contains the form of distinct judgments (cf. *FTL*,
p. 63 [56]). The evidence of distinctness is the evidence proper
to a judgment that is explicitly and actually performable as a
meaningful judgment. It therefore excludes in its originariness
the "non-sense" which implies a complete absence of meaning,
both formal and material; but it does not exclude material
counter-sense or contradiction. That is, the meanings included
in the judgment can be contradictory among themselves in
such a way as to constitute a proposition which is objectively
false but which is valid qua meaningful judgment (*FTL*, p. 65
[57]).

But from this it appears that the only new element brought
to the morphology of meanings by the evidence of distinctness
is the fact that this evidence makes explicit both the contradiction and the noncontradiction of the judgment, and it does this
by actualizing the judgment that is guaranteed a priori by the
morphology. This is what exactly defines the domain of the
logic of consequence (*Konsequenzlogik*), the logical discipline
which is set above the morphology of meanings (*reine Formenlehre der Bedeutungen*). The latter studies the essential formal
aspect of the judgment, while the former has as its object
only relations of consistency and inconsistency between the
meanings composing the judgment (either simple or composite,
i.e., syllogistic) (*FTL*, p. 63 [56]). The formal law of meaning
of the judgment thus takes its explicit form and becomes the
law of the consistency or inconsistency of the judgment. But it
must be noted that in both cases we have the same requirement for the essential possibility of the judgment. Only formal
counter-sense is excluded, not material counter-sense. The ideal
existence of the explicit judgment is what the principles of the
logic of consequence govern. Hence these formal principles (of
noncontradiction and excluded middle) are the laws of the
analytic or "mathematical" existence of judgments (*FTL*, pp.
334 f. [293], 140 [125]; and cf. § 20).

On the other hand, it appears that the morphology of meanings cannot disregard the evidence of distinctness, since the
latter is the proper evidence or originary categorial experience
in which the meaning form of the judgment, which is constructed a priori by the system of the morphology, is constituted
and manifested (*Auftreten als es selbst*). Hence the morphology
implicitly appeals to the evidence of distinctness. When the
logician wants explicitly to construct a certain form of judgment

which is guaranteed by the morphology of meanings, he makes use of the evidence of distinctness. Insofar as he constructs a categorial meaning form which is guaranteed a priori by the *reine Formenlehre*, he remains within the domain of apophantic morphology; insofar as he makes use of the evidence of distinctness, he is already in the domain of the logic of consequence. The *reine Formenlehre der Bedeutungen* is consequently not self-sufficient. The meaning forms that it yields a priori are guaranteed only as to their essential possibility, while their actuality is given only in the evidence of distinctness. This is why the logic of consequence is a higher logic of the judgment which makes fully explicit the virtualities of the first and elementary discipline, apophantic morphology (*FTL*, p. 53 [46]). It is based on the latter, and their close connection constitutes a single logical discipline which is "closed on itself" (*abgeschlossene*), i.e., autonomous and self-sufficient. This discipline is apophantic analytics or pure formal analytics, whose exclusive domain is the sphere of judgments as pure apophantic senses. Pure analytics is therefore a pure theory of the region of senses (*FTL*, pp. 136 f. [121]). This is the complete morphology of meaning forms under the formal aspect of possible performance of the explicit and distinct judgment and no longer only under the aspect of the a priori possibility of every form of judgment having meaning. Between the point of view of the a priori possibility of every meaning form and that of the possible performance of the distinct judgment there is the difference which separates the universal from the particular—that is, the difference which separates the multiplicity which is defined a priori from the individual unity whose originary givenness is formulated in its possibility if not effected in its actuality. Pure analytics is therefore a higher morphology, which takes up the entire system of possible meaning forms elaborated by the *reine Formenlehre der Bedeutungen* and reformulates the originary forms of the latter discipline as well as their correlative operations. By putting to use the law of operational iteration, it investigates all the possible forms of explicit judgments "strictly speaking." By an actual systematic construction of existing forms, it nomologically determines—and governs—all judgments in the evidence of distinctness. Pure analytics thus complements the morphology of meanings by working out the new formal point of view of consistency and inconsistency. It exploits the elementary morphology and makes it truly an apophantic morphology (*FTL*, p. 336 [294]).

The morphology of meanings and the logic of consequence—in a word, formal apophantic analysis—thus have one and the same theme, the distinct judgment, from the point of view of its essential a priori possibility and from that of its effective actuality (i.e., its originary givenness). These two points of view come together in the evidence of distinctness, since the latter assures and actually constitutes the ideal existence of the judgment that is guaranteed as to its essential possibility by the a priori system of possible meaning forms (*FTL*, pp. 62 f. [55]). Thus the *reine Formenlehre* and the *Konsequenzlogik* each play the role of possible science, of potential formal logic, with respect to the fully formulated and completed formal logic which is apophantic analytics. The union of the two disciplines constitutes pure formal logic or pure formal analytics and describes the a priori sphere of distinct judgments (cf. *FTL*, p. 65 [57]). Only the morphology of meanings and the logic of consequence can make up formal analytics, since only these two disciplines do not take into consideration the synthetic point of view of truth (verification by adequation). The logic of consequence is based on the morphology of meanings, and, conversely, the latter is completed only in the former. Each is an apophantic morphology, and each constitutes a formal science of senses—the one from the point of view of the fundamental condition of the elementary meaning, the other from the more highly elaborated point of view of the compatibility and incompatibility of judgments or meanings among themselves.

As a matter of fact, these two disciplines seem to be so closely imbricated that we may no longer see any use in distinguishing them. Perhaps we should see this distinction as a survival of the first formulation of formal logic in the *Logical Investigations*, since it is in the appendices to *Formal and Transcendental Logic*—apparently after he had been criticized for having used ambiguous terms, too reminiscent of traditional logic—that Husserl most strongly affirms the unity of the morphology of meanings and the logic of consequence (cf. *FTL*, Appendices I and II). But this is not a sound explanation, since the tripartite division (*dreifältige Schichtung*) of formal logic given in *Formal and Transcendental Logic* is not that of traditional logic. It is instead the result of Husserl's own clarification of traditional logic (*FTL*, p. 71 [62]). In order to reconcile the two positions, perhaps we should say that the morphology of meanings and the logic of consequence are indeed each a logic of pure meaning forms. But the first yields only the *essential characteristic* of the judgment, and the second yields only the *relations* of consistency and inconsistency (*FTL*, p. 63 [56]). In this sense, the logic of consequence "narrows" the morphology of meanings, the more so as it is extended in a logic of possible truth (*FTL*, p. 70 [62]). Or should we say instead that apophantic analytics is specified by the evidence of distinctness (i.e., by the distinct judgment) and that the logic of consequence is only a part of apophantic analytics, which therefore involves the evidence of distinctness—but from the exclusive point of view of noncontradiction? The difficulty is as follows. The evidence of distinctness is already involved in the morphology of meanings, and in itself it is independent of any consistency or inconsistency. It simply formulates the consistency or inconsistency of judgments, excluding nothing but formal counter-sense (cf. *FTL*, pp. 66 f. [59], for example). But the logic of consequence is a logic which, when fully developed, excludes even material counter-sense. If it also involves the evidence of distinctness, this will be an evidence of distinctness restricted to the exclusive concern with contradiction of meanings among themselves (exclusion of material counter-sense).

Husserl's threefold formal logic must therefore be presented as follows:

First (fundamental) level: morphology of meanings (*reine Formenlehre der Bedeutungen*), the elementary morphology, concerned only with the formal condition of meaning of the judgment form.

Second level: "logic of distinctness" as such, or *Konsequenzlogik* in the broad sense, concerned only with demonstrating the material consistency or inconsistency of judgments, without admitting the exclusive point of view of noncontradiction.

Third level: *Konsequenzlogik* in the narrow sense, i.e., "logic of distinctness," exclusively concerned with noncontradiction (*Logik der Widerspruchslosigkeit*).

Thus there will be an apophantic analytics or apophantic morphology completed from the two points of view, that of the essential possibility of the judgment and that of the evidence of distinctness (actual originary givenness) of the judgment; and there will be a *Konsequenzlogik*, the ultimate morphology under the aspect of noncontradiction—the cornerstone for a logic of possible truth.

This is a felicitous solution, since it conforms to the ternary division of Husserlian formal logic. But unfortunately it is not entirely admissible, since the evidence of distinctness is introduced within the logic of consequence (cf. *FTL*, § 14). Moreover, the evidence of distinctness seems at first sight to imply an exclusive consideration of noncontradiction. The logic of consequence is what is qualified as *Sinneslehre* and is consequently what comes together with apophantic morphology to the extent that the two form a single autonomous science (cf. *FTL*, pp. 137 f. [121 f.], 330 f. [289 f.]). But there seem to be no insuperable difficulties in this, and a formal logic could very well follow the schema outlined above. To show this, we would apparently have to follow the letter of Husserl's exposition less closely than we are trying to do here.

Thus we arrive at a conception of the evidence of distinctness as being indifferent in itself to consistency or inconsistency. This view is confirmed by the fact that according to Husserl the process of *Verdeutlichung* may or may not be contradictory (*FTL*, p. 58 [51]; and cf. p. 215 [191]). The problematic of consistency and inconsistency is further worked out by giving priority to noncontradiction in the logic of noncontradiction. The latter is therefore the finishing touch to a completed morphology, which is coextensive with apophantic analytics and contains the morphology of meanings as well as a "logic of distinctness." In the latter, two exercises of the evidence of distinctness must be distinguished, one in which it is exercised as such (originary givenness-construction of the judgment) and another in which it is exercised under the exclusive aspect of noncontradiction.

§ 30. *Pure analytics and logic of truth. Phenomenological sense of the tripartite division of formal logic. The evidence of clarity of the judgment*

IF THE EVIDENCE OF DISTINCTNESS in itself has nothing to do with consistency or inconsistency, this is because the completed morphology is independent of any question of truth. Nevertheless, the evidence of distinctness itself may respect the criterion of noncontradiction. The logic of consequence is a logical discipline establishing the formal laws of predicative meanings which are consistent among themselves. It excludes formal contradiction, and in virtue of its very formality it allows the possibility of a material counter-sense (cf. *FTL*, p. 65 [57]). But this formal noncontradiction does not imply any concern with possible truth. The thematic of truth, even possible truth, is in itself foreign to the logic of consequence. The logic of consequence is not by itself a logic of truth. In fact, Husserl insists on this point: the logic of consequence, and apophantic analytics in general, is not to deal with the truth or falsity of the propositions it takes into consideration (cf. *FTL,* pp. 54 f. [47 f.], 62 f. [55], 65 [57], 66–68 [59 f.], 71 [63], 196–98 [174 f.], 333 [291], 337 [295]). Relations of consistency and inconsistency are exhibited most clearly in syllogistics, that part of logic which deals with entailment of propositions. Consistency here is purely formal and analytic; it means only inclusion of the conclusion in the premises. Inconsistency, on the other hand, resides solely in the fact of incompatibility of the conclusion with the premises. In fact, traditional logic saw immediately in these analytic relations of consistency and inconsistency formal conditions of possible truth or falsity (*FTL,* p. 53 [47]). For when the judgment that is considered formally by logic is "materialized" or concretized by being filled with objective meaning, the formal connections of consistency and inconsistency determine a compatibility or incompatibility of real judgments. It is then that the knowledge interest is reintroduced and that meaning takes on its value as meaning of an object.

However, this problematic of possible truth is taken up by another independent discipline. Logic is traditionally held to be the science of possible truth, and Husserl himself takes over this first definition. Despite this, traditional logic represents itself as a *pure* logic of noncontradiction. But it cannot be a pure logic of noncontradiction if it includes the concern with possible truth (*FTL,* p. 53 [47]). A distinct problem appears in this logical study, the problem of consistency and inconsistency of judgments among themselves. This problem by no means includes that of the possible truth or falsity of these consistent judgments, although the latter problem is consequent upon the former (*FTL,* p. 53 f. [47]). Only the possibility of judgments among themselves is examined, from the point of view of their performability (*Vollziehbarkeit*); only the actual ideal existence of the explicit judgment is considered, the mathematical existence of the predicative meaning, apart from its relation to the real object. More exactly, we must distinguish in this essential possibility of judgments between (1) the formal *noncontradiction* of the judgment as such and (2) the *consistency* of judgments among themselves. The consistency of judgments among themselves is clearly an extension of the noncontradiction of the judgment as such to a set of judgments making up the unity of a complex judgment. The concept of consistency is therefore subordinate to that of noncontradiction (*FTL*, p. 331 [290]). A consistent system of judgments necessarily supposes the noncontradiction of the component judgments. Pure analytics is therefore a logic of noncontradiction as well as a logic of consequence (*FTL*, p. 332 [291]). In any case, it excludes any reference to the true and the false (even possible), and it determines in a universal manner the compossibility of judgments as such (*FTL*, p. 333 [291]; and cf. pp. 62 [55], 334 [293]).

With the evidence of distinctness, then, logic considers only the *Ideal-objektivität* of the meaning and not its *Gegenständlichkeit* (i.e., its objective relation to the *Gegenstand*). Husserl claims sole authorship of this distinction between logic of consequence (in the sense of pure analytics) and logic of truth within what traditional logic regarded as a single identical discipline and not even as two aspects of the same science (*FTL*, p. 71 [63]). It is based upon the genuinely phenomenological distinction between meaning as such (linguistic meaning) and meaning as meaning of the object. This distinction occurs within the concept of meaning, just as the distinction between logic of consequence and logic of truth occurs within formal logic. The division in the object necessarily brings with it a corresponding division in the science of this object.

However, this division does not absolutely separate the elements distinguished. We are about to see for the first time a case in which Husserl reconsiders what he has said. The logic of noncontradiction is in fact a fundamental part of the logic of truth, since the relations of consistency and inconsistency or of noncontradiction and contradiction are in effect essential conditions of possible truth (as traditional logic held). Husserl does not so much turn away from traditional logic as try to mark better the divisions that it ignores. Incompatibilities with respect to meaning form can only result in material incompatibilities, and hence in falsities, when the meaning form is filled by a determinate meaning. Formal anticipation here guarantees possible truth or falsity. The requirements of possible truth thus limit the "arbitrariness" of apophantic morphology. If pure analytics is a condition of the logic of truth (*FTL*, pp. 55 [49], 65 [57])—that is, if genuinely philosophical logic is not to be allowed to be a mere symbolic game, independent of any application (*FTL*, pp. 108–10 [96 f.])—this is because not every judgment that is possible in the evidence of distinctness is necessarily possible in the logic of truth (*FTL*, p. 70 [62]). Formal logic must be capable of application to the object, and the laws of formation of syntaxes which are elaborated by pure analytics are subordinate to the laws expressing the conditions of possible truth (*FTL*, pp. 106 f. [95]). The logical intentionality is a philosophical intentionality, directed to the object, and this means that it is a knowledge interest (*FTL*, pp. 139 [123], 142 f. [127], 109 [97]). On the other hand, the conditioning of possible truth by pure apophantic analytics is clearly indirect, since apophantic analytics is oriented toward the judgment as such and only mediately toward the object of this judgment.[11]

We must return to what we have seen concerning the subjective modes of givenness of the judgment. We saw that language constitutes an indication or anticipation of the meaning as such. This anticipation is fulfilled synthetically by a progressive coincidence (*Deckung*) with the effectively performed meaning. We are then at the level of the evidence of distinctness, the level of the meaning as such. But what is a meaning if not a meaning of an object? The intentionality of language to meaning is continued in the intentionality of meaning to object meant. The meaning as such is therefore an anticipation or empty consciousness of the object. The object is only intended (*vermeint*) by the meaning, it is not yet possessed by it. There is possession of the object only when the meaning "covers" (*deckt*) the object that is originarily given, i.e., when the anticipation or empty consciousness is fulfilled by a progressive synthetic coincidence with the object itself. At the point when this occurs, the intentionality reaches its telos, the thing itself (*Zu den Sachen selbst!*). Here knowledge is consummated.

Hence, three levels must be distinguished: language—meaning—object. And we must therefore distinguish two intentional movements: from language to meaning (evidence of distinctness) and from meaning to object (evidence of clarity). This, as always, implies the same distinction within the meaning: meaning as such and meaning as meaning of the object (i.e., in Husserl's language, *die vermeinte Gegenständlichkeit als solche* and *die vermeinte Gegenständlichkeit schlechthin*). And since it is an objectivity for me only when I have constituted it

11. Here we have the problem of the relation between formal apophantics and formal ontology, which we will encounter again below. Cf. *FTL*, pp. 65 f. (58), 129 f. (115 f.), 135 (120), 144–47 (129–31).

(or constituted its meaning) in my consciousness, this distinction leads to the following: meaning—object or *Sinn* (*Vermeintheit, Meinung, Bedeutung*)—*Gegenstand*. (Cf. *Ideas*, §§ 42, 44, 46; *EJ*, § 65; *FTL*, § 47; *LI*, pp. 431 [II/1, 222], 517 [II/1, 327]).

Husserl's logic is erected on the basis of this articulation of intentionality. We have seen that this logic has the meaning as its object. To the levels distinguished just now there correspond the three levels of formal logic: the morphology of meanings, the logic of consequence, and the logic of truth. To the intentional movements that we distinguished there correspond the evidence of distinctness and the evidence of clarity, since the movement indicated above is a movement passing from the confused judgment to the distinct judgment and then to the fulfilled (clear) judgment. The distinct judgment being the theme of the logic of consequence, the confused judgment and the clear judgment remain.

The confused judgment, the judgment in the broadest sense, is the object of the morphology of meanings. By "confused judgment" we are to understand (1) every confused perception of a judgment and (2) every judgment that possesses a unity of sense, even one that is materially contradictory. These two senses of confused judgment do not have the same import. The contradictory judgment is already a distinctly understood judgment, whereas the confused perception of a judgment is a nonexplicit judgment. The latter is an improper originary mode of givenness of the judgment; the former is a proper originary mode of givenness of the judgment. A confused judgment in the first sense is not yet understood in an articulated manner; a confused judgment in the second sense is an articulated and distinct judgment. For example: "No square has four sides," "All *A*'s are *B*, therefore some *A*'s are not *B*." There is in such a case an understanding which is distinct, since it is the result of the actual performance (*Vollzug*) of the judgment in a syntactic form which conforms to the formal law of meaning. But it is nevertheless a contradictory understanding. The evidence of distinctness does not yet imply the exclusive quest for noncontradiction. The logic of noncontradiction would of course reject such a judgment.

If we say that the object of the morphology of meanings as pure grammar is the confused judgment, this must be made more precise. For in the passage from confused judgment to distinct judgment, it appears, in an originary evidence, that the distinct judgment is identical with the judgment which was previously intended in a confused manner. The form of the same (*dasselbe*) appears in an originary manner, and a "third" evidence manifests the identity of a judgment which is in itself indifferent to the modes of confusedness, distinctness, and clarity and which consciously abstracts from these various modes of givenness. But *for us* a judgment is necessarily given in a particular mode of givenness; and this judgment, or this concept of judgment with the most extended sense, is consequently an idea, the *idea of the judgment,* which all factual judgments —confused, distinct, or clear—approach asymptotically. This judgment is realizable ad infinitum, which means that it is not realizable in practice. It is best represented in fact by the confused judgment, which includes in its concept all possible judgments, those which are to be made distinct and those which are to be clarified (*FTL,* § 21). This idea is conscious as such, since it abstracts consciously from the various modes of factical givenness; it is the ideal identity, the intentional unity (*Ideal-identisches*) that plays, in the various successive formations of judgments (confused, distinct, clear)—that is, in a pure apophantic point of view—the same role as the thematic object plays in the ontological point of view. The thematic object, too, appears in the course of successive identifications as "the same differently formed" (*FTL,* p. 113 [100]). In each case we have to do with a "synthetic open infinity of possible modes of consciousness of the same." [12] But the idea is always more or less realized. The idea of the judgment is realized either in the mode of distinctness, in the mode of clarity, or in the mode of confusedness. Each of these modes "narrows" the ideality of the judgment in itself. But the confused judgment is the "broadest" of the three modes of givenness, the one that factically most nearly realizes the idea of the judgment, which by itself is indifferent to confusedness, distinctness, and clarity. This is why it can be said that the morphology of meanings has as its proper object the judgment in the broadest sense, i.e., either the idea of the judgment or else the realization of this idea which best respects its ideality. [13]

12. *FT,* p. 316 (277). Thus it turns out that we are dealing with a particular case of transcendental constitution, every constituted objectivity being the ideal unity of a multiple subjective constitution.

13. Cf. *FTL,* pp. 70 f. (62). Our exposition here is obviously an interpretation, since Husserl does not say—at least in *FTL*—that the broadest concept of the judgment coincides with the idea of the judgment. Husserl again takes up the theme of the idea of the

However, this tripartite division cannot be maintained in such a rigorous way. For the second time, Husserl seems to turn back. (1) We must not forget that meaning as such is the linguistic meaning. But language independent of its meaning is not a logical theme. This is why the ideal language that enters into pure grammar is a language which has a meaning. Furthermore, the formally distinct judgment is given only in the evidence of distinctness. We cannot absolutely separate the science of an object from the science of this object's originary givenness. This is why the morphology of meanings implies a "logic of distinctness" and is ultimately completed in a logic of consequence under the aspect of noncontradiction. (2) Meaning as meaning of an object immediately gives rise to a problematic of evidence or of truth. Meaning thus conceived brings in the verifying experience of the object. The logic of consequence, which is an essential formal condition of the logic of possible truth, brings us in the last analysis into a transcendental thematic, that of originary constitution of the objectivity in general and of the categorial objectivity in particular.

It should be emphasized again that this distinction occurs within the meaning, that it is within the meaning that the genuinely phenomenological separation of formal logic and transcendental logic has its beginnings. For it is clear that pure apophantics is and remains a purely formal logic. Husserl's insistence on leaving out of pure apophantics any question of truth, even possible truth, and hence any question of verification by possible synthetic adequation, proves this. The analytic logic of the judgment is a mere explication of knowledge and not an

---

judgment in *EJ*, but from a different viewpoint. In this work he gives it the following definition: the idea of the judgment is the completely fulfilled judgment, i.e., the judgment in which the state of affairs (*Sachverhalt*) and the proposition (*Urteilssatz*) coincide. This can occur, of course, only in the originary form of the judgment. In this case alone, "The concept of the state of affairs designates from the first the identical thematic skeleton which all judgments have in common . . ." (*EJ*, p. 244 [291]; cf. *EJ*, § 69 and *FTL*, § 89(a)). It is the limit case or zero case (*Grenzfall, Nullfall*)—that is, the ideal case. The idea of the judgment is thus the originary judgment "*S* is *p*," and again we find the theme of the *reine Formenlehre der Bedeutungen*. This primary and ideal originary form (*Nullfall*) is never realized in its perfect ideality but always appears in various immediate modes of givenness from which intentional analysis (ideation) extracts the corresponding eidos (cf. *FTL*, p. 63 [55]). Once again we find another aspect of exemplarism.

increase of knowledge. This is the Kantian distinction between the analytic judgment and the synthetic judgment. Only judgments of the latter kind constitute progress for science. In an analytic judgment, knowledge finds only what it already had— but in a more explicit manner. In Husserl's words, there is progress of knowledge only in clarity and not in distinctness. This is what underlies the tautological character of analytic logic (cf. FTL, App. III, § 3).

If the logic of noncontradiction is in a way tautological, what about the logic of truth? It may be said that the logic of truth is primarily a logic of possible truth. But even this is ambiguous, since the forms of connection of judgments govern actually fulfilled judgments, or at least those which are to be actually fulfilled; and this presupposes at least the possibility of a synthetic fulfillment of the empty judgment (anticipation or empty meaning) and hence the possibility of the originary experience of the object. The logic of possible truth is in turn only a cornerstone, so true is it that intentionality is an irrepressible movement that does not cease before reaching its telos, the *Sache selbst*. Pure formal logic itself requires that it be continued in a transcendental logic and therefore in a synthetic logic of truth. Thus, the ternary division established by Husserl, while it has a genuine formal value, takes on a transcendental sense as well. It amounts to the essential division between formal logic and transcendental logic. And this division is what specifically characterizes Husserlian logic. This is what constitutes the profound intentional sense of the division between the logic of noncontradiction and the logic of truth. A complete elucidation of the latter distinction cannot fail to lead us to the distinction in the properly phenomenological sense which we have indicated here (cf. FTL, p. 71 [63]).

To show this in a definitive way, we must take up the third level we distinguished above: that of meaning as meaning of an object, corresponding to the logic of truth. We have looked at the confused and distinct givenness of the judgment, and clear givenness remains.

Even when the linguistic indication is fulfilled by an explicitly performed meaning, we still have an empty consciousness. An empty consciousness itself can be either confused or distinct. The meaning as such is already a "full" consciousness, in a way; it is the result of the fulfillment of the indication of language. But as meaning of an object it is still an empty consciousness of the object, since the object is not yet possessed in its originary presence. The distinct judgment is thus an anticipation which needs to be fulfilled or verified. The judgment in general can therefore be given in yet another manner: in the mode of clarity. In this case it is not the judgment as judgment that is originarily given but rather that which the judgment as categorial meaning intends: the object, the unique telos of knowledge (*FTL,* p. 60 [53]). This object is obviously given in its originary presence only by and in an originary experience. Only thus can it adequately fulfill the meaning anticipation which previously intended it. So only the originary mode of givenness of the clear judgment constitutes knowledge strictly speaking, actual knowledge, which thus shows itself to be an adequation of the judgment meaning to the originary experience of the thing meant (*FTL,* p. 61 [53 f.]). A new distinction must be introduced, however. The clear judgment as we have described it is a genuine evidence, and as such it is a true cognition. But it may happen that the process of verifying experience does not actually occur, that it does not accompany the positing of the distinct judgment. This does not mean that we remain with the distinct judgment alone. A possible clarity may appear, an originary givenness of the judgment in which the latter is not in fact actually verified by confrontation with the reality of experience but in which this verification is conceived as possible in an *anticipated clarity.* Here the clarity is not actual; it is prefigured. The evidence is not genuine, in the full sense of the word, but only intended. Clarity itself has its degrees of perfection; every scientist knows that evidence can be perfect or imperfect (intended) (*FTL,* pp. 61 [54], 125 [111]).

This assertion has an obvious consequence with regard to the continuity between the logic of consequence and the logic of truth. Only the judgment that is verified in adequation to the originary experience of the thing is clear and actual knowledge. But this clarity can be diminished; clarity is an infinite idea, and it has degrees. These degrees can, according to what we have seen, reduce to unclarity. The unclear judgment is an (imperfect) mode of the clear judgment. But the distinct judgment is an unclear judgment. It is a judgment which is in no way concerned with any adequation to the originary thing, a judgment which leaves to one side the question of truth and objective evidence. It can thereby be shown that the distinct judgment is already a clear judgment or is at least a judgment which possesses the clarity of anticipation. The distinct judgment may be intuitive (*anschaulich*); it may be by itself "still imperfectly intuitive, or even completely unintuitive." If it is intuitive by itself, this is because the evidence of distinctness is already by itself an evidence of anticipated clarity. If it is imperfectly intuitive or not intuitive at all, the distinct judgment can be modified into a judgment endowed with the clarity of anticipation. That is, the distinct judication can continue in a unitary process of intuitive prefiguration. This synthetic transition potentially "realizes," it "ideates" or "idealizes," the intentional telos of the judgment in the ideality of anticipation. It is the clarification (*Klärung*) of the judgment—a primary, ideal, anticipatory *Klärung* which is followed by a second, definitive, "absolute" *Klärung*. The latter is the evidence of clarity of possession, in which the intention reaches its goal (*Endziel*) and is actually realized (*FTL*, p. 61 [54]).

The synthetic passing from distinct judgment to clear judgment can therefore terminate in different degrees of clarity (cf. *FTL*, p. 62 [54], n. 1). It is subject to the regulation of the idea of clarity. And it is realized in two ways, corresponding to the two modes of the evidence of clarity. The evidence of clarity of possession and the evidence of clarity of anticipation are two ideas, each of which pre-scribes a process of clarification (*Klärung*) (*FTL*, p. 61 [54]). But in virtue of intentionality, we must add, these two clarifications are continuous with each other. The evidence of clarity of anticipation is the potency of which the evidence of clarity of possession is the act. Here as elsewhere in intentionality we find the dialectical schema of *dynamis* and *entelechy*. This schema can be expressed at the level of the evidence of distinctness; here it is expressed at the level of the evidence of clarity. In any case, we can just as well say that the evidence of distinctness is the potency of which the evidence of clarity is the act. It may be held that there is only one clarification which has two modes, one imperfect (potency) and the other perfect (act). Or again, it may be held that either clarification actually occurs or else it does not occur. If it does not occur, the distinct judgment remains just as it is; and as a mode of clear judgment, i.e., as an unclear judgment, it is already a clear judgment. If it does occur, the clarification of the judgment goes through all the modes of perfection of clarity until it ideally reaches genuine clarity. Only the latter merits the title of actual clarity (the act is conceived as ideal by Husserl, as we know) and hence exemplary clarity; all the other modes are only anticipatory participations.

We can now connect the logic of consequence with the evidence of distinctness, the logic of possible truth with the evidence of clarity of anticipation, and the synthetic logic of truth (transcendental logic) with the evidence of clarity of possession. We see how the logic of consequence is a cornerstone for the logic of possible truth and how the logic of possible truth is a cornerstone for transcendental logic. If the telos of intentionality is the unique object as such, the telos of formal logic is the unique transcendental logic. Intentionality is to be seen here as a continuous teleology—that is, as a single dialectical movement whose moments are not irreducible levels but only stages which transcend one another. Similarly, each stage of formal logic must be seen as a provisional level in which the following level is "preconstituted" and in which the logic of truth in particular (analytic and synthetic, objective and subjective) is preconstituted. There is only one formal logic, but it has many strata. Likewise, there is only one logic, which nonetheless has two moments, one formal and the other transcendental. This teleology is precisely that of factical example toward ideal exemplar. The telos thus plays the role of limit, the role of idea or norm. For Husserl, the concept of limit implies that of ideal norm; the idea is always regulative, it is a motive of realization. The exemplar is always a transcendental motive (cf. *FTL*, p. 62 [54], n. 1).

Once again we see that meaning is the pivot of the various Husserlian thematics, in this case formal logic and transcendental logic. We need only orient our critical attention differently to be dealing with formal logic on the one hand or with transcendental logic on the other. The same notion will enable us to draw the distinction between formal apophantics and formal ontology. This change of attitude alone is what justifies the distinctions made within logic despite its essential univocal continuity. In any case, it is certain that the evidence of clarity, like the evidence of distinctness, implicitly brings up a transcendental thematic—one which is still very slightly developed in *Formal and Transcendental Logic*, a work which is reserved for formal logic. This transcendental thematic is that of truth or originary evidence. As such it will be placed under the general heading of a logic of truth, even though the latter must at first be considered as a formal logic of possible truth.

§ 31. *Analytic logic as "mathematics" of senses*

THE LOGIC OF NONCONTRADICTION is most expressly
formulated in syllogistics. This is where relations of consistency
and inconsistency are worked out most immediately. The subject matter of syllogistics is analytic inclusion or exclusion of
judgments among themselves and is therefore purely formal.
However, according to Husserl the law of consistency and inconsistency applies also to the simple judgment, the judgment
whose members are not composed of other simple judgments
which are nominalized or joined by the particles "and," "or," etc.
The simple judgment or autonomous *apophansis* is likewise
subject to the law of consistency and inconsistency (*FTL*, p. 54
[48]). It appears in this form in the evidence of distinctness
(understood in its first extended sense). Or, in terms of the logic
of consequence in the narrow sense, it appears in the distinct
originary form of noncontradiction. But what does consistency
mean in the context of the simple judgment?

Since we have to do with the simple judgment, consistency
cannot be a compatibility with other judgments. Consistency
must be solely an internal noncontradiction. However, it can
no longer be a matter of formal consistency. We have seen that
contradiction is understood by Husserl in two senses: either as
a formal contradiction or as a material contradiction, either as
an *analytischer Widersinn* or as a *sachlicher Widersinn*. Syllogistic consistency is above all an extrinsic formal consistency.
The consistency of the simple judgment will be, on the contrary,
an intrinsic material consistency. The simple judgment actually
has two ways of being noncontradictory (of avoiding counter-
sense), formally and materially. The formally noncontradictory
simple judgment is the judgment that conforms to the elementary law of meaning; it is a genuine meaning or sense (*Sinn*),
originarily given in the evidence of distinctness (in the broad
sense). It can therefore be materially contradictory as long as
it is a single meaning, as long as it is not non-sense (*Un-sinn*).
But the materially noncontradictory simple judgment is a judgment whose component terms are compatible in their own individual meaning, i.e., one whose members S and p are two
meanings which do not objectively exclude each other. For the
logic of the simple judgment, the law of noncontradiction there-

fore extends to the members of judgments (*Urteilsglieder*), which are not, strictly speaking, autonomous judgments but are nevertheless subject to the law of the judgment (*urteilsmässig*). Compatibility of judgments among themselves here becomes compatibility of the members of the judgment among themselves; they too must be posited in the evidence of distinctness (*FTL*, p. 63 [56]).

We see, then, that the notion of noncontradiction differs according to whether it is applied to composite judgments (syllogistic ensembles) or to simple judgments. Either it is primarily formal, implying as substructure a material noncontradiction of the various judgments which enter into composition; or else it immediately implies an objective "reference," while conforming to the law of meaning. In the case of a syllogistic ensemble, noncontradiction is primarily formal and secondarily material. In the case of the simple judgment, noncontradiction is immediately material, since formal contradiction is immediately a non-sense. This means that noncontradiction applies immediately to meanings, to the meaning content of meanings, and no longer to the form of connection of meanings.

But meaning is at the same time meaning of language and meaning of the object. It is either a terminus of the evidence of distinctness or an anticipation of the evidence of clarity. It is essentially intermediate. Formal logic, being situated at the level of the evidence of distinctness, is therefore concerned with the meaning as such (this will be pure formal apophantics) and not with the meaning as meaning of an object. Its theme is more precisely the judgment as pure meaning, *als blosse Vermeintheit*. But does this suppress its "objective" value? If we consider the meaning as such, we do stress especially the fact of being meaningful; but meaning is still necessarily meaning of an object. The objective reference is simply no longer immediate (as is the case in formal ontology) but is instead indirect. The intentional object is suspended, as it were, by a reduction to the pure sense. The meaning is then considered as a meaning (of an object), i.e., as a sense. As in the case of artistic expression, language comes into being; and meaning thereby keeps an objective content. The judgment, even *als blosse Vermeintheit*, is a sense. Formal logic conceived as formal apophantics is thus a pure theory of the region of senses (cf. *FTL*, p. 137 [122]). (This assumes that the "absolute" division between meaning and object has been carried out.)

The meaning is therefore "objective" without having any

explicit relation to the object (*Gegenstand*).[14] It has a sense in itself, and this sense appears in the originary evidence of distinctness. The evidence of distinctness is thus the evidence proper to the meaning as such and, more specifically, to the predicative meaning (cf. *FTL,* pp. 176 f. [157], 203 [181]). The evidence of distinctness is therefore what originarily manifests the ideal objectivity of meanings and determines formal apophantics as an "ontology" of judgments qua senses (cf. *FTL,,* p. 144 [128]). Husserl gives a striking illustration of this. He speaks of judgments which can be reactivated by and in an evidence of distinctness, judgments which are in themselves false or at least no longer verifiable in an originary experience. Their sense can nevertheless be reconstituted in distinctness, independently of any verifying experience and hence independently of the object strictly speaking (*EJ,* p. 261 [313 f.]). The evidence of distinctness is therefore really a certain originary grasp of the meaning as such, an originary evidence of the sense. This position corroborates and implies the thesis of the ideal objectivity of logical configurations.

This character of objectivity independent of the object, of *Objektivität* independent of *Gegenständlichkeit,* which the logic of the meaning as such possesses, is the basis of the unity of formal apophantics and formal mathematics (*FTL,* p. 79 [70 f.]). Each of the latter disciplines may be regarded as symbolic thought, i.e., as thought without intuition (*LI,* pp. 303 f. [II/1, 66 f.]). A symbolic thought is a thought devoid of objective evidence. Although as ideal objectivity it possesses an evidence which manifests its *Selbst,* it cannot as such have the evidence of its *Gegenstand.* Though it has an evidence of distinctness, it has no evidence of clarity (cf. *LI,* p. 366 [II/1, 141]). Because it is a thought without actual relation to its object, symbolic thought is empty (*LI,* p. 400 [II/1, 183]) or blind (*LI,* p. 366 [II/1, 141]). It is thought in an improper sense (cf. *LI,* pp. 509 [II/1, 315], 653 [II/1, 500 f.]). It does, of course, have a complete eidetic freedom, since it is not bound (*gebunden*) to the object. But this freedom is the freedom of play or freedom of gratuitousness, which conflicts with the philosophical sense of logic (cf. *FTL,* § 40).

14. This is what enables language to communicate without expressing, as Q. Lauer points out in *Phénoménologie de Husserl* (Paris: Presses Universitaires de France, 1955), p. 61.

If a formal logical discipline is worked out at the level of the symbol (i.e., at the level of mere meaning, independent of the object meant), it becomes an apophantic mathematics.[15] That is, it will be an apophantic analytics worked out on the model of mathematics, ultimately in itself and independently of any possible application (cf. *FTL*, p. 109 [97]). It is consequently a mere intellectual game. In that case we fall into the error of technization that is brought up in the *Crisis*, that is, the loss to a science of its originary sense.[16] But technization is truly dangerous only when it is unconscious, when it is involuntarily performed (*Crisis*, p. 47 [46]). The profound sense of logic is the interest in the object, a philosophical interest which may be expressed in two ways: one formal (formal application to the object, possible truth by normation) and the other transcendental (elucidation of the phenomenological origin of every objectivity). But a logic can be conceived which would quite consciously and consistently disregard the question of possible truth and would keep of the logical interest only the interest in judgments as such and mere relations of consistency and inconsistency as such. A logic of this kind can then legitimately and freely be developed as a pure formal mathematics of judgments qua senses. It is legitimate if it consciously disregards the properly logical interest in application to the objective domain, i.e., if the logician admits its extralogical character (*aüsserlogische Mathesis*). Such a *mathesis* is outside the domain of the *Wissenschaftslehre*. It does not have the seriousness of a genuine science but is a sort of game, a "mathematics of mathematicians" (*FTL*, p. 140 [124 f.]). It is not oriented toward "possible domains and a possible knowledge of them, nor toward possible systematic theories." It does not have the theoretical orientation that characterizes logic strictly speaking, and it is not a logic strictly speaking (*eigentliche logische Mathesis pura;* cf. *FTL*, p. 139 [123]). It acquires this orientation only by being subordinated again to logic as *Wissenschaftslehre*, only if its laws of consistency and inconsistency pure and simple are transformed into laws of possible material truth—in

15. This is the goal of the perfect development of traditional logic (*FTL*, p. 76 [67]).

16. Cf. *Crisis*, § 9(g). Although mathematics is a symbolic knowledge, it can nevertheless be applied and is therefore not technized on its own account. Its original sense is therefore a logical sense (*FTL*, p. 110 [97]).

short, only if the essential relativity to a possible objectivity is restored to the entire mathematical system of logic (cf. *FTL*, p. 143 [127 f.]).

Thus we see that the very sense of formal logic is the sense of "being applied to the possible object," and that formal logic is essentially a logic of truth. This does not mean rejecting the preceding pure morphological disciplines. These disciplines are necessary as conditions *sine qua non* of the logic of possible truth (cf. *FTL*, pp. 55 [49], 64 f. [57] and passim). Despite all this, however, we may question the utility of such a straightforward distinction between the logic of consequence—i.e., pure analytics of meanings as such or logical "mathematics"—and the logic of possible truth, since Husserl's aim is precisely to establish a philosophical logic, and since the logical interest is a philosophical interest in the object.[17] We should see here the concrete application of what we have already encountered. Logic is in itself a theoretical science, but it has a normative function. Similarly, the laws of consistency and inconsistency are in themselves purely analytic-mathematical, but they take on a genuine logical function when they include the concept of (possible) truth. Hence the logic of truth does not represent an extension of apophantic analytics but only the exercise of a properly logical function (*FTL*, p. 191 [169]; and cf. above, § 18).

Husserl's project of constructing a *mathesis universalis* is to be understood in this spirit of "possible application of mathematical-logical analytics." Here again Husserl takes his place in a venerable tradition—a tradition which extends from Plato to Leibniz, passing through Lully and Descartes. This is a part of Husserl's logic which we shall leave to one side, even though it acquires some importance in *Formal and Transcendental Logic*. We point it out, however, since it is the ultimate elaboration of mathematical-logical analytics. Only the unity of pure apophantics and mathematical analytics can make it possible to construct a system such as the *mathesis universalis*. We should not be surprised that Husserl gives the *mathesis* deductive form as its definitive form.[18]

17. Cf. the seeming contradiction between passages in *FTL*, pp. 53 (47), 55 (48), 65 (57), 71 (63), 134 (119), 333 (291), on the one hand; and, on the other hand, passages in *FTL*, pp. 53 (46), 55 (49), 65 (57 f.), 106 (95), 109 (97), 130 (116), 139 (123), 143 (127), 191 (169), and 306 (269), n. 1.

18. *FTL* therefore realizes the program outlined in *LI* (Prolegomena, §§ 67–70).

The collusion of logic with mathematics has therefore been to the advantage of logic. It made it possible for logic to be completed in a *mathesis universalis;* and above all it enabled logic to become aware of the ideal objectivity of its theme, by affirming the irreal *Gegenständlichkeit* of every logical configuration. This is the open way to formal ontology. Thus the kinship of these twin sisters, logic and mathematical science, is concretely shown.[19]

§ 32. *Formal logic as formal apophantics and formal ontology*

FORMAL LOGIC AS PURE ANALYTIC APOPHANTICS is a science that deals with the judgment as ideal object, as *urteilend vermeinte Gegenständlichkeit als solche*. It operates under the aspect of the evidence of distinctness. Despite the absence of any actual relation to the real object (in verifying experience, for example), it applies to objective determinations. The meaning as such is in fact an objective sense. However, these determinations are studied from a formal point of view and not in their concrete individuality. Apophantic analytics is a formal logic. If it is a science of predicative meanings, it is therefore a science of objective determinations entering into syntactic composition. In short, if it is a formal science of predicative meanings, it is for this reason a formal science of these objective determinations. The objective determinations and the objective sense which it considers in the meaning as such are therefore studied in a purely formal manner, as modes of the object in general. And here we witness the genesis of formal ontology.

To gain entrance to the difficult study of the relations between formal apophantics and formal ontology, let us recall the principle with which we set out in order to enter into formal logic in general. Logic is the science of science. In this sense it is the idea of science, the eidetic sphere that must be associated

19. *LI*, p. 179 (I, 170). This kinship between formal logic and mathematics therefore makes it possible to account for the deepening of formal logic as both pure apophantic analytics and formal ontology. Cf. S. Bachelard, *A Study of Husserl's "Formal and Transcendental Logic,"* trans. Lester E. Embree (Evanston, Ill.: Northwestern University Press, 1968), pp. 85 f.

with science as such in order for the science of science to be possible (*Ideas*, p. 175 [140 f.]). But science implies its object, by a necessity of the intentionality of consciousness. An eidetic study of science therefore necessarily requires an eidetic study of the object of science. The object is considered here in a purely formal manner, of course, since the object in its material concreteness (*hic et nunc*) is suspended by the epochē (cf. above, § 17). Formal logic will therefore necessarily have two dimensions, and Husserl is well aware of this from the beginning of his inquiry. In fact, already in the *Logical Investigations* he shows how the first task of a formal object is to fix the pure categories of meaning and the pure categories of objectivity. By the former he means all those categories which make possible the unity of a theoretical discourse, whether at the level of simple judgment or at the level of theoretical deduction. The most primitive concepts in this domain are those of concept, proposition, truth, and so on. But even simple judgments, and *a fortiori* the syllogistic ensemble, are composed of a certain interconnection of elementary concepts, such as predicate, plural, conjunctive connection, disjunctive connection, hypothetical connection, and so on. In this way the domain of formal apophantics strictly speaking is pre-scribed, i.e., the domain of the apophantic a priori. Corresponding to this domain, we have so far seen in detail the morphology of meanings and the logic of consequence, hence pure apophantic analytics.

In the second group of categories that are constitutive of formal logic, we find those which designate the various modes that the object in general can take: *Gegenstand*, state of affairs, unity, plurality, number, relation, and so on. These are the formal objective categories, which are applied in formal logic independently of any determinate matter of knowledge. Moreover, it is by reason of this independence that their presence in an eidetic science is justified. It is the ontological dimension strictly speaking that opens to our logical inquiry here (cf. *LI*, Prolegomena, § 67; *FTL*, § 27). But this is a problem that raises difficulties; we have dealt with it in Part II. The ontological dimension of formal logic is an innovation which Husserl claims for himself, and it manifests the surpassing of traditional logic in a logic of the object. Even at the purely formal level at which we are now situated it manifests the broadening of logic into a philosophy. It takes on all the greater importance in phenomenology because it opens up the transcendental thematic of the constitution of the object. It therefore goes beyond traditional logic by initiating a formal logic of the object and by pointing the way to the transcendental thematic. In a word, it realizes the properly logical interest at the analytic level and leads up to its transcendental philosophical outcome.

This is one aspect in which mathematics has been of more than a little help for the broadening of traditional logic. In fact, as soon as the ideal objectivity of logical configurations is recognized, it is also recognized that they can be dealt with as mathematical entities (cf. *FTL*, pp. 76 [67], 78 [69], 81–83 [71 f.], 167 [149]). Obviously this is in the first place a matter of predicative categorial objectivities alone, since the traditional logic descending from Aristotle took only the predicative judgment into consideration. But the concept of the judgment is broadened to include every nonapophantic syntactic objective configuration, and in this way all the mathematical objectivities of arithmetic, geometry, etc., enter into formal logic. Purely logical analysis is thus broadened into a more universal pure analysis, which extends to the mathematics of quantities, combinations, permutations, cardinal and ordinal numbers. Activities such as collecting, counting, combining—although in themselves nonpredicative—are also to be regarded as logical activities, and their correlates are to be regarded as logical configurations. As a matter of fact, we no longer have to do with judgments in the sense of traditional logic but with judgments in the broader sense of a "pure" mathematical analysis (*FTL*, pp. 76 f. [67], 106–8 [95 f.]).

The extension toward a mathematical logic continues, then, in the direction of a formal ontology. Mathematics considers in a general way a variety of ideal objectivities (quantity, number, etc.). Obviously, it will sooner or later come to pose the problem of the unity in principle of its objective domain. In doing this, it arrives at the conception of a pure formal domain which is delimited by the various derivations from an object in general and which is defined a priori by this concept of the *object in general*. All material concreteness is of course excluded; the object in general is a purely formal concept. Nonetheless, by virtue of this originary (primitive) concept, the mathematical objective domain finds a strict unity of meaning, since every "material" objectivity that this science may consider is found to be a pure derivation from the highest formal concept. And thus the various mathematical sciences (theories of sets and of numbers: *Mengenlehre, Anzahlenlehre*) have their title as formal sciences assured by the fact that their object is a derivation from *something in general*. This is how the idea is born of an "a priori ontology" of the formal mathematical domain, an a priori universal ontological science which will completely realize one of the dimensions (the objective) of the idea of science— that is, one dimension of logic—and which will be defined in a universal manner by the concept of the object in general. The whole series of formal derivations can be constructed a priori on the basis of this concept. This universal ontological science is actually a formal mathematics in the most comprehensive sense; it is a pure formal ontology dealing with the object in general and its pure derivations. Thus, along with the purely mathematical concepts, we will find formal concepts that are still more universal: relation, series, part, whole, object, etc. By way of mathematical science we have therefore obtained a guiding idea for the logic of the object. We have seen the possibility of such a logic by showing the possibility of a universal form of the object. We now have the idea which will enable us to realize this formal ontology. All that is needed is to broaden formal mathematics to an essential (*wesensmässig*) universality. Formal mathematics, insofar as the unity of its own objective domain is explicated in terms of the identity of the highest category "something in general," is already formal ontology (*FTL*, pp. 77 f. [68]). It remains only to explicate this universality.

However, we must observe that, even though formal ontology is the extension of mathematical analytics, it does not retain the symbolic and "gratuitous" character of a "pure" mathematics. With formal ontology the concern with the object is again introduced, albeit in a purely formal way. By bringing to light the possibility of the formal logic of the object, formal ontology gives the logic of possible truth its full sense[20] and makes it

20. *FTL*, p. 191 (169). We find here a confirmation of our interpretation of Husserlian formal logic, which is divided into a *Konsequenzlogik* in the broad sense (including the *reine Formenlehre der Bedeutungen* and the "logic of distinctness") and a *Konsequenzlogik* in the narrow sense, the logic of noncontradiction. The logic of actual truth being necessarily transcendental, the formal logic of possible truth can be worked out only on the basis of a formal ontology. Husserlian formal logic is therefore twofold, apophantics and ontology, as our study of the idealizing presuppositions will also confirm. The tripartite division of formal logic thus reduces to the two-dimensionality of apophantics and ontology. The difficulty is not even pointed out by *FTL*, and S. Bachelard is also silent on this point in *A Study of Husserl's "Formal and Transcendental Logic."* Cf. below, pp. 208–9.

possible to reintegrate pure apophantic analytics (mathematics of senses) into the logical *Wissenschaftslehre*. The knowledge interest, or interest in application to the possible object, therefore once again specifies formal logic. The final sense (*Endsinn*) of formal logic is thus found to be not formal apophantic logic but formal ontological logic (*FTL*, pp. 144 f. [129]). Thus Husserl shows the difference between pure apophantics and formal ontology on the basis of this objective concern (or, more specifically, its two modes, direct and indirect). At first sight, in fact, the new formal ontology seems radically different from apophantics (*FTL*, p. 78 [68 f.]). However, it is not. Formal apophantics and formal ontology are inseparably bound together.

Let us begin with the fact on which all of formal logic is based. Formal logic in general has as its proper theme the predicative judgment. But what happens in the judgment? The judgment is the second operation of the knowing consciousness. It therefore presupposes a first operation: experience. In experience an objectivity is given to us originarily, but this objectivity is not yet strictly speaking known. There is knowledge strictly speaking only in the judgment, when the experienced objectivity "enters into" a judicative process and lets itself be categorially (syntactically) formed. The judgment is therefore a knowledge of categorially formed objectivities. Hence it has both an apophantic dimension and an ontological dimension, but the two dimensions are closely interrelated. If the judgment is a certain syntactic form, this form is the form of a categorial objectivity. Form and matter here constitute an indissoluble whole and mutually determine each other. Thus every categorial objectivity enters into the judgment considered as categorial syntax. In terms of formal logic, this means that every form of *Gegenstand*, every derivation from the object in general, necessarily enters into formal apophantics (*FTL*, p. 79 [69]). It must further be said that the categorial objectivity as such is categorial precisely because it has been syntactically formed by the judicative process. The judgment itself is what constitutes the categorial objectivity as such, and this is why the latter must come within the domain of formal apophantics. In fact, for the knowing subject there are only *categorial* objectivities in the judgment; there is no sense in wanting to find any other kind of objectivity in it (*FTL*, p. 146 [130]). The syntactic form itself therefore determines the categorial objectivity. If the latter is a mode of the object in general, then formal apophantics syntactically determines the derivations from the object in general, and the entire domain of formal ontology (the object in general and its syntactic derivations) comes under formal apophantics. Husserl has no intention of denying this fact (*FTL*, pp. 110 [98], 107 [95]). He himself shows that the syntactic (categorial) formation of the object is what constitutes the categorial objectivity, whether this objectivity is explicated at the pure formal level (*überhaupt*) or is simply considered in everyday practice (*FTL*, pp. 113 f. [101]). In fact, every object, insofar as it can be logically or predicatively explicated, necessarily takes a certain categorial form. From this syntactic formation there results a certain categorial objectivity which—formally-generally expressed—has its place in a syntactic category (thing, state of affairs, etc.) (*Ideas*, p. 69 [29]).

However, there is another fact which Husserl has no intention of denying. Even though categorial objects result from an apophantic process, they are, nonetheless, objectivities. The categorial objectivity qua objectivity refers back to a primary experience which constitutes it originarily; and, as categorial, it refers back to a syntactic formation (*Formung*) which comes within the domain of formal logic. As an objectivity, of course, it ultimately refers back to a transcendental thematic. But it is also subject to the universal formal laws that determine the formal (*wesenseigentliche*) aspect of every object. This objective point of view is for the time being first for us. Husserl expresses it in a synthetic manner when he says that the categorially formed objectivity is an ontological concept and not an apophantic concept.[21] It is apparent from this that it belongs to a science of the object, but a formal science: formal ontology, an essential and integral part of formal logic. The judgment considers only categorial objectivities. It is itself a categorial objectivity, since it is a unitary predicative meaning. Here we may use the same minor premise that we used above: there is no sense in wanting to find anything but categorial objectivities in the judgment. So the judgment itself, which turns out to be a categorial objectivity, comes under formal ontology (*FTL*, pp. 120 f. [107]). We seem to be in an inextricable predicament. On the one hand, formal ontology reduces to formal apophantics, since the syntactic form is what determines the categorial

21. But the categorial objectivity is ambiguous; it is both an *objectivity* and *categorial*. This is why Husserl immediately adds that this ontological concept has an apophantic origin (*FTL*, p. 145 [129]).

objectivity. On the other hand, formal apophantics reduces to formal ontology, since in the judgment there are only categorial objectivities, and the judgment itself is a categorial objectivity, i.e., it represents a genuine formal-ontological concept.

We are witnessing here a mutual reflection of the difficulty (a *Zig-zag*, in the words of the *Crisis*). This means simply that we are once again about to encounter the exemplary reciprocity of the two dimensions of intentionality.[22] Formal apophantics and formal ontology amount to two equivalent disciplines within one and the same science, formal logic. This equivalence denotes a concrete correlation or convertibility and therefore a unity (if not an identity).[23] Formal apophantics and formal ontology must *be* one and the same science, then, but regarded from two different points. With this science we do not leave the strictly formal domain of logic. However, since intentionality is apparently to be involved, our inquiry is going to take on a more distinctly phenomenological air. This is why Husserl calls the elucidation of the relations between formal apophantics and formal ontology a phenomenological clarification of the two-sidedness of formal logic as formal apophantics and formal ontology (*FTL*, p. 105 [93]). It is a question of understanding how the two formal dimensions are correlative, how they are both one and distinct within the same intentional movement toward the thing itself, and how they mutually refer to each other.

Let us begin, then, by explicating formal ontology on the basis of apophantics, i.e., on the basis of the formal objective dimension of the judgment. Every object *is for us,* insofar as it *is* and is *as* it is, only in an appropriate mode of consciousness. Thus judging is a mode of consciousness which affirms the being of a certain object or its relation with a certain other object (*FTL*, p. 111 [98 f.]). Judging in general has an objective

22. We also seem to find here an echo of Husserl's debate with psychologism. This philosophical error consists in reducing the object to its subjective constitution; whereas it is of course necessary to maintain the subjective constitution but also to assert, correlatively, the transcendent ideality of the constituted object. It cannot be denied that the categorial objectivity is constituted in some way by syntactic (apophantic) *Formung,* but the ontological specificity of this objectivity must also be safeguarded.

23. Cf. *FTL*, pp. 110 f. (98), 147 (131), 149 (133), 191 (169); *Ideas*, pp. 68 (28), 409 (362). We must not forget that what is bound together essentially is concretely one in the unique and absolute concretum, transcendental subjectivity (*CM*, p. 84 [117]).

orientation; and since the characteristic of formal ontology is to be a science of the object in general, the judgment qua judgment of a certain thing or state of affairs falls within formal ontology. The logician is concerned with the object of the judgment, then, and his orientation is *gegenständlich*. The object of formal ontology is therefore the *Gegenstand worüber*, the *schlichte Gegenstand* of the judgment (*FTL*, pp. 78 [69], 112 [99], § 48), or, more exactly, the intended objectivity as objectivity (*vermeinte Gegenständlichkeit schlechthin*); and the performing of the judgment is judging strictly speaking (*Urteilen schlechthin*) (cf. *FTL*, p. 132 [117]). Judging is the judging of something by consciousness. With judging and the object of judging we do not go outside consciousness, in virtue of the intentional correlation of the object and consciousness. The object is therefore immanent in consciousness, although irreally transcending the multiple process of its constitution (*FTL*, p. 111 [99]). The object of the judging consciousness is therefore a judicatively intended categorial objectivity,[24] which is the objectivity pure and simple (*vermeinte Gegenständlichkeit schlechthin*) and which is essentially distinct from the judicative intention of the categorial objectivity (*vermeinte Gegenständlichkeit als solche*). On the one side we have the *Urteil*, on the other the *Urteilsmeinung* (cf. *FTL*, p. 132 [117]). This distinction proceeds from the transcendental fact that there is being only in and for my consciousness. If we keep in mind the phenomenological principle, we can conveniently simplify the distinction used here and replace it with the distinction between object and sense.[25]

Now, the theoretical attitude oriented toward the object (*schlichte Gegenständlichkeit*) pertains to formal ontology, and the attitude oriented toward the sense (*Sinn*) pertains to formal apophantics. We have to do only with intentions of consciousness. These may be direct and give the object *schlechthin* immediately (the ontological attitude), or else they may be indirect and give the object only mediately (the apophantic attitude). In a simple judging, the subject's attention is entirely oriented toward the object of his judgment. This will, of course, be a categorial object; but it will be one which is, nevertheless, the final goal of the judging intention. In this sense, logic, inso-

24. Cf. *FTL*, p. 134 (119): "die geurteilte, die urteilend vermeinte kategoriale Gegenständlichkeit."
25. We have often seen this distinction; cf. above, p. 173.

far as it explicates the scientific knowledge interest, ends with judging *schlechthin*, i.e., with actual knowledge of (categorially formed) objectivity. Formal ontology is thus the final sense of logical analytics (*FTL*, pp. 144 f. [129]). This attitude has an immediate and unreflective character, which Husserl calls naïve.[26] It is the attitude originating in the knowledge interest, which tends directly toward the thing itself. This is why the reflective attitude, which is oriented toward the judgment as such,[27] can be only intermediary. For if the judging subject immediately intends the object, it is also obvious that he can do this only because he in a way "goes through" the judgment as such, because he uses the judgment as a "passage" or a means for reaching the object. In the attitude of formal ontology, the judgment as such—as it comes within the domain of formal apophantics—is implicitly performed, but the attention (*der thematische Blick*) of the one who is judging is not directed on it. Hence it remains "in the background." We are therefore in a logic strictly speaking (the application of the logic of truth) but one that explicitly puts in play the direct attitude of the judgment (*gerade urteilende Einstellung*). The knowledge interest is immediately realized without passing through an intermediary thematization of the judgment as such. The judgment sense (*Urteilssinn*) is thus a means which is implicitly performed but necessary to the logical knowledge interest (*FTL*, pp. 134 f. [119 f.]; cf. pp. 129 [115], 145 [129], 147 [131]). Logic immediately takes on its philosophical character (as opposed to the gratuitous character of the "playing with thoughts," the *Gedankenspiel*), since it reaches the thing itself in an immediate evidence.[28] The formal ontological attitude brings to light the first concept of truth, the concept of the *truth of being* (*Seinswahrheit*), of which real truth is a particular case. By "first" concept we are to understand not only first in the genetic sense but first in itself. The truth of being is not only the first concept of truth that the logical inquiry encounters; it is the exemplary truth by which all other truth is measured (in particular, "apophantic" critical truth) (*FTL*, pp. 127 f. [113 f.]).

26. Without, however, giving this word the pejorative nuance usually attached to it. Cf. *FTL*, p. 121 (108), "die Einstellung des naiv-geradehin Urteilenden"; and p. 133 (118).

27. "Urteilseinstellung in der Sinnesreflexion," *FTL*, p. 133 (118).

28. Even if logic is not yet directed toward possible application, it is already philosophical; cf. *FTL*, p. 109 (97).

And correlatively with this first concept of truth we discover the first concept of evidence (which is also first in itself), the concept of the originary possession of true and real being (*Ursprüngliche Selbsthabe von wahrem oder wirklichem Sein; FTL*, p. 128 [113]). In the judgment that is immediately directed toward things, then, we originarily have a truly existing state of affairs in the mode of self-givenness.[29] This evidence is precisely the evidence of clarity (cf. *FTL*, p. 133 [118]); it is the immediate givenness of the categorial objectivity in its predicative syntactic form.

This is what characterizes the formal ontological attitude of the judging subject. What occurs in concrete practice (and what we have just described phenomenologically with Husserl) has only to be "ideated" and we will have justified pure formal ontology. The ideation will use as its exemplary support a certain clear and true immediate judgment, i.e., a certain originary givenness of a categorial objectivity (cf. *FTL*, pp. 41 [36], 62 f. [55], 247 [218], and esp. 192 [170]).

Obviously, the apophantic attitude appears sinuous and complex by comparison with the immediacy of the ontological attitude. We have just seen that the scientific knowledge interest uses the judgment as a means. The ontological attitude does not thematize the judgment as such; it "goes through" the judgment and thus implicitly assumes it to be actual. It is nevertheless possible to thematize this judgment as such. This takes place in a reflective judgment, in a judgment at a second and critical level (*FTL*, pp. 112 [99 f.], 132 [117]). Now it is no longer the objectivity pure and simple (*schlechthin*) that is thematized but the judgment as such, the *blosses Urteil*, the judgment pure and simple (cf. *FTL*, p. 130 [116]). Note that the object thematized in the ontological attitude is necessarily intended (*vermeinter*), but in our attitude it is precisely this *intended as intended* that is the theme, the *vermeinte Gegenständlichkeit als solche*.[30] The knowledge interest in the apophantic attitude no longer has the directness that characterizes the ontological attitude. It is inflected, or rather reflected, and takes on a critical mode (*FTL*, §§ 44–49, 542, 546). The judgment "as such" becomes the principal concept. "Judgment" must

---

29. "Wahrhaft seiender Sachverhalt im Modus der Selbstgegebenheit" (*FTL*, p. 146 [130]).

30. *FTL*, p. 126 (112). Among these *Vermeintheiten als solche*, Husserl prefers a narrower concept, that of the predicative judgment.

be taken here in both possible senses of the word: in the broad sense, as the "nonpredicative" judgment or the noematic result of syntactic operation other than judication, and in the narrow sense, as the predicative judgment strictly speaking. Now we are no longer dealing with the categorial objectivity itself but with the judgment sense. The apophantic attitude is a critical attitude which considers the entire sphere of judgments qua apophantic senses.[31] Formalized as apophantic logic, this attitude will consider the formal region of senses and will be in its own way a formal ontology, an ontology of pure senses.[32] This is possible in virtue of the objectifying thematization of judgment senses, i.e., in virtue of the ideal objectivity of predicative configurations. A conversion of interest occurs in the apophantic attitude, a conversion that results in positing the senses themselves in a certain *positional evidence* (*FTL*, pp. 135 f. [120 f.]). For the critical attitude we are now studying consists in a "modification of direct themes," and, as we know, every modification can in turn be considered as originary element and can thus appear in a doxic evidence.[33]

The ontology of apophantic senses is a pure mathematics of noncontradiction, however, and in this sense it is an extralogical *mathesis* and is separate from the apophantic attitude itself. The latter is in fact a logical (*wissenschaftstheoretische*) attitude, and it implies concern with the object. It does entail a modification of direct themes, a reflection on the ontological attitude; but it does not thereby abandon the telos of the ontological attitude. Even as a modification of direct themes, it in a way shares their immediacy. In a word, the apophantic attitude, too, manifests the intentionality of knowledge which ends in the object. Rather than directly reaching the object by a nonthematized judgment, it reaches the object indirectly by the intermediary of a criticism of the judgment, i.e., after having thematized it and compared (measured) it with the originary givenness of

31. "Die Urteilssphäre als Reich der apophantischen Sinne" (*FTL*, p. 137 [121]). Apophantic analytics is a "universale und reine Wissenschaft von den apophantischen Sinnen" focused on the "Apriori der Sinnessphäre" (*FTL*, p. 137 [122]).

32. Cf. *FTL*, pp. 184 (163), 132 (118), 36–42 (31–37), 144 (128). This is an ontology that is not "objective" but "mathematical," dealing with senses as such taken as symbols. Cf. above, § 31.

33. *Ideas*, § 105. This section reconfirms an important thesis in phenomenology, the thesis that nonbeing is a mode of being (first attitude), i.e., that nonbeing is (second attitude).

the object. In other words, the judgment is first regarded as simply a judgment (*blosses Urteil*), as a mere truth claim or possible truth and not as an actual truth. The thematization of the judgment on its own account must be followed by its adequation to reality; or rather, the very goal of the thematization of the judgment on its own account is this adequation.

The apophantic attitude is therefore essentially critical. It is directed immediately on the judgment and mediately on the objectivity itself, i.e., on the judgment as essential condition of its own possible adequation to reality (*FTL*, pp. 130 f. [116]). This is the attitude of the scientist, and Husserl correctly calls it a scientific attitude (*eine wissenschaftliche Einstellung*). Only the scientific judgment needs to be adequate to the reality that is signified by the judicative meaning (*Urteilsmeinung*); and this adequation must be actual, it must conform to the originary givenness of the objectivity. The scientific attitude is thus a theoretical criticism of the meaning taken as object. It differs from the attitude of "everyday judging" (*alltäglicher Urteilende*) and consists, in short, in seeking the evidence of clarity of judgments as such by an adequation to the originary reality (*FTL*, pp. 124 f. [110 f.]). In this sense, apophantic logic and the judgment thematized on its own account are only means in the service of determining the objective domain. The thematic of predicative propositions as such is necessarily an intermediate thematic. Its entire sense lies in its application to the object, in adequation to the object in a possible evidence of clarity (*FTL*, p. 129 [115]). And precisely to the degree that the apophantic attitude is actually oriented toward the clarification of judicative intentions (*Urteilsmeinungen*) does it take on a formal ontological significance, but without itself being formal-ontological. The critical attitude is always in the service of the primary interest in the things themselves, and logic in its ultimate sense is always formal-ontological rather than formal-apophantic.[34]

The mode proper to the formal-ontological attitude is immediacy; the mode proper to the apophantic attitude is reflective and critical. But clearly we are dealing here with a reflection on the basis of the direct mode. The apophantic attitude presup-

---

34. *FTL*, p. 144 (129). Logic therefore has two ways of being genuinely logical, either in the ontological mode (direct intention to the object) or in the apophantic mode (mediate intention to the object)—i.e., the "mathematical" mode in an ontological sense.

poses the ontological attitude. In order to criticize the judgment, we must first have the judgment. The ontological attitude is therefore both the first and the last step of formal logic, i.e., it is both the first and the last step of knowledge. This is why truth in the apophantic attitude is a critical truth, and evidence is a critical evidence. In other words, it is a matter of measuring the meaning of the judgment thematized as such by the originary givenness of the thing. Actual adequation is what defines the critical concept of truth for Husserl (*FTL*, p. 127 [113]). It would even be better to speak of verification rather than truth. As a matter of fact, the critical-apophantic attitude necessarily implies an interest in verification (*FTL*, p. 123 [109]). The interest in possible truth is always an interest in verification (*FTL*, p. 65 [57]). Critical truth in general, since it is truth resulting from adequation, is necessarily the verification of a judicative intention.

This manner of speaking makes it easier to understand the essential "secondariness" of critical truth, which is a participation in truth in the immediate and primary sense of the ontological attitude. This second concept is that of the *truth of the judgment,* the truth of correctness of the judgment.[35] Correlatively, the concept of evidence is here the critical concept of adequation of the judgment as categorial objectivity to the originary actuality of the corresponding reality. There is here a consciousness of truth, a relation of one truth to another truth or of one evidence to another evidence. The evidence proper to apophantic senses is the evidence of distinctness, which originarily gives the apophantic sense, the pure and simple judgment as meant. The evidence proper to the objectivity as such is the evidence of clarity. Critical evidence is thus the verifying adequation of the first evidence (of distinctness) to the second evidence (of clarity), just as critical truth is measured by the truth of being, which alone is first in itself. Critical evidence is, to be sure, a kind of evidence of clarity, since there is possession (*Selbsthabe*) of the thing. But it is critical in the sense that it entails the thematization of the judgment as sense in the evidence of distinctness and the fulfillment (which is critical strictly speaking) of this evidence of anticipation by the immediate evidence of the thing (evidence of clarity in the first, ontological sense). From the apophantic point of view, the evidence of

35. "Kritischer Wahrheitsbegriff der Urteilsrichtigkeit" (*FTL*, p. 127 [113]).

distinctness is first, and it is verified in the evidence of clarity. From the ontological point of view, the evidence of clarity is first, and it is "criticized" in reflection on the judicative intention (*Urteilsmeinung*), i.e., in the evidence of distinctness (*FTL*, pp. 128 [113 f.], 146 [130]). The truth and the evidence proper to the apophantic attitude are therefore second and dependent with respect to the truth and the evidence of the ontological attitude. The latter is the ideal exemplar and hence the telos of the former. There is evidence and truth in each case, but it is immediate in the one case and mediate in the other. Participation in the ideal exemplar always allows a common formal determination to subsist in two different concrete modes.

Thus it remains that critical truth is measured by a truth which Husserl qualifies not as critical but as *naiv-gerade*. This clear truth in naïveté is the beginning of wisdom but not the end of wisdom. It needs to be confirmed by a thematization of the judgment as such, to be critically measured by the originary givenness of the object (cf. *FTL*, pp. 278 f. [246]). Critical truth is that of the judgment that conforms in its meaning with the originarily given object. "Immediate" truth is the truth of being. This simply reflects ad infinitum the difficulty of the problem of truth. This is so because (1) the verifying adequation that results in critical truth is an infinite process whose telos is ideally anticipated and (2) the truth of being is the truth of experience "fixed" in the judgment, and the process of experience that results in knowledge of the *Selbst* of the thing (and hence in a true knowledge of the thing) is also anticipated in an idea of the object in its "itself." Rather than a doctrine of truth, phenomenology more readily yields a *motive of realization*. Truth is in fact an infinite idea (cf. *FTL*, pp. 127 [113], 198 f. [176], 277 [245]). The infinity of the critical process of verification of the scientific judgment reflects the infinity of the process of originary experience. The ideality of the first extends univocally into the ideality of the second. The apophantic attitude and the ontological attitude are thus continuous, and they both manifest the same intentionality of knowledge of the object. This intentionality passes through various levels, which are, as we know, not irreducible stages but dialectical moments mutually transcending one another. From language to the object we have the morphology of meanings, the "logic of distinctness,'" the logic of consequence, the logic of possible truth. That is, we have a pure analytics of meanings which is fully worked out in its two dimensions, the apophantic and the ontological.[36]

But traditional logic stops with apophantic logic. By reason of its exclusive orientation toward judgments as such, it is situated from the first in the critical attitude (cf. *FTL*, pp. 130 f. [115 f.]). But this cannot be a genuine critical attitude. Traditional logic ignores intentionality. More exactly, it truncates intentionality by regarding itself only as a formal logic of possible truth, whereas by its transcendental extension it includes a (synthetic) phenomenology of the object itself. Our latest reflections already place us in a transcendental point of view. The concepts of evidence and of truth are no longer concepts of formal logic strictly speaking but of transcendental logic, whether they are understood in a naïve and immediate sense or in a critical and reflective sense. Thus it is quite true that the relations between formal apophantics and formal logic can be grasped only in a phenomenological clarification, i.e., formal logic is explicated and can be explicated only in transcendental phenomenology (*FTL*, p. 178 [158]). Traditional logic wished to remain purely formal and had no conception of its possible transcendental extension. It did not even clearly discern its possible formal extension in formal ontology, i.e., in a logic of possible truth as logic of the object. In that case, the only means of arriving at formal ontology is to reintroduce objective concerns in formal logic, which cannot fail to open the way to transcendental investigation. Thus logic, lacking formal ontology, lacked transcendental logic. This is, in short, why traditional logic is not genuinely critical but only formal and objectively normative.

There is yet another important point to be noted. The verifying adequation of the judgment as such to the originary objectivity is the adequation of the judgment as intended to the corresponding categorial objectivity (cf. *FTL*, pp. 65 [58], 127 [113], 146 [130], 327 [287]). But the judgment as such (*blosses Urteil*) is also a categorial objectivity. What is more, it is the same categorial objectivity as that by which it is measured. In fact, only their modes of givenness are different. In the judgment as such, we have to do with the evidence of distinctness,

36. This theme of the continuity of intentionality is the same as what Husserl called the shifting of intentionality (*Verschiebung der Intentionalitäten*). We have already come across it above, pp. 101, 172, 175–79. Cf. below, § 33.

the evidence proper to the apophantic sense. In the case of the judgment as object, we have to do with the evidence of clarity, the evidence proper to categorial objectivities, i.e., objectivities entering originarily into a process of judication. In the first case we have a revivification of already constituted apophantic senses; in the second case we have an originary constitution of these same categorial objectivities. In the first case we encounter once again the intentional method in the mode of *Nach-verstehen*, while in the second we immediately have the intentional method in the mode of originary constitution. In short, determination of the mutual relationship between formal apophantics and formal ontology brings out the two dimensions of intentionality. On the one hand, we recover the originary constituting experience, setting out from an element which is already given or "already there" (in this case, the judgment as such given in language in the evidence of distinctness). On the other hand, we end with the object constituted by an appropriate "experience" (here again the judgment as such proceeds from reflection on the ontological attitude in the evidence of clarity), setting out from the fundamental intention of knowledge—that is, from consciousness itself. If the latter thought process is compared with the former, it will of course seem "more originary," since what is more originary is transcendental consciousness. But the method that consists in proceeding from a meaning as such (*blosses Urteil*) to its subjective constitution also supposes an originary experience, that of the evidence of distinctness. With respect to the thing itself (*Sache selbst*), originary evidence is the evidence of clarity; with respect to the meaning itself (*vermeinte Gegenständlichkeit als solche*), originary evidence is the evidence of distinctness. The evidence of distinctness and the evidence of clarity reciprocally take primacy in point of originariness depending on whether we take the descriptive-phenomenological or the transcendental-phenomenological point of view on intentionality. Thus we do not find absolute priority on either side. If Husserl can say that the truth of being is first in the absolute sense and that critical truth is therefore second, this is because he here places himself exclusively in the ontological and transcendental point of view, which is that of the originary constitution of the *Gegenstand*. From this point of view the evidence of clarity is obviously first. But in the constitution of the *Sinn* the roles are reversed, and the evidence of distinctness takes first place. These observations have only a relative validity, however. The only absolute point of view is that of concrete consciousness, the life of consciousness. From this point of view we have an equivalence of two correlative thematics (cf. below, "General Conclusion"). There are two originary modes of givenness of explicit judgments (cf. *FTL*, pp. 324 f. [285]); there are two types of objectivity (real or empirical and irreal or ideal); there are two types of genuine knowledge (science and logic-philosophy); there is but one transcendental consciousness, the originary and absolute source of all constitution. In short, the two dimensions of intentionality and all its concrete applications—the two-sidedness of transcendental logic in *Experience and Judgment* and *Formal and Transcendental Logic* as well as the two-sidedness of formal logic as formal apophantics and formal ontology—are always to be regarded from the point of view of transcendental consciousness. Thus we come to the conclusion that, within formal logic, apophantics represents the descriptive-phenomenological dimension and ontology represents the transcendental-phenomenological dimension of intentionality. The first sets out from the constituted judgment as *blosse Bedeutung,* given (confusedly) in experience; the second, on the contrary, immediately shows the originary constitution of the categorial objectivity expressed predicatively in the judgment.

But we also know that *Formal and Transcendental Logic* represents the descriptive-phenomenological dimension and that *Experience and Judgment* represents the transcendental-phenomenological dimension. There is therefore a certain relationship between *Formal and Transcendental Logic* and apophantics, on the one hand, and between *Experience and Judgment* and formal ontology, on the other. *Formal and Transcendental Logic* and *Experience and Judgment* are two modes of a single transcendental logic; formal apophantics and formal ontology are two modes of a single formal logic. Each pair is originary; that is, each rests on an originary evidence. *Formal and Transcendental Logic* and apophantics rest on the originary experience of the meaning as such, the experience of language, and are intuitively grounded in the evidence of distinctness. *Experience and Judgment* and formal ontology rest on the originary experience of the *thing* and are intuitively grounded in the evidence of clarity. Thus we can definitely resolve the apparent difficulty which arose above (cf. § 21). The two dimensions of Husserlian formal and transcendental logic are each originary but are originary in different ways, since intentionality appears in both its dimensions and correlatively requires two types of originary evidence, the evidence of distinctness and the evidence of clarity. This is why the following parallel or proportion can be drawn between the two pairs of divisions within formal logic and transcendental logic, respectively: formal apophantics is to *Formal and Transcendental Logic* as formal ontology is to *Experience and Judgment* (cf. above, p. 138).

PART IV

Transcendental Logic

1 / The Presuppositions of Formal Logic

§ 33. *Equivocations of language and shifting of intentionality*

OUR PRECEDING INQUIRY was intended to show the progressive movement which goes through formal logic. Formal logic is divided into levels which are distinct but not irreducible. Each formal level is completed with a perfect continuity in the following level. The movement followed by logical thought goes from meaningful language to the object. Formal logic cannot fail to deal with the problem of evidence. Of course it deals with this problem without thematizing it as such, since the thematization of evidence comes within the exclusive domain of transcendental logic. Insofar as logic is the science of science (i.e., of theory), it supposes the object to be given; that is, it presupposes the dator evidence of its object. It implies and exercises in an anonymous way the dator evidence of its proper object without explicitly reflecting on this evidence. It therefore presupposes a transcendental thematic. It admits the results of the originary dator evidence as if they were given in themselves, whereas they refer as index to corresponding subjective and constitutive a prioris. This is not a deficiency on the part of formal logic qua formal logic; but it shows the dependence of formal logic with respect to transcendental logic, the phenomenology of consciousness or science of evidence, i.e., science of sense-giving (*Sinngebung*). In a word, the method of formal logic remains "naïve." It rests upon a concealed presupposition which is "anonymous" and not clarified (cf. *FTL*, p. 187 [166]).

[205]

Now, this presupposition is articulated along the same lines as the partition that Husserl finds within formal logic. But it seems that this amounts to reinstating a multiplicity in transcendental logic, which is contrary to the unity that seems to be implied in the idea of absolute science. Here again we are going to witness the reduction of multiplicity to unity or, more exactly, a surpassing, in immanence, of multiplicity by the teleological dialectic of intentionality.

We know that the morphology of meanings is an elementary and fundamental logic which needs to be actually explicated by way of the evidence of distinctness; this evidence specifies a "logic of distinctness" or logic of consequence in the broad sense. This logic, by elucidating the exclusive point of view of non-contradiction, becomes a logic of truth, since the forms of non-contradictory predicative thought are norms of objective truth. Each formal discipline thus "fits" into the one preceding it and extends naturally into the one following it. Formal logic is fashioned by an internal motive which is simply the logical interest in the object. This is why logic comes to an end, or reaches its telos, only when it formally thematizes the object. Formal ontology is the final sense of formal logic. But the interest in the object, the teleological movement in virtue of which the various logical disciplines succeed one another up to the formal logic of the object (and finally up to the constitutive logic of the object), is nothing but intentionality. We have therefore seen only a first "part" of the logical interest in the object. Its end or last stage, transcendental logic, remains to be seen. The one entails the other. To perform and anonymously presuppose evidence is to engage sooner or later in thematizing this evidence and establishing a subjective-phenomenological logic (*FTL*, p. 270 [239]).

However, what we have seen enables us already to understand the properly transcendental value of the inquiry we conducted concerning formal logic. Was this inquiry not an intentional clarification of the sense of traditional logic? And did this clarification not issue in the problematic of evidence (in its two modes, distinctness and clarity)? Our preceding investigations are therefore subjective-phenomenological, since they establish three subjective attitudes of judication, three evidences, three strata of constitutive concepts (*FTL*, p. 178 [158]). The essential multiplicity of formal logic thereby appears.

Nevertheless, formal logic has the judgment as its exclusive theme. If it divides into three specifically different levels, equivocations in the language of logic must necessarily follow. The same concept of judgment is used three times with different meanings. The morphology of meanings, the logic of consequence, and the logic of truth do not have the same formal point of view on the judgment. Equivocation therefore takes place. However, this equivocation is an essential necessity. It simply expresses in the domain of language the univocal continuity of the logical interest of formal logic (*FTL*, p. 178 [158]). It reflects a *shifting of intentionality* (*Verschiebung der Intentionalität*). In fact, each formal discipline has its own object, its own intentionality. If each discipline extends into another which is immediately contiguous with it, its intentional movement extends to the telos of the intentionality of the second discipline. The intentionality of the first discipline is transposed; and, in virtue of the continuity we have already exhibited among the various logical disciplines, we have the same intentionality explicated and developed in a continuous manner. There is only a single intentional movement, which takes on different modes corresponding to the various levels. In the morphology of meanings, this is an evidence in the rhythmic aspect of verbal articulations; in the logic of consequence, it is an evidence of distinctness of articulated meanings; in the logic of truth, it is an evidence of clarity in the adequation of meanings to categorial objectivities (cf. *FTL*, pp. 178 f. [159]). All these evidences interpenetrate to such an extent that the evidence of clarity cannot be without the evidence of distinctness or without the evidence of verbal articulations. There is a single movement, a single univocal reality, but there are several manifestations in the several evidences, respectively. On the other hand, we can speak of equivocation, since formal logic considers only the judgment as its sole object and since this judgment is realized in several different ways. The linguistic equivocation thus merely expresses the univocal oneness of intentionality. Hence this equivocation is inevitable, precisely by reason of the univocity of the reality signified.[1] To justify it and overcome it, it

----

1. *FTL*, p. 177 (158). Similarly, in a pantheism like Spinoza's, the univocity of the object entails the equivocity of language. The same is true of Platonic idealism: the word "horse" is equivocal, but the horse as a reality is univocal, since between the horse in itself and the empirical horse there is identity as to essential determination but diversity in ontological mode of subsistence. This shows that in an exemplarist system it is impossible to escape from this "dialectic" between the univocal and the equivocal; language

is therefore necessary to exhibit the shifting of intentionality. This will involve (1) reflectively distinguishing the various stages of intentionality (the various logical disciplines) and (2) affirming their continuity, the intentionality of formal logic —that is, recognizing that the change of sense (*Sinneswandlung*) we are considering is at both a shifting and a coincidence (*Überschiebung* and *Deckung*) (cf. *FTL*, pp. 178 f. [158 f.]). Hence the shifting of intentionality is what explains the linguistic equivocation and at the same time makes it possible to overcome this equivocation. It clearly shows the surpassing of the analytic-objective multiplicity of logic in the subjective unity of consciousness (*FTL*, pp. 177–79 [158 f.]).

It is to be noted, however, that the expression "shifting of intentionality" is legitimate only in connection with formal logic, in which a multiplicity of disciplines are distinguished. It is no longer strictly legitimate from the phenomenological point of view of intentionality. The latter is in essence a shifting or *dynamic self-transcendence*—a characteristic which essentially defines consciousness itself (cf. *CM*, p. 46 [84]). And this shifting is itself unique because it tends toward an intentional unity pole. The movement is the uninterrupted succession of its dynamic "parts" (moments). From the analytic point of view it makes sense to affirm the multiplicity of these moments and set them out as independent parts (*Stücke*). But the intentional point of view prohibits such an analysis; the "part" must be a "moment" (cf. above, § 12). The radical unity of intentionality is thus compatible with the multiplicity of its moments. The final sense of formal logic is indeed formal ontology, but formal logic is nevertheless partitioned in three distinct levels. This ternary partition is an accomplishment of Husserl's formal logic. Each of the formal disciplines is autonomous and rests upon its own constitutive concepts. These concepts are laid down by formal logic, but they have not yet undergone the intentional clarification which alone can guarantee their validity and legitimize their status. It is to be noted in particular that each of the formal disciplines presupposes its object without itself being able to justify the transcendental legitimacy (the dator evidence) of this object. It now falls to the logician to bring to light the hidden presuppositions, the naïve implications, and the anonymous methods implied in formal logic. Here again we see how

---

cannot be adequate to reality—or at least this adequation is an infinite idea.

transcendental logic extends formal logic "intentionally" without conflicting with it, and we see that the sense and even the legitimacy of formal logic can be guaranteed only by transcendental logic.

It seems at first sight that the presuppositions of formal logic correspond to the three levels of intentionality: language—meaning—object. Thus each formal discipline (*reine Formenlehre, Konsequenzlogik, Wahrheitslogik*) requires the elucidation of its ideal a priori. However, we know that, although intentionality has three levels, these levels determine only two intentional movements, i.e., two evidences. These are the evidence of distinctness and the evidence of clarity, of which the first is the telos of the teleology from language to meaning while the second is the telos of the teleology from meaning to object. For it must be taken into account that language is verbally articulated only insofar as this articulation of words reflects the coherent articulation of their senses. The evidence of the rhythmic aspect of verbal articulations is therefore always assumed by the evidence of distinctness of meanings. If Husserl distinguishes between them, this is only in order to show that the evidence of articulations is the verbal or "material" aspect of the evidence of distinctness of meanings. Just as the morphology of meanings combines with the logic of consequence to constitute a single apophantic morphology, so the evidence of the rhythmic aspect of verbal articulations is assumed by the evidence of distinctness. This is why formal logic is really divided into *two* disciplines, which are the logic of consequence in two senses: in the broad sense, which includes an elementary morphology, and in the narrow sense, in which it becomes a logic of possible truth. Similarly, intentionality is in fact a movement which goes from meaning to object, language being only the material expression of meaning (and hence an element which is secondary and dependent on meaning). Thus we speak only of *two* levels of formal logic. But if the effective partition of formal logic is a division into two parts, there must correspond to the formal disciplines two series of constitutive concepts, hence two and only two presuppositions. Finally, since the evidence of distinctness is the originary givenness of meanings, and the evidence of clarity is the originary givenness of the object meant, it follows that the presuppositions of formal logic are those of the ideal identity and the truth of logical configurations—that is, the *being in itself* and the *truth in itself* of predicative meanings. Husserl explicitly asserts this (*FTL*, p.

243 [215]). But here, too, the multiplicity is provisional. If the diversity of formal disciplines and the multiplicity of intentionalities from which it results are really surpassed by the teleological unity of the interest in the object, it is a priori impossible that the presuppositions articulated along the same lines as the diversity of formal logic should not reduce to unity. As a matter of fact, we are going to see that the exposition of the two presuppositions emerges in each case in a thematic of experience or originary evidence and that, by the intermediary of a criticism of analytic logic, we pass from formal logic to a transcendental logic or phenomenology of reason. In other words, the two presuppositions of formal logic each refer to the subjective a priori of experience and, in the end, to the unique absolute presupposition, the transcendental ego.

A. THE FIRST PRESUPPOSITION OF FORMAL LOGIC

§ 34. *The ideal identity of the meaning*

OUR PRESENT INVESTIGATION consists in a constitutive criticism of the fundamental concepts of formal logic, either as logic of pure meanings or as implying an interest in the object. One series of presuppositions will therefore correspond to "pure" analytics (mathematics of senses), another series to the logic of truth. Each of these presuppositions will be the index of constitutive investigations in its respective domain, investigations which end by transcendentally justifying the fundamental concepts of the logical disciplines.

Now pure analytics considers the judgment as pure meaning, and it attends solely to the meaningful unity of the judgment as such. In other words, far from concerning itself with any actual reference to the object (*Gegenständlichkeit*), it is interested only in the *Objektivität* of predicative meanings, their consistency or inconsistency. We have seen that the judgment as a logical configuration (*logisches Gebilde*) is an objective identity giving itself as such in an originary evidence. The schema of evidence in general is reproduced here. Just as the object is the unity of the noetic multiplicity of its modes of givenness, so the judgment as *logisches Gebilde* is a unity constituted in a multiple subjective process. As the unity of a multiplicity, it transcends this constitutive multiplicity or multiple constitution. Considering that the judicative process of constitution is real [*réel*], we must further say that the transcendence of the intentional unity (in this case the judgment) implies a certain ideality. The judgment, as a *logisches Gebilde* constituted in a noetic manifold, is thus an ideal objectivity (*Ideal-Objektivität*) which implies as its essential property an identical being, an ideal identity. It is in virtue of this that the judgment is identifiable ad infinitum in acts which are numerically distinct but qualitatively identical, and that the judgment in its qualitative and numerical identity constitutes a permanent acquisition that is forever "within reach" (cf. *FTL,* pp. 185 f. [164]; see also above, § 22). However, this aspect of the matter is not in the domain of formal logic. Pure analytics supposes the ideal objectivity of logical configurations, the ideal identity of meaning as such, without thematizing its originary givenness. It is oriented toward the product of constitution, the constituted, and does not itself go from the constituted to its constitution. Here we see the "naïve" presupposition: the admission of the ideal identity (being in itself) of the judgment as an evident and absolute given, without thematizing the subjective method which stood over its transcendental constitution.

However, this constitution is required by the very essence of the constituted. The constituted necessarily indicates (is an index of) an originary constitution, and this originary constitution is precisely its *subjective a priori.* In thematizing the constituted on its own account (the judgment as ideal and identical meaning), pure analytics yields to the naïveté of the natural attitude without seeing that this attitude implicitly rests on a constitutive subjective a priori. The "naïve presupposition" must be subjected to criticism and clarified by the subjective a priori. Only in this way can we assure ourselves of the legitimacy of the ideal identity of the judgment as such (in a universal way, the ideal identity of pure meanings), and only in this way can formal logic be grounded in its "pure" thematic. This grounding will no longer be objective-analytic, but rather transcendental-synthetic. Investigation of the presupposition of mathematical analytics thus consists in intentional clarification of the judgment (of the pure meaning) as an ideal identity. This identity, when taken as theme of a transcendental criticism, is the index of a system of constitutive intentionalities, since the given necessarily presupposes givenness. This system is going to confront us with new difficulties. For the ideal identity eludes the process of its constitution, i.e., it is never genuinely or adequately constituted. The a priori of analytic logic can evidently be only an "idealizing" presupposition, an idea, precisely because constitutive intentionality is infinite.

The judgment as a transcendent ideality is never given in a perfect manner. It is pre-scribed as the ideal telos of an originary process of judication; but its "itself" (*Selbst*) is never fully and adequately grasped, simply because it is ideal. Thus the constitutive criticism of the presupposition of the being in itself of the judgment takes on the appearance of an infinite regress. If it is true that the identical ideality of the judgment as such transcends the subjective process of its own constitution, what guarantee do we have of its identity (*FTL*, p. 185 [163])? A new evidence would be necessary, one which would originarily justify this transcendence in its "itself"—that is, this transcendence as transcendence and not as this or that ideal object (pure judgment or meaning). But then we have an endless spiral. If we assume a new evidence in order to justify transcendentally the transcendence of the meaning as transcendence, this new object is in turn a new transcendence for the new corresponding givenness. The transcendence of the meaning is as such a new intentional unity transcending the second-degree evidence which we must assume in order to motivate it. Thus the ideal identity of meaning has its legitimacy "postponed" ad infinitum. The critical-constitutive investigation of presuppositions dissolves in an infinite regress (*FTL*, p. 186 f. [165]; cf. *Ideas*, p. 378 [332]).

As a matter of fact, this situation must be accepted. The adequate justification of the ideal identity of the judgment as pure meaning is an idea that is realizable ad infinitum, i.e., that is actually unrealizable (*FTL*, p. 187 [166]). This "opening onto the infinite" or *processus ad infinitum* in the constitutive investigation merely expresses in another way the ideality of intentionality and of its telos. The intentional unity is in fact by definition an ideality transcending the process of its own constitution (*FTL*, p. 165 [148]). But the intentional movement can have only a unity of order. Reference to the object is what unifies and orders constitution. The object, the telos of its own constitution, is hence an intentional unity; that is, it is, strictly speaking, an ideal principle of order. The intentional movement of its constitution teleologically acquires an *ideality* which it progressively *realizes* in proportion as the object is determined beforehand in its *Selbst*. The unity of the intentional movement is therefore formulated in an idea which thematizes in a unitary way the infinite totality of the movement itself and which pre-scribes for this movement its *de facto* realization. Consequently, no evidence will ever be adequate to the transcendent object that is correlative with it. The reason for this is that originary evidence or constituting sense-giving only manages to pre-scribe ideally its own telos, i.e., the telos of the intentional movement which would actually give us the "itself" of the object. The sys-tem of constitutive intentionalities only approaches this ideal telos asymptotically. The object in general and the *logisches Gebilde* as ideal objectivity are only infinite ideas. Hence it is not pertinent to say that a new evidence is necessary in order to constitute the ideal transcendence in its "itself" (adequately). It would be more correct to speak of an evidence continued in the ideal mode of the "and so forth." This does not enable us to avoid the *processus ad infinitum,* but it does at least make it possible to thematize it as an ideal unity, as an idea.

This is where Husserl chooses to introduce the doctrine of the ideal infinity of the intentional movement. We have come across the essential characteristic which intentionality possesses, the characteristic of transcending itself. If this is really an es-sential property, this self-transcendence must be infinite, as we can infer from what we know about the shifting of intentionality. Husserl now seeks to resolve this problem: how to thematize in a finite notion an infinite movement which in its very in-finitude remains essentially potential? In other words, how can the idea be a finite notion if it is in reality infinite (cf. above, § 13)? The ideal form of "and so forth," which is a fundamental struc-ture of the sphere of judgments, is just what enables us to thematize an absence of limits in a process. In reality, the "and so forth" as an ideal structure expresses an infinity and coincides with the idea itself. Thus the "and so forth" specifies the property which the idea has of being an anticipating idea(liza)tion of an infinite process (evidence, experience, explication, judica-tion, flow of experiences, etc.) (cf. *FTL,* pp. 188 f. [167]; *EJ,* § 51b; *Ideas,* §§ 83, 149, and passim).

Obviously this ideal form of the "and so forth," which thematizes a fundamental structure of consciousness, is valid far beyond the single problem of the ideal identity of categorial meanings. All evidence and all intentionality—in short, all consciousness—falls under it. Intentionality is universally a unique and infinite movement tending continuously toward one and the same telos. Here, too, the evidence guaranteeing the ideal identity of meanings (their being in itself) is one and the same evidence, which approaches one and the same ideal telos ad infinitum. An idealization is obviously involved here, since in fact no one can continue ad infinitum the movement that is initiated.[2] The constitution (or the constitutive criticism) of the presuppositions of mathematical analytics is therefore an infinite task which the intentional method enables us to thematize ideally in the form of the "and so forth," i.e., in the form of the idea. Application of the ideal infinity of the "and so forth" to the constitutive investigation of the a priori of pure analytics is therefore a key part of the intentional criticism of the constitutive concepts of formal logic. Ideality (and hence this infinity in the mode of "and so forth") is for this reason implied in the sense of all the fundamental concepts of formal logic. Here we have seen its application to the fundamental concept of pure analytics, the ideal identity of judgments as such. But the same ideal infinite structure—that is, the same intentional structure—is found in every concept of formal logic (for example, the concept of truth in itself), as well as in every objectivity in general (*FTL*, p. 188 [166]).

§ 35. *The possibility of the evidence of distinctness*

THE JUDGMENT can also be considered as a copulative connection of two simple meanings or else as a judgment included in a syllogistic ensemble. The *logisches Gebilde,* which has so far been regarded as a meaning, is now given as a meaningful connection bound by the necessities expressed in logical principles, such as those of noncontradiction and excluded middle. By this we must understand the logical principles of the logic of consequence in the broad sense. Hence these

2. Cf. *FTL*, p. 188 (167). The infinitude which Husserl holds to be the distinctive feature of the idea and of the "and so forth" here reveals its quantitative (mathematical) origins. If any doubts remain on this score, even after Husserl's assertion that the idea cannot be actually realized (*FTL*, p. 187 [166]), we need only read the example given by Husserl in *FTL* (p. 188 [167]): the infinite series of numbers, in which the structure of the "and so forth" is to be found in the form "$a + 1$." Moreover, if the "and so forth" is a constructive infinity, where would it be realized better than in mathematics—which is the domain of constructive infinities? These conclusions corroborate those given above (§ 11).

govern only the ideal existence of the judgment, i.e., in the simplest case, the predicative connection of two meanings. Now, the ideal existence of the judgment is given in the evidence of distinctness, and the logic of consequence qua pure analytics is the logic of this evidence. Since its theme is the judgment, the logic of consequence admits as a fundamental principle that every judgment can be brought to the evidence of distinctness— which may appear to be a necessary truth if we recall that the evidence of distinctness is of itself indifferent to contradiction as well as to (material) noncontradiction. The evidence of distinctness simply expresses the ideal mode of existence of the distinct judgment, and such a judgment can be contradictory with respect to other judgments or even internally inconsistent without thereby in the least losing its ideal existence as a meaning. This is what Husserl means when he writes that every judgment is capable of being elucidated in an evidence of distinctness in either a positive or a negative sense, since we are still on a level of formal logic which precedes the introduction of the concept of truth (*FTL*, p. 215 [191]).

Hence, just as pure analytics was shown above to suppose the ideal identity of meanings without asking the "how" of it (the subjective a priori), so here the logic of consequence (in the broad sense) admits as a presupposition that every judgment can be brought to the evidence of distinctness in itself without clarifying the presuppositions upon which such an assertion rests. Just as the pure analytics of meanings supposes the object to be given and posits the object's ideal identity without reflectively thematizing its originary givenness, so here the pure analytics of judgments as connections of meanings under the aspect of logical principles admits in a naïve way the possible distinctness of the judgment without investigating the profound intentional motivation of this possibility.

To be sure, this is not a matter for formal logic. Only transcendental logic undertakes such a constitutive and critical investigation. It remains true, nonetheless, that distinctness itself, which seems to be the essential property of every possible judgment, is also a "given" which must be clarified and justified. In other words, the question of the possibility of the evidence of distinctness now arises. We shall proceed, as we just now did, from a naïvely admitted "given" or anonymous presupposition to a constituting givenness. It must be noted, however, that we are penetrating farther and farther into the transcendental thematic. Just now we had to do with an actual given, an ideal and identical object, and hence a genuine constituted object. Here we are to trace to its constitutive origins an evidence which is considered as a mere immediately admitted presupposition. Constitutive (critical) investigation in general takes its point of departure in an object or a factical given which plays the role of thematic index. In the present case, the factical given—the index of the constitutive evidence—is itself an evidence. The evidence of distinctness itself is, with respect to its own index (language), a constitutive system of intentionality; it already corresponds to a transcendental thematic. To put it in question is in turn to submit a subjective thematic to criticism. This is to radicalize once more the process of constitution. Our present investigation is therefore the constitutive criticism of an evidence, the investigation of the evidence of the evidence of distinctness.[3] In this way there reappears the historicity of consciousness, which is sedimented in the various levels of its *Leistungen*. Just as the constituted object expresses the sedimentation of objectified consciousness, so also the evidence of distinctness, as it is presupposed here by pure analytics, is the subjective expression of a still deeper intentionality.

The evidence of distinctness originarily gives the unitary sense and the ideal existence of the judgment—that is, it originarily explicates the ideal modes of connectedness among relative terms in judgments and among judgments *inter se*—in a contradictory or a noncontradictory manner. But what is meant by the "sense" of a proposition? An equivocation crops up here, since the sense of the judgment can be the judgment itself as well as the content of the judgment. The judgment as such is capable of assuming several modes: the simple certainty of the categorical assertion (the originary judgment) may become uncertain, doubtful, probable, etc. However, all these modes preserve a priori the same content, i.e., a common meaning content which remains identical despite the successive changes of doxic modalities (*FTL*, pp. 216 f. [192 f.]; cf. below, § 44). "The sense of the judgment" can therefore be taken in two senses, and these two senses extend to all positional spheres in an analogous manner. We must distinguish in every judgment between the judgment as such and the content of the judgment, that is, between the modal quality and the matter of the judg-

3. Perhaps it can be said simply that here we are investigating the evidence of distinctness, differentiating between distinctness (as noematic result) and the evidence in which it is constituted (noesis).

ment. The two are inseparable in the concrete judgment, and together they constitute the unity of the judgment under consideration. That is, they constitute the judgment strictly speaking (its intentional being).[4] There is only one judgment in which quality and matter merge in an identity, and this is the *idea of the judgment*. This originary case of the ideal judgment, in which the matter is itself quality, is realized in the simple categorical assertion, formally expressed as "S is p." Here there is an identity between the assertion and what is asserted; the *Urteilssatz* is identical with the *Sachverhalt*. This judgment in which the *Sachverhalt* is identical with the completely fulfilled judgment is a limiting case or zero case. The simple judgment is an act of such a kind that its quality coincides with its intentional being, since its matter and its quality are identical (*EJ*, §§ 60, 68, 70; *LI*, p. 600 [II/1, 430]; and cf. below, § 48). In every other judgment there is a dissociation between what is identical in the simple judgment; the quality is something other than the matter. The matter is not immediately quality by itself,

4. The quality of an act of consciousness is the specific character of the act which determines it as a mere representation, a judgment, a sensation, etc. (*LI*, pp. 586–88 [II/1, 411–14], 604 [II/1, 436]), as positional or nonpositional (*LI*, pp. 626 [II/1, 465], 639 [II/1, 481], 643 [II/1, 487], 646 [II/1, 491]). It is an abstract moment of the act and has no bearing on the objectivity of the act (*LI*, pp. 589 [II/1, 416], 604 [II/1, 436], 621 [II/1, 457]). Hence the quality complements the matter and together with it forms a complete act (*LI*, pp. 617 [II/1, 453], 620 [II/1, 457 f.], 637 [II/1, 478]). The matter of an act is the act's intentional content (*LI*, p. 578 [II/1, 399]) and gives the act its objective reference (*LI*, pp. 588 f. [II/1, 414 f.], 598 [II/1, 427], 648 [II/1, 494]); it remains identical even if the quality should change (*LI*, pp. 586 [II/1, 412], 627 [II/1, 466]). In it we must distinguish between reference to the originary *Gegenstand* (originary *quid*) and objective determination of the *Gegenstand* (noematic *quomodo*), which together make up the complete matter or noematic sense (noematic *quid*); cf. *LI*, pp. 588 f. (II/1, 414 f.). That is, we must distinguish between the object pure and simple (= X) and the object in the *quomodo* of its objective determinations (*Sinn*), in the words of *Ideas*, § 131 (cf. below, § 45). *EJ* distinguishes in the judgment between the content or matter of the judgment and its thetic character. These two elements together yield the complete judgment noema, consisting of the matter (noematic *quid* with its various strata of determinations) and the act character or quality (pp. 286 f. [345]). In every act the complete noema is made up of the noematic *quid* and the noetic *quomodo* (subjective mode of givenness); cf. *Ideas*, § 132. This conjunction of quality and matter is what makes up the intentional essence of the act (*LI*, p. 590 [II/1, 417]; *Ideas*, § 133).

and what is asserted is not by itself the assertion; rather, the matter takes on a special modality in order to be an intentional being, an assertion. The matter remains identical in itself. It undergoes a modalization, since its quality changes and the judgment is no longer identical with its quality. This modalization itself constitutes a modified judgment—a judgment which must be distinguished from its content (the originary judgment), since the intentional being of such a judgment no longer coincides with its matter.

Now, every modalization is relative to the originary form and is determined as a function of it. Every judgment other than the simple categorical is therefore relative to the originary judgment of which it is a modalization. The question of the possibility of the judgment in distinctness thus arises differently in the case of the simple judgment than in the case of the modified judgment. In the former, it is immediately and inseparably the question of the possibility of the quality *and* the matter, since the two coincide. In the latter, the possibility of the judgment is grounded in the possibility of the matter of the judgment. Hence in each case it is a matter of grounding the possibility of the intentional being of the judgment. But in the simple judgment this grounding concerns the quality and the matter inseparably, while in the modified judgment it concerns only the matter (the content of the judgment). In other words, the modified judgment is possible only if its matter is possible. The ideal existence of the judgment as such therefore presupposes the ideal existence of the content of the judgment, and the evidence of the former is based upon the evidence of the latter.[5]

Thus, when the logic of consequence lays down the principle that every judgment is capable of the evidence of distinctness, it must be added that every explicit judgment implies as a presupposition the evidence of the judgment's content. But putting the matter of the judgment in question forces us to go beyond the framework of a pure analytics, since we are thereby emphasizing the importance of material cores for the possible performance (*Vollzug*) of distinct judgments (*FTL*, pp. 217 f. [193 f.]). Formal logic formalizes or "algebraizes" the material

5. *FTL*, p. 217 (193). It is easy to construct a parallel argument for the simple judgment, in which the matter is itself quality, although Husserl does not do so.

cores and empties them of their respective material content [*teneur*] (cf. *FTL,* p. 48 [42]). The evidence of distinctness of the judgment depends upon the evidence of the judgment's content. But this content is objective, and thus we return to the position we have already come across: that the evidence of distinctness is ultimately grounded in the originary evidence of the thing as it is verified in the evidence of clarity. In trying to clarify intentionally the possibility of the evidence of distinctness, then, we emerge in the world of *experience.* We have thereby gone through in reverse order (reflectively) the sense genesis which was responsible for the originary constitution of the distinct judgment, and we have brought to light the intentional foundations of the judgment (*FTL,* p. 218 [194]). With our interest in the object we have in fact gone beyond the "pure" analytic framework of formal logic and are squarely within transcendental logic.

This is not all. In order to ground the evidence of distinctness of the judgment, the syntactic matters must maintain certain relations among themselves (relations of either concordance or exclusion). But these relations, the fact that syntactic matters "have something to do with one another," are in the final analysis grounded in the fact that every judgment presupposes a universal basis of experience which is itself regarded as a concordant unity of possible experience. And in this universal basis of experience of the world, everything is related to everything (*FTL,* p. 218 [194]). That is, the relations—whatever they may be—which the syntactic matters of the judgment maintain among themselves are a priori grounded in the concordant unity of universal experience (*FTL,* p. 219 [195]).

Thus the ideal identity that characterizes meanings and judgments is intentionally rooted in primordial experience. The presupposition of the being in itself of the meaning, whose absolute evidence in an imperfectly clarified distinctness the natural attitude uncritically admits, refers back to a subjective a priori, a transcendental and originarily constitutive presupposition. As a matter of fact, we will have to proceed even farther—from experience to the ego—to fully complete our reflective criticism of the presuppositions of formal logic. The intentional method which proceeds from the evidence of distinctness to experience is nothing but the transcendental reduction itself.

B. THE SECOND PRESUPPOSITION OF FORMAL LOGIC

§ 36. *The possibility of adequation of the judgment*

THE SAME QUESTIONS that we posed with respect to pure analytics we can now pose with respect to the formal logic of truth. We can thereby undertake to bring to light the subjective problematic of this higher formal logic.

Let us clearly situate the formal logic of truth. Mathematical analytics is an autonomous formal discipline; it does not become a new discipline when we go from the logic of consequence to the logic of truth. The logic of consequence simply undergoes a sort of "change of sign" when it integrates the problem of truth. Only the subjective attitude changes, and it is really the logical intentionality or logical function that is brought into play again by the logic of truth. It is in virtue of this function that the laws of mere noncontradiction become conditions of possible truth. It is also in virtue of this function that pure analytics becomes a *Wissenschaftslehre* strictly speaking—or, what is equivalent to this, a formal ontology (cf. *FTL*, p. 191 [169]).

Hence our present critical inquiry bears upon the subjective attitude presupposed by the formal logic of truth. Here, as before, we will encounter a presupposition which is naïvely thematized by the formal logic of truth and which anonymously presupposes a subjective a priori. The logic of truth is an objective formal discipline, and hence we cannot immediately bring up the constitutive thematic of truth. Truth is in fact the ideal telos of an originary dator evidence, the telos of the adequation of the judgment to the thing itself. But formal logic by definition disregards concrete material cores and considers only empty forms. Hence it cannot thematize truth subjectively. However, even as formal logic of truth it effects a certain objective thematization of truth. More precisely, it effects an idea(liza)tion of particular true judgments in order to elicit from them the logical principles of possible truth. The logic of truth thereby accepts an ideal formulation of possible truth; it accepts truth as an absolute immediate given, without concerning itself with the dator evidence in which it is constituted.

Formal logic cannot operate in any other way. Only subjective-phenomenological logic can effect the thematization of an intentional structure considered in its genuine sense as a constitutive and dator structure. In a word, formal logic can ideally formulate the logical principles, but only transcendental logic can intentionally motivate them. Only phenomenology is a subjective science of the subjective.

Hence we must begin by considering the way in which the logic of truth explicates the fundamental concept of truth in its logical principles (*FTL*, pp. 191 f. [170]). In this way we will discover the second presupposition of formal logic. Here is the statement of the principle of noncontradiction: "If a judgment is true, its contradictory is false." And the principle of excluded middle: "Of two contradictory judgments, necessarily one is true." If these two principles are brought together in a single statement, we obtain the following principle: "Every judgment is either true or false" (*FTL*, p. 66 [59]). The evidence of these principles must necessarily be subjectively grounded in the evident constitution of the concepts of truth and falsity. This means that we are going to investigate in a subjective attitude the *analogon* of the objective logical principles, which we can do by showing that the logical principle of noncontradiction is concretized in a process of adequation. Hence we obtain the following result: if a concrete judgment in positive material evidence can be brought to adequation, it must a priori be the case not only that its contradictory is impossible as a judgment at the level of the logic of consequence (in the narrow sense) but also that its contradictory cannot be brought to verifying adequation (*FTL*, p. 193 [171]. Thus only the noncontradictory judgment is capable of being brought to adequation. But we have thereby justified only the concept of truth. The concept of falsity can apparently be justified only by the exposition of a negative adequation. The constitutive criticism of the principle of excluded middle is what will give proof of it. "Of two contradictory judgments, one is true and the other is false." Hence we must, as before, suppose an adequation. But in this case, adequation is sometimes positive and sometimes negative, whereas, in the preceding case, it was only positive, since it a priori excluded contradiction. In the case of negative adequation, the concept of falsity is transcendentally justified. The principle of excluded middle therefore implies that every judgment can be brought to adequation, in either a positive mode or a negative mode. But this result clearly shows its extreme importance once it is expressed in a second and more direct formula: "Every judgment is capable of adequation." This is a presupposition which formal logic immediately admits, but without giving an account of it. It is the presupposition which makes the logic of truth itself possible but which condemns this logic to naïveté if the presupposition is itself not criticized and subjectively legitimized in turn (*FTL*, pp. 193 f. [171 f.]). Only then will this essential possibility of adequation on the part of every judgment become a genuine constitutive condition, legitimized as a subjective a priori.

§ 37. *The truth in itself of the judgment*

THIS IS NOT ALL. The judgment as such, in the strict sense of the word, is the judgment of the evidence of distinctness, i.e., the judgment of the logic of consequence. But the definition of the latter in no way implies the predicates of truth or falsity. Truth and falsity are not constitutive characteristics of the judgment strictly speaking. What is more, the judgment in itself implies no truth claim. The judgment is the telos of a judication; it is mere categorial belief (cf. *FTL*, pp. 121 [108], 196 [174]), which has no need of being constituted in an experience, in a "being persuaded in the presence of things that they are really such and such," in order to enjoy the ideal existence that is essential to the judgment strictly speaking. So, too, the logic of consequence or "pure" analytics is not a logic of truth but rather a logic of distinctness in the broad sense. However, just as the logic of consequence can take on its own logical function, so the judgment can admit a practical intention of verification. Thus it can undergo a subjective process of evident confirmation (*FTL*, pp. 196 f. [174]). This is a *functional* (i.e., intentional) extension (cf. *Ideas*, § 86), like the logical function of mathematical analytics. This interest in the object is nevertheless already written into the originary sense of apophantic logic, and the logician is thereby warranted in regarding every judgment as an assertion to be verified—that is, in short, as a truth claim (*FTL*, p. 197 [174]). Thus we are faced with a paradoxical situation. On the one hand, the judgment strictly speaking (in the evidence of distinctness) essentially involves no truth claim. On the other hand, its very essence—in virtue of the sense of apophantic logic—is to be a truth claim.[6]

This "remarkable" contradiction manifests itself again in another way. The two logical principles are summed up in a single formal statement: "Every judgment is either true or false." This does not mean simply that the scientist has the subjective (psychological) conviction that every judgment must be either true or false; it means that every judgment is *in itself* either true or false. The very essence of the judgment entails that it be either true or false. Every judgment is in itself and a priori determined or decided (*entschieden*) as to its truth or falsity. This decidability (*Entscheidbarkeit*) of the judgment, its character of being true or false in itself and a priori, is the formulation of the "naïve" presupposition of the logic of truth. The principle "Every judgment is either true or false" makes no reference to the possible adequation which alone could legitimize a judgment as true or false. It is admitted uncritically, as an evident and absolute given which apparently has no need of an intentional motivation.

This does not prevent Husserl from stating in the same passage that neither truth nor falsity is a constitutive characteristic of the judgment. The judgment is in itself neither true nor false; it includes no truth claim. On the other hand, the judgment is a priori true or false; its truth or falsity is decided a priori. This situation is indeed remarkable (*merkwürdig*), to say the least![7]

But we do not really have a contradiction here. Instead, we have an aspect of intentionality which cannot fail to give the appearance of a contradiction when it is expressed in analytical-logical language. Let us recall what we saw concerning the motif which shapes science and leads it infallibly, as it were, to its ideal telos. This motif is represented in our present study by the inexorable movement of surpassing on the part of the logical intentionality: from language to meaning, from meaning to object. Strict as the distinctions drawn by Husserl may be

6. Again we find the thesis that the evidence of distinctness is an evidence of clarity since, being unclear, it participates in clarity. Cf. above, § 30.

7. *FTL*, pp. 196 f. (174 f.). Notice in this passage the two points of view, *für uns* and *an sich*. This distinction should lead us toward the solution of this apparent contradiction by calling to mind the two dimensions of intentionality.

(and they seem all the more irreducible because they are expressed in an analytic language), they are nevertheless absorbed in a single intentional movement, that of the shifting of intentionality. Our present difficulty must be set within this dynamic dialectic. The judgment as such is traversed by an intentionality toward the object, that is, by an interest in verification or a truth claim. The judgment can always be regarded as a passive bearer (*Mit-träger*) of intentionality; in this case, the judgment is put "out of the circuit" of intentionality, and all claim to truth is removed from it. Thus it appears that intentionality itself is what determines a priori that the judgment is to be brought to adequation. The "naïve" presupposition must therefore be constitutively clarified in a subjective a priori. The truth or falsity of the judgment is indeed intentionally (teleologically) determined. But when the judgment is considered apart from intentionality (hence from a point of view which is that of formal analytics), it remains outside of validity (*ausser Geltung*). Formal logic considers the constituted product rather than the constitution. Thus the true and the false are determined in themselves by intentionality and will therefore be justified (evident) in a subjective thematic. But from the objective analytic point of view they do not represent constitutive characteristics of the judgment. Immediate inspection of the judgment does not disclose them; they are not seen (*angesehen*) in the judgment strictly speaking, that of the evidence of distinctness. As long as the intentionality of the judgment remains hidden and anonymously exercised, the ideal telos (truth or falsity) remains undetermined for it. This is a first, preliminary way of explaining how the judgment can by its essence (*eigenwesentliches*) exclude the predicates "true" and "false" while nevertheless being intentionally true or false. The analytic point of view in effect brackets the concrete intentionality that makes it effectively possible to determine the true and the false with respect to the judgment by revealing their evident reality.

But the judgment can also be regarded as being dynamically integrated in the intentional movement. In this respect it is a moment of intentionality and effectively participates in it while by itself partially realizing it. As an integral part of an ideal dynamic (intentional infinite) whole, it is pre-scribed eidetically or a priori.[8] Hence its telos can be ideally anticipated

8. Since everything, absolutely everything, is eidetically prescribed. Every objectivity, being transcendentally constituted, is

in an a priori form. Conversely, this ideal telos pre-scribes the process of its own realization. But what is the telos of a judication but adequation, positive or negative—that is, truth or falsity? The truth or falsity of the judgment is therefore pre-scribed a priori by the judication itself. This is another way of expressing the decidability of the judgment; the judgment is true or false in itself and a priori. Let us call to mind the results of Part I. The in-itself of real science in process of development, of the teleological movement of science, is ideal science, the idea of science. This idea is both eidos and telos, form and end; that is, it is the exemplary norm of science. For Husserl the in-itself is necessarily an extrinsic exemplary form. Hence, to say that the judgment is true or false *in itself* is to say that truth or falsity are *pre-scribed* by the present judgment—even though it is not known, in the absence of effective adequation, whether this judgment is actually true or false. If the presently actual judgment is regarded as such, it is neither true nor false; if it is regarded as anticipating its ideal in-itself, which is at the same time its telos, it is true or false in itself. In the one case there is a truth claim; in the other there is not. But conversely, the ideal telos of the judgment motivates and eidetically pre-scribes the process of its realization. The fact that the judgment is true or false in itself therefore implies that there is, *in itself*, with an equally compelling necessity, an intentional way which makes it possible effectively to attain positive or negative adequation of the judgment, i.e., its truth or falsity. This intentional way, which is simply that of the interest in verification, is therefore a priori possible and a priori determined (pre-scribed), even though it has never been followed to its end. This too is an astonishing (*erstaunlich*) a priori, since it implies that we know a priori that unknown intentional structures exist which have never been discovered in fact, since it affirms a priori the existence of unknown teloi and equally unknown ways of access (*FTL*, p. 197 [175]). Teloi and ways of access are therefore at the same time both determined and undetermined. Critical investigation and intentionality have a line of advance which is determined in itself as to the intentionality itself but which is presently undetermined for the actual and existing judgment. Hence, to say that the judgment is true or false in

the telos of the prior constitutive system of intentionality; and it anticipates its ideal and definitive telos, which is precisely its eidos, the idea in its full and perfect actuality. As in Plato, everything has its corresponding idea. Cf. *Ideas*, p. 376 (330).

itself implies that the telos of adequation, insofar as it is ideally anticipated, is a mere possible. Notice the form of the word *Entscheidbarkeit,* which expresses a potentiality. The truth or falsity in itself of the judgment is a mere presently ideated possible. The form *Entschiedenheit* would be misleading, since it would give the impression that the truth or falsity of the judgment is presently determined.[9] The intentional way to adequation that is pre-scribed a priori thus has us follow the infinite realization of a goal which is both determinate and indeterminate, to use Merleau-Ponty's words.[10] It commits this realization to a sort of teleological determinism on the part of intentionality itself, for which only the telos is determined in itself and which alone can infallibly have access to this telos. Everything happens, in short, as if intentionality were substituted for judgments (i.e., for judging subjects themselves, which become simply the bearers of intentionality) (cf. below, "General Conclusion").

Hence we have here a second way of justifying—this time in and by intentionality—why and how the judgment can be said to be true or false without thereby essentially attributing truth or falsity to it as constitutive characteristics. The judgment considered in its facticity cannot be said to be true or false in itself. Only the ideal judgment, the judgment idealized or ideated as having reached its telos, is true or false in itself. This is why Husserl writes that the predicates of truth and falsity pertain to the essence (*Wesen*) of the judgment. If this *Wesen* is the idea of the judgment, the ideal telos of the infinite process of judication, then naturally neither truth nor falsity can be constitutive characteristics of any actually existing judgment whatever.[11] The decidability (*Entscheidbarkeit*) of the judgment as true or false in itself is only the ideal anticipation of its effective adequation, positive or negative. It is established, then, that the truth (or falsity) in itself of the judgment is an

---

9. If we keep in mind the distinction between the descriptive-phenomenological and the transcendental-phenomenological points of view, however, we can accept as an alternative the form *Entschiedenheit.* In fact, the exemplary in-itself implies a perfect actuality, which is that of the value act. And we know that value act is only potency from the point of view of existence act.

10. Maurice Merleau-Ponty, *Phenomenology of Perception,* trans. Colin Smith (New York: Humanities Press, 1962), p. 446.

11. Cf. *FTL,* p. 197 (175): "kein konstituierendes Merkmal irgendeines Urteils als Urteils."

idealizing presupposition of the logic of truth. Even though Husserl does not continue his constitutive criticism, we can easily see that this presupposition brings us to the transcendental problem of adequation or verification—that is, the problem of *experience*.

§ 38. *Transcendental logic: subjective a priori of formal logic. Reduction of the judgment to experience*

THUS THE TWO PRESUPPOSITIONS we discovered in formal logic—that of the identical being in itself and that of the truth in itself of judgments—both lead us to the subjective a priori of experience, to nonpredicative evidence. The identical being of judgments (i.e., the *Objektivität* of logical configurations) amounts to an ideal (mathematical) existence which is originarily given in the evidence of distinctness and in the eidetic forms this evidence can assume in the various logical principles of a "pure" analytics. The truth in itself of judgments is also expressed in various ways in the various principles of the logic of truth. But principles of the logic of truth and principles of the logic of consequence are all principles of a single logic which is shaped by a single intentional motive, the interest in the object. Sooner or later there must therefore appear a reference to the objective, an explicit *Gegenständlichkeit*. This reference will be indirect in the logic of consequence, since it presupposes an intermediary thematization of the categorial meaning as such; in the logic of truth it will be direct, since truth is by definition the telos of adequation. In the first case, we have therefore discovered the presupposition of logic as formal apophantics; in the second, we have the presupposition of logic as formal ontology. But the two disciplines have one and the same subjective a priori: experience. The first supposes experience as a condition of the possibility of the evidence of distinctness; the second supposes experience as a condition of the possibility of truth in the evidence of clarity.

These two presuppositions must, however, be actually clarified and justified, and this requires the actual performance of the originary evidence in which they are constituted. The being in itself and truth in itself of categorial meanings are expressed formally in the principles of logic. These principles result from a generalizing-formalizing variation of a factical example. By definition, they are not at all concerned with the importance that the fundamental material core of every categorial meaning can assume. They consider only an empty form, the meaning of a "something in general," which any object taken at random (*beliebig*) may exemplify. The logic of consequence will take as example a factual identical categorial meaning, a certain factical judgment in its pure *Objektivität*. The logic of truth will take a true judgment, an evidence in its actual (imperfect) clarity. It remains only to vary these examples freely to form the mode of consciousness "judgment in general" and to read from it the fundamental laws of the eidetic sphere of judgments (*FTL*, pp. 214 [190], 192 [170], 198 [176]). Every such procedure is an idealization and presupposes the factical departure example (*Ausgangsexempel*). But these two features of the procedure raise a problem.

On the one hand, the example is *already there*. We have it "in hand" as the terminal product of a constituting intentionality, and it does not seem to require any intentional clarification (*FTL*, p. 214 [190]). In fact, formal logic does not seek any farther and does not pose any questions of constitution; it does not seek to establish a subjective thematic. It simply supposes the intentionality that is naïvely exercised and hidden in its sedimented result without investigating this intentionality, without even thinking that it should be investigated, indeed without even suspecting its veiled presence or its secret efficacy (*FTL*, pp. 200 [177], 214 [190]). This is the naïveté of formal logic, which recalls the one-sidedness of the positive sciences and ranges objective logic among the latter (cf. *FTL*, §§ 79–81). However, the logician obviously cannot be satisfied with so little. He will undertake to criticize the genuine sense of formal logic by uncovering its intentional genesis (*FTL*, p. 214 [190]).

On the other hand, logic accepts the idealization of the example without seeking the exact phenomenological status of this operation and its products. The logical principles are admitted as "self-evident," perhaps because they conform to a certain "common sense," which is held to be infallible since it is natural. But the question is precisely one of intentionally motivating this infallibility of common sense and criticizing these "obvious truths" that seem so self-evident. Husserl undertook this procedure, and we saw the difficulties that forthwith arose: the identity of meaning, for example, implies an ideal (intentional) structure thematized in the form of the "and so forth."

The critical and constitutive investigation thus has two tasks to accomplish. The first is to show that the "obvious truths" admitted as absolute principles of formal logic are in reality merely presupposed. The other—second, but more radical, since in the last analysis it grounds the former inquiry— is a reductive procedure which moves from the judgment as such to its motivating origin in experience and which therefore submits the sense of the judgment to an intentional criticism designed to reveal its genetic constitution from experience. Now that we have distinguished the various fundamental modes of the judgment, which partition formal logic into so many distinct formal disciplines, and now that we have further disclosed their constitutive concepts or "idealizing presuppositions" (being in itself, truth in itself), we must, finally, examine the constituting sense genesis that is implied in them (*FTL*, pp. 206 f. [183 f.]).

From this latter point of view, syntactic matters—that is, in fact, the individual as such—take on great importance (*FTL*, p. 214 [190 f.]). Formal logic can consider only universal forms from which the material content has been removed. A formal concept is therefore indeterminate as to the concrete individual to which it refers or can refer. Thus it cannot be known analytically whether S and p result from the formalization of an elementary syntactic matter or from one that is complex (a nominalized judgment, for instance). The form S is, however, essentially relative to the object (in an indeterminate mode). The effective relation to a certain object is explicitly suspended; the objective reference of the universal form is not individuated in any way. This is why formal logic can say nothing about the individual (*FTL*, pp. 203 f. [181]). The individual can be given only in an experience (which is the effective relation to the individual object) and in the particular judgment of experience (*FTL*, p. 206 [183]). In order to be able to trace the judgment to experience, we must make the ultimate elements of the judgment (the syntactic matters) "intuitive" in adequation by an evidence of clarity. But our last statement is not an "analytic" statement; it already goes beyond the framework of a formal logic. With the experience of the individual we are in transcendental logic. Since experience is what makes adequation (i.e., the truth of the judgment) possible, the genuine logic of truth is transcendental logic—which alone can include a *logic of experience* (*FTL*, p. 203 [180 f.]). Analytically, it can be said only that the sense of the judgment presupposes ultimate cores which are in necessary connection with individual objects. But the actual reduction to these ultimate cores goes beyond the analytic domain.

Only a critical reflection can recover the objective reference of the judgment, by tracing the genesis of its sense. Only an intentional analysis, in a phenomenological reduction of the judgment to experience, can regard the judgment not as mere *Objektivität* but as intention of an object. This reduction is at the same time clarification and motivation. Every judgment form, however universal it may be, is traced back to an individual judgment and thereby to experience. In particular, every universal subject form is intentionally reduced to an originary and primary form, which is that of the ultimate substrate—the immediately experienceable, simple, elementary substrate. Correlatively, every predicate form is traced back to an ultimate predicate, one which is no longer constructed from other predicates—a predicate which is likewise simple and elementary. The critical investigation here takes a course which is the reverse of formalization. It is the return to the concrete individual, the return to the object-about-which (*Gegenstand-worüber*) (*FTL*, pp. 202 f. [180]).

This return takes on different aspects depending on whether we have to do with formal configurations corresponding to a material a priori or with those corresponding to a formal a priori. The problem of evidence and truth (of clarification by return to the individual) is different in the two cases as a result of the different constitution (genesis) of the two a prioris. The material a priori originates in the reduction of an individual taken as factical example to its essential hyletic core. The formal a priori originates in the immediate formalization of any individual as a "something in general" (universal objective form). Consequently, the constitutive criticism of the first requires an exemplary intuition of its real point of departure, hence an at least possible real [*réale*] experience (*FTL*, p. 213 [189]). The constitutive criticism of the second needs only a free (arbitrary) illustration by any objectivity whatever.[12] In the one case a determinate individual intuition is needed. In the other case the

12. *FTL*, p. 213 (189 f.). The logical principles are obviously formal a prioris and are instantiated by any "individuals" whatever. This is why Husserl speaks in this passage of *Kategorialien* illustrating analytic a priori laws. Some judgments are material a priori; for example, scientific laws bearing on determinate material domains.

individual intuition is indeed necessary, but it is neither determinate nor limited to a certain material order of reality. Thus I can illustrate the object in general by an apple as well as by Spinoza's *Ethics*. In the one case the a priori preserves a certain hyletic content; in the other it does not.

Thus the reduction shows in general that every judgment has a priori a reference to an individual, in whatever way this referential relation is realized (*FTL,* p. 204 [181]). It follows as a correlative a priori that every truth pertaining to a universal judgment leads back to an individual truth—that every truth in general relates to a world of individuals (*FTL,* p. 204 [181]). This is how Husserl's statement that every judgment leads back to experience is to be explicated.

This reduction is, moreover, real [*réelle*]. It has a real terminus, not an ideal one located at infinity. The reductive procedure (at least the one we are looking at here) is finite; the ultimate substrate is a reality, not an idea (*FTL,* p. 204 [182]). For logic in its final sense is formal ontology, and it is here that this teleological sense appears. The effective reduction of the judgment to the individual judgment proves that formal logic itself inclines, in an ultimate (*letztlich*) way, to the service of a genuinely scientific interest. This is why it applies teleologically to the sphere of individuals (*FTL,* p. 205 [182]). Without this essential relativity to the individual (applicability) in the meaning of every logical intention (*Vermeintheit*), how would such an intention have a formal-ontological value (*FTL,* pp. 213 f. [190])?

Moreover, this reduction is at the same time a transcendental motivation; it exhibits the intentional foundations implied in universal (formal) judgments. It grounds the predicative universal in the predicative individual, then in the prepredicative individual. In a word, it grounds the judgment in experience.

In fact, the most immediate foundation the inquiry discovers is the individual judgment. The formal concepts of subject and predicate are grounded first of all in ultimate substrates and predicates. But here we are concerned with individual syntactic matters, and the direct relation to the individual is precisely experience. It must therefore be acknowledged that the individual judgment is a judgment of experience (*Erfahrungsurteil*) which is itself based on experience. For this is the originary evident judgment, which is immediately grounded in the correlative evidence of the experience of the *Sachverhalt* that is intended, i.e., in simple individual evidences. This is the judicative consciousness in the mode of originary givenness, and as such it precedes and grounds every other judgment.[13] This is why Husserl speaks of it as the origin judgment (*Ursprungsurteil*), as the "originary part" of the total judicative process.[14] The reduction of judgments to ultimate judgments therefore results in a reduction of judgments to experience. Three evidences are apparently involved in this intentional movement: the evidence pertaining to the formalized judgment, the evidence of the judgment of experience, and the evidence of experience itself. The reduction is thus progressively radicalized in passing from the first evidence to the second (both of which are predicative) and then to the third (which is prepredicative). We pass from the predicative world (more or less idealized in pure formal meanings) to the *individual life-world*. Reduction of the judgment to experience corresponds, as we will see later, to the reduction of science or of the idealized world (mathematized in a framework of rigid formulas) to prescientific originary experience, to the originary life-world. Science is necessarily situated at the predicative level of the judgment (since there is knowledge only in the judgment), and the world of experience is situated at the level of prepredicative experience—which is the level of what Husserl calls the *Lebenswelt*, the originarily lived world, the world of individuals and of individual truths.[15]

It must not be thought, however, that the *Lebenswelt* is situated purely and simply at the prepredicative level, on the hither side of all possible knowledge. It too implies a certain immediate knowledge, since it includes the judgment of experience. In an ultimate critical effort, reflection discovers an essential broadening of the concept of judgment to that of experience. Of course, as in any other manifestation of consciousness, the originary mode of givenness takes primacy; thus, in this case, the evident judgment takes primacy. But it must be added that

13. *FTL*, pp. 208 f. (185). Applying the general doctrine of consciousness, it can be said that in the predicative order this originary judgment is a "*Bewusstsein im Modus der Selbstgebung*" which precedes (*vorangeht*) every other judicative mode of consciousness.

14. *FTL*, p. 211 (187), and cf. § 86 passim. Likewise *EJ* sees in the judgment the "originary cell" (*Urzelle*) of thematic determination (pp. 63 [65], 212–15 [250 ff.]). Moreover, *Urteil* means "originary part" (*Ur-teil*).

15. We are using the word *Lebenswelt*, which is absolutely untranslatable, to designate the "place" where human theoretical life has its roots.

the judgment can be evident at a high level of formality. In this case, it is founded on prior judgments which are also evident, among which the judgment of experience is to be found. The evidence of the judgment in general is necessarily relative to that of the judgment of experience. But the latter is evident by virtue of adequation to its object. The individual judgment, which is what we are concerned with here, will be evident precisely by virtue of the evidence of its individual object. The evidence of the individual judgment is simply the evidence of experience (*FTL*, p. 209 [186]). The very concept of the evidence of the judgment in general therefore involves the evidence of experience, and the judgment of experience thus motivates a broadening of the concept of the judgment in general (*FTL*, p. 210 [186]). It is *in* the judgment, and not *alongside* it, that experience functions (*fungiert*) to insure the individual judgment of its evidence (*FTL*, p. 211 [188]). The judgment of experience is therefore in experience; it is a constitutive part of experience. Rather, it *is* an experience, and this is why formal logic must include a theory of experience. It is on the basis of the judgment itself that we discover that all the predicative categories traditionally attributed uniquely to the sphere of judgments belong already to the sphere of experience: assertion, negation, relation, certainty, modalities of certainty, and so on. All these determinations are preconstituted in prepredicative experience and are not the exclusive property of the predicative sphere.[16]

The reduction we have just carried out is therefore, in short, a turning from the evidence of logical principles to the evidence of experience (cf. the title of chap. 4 of *FTL*, Pt. II). That is to say, it is a return from the evidence of distinctness to

16. Cf. *FTL*, p. 209 (186). It is important to emphasize that *FTL* makes this discovery on the basis of the judgment. *EJ* asserts the same thesis, but on the basis of perception. This is a way of exhibiting once more the reciprocal unity of the descriptive-phenomenological and the transcendental-phenomenological points of view. Note again that the judgment in general is an "experience" insofar as it is evident. But, in the case of formal judgments, this "experience" is the originary experience of the individual not immediately but, as it were, intentionally—by way of the genesis of its own specific sense. In any case, the intentional structure of experience in general (the ideal infinity of the "and so forth") is found even in the formal judgment, since it too is an *Ideal-Objektivität*, the transcendent pole of a correlative noetic constitution.

nonpredicative evidence by way of the intermediary of the evidence of clarity. So the cornerstone of a theory of the judgment is the theory of experience, i.e., of nonpredicative evidence. This is a transcendental theory, a constitutive criticism which exhibits —although reflectively and "backwards"—the progressive line of advance leading from pure and originary experience to the idealized forms of formal logic. The transcendental theory of the judgment brings to light the sense genesis of judgments and reveals the various moments of their constitution. Judgments will now appear in their genuine sense as products constituted by an intentional genesis. And since it is a movement which has several stages (experience, judgment of experience, idealized judgment), the intentional genesis is a veritable *history* (*FTL,* pp. 207 f. [184]). This history is obviously sedimented in its own results, just as geological layers are stratified. But this sedimentation is the index of their historical constitution. All of intentional analysis consists in tracing the various moments of this history in order to reactualize it in its motivating entirety[17] and thereby provide a transcendental understanding of its sedimented results. In this reflective operation (*Nach-verstehen*) the products (in this case, the constituted judgments) are the guiding threads or indices for intentional analysis. The sense genesis itself makes it possible to discover the various constitutive evidences—each of which is found to provide a certain moment of the total constitution—and to order these evidences according to the objective level at which they have played a part in constituting the total product. This historicity of constitution is, moreover, a universal property of consciousness. The object in general, being an intentional unity, is the telos of a constitution and therefore the terminus of a historicity or intentional teleology. It is because there is a historicity of senses that there can be a reductive method (intentional analysis) that goes from what is constituted to its constitution (*FTL,* p. 208 [185]). The entire reflective and constitutive investigation we are conducting with regard to logic assumes the historicity of consciousness—which is, moreover, just another expression for intentionality itself.

We have now arrived at the positive result of our inquiry

17. In fact the motivation must be total. This brings us back to the structure of "and so forth," since an intentional totality is necessarily infinite and therefore ideal. Our current investigation is simply formulating the concrete subjective infinity of what Husserl has called the idealizing presuppositions of formal logic.

on the subject of the presuppositions of formal logic. The judgment as such is traced back to experience. This reduction is constitutive and motivating, since experience transcendentally grounds the judgment. It has two intentional moments. The inquiry first moves to the ultimate judgment, which is the judgment of experience. Then it establishes that the judgment of experience is immediately grounded in experience itself and that their mutual "proximity" is so great that we may unhesitatingly broaden the notion of judgment to include experience. This is why the transcendental theory of the judgment is essentially a theory of experience. The intentional theory of the judgment (*FTL*, § 91) is therefore a *logic of experience* or transcendental logic. Just as experience is the subjective a priori of the ideal presuppositions of the judgment, so transcendental logic is the subjective a priori of formal logic.

Now, all of phenomenology presupposes the phenomenological reduction. Hence we have here the *second reduction* of logic. The intentional analysis of science that we presented in Part I is an analysis within the reduction; consequently, the logic which that analysis made it possible to establish is likewise a logic within the reduction. This is immediately apparent for transcendental logic, but it is no less the case for formal logic. The latter is indeed a logic, a theory of science reduced to its noetico-noematic structure. Science thus reduced is inscribed in the flow of experience [*vécu*] or constitutive consciousness as one of its own *Leistungen* (of higher type, more or less idealized). As a science of a reduced object, logic is itself a reduced science. However, even though this reduction is primary and fundamental, it is only preliminary. From a radical and phenomenological point of view, the reductive process must be continued up to transcendental subjectivity—the only ultimate and therefore irreducible foundation.

Objective formal logic is thus put in question and its sense genesis is explicated. But it must not be forgotten that logic is science "formally considered" (*FTL*, p. 108 [96]), science in general, the science of science, the form and norm of every other science. If the *Wissenschaftslehre* is not limited for Husserl (as it is for the classical tradition) to a purely objective formal logic but is continued in a subjective criticism, it is therefore also the transcendental criticism of science in general. It insures the transcendental foundation of all the sciences and their unity in principle. But this foundation is unique and universal, and it is likewise valid for logic itself. Husserlian logic is therefore a transcendental criticism of science as well as a constitutive self-criticism.[18] This is why what we have seen concerning the reduction of logic to the *Lebenswelt* and to experience is true in general for every science as well. Reduction of the judgment, the object of formal logic, to experience is the form or eidos of reduction of the special sciences to the world of immediate experience. The constitutive criticism of formal logic therefore elicits the subjective form of science in general, its *subjective a priori;* it is a genuine *subjective formal logic,* a transcendental logic. Logic is therefore not one special science among others. It is what makes the sciences into sciences; it is the formal science par excellence. This formality manifests itself in two respects. As objective formal logic, logic norms science in general in an objective exemplary manner. This normation of science by logic, of factical science by ideal science, of fact by idea, is what insures the genuineness of science (*FTL*, p. 174 [156]). As subjective formal or transcendental logic, it norms in a subjective exemplary manner, since it elucidates the universal structure of intentionality which each objectivity will subsequently concretize in reality [*réalement*]. Logic is therefore the formal science from the analytic as well as the synthetic point of view, from the objective as well as the subjective point of view. It is normative both objectively and subjectively, since it is the universal theory of science (cf. above, § 20; below, § 51; and *FTL*, p. 173 [154 f.]). But this primacy is brought out in a more striking manner from the subjective point of view. A special science can be a valid science without being transcendentally justified (cf. *Crisis,* p. 26 [23]); but logic, which is the science of science, cannot be a valid logic without extending into a subjective thematic which clarifies its intentional implications. Logic is therefore in the highest degree self-criticism, and as such it is by definition a *Wissenschaftslehre.* Thus it is transcendental criticism of science in general.

Although logic formally insures the criticism of science by carrying out its own criticism, the one can nevertheless be studied separately from the other. That is, the criticism of science can be considered separately from the criticism of logic. Two of Husserl's works answer to these diverse concerns: the *Crisis* and *Formal and Transcendental Logic.* The first shows

18. This is the difficulty raised by *FTL* (pp. 173 f. [155]). We encountered this duality of Husserlian logic, which is also that of transcendental phenomenology, above (§ 19).

the reduction of science to experience (then to the ego); the second shows the reduction of logic to experience (then to the ego). With these two works, as we have already seen, we remain within the same dimension of phenomenological investigation—the descriptive-phenomenological point of view, which starts out with description of the given fact and ends, by way of (retrogressive) intentional analysis, with the constitutive origin of this fact. Only the exemplary value of the two procedures is different. Reduction of science to experience is a factical illustration of ideal reduction to experience, a reduction which logic considers in its eidetic generality and which we have just carried out. Hence it has a logical value; and again we find science in the legitimate sense of the word to be a particular case of science in general or of logic. With the reduction of science, then, we have a real (not an ideal) case of reduction to the experience of the *Lebenswelt*—the process of ideation, which is always possible, enabling us at any moment to reach the ideal level of logic. In other words, the reductive movement in *Formal and Transcendental Logic* is the eidos of that in the *Crisis*. Here again we find an especially clear manifestation of Husserlian exemplarism.

But how does this reduction of science to experience in fact take place—this second reduction, which begins to realize what the phenomenological suspension inaugurates?

2 / The Transcendental Reduction

§ 39. *The epochē of objective science*

IF IT IS TRUE that science is a particular case of logic, inasmuch as logic is science in general, we must expect to find a parallel movement here. Science too assumes an unclarified presupposition and thus leads us back to the subjective a priori of experience.

Science is guided by the idea that its object, the nature of things, is determined in itself and that consequently it is possible to elaborate a knowledge of this object which is true and absolute in itself. In a universal way, all knowledge pre-scribes its ideal telos of perfection, a state in which it would possess its object in an exhaustive and adequate manner (*Selbsthabe*). A teleology is therefore latent in all knowledge, even empirical knowledge. All knowledge aims at a perfection and exactness which it does not presently have and which remains a factually unattainable limit.[1] But this does not mean that this limit is an idea. This intentional structure implicit in every cognitive operation has not yet found adequate means of expression or rigorous thematization. It remains within the "approximately" of the empirical *type*, without attaining the pure eidos or idea as such.[2]

1. Husserl acknowledges a certain naïve intentionality prior to the phenomenological suspension; cf. *Crisis*, p. 236 (239).
2. Cf. *Crisis*, p. 25 (22). The type is therefore the empirical idea, so to speak; it is a general schema which defines the in-itself of a thing approximately by descriptively expressing what is not amenable to empirical comparison. This in-itself is obviously capable of growth if a new character of the object makes its appearance.

The application of mathematical science to knowledge, and to physical science in particular, is what makes it possible to thematize and adequately express this tendency to exactness which shapes even the natural attitude. And this application is at the origin of the unprecedented development of modern science.

Euclidean geometry already represented the ideal type of exact knowledge in antiquity and for Renaissance man. Its object is determined in itself and in an absolute manner; no approximateness is possible for the object of geometry. Moreover, the infinite world of mathematical being is pre-scribed in such a way that an ideal method of deductive-constructive thought can "discover" a priori the forms which already "exist" ideally and in truth (*Crisis*, p. 22 [19]). Geometry thus represents a type of a priori science which is independent of the real [*réel*] and which is capable of constructing an infinite domain of possible forms (*Gestalten*). The construction of this domain is at the same time the proper knowledge of the mathematical object, since the mathematical object is known only insofar as it is made or constructed. Can this not be seen as an adumbration or factical example of phenomenology as subjective and constitutive science of the sense of the world? However, mathematics cannot stop at mere ideal knowledge of a possible mathematical world. The geometer, aware of the ideal exactness of his constructions and concepts and (if he is something of a philosopher) aware of the striving of nonmathematical knowledge to attain an ever greater exactness, could not fail to think of applying his mathematical method to knowledge of the real world and thereby to the universality of being (*Crisis*, p. 22 [20]). This bold synthesis made it possible, on the one hand, to bring to physical science the exactness which it did not have, the ideality toward which it tended, and, on the other hand, to furnish mathematics itself with a material fullness (*Fülle*) which it lacked. The application of mathematics to physics, the mathematization of corporeal nature, is therefore advantageous to both mathematics and physics. By this means the material world can gain access to ideality, and physical knowledge can gain access to rationality. This is the principle of Galileo's physics (cf. *Crisis*, pp. 22 f. [20 f.]).

However, the mathematization of nature is not without complications. It introduces into physical-mathematical knowledge a relativity, an in-finitude, which pure mathematics by itself does not have. The mathematical world is, to be sure, infinite, since it is a possible world. But the mathematical object itself, this or that *Gestalt*, is determined in itself. It does not need to turn to an extrinsic principle for its own determination. The determination of mathematical being is an *absolute intrinsic determination*. The triangle is what it is, in itself and absolutely, and its characteristics accrue to it absolutely. The exactness of the mathematical object is an exactness in itself, not by participation (*Crisis*, p. 27 [24]). This absoluteness of mathematical science follows from the essential homogeneity (univocity) of mathematical being, which is purely ideal. But the application of mathematics implies by definition the connection of mathematics with a heterogeneous material domain. Physical-mathematical science is not univocal in the same respect as pure mathematical science. It tends toward a perfect homogeneity, which is ideal mathematization. But this is precisely a *tendency* toward an ideal or an ideal teleology. The mathematization of nature therefore amounts to an idealization by participation in the pure ideality of mathematics. The exactness of physical objects (that is, of physical cognitions) will be an exactness by participation in mathematical exactness. The latter normatively regulates the former (*Crisis*, p. 34 [32]).

Now, this idealizing teleology of physical-mathematical science brings out a certain dialectical duality between fact and idea, since mathematics applied to knowledge of the physical world abstracts the immediately mathematizable identical form (*Gestalt*) of this world. But this operation corresponds to a particular point of view, which is not that of the originary experience in which we are given natural objects. These objects are given to us originarily in a sensory fullness (*sinnliche Fülle*) which in some way "fills" the "form" that is abstracted by mathematical science. There is therefore one part of the material object which physical-mathematical science cannot consider: the sensible qualities of the object (color, sound, odor, etc.). The rationality and ideality of physical-mathematical science thus seem to be tied to an essential limitation of its object. They exclude everything that is the proper object of the senses, i.e., the proper sensibles (*aisthēta idia*), and retain only the common sensibles (*aisthēta koina*), such as extension and quantity (*Crisis*, pp. 29 f. [27]). In this way the distinction appears between the sensible thing (*Sinnending*) and the physical thing (*physikalisches Ding*), the former corresponding to sensible *imaginatio* and the latter to physical *intellectio* (cf. *Ideas*, p. 161 [127]). The tradition has completely transformed the sense of this distinction by substituting for it the distinction between secondary qualities and primary qualities. By attributing these two kinds of quality to specifically different orders of reality, as we shall see, the tradition has set the former aside as purely subjective and has made the latter the only transcendent (extramental) being.

Husserl believes instead that Galileo's undertaking consisted precisely in affirming the complete rationality of physical reality, i.e., the possibility of a complete mathematization of physical reality. Consequently, Galileo's thinking implied a radical continuity between *Sinnending* and *physikalisches Ding*, between what were later called secondary qualities and primary qualities. Although the latter have a certain privilege, in that they are immediately mathematizable, the others are at least not irreducible to them, since they are mediately mathematizable (*Crisis,* § 9c). Physical reality is therefore rational indeed; but this rationality, coming from the application of mathematics to the material domain, is an idea. That is, physical reality tends ad infinitum toward a complete mathematical rationality. This rationality is therefore exemplary; it does not determine the material domain in itself and absolutely but rather determines it extrinsically by mensuration or exemplary normation. The physical world tends toward rationality, toward mathematization. It can be said to be mathematical, or rational in itself, if this expression is given the sense it has in an intentional or exemplarist perspective, in which the in-itself is the ideal telos.

More profoundly, the (intentional or teleological) continuity in rationality and mathematical ideality is grounded in the evidence that the sensible thing (*Sinnending*) is not separable from the physical thing (*physikalisches Ding*). The sensible thing is certainly not the sign of the physical thing, since a sign never gives what it signifies in its "itself." But the sensible thing does manifest the physical thing, and the latter can be manifested only in it (*Ideas*, p. 160 [126]; *Crisis*, p. 33 [31]). In other words, the physical thing can be given only in a sensible manner, in the various sensible appearings which are, precisely, the sensible *Ding*. The physical thing is thus implied in the appearing of the sensible thing. It transcends the originary process of givenness of the latter, but it is not thereby transcendent to the sensible world given in consciousness or to consciousness itself (*Ideas*, pp. 161 [127], 163 [129]). Reason explicates in the nature which appears the physical nature which does not appear but which is manifested in it. Physical nature therefore has a transcendence that is higher than that of the sensible thing (*Ideas*, p. 162 [128]), but the two are mutually immanent in each other. What presents itself to consciousness in a bodily fashion is not only what strictly speaking *appears* of the thing but, quite simply, this thing itself, the whole of the thing in its global sense (*Ideas*, p. 384 [338]). And in this global sense, as one of its constitutive strata, the physical thing—the proper substrate of the exact determinations of physical science—is necessarily implied.

But the philosophical tradition did not take this orientation. It took into consideration only the radical distinction between *Sinnending* and *physikalisches Ding*. The latter alone was the true being of things, hence physical science alone determined the true being of things in themselves. The *physikalisches Ding* (i.e., the primary quality) transcends the entire content of the thing as it is given to us in the experience of its bodily presence (*Ideas*, § 40). Nature in its true in-itself is therefore mathematical. Every other (secondary) quality could be only subjective and could not meet the requirements of objectivity of a genuine science (*Crisis*, pp. 52 f. [53 f.]). Mathematical physics, guided by the idea of objective science, discards everything it considers to be dependent on the subjective sensible aspect of things, the data of sense perception, sound, color, odor, etc. It retains only extension (i.e., quantity) and makes this the very essence of the physical world. However, even though physics thus conceived sets aside all sense data as pertaining to the subject and consequently makes them the object of psychology (the science it deems to be concerned with the subjective), and even though it retains only what it considers to be the rational (mathematical) in-itself of material bodies, it nevertheless regards this rational in-itself as the *efficient cause* of the subjective data of perception (*Ideas*, p. 158 [122 f.]). This is why the philosophical argument has flourished which claims to infer the existence of the external world (i.e., the external world in its more or less known in-itself) from these subjective data of perception. This is an argument for which Husserl cannot find strong enough words of criticism. For him, a bond of causality between *Sinnending* and *physikalisches Ding* is an absurd or mythical conception (*Ideas*, p. 162 [128]; *FTL*, pp. 230 [204], 280 [247]), a blindness to the nature of external experience (*FTL*, p. 162 [144 f.]), a confusion between the ego and the human soul (*FTL*, p. 230 [204]; *CM*, § 10; *Crisis*, § 18)—and consequently between a priori intentional correlation and psychophysical causality (*FTL*, p. 252 [223]; cf. *LI*, pp. 593–95 [II/1, 421–24], *CM*, pp. 81 [115], 85 [118]). There are two reasons for Husserl's animosity. The argument in question in effect recognizes the distinction between secondary qualities and primary qualities as a real distinction in nature, whereas it is a matter of difference in degree of objectivity (a matter of an intentionality). Furthermore, it ends by substituting for the real and material world of physical bodies an idealized nature, a formalized and immediately mathematizable substrate, which for this reason appears only in its mathematical formulation. The world thus becomes an absolutely determined mathematical world. It no longer appears in its material, empirical, immediately experienced concreteness (*Lebenswelt*) but in a rigid brace, an ideal system adequately expressed in the mathematical formulas of a technized science which has lost the sense of its intentional origins. The immediate data of perception no longer have any objective or scientific value; they are "merely subjective." [3] Only idealized nature is in itself; only it is endowed with an absolute truth and an ideal exactness. This is the "naïve" presupposition of science: the *determinateness in itself of the physical world,* that is, the affirmation that the essence of the physical world is mathematical and is the object of an exhaustive ideal science endowed with an absolute truth. This presupposition has become quite "natural" in our generation. That is, it passes as a "self-evident" evidence, a primary and absolute truth which has no need of intentional clarification. The idealizing presupposition of physical science, and in general every ideal presupposition admitted a priori, is in short a *technization,* in the words of the *Crisis*. The criticism of the being in itself and truth in itself of the judgment in *Formal and Transcendental Logic* and the criticism of the technization of science in the *Crisis* are parallel (*EJ*, pp. 42–44 [40, 42]).

According to Husserl, the error is to have drawn such a radical distinction between secondary quality and primary quality, between *Sinnending* and *physikalisches Ding*. To make them two objects of different natures is to go contrary to intentionality itself. The first mistake, too—the technization of mathematics—is an obliviousness to intentionality and to the genesis of senses. It must never be forgotten that mathematics has its motivating origins in an empirical art of measuring areas (*Feldmesskunst*),

3. As if mathematical formulas (i.e., idealized nature), being constituted, were not subjective!

as the word "geometry" indicates (*Crisis*, pp. 27 f. [24 f.], 49 [49]). Thus it was, in the past, an elementary technique immediately applied to a practical interest. But the technique of measurement developed, and the art of calculating that is correlative to it benefited from this progress. From this point on a process of mutual influence is set in motion between the progress of geometrical technique and the mathematical art that it puts to work. For measuring an area involves in practice a certain science of calculation. If this science develops, measurement becomes easier. But conversely, measurement needs a science of calculation which is ever more advanced, and hence it requires the progress of mathematics. Geometric science is born for its own sake at the point when the art of calculation necessary to the art of measuring areas begins to develop independently, that is, when it becomes *technē* and method on its own account. It then exhibits an almost infinite spontaneity, which advances it ever farther in the discovery of its own ideal domain.[4]

But at this point the motivating origins in the world of immediate experience disappear little by little. Mathematics tends to consider its *de facto* autonomy as a *de jure* autonomy. It is technized, and it loses the sense of its origins; the memory of the constitutive genesis of its own sense grows dim. It then sets itself up as an ideal and self-evident a priori. There is a certain dogmatism *von oben her* in this attitude (*Crisis*, p. 49 [49]). But it is this already technized mathematics that is applied to physical science. This is the mathematics that is at the origin of idealized nature, of the system of mathematical formulas which is in fact substituted for the life-world (*Lebenswelt*). And if mathematics in itself has lost the sense of its own intentional origins, how could it be expected, under these circumstances, that physical-mathematical science—which is in a way born of mathematics—should have retained this sense and should not present itself as an absolute, determined and evident in-itself. It is the science of the world, indeed, and it thinks it has justified its undertaking when it has shown that its object is the world. But this reduction to a subjective a priori, which would be the a priori of the *Lebenswelt* (or, more precisely, of lived experience), stops too soon in an idealized world or mathematized nature (*Crisis*, pp. 48 [48], 50 [50]; *EJ*, p. 45 [43]). This has a great advantage from the point of view of mathematical-physical

4. *Crisis*, pp. 40 f. (40), 46 f. (46). This tendency is, moreover, necessary to every method; *Crisis*, p. 48 (48).

science, since physics seems to be motivated by this apparent reduction to the world, and, further, since this world (which is in fact an idealized world) is adequately expressed in the correlative science. In short, it appears that the world and the physical body are really determined, each one in itself, and that science itself reaches this in-itself in an absolute truth.

But there is an equivocation here. The world that mathematical physics considers is not the originary life-world (*Lebenswelt*). The "reduction" of mathematical physics to the "world" is not a reduction. The idealized world is nothing but the result of the very method of idealization. It is a "cloak of ideas" which has been substituted for the life-world, for lived experience, and which makes it possible to affirm the absolute intrinsic rationality of the world. This world is therefore nothing but science itself or, rather, its results. What we have here is a matter of noesis-noema correlation. If the object is determined and constituted in and by the noetic method, why be surprised that the object is adequately expressed by science? It is thus that—far from rising to intentional sources in the *Lebenswelt*—mathematical physics substitutes for the *Lebenswelt* a mathematized world, a garment of ideal formulas (*Ideenkleid*) that is the noematic result of a mathematical method of idealization. What physical science regards as the true being of the world is therefore nothing but method, method taken absolutely by itself, whereas this method is understandable only by and in its intentional reference to the *Lebenswelt* and to the experience of the *Lebenswelt* (*Crisis*, pp. 51 [52], 50 [50]; *EJ*, pp. 43 f. [41 f.]).

It is therefore a question of dismantling or "destroying" (*Abbau*) this ideal presupposition. The presupposition is dismantled when it is traced to its subjective a priori, when the idealized world of mathematical physics is intentionally clarified by showing what it actually is (*EJ*, § 10). We need not deny or suppress physical science. We must submit to intentional analysis the idealized world it presents and must exhibit the constitutive intentionality or historicity of mathematized nature. This intentional analysis by no means amounts to a depreciation of physical science or idealized nature; the movement leading from mere *doxa* to *epistēmē* is perfectly legitimate (*EJ*, p. 46 [44 f.]). A reflective procedure is necessary in order to rediscover the subjective a priori of mathematical physics. This is the reduction of objective science to the correlative a priori of the *Lebenswelt* (*Crisis*, p. 140 [143]; *FTL*, pp. 182 f. [162]). Mathematical rationality is then no longer the (intrinsic) determinateness in itself of the idealized world; the object is no longer the method. Rationality is the telos of an intentional process of rationalization of the *Lebenswelt,* and the object in itself is the terminus of the method.

§ 40. *The life-world* (Lebenswelt): *fundamental phenomenological problem*

IN SHORT, whether we propose to criticize logic as such (*Formal and Transcendental Logic*) or physical science (*Crisis*), we arrive at the same fundamental a priori: the *Lebenswelt.* Every science necessarily involves a motivating reference to the world of lived experience. The genesis of its sense, once explicated, shows a superposed series of more or less idealized evidences, each of which presupposes a primary evidence that is not idealized, an experience in an ultimate and originary sense (*EJ,* p. 45 [43 f.]). Every constitutive thematic of science and every logic thus necessarily extends to this originary world of experience. The reduction of objective science and clarification of its sense manifest the fundamental presence of the originary world. The *Lebenswelt* is pregiven to all scientific knowledge; it is the result of a simple act, the primary foundation of every composite act. Moreover, the word "pregiven" (*Vorgegebenes*) is completely legitimate only from this reflective-constitutive point of view. Every science is thus grounded and has its logical sense legitimized by and in its explicit reference to the *Lebenswelt.* The reduction of a science is a grounding of its validity (*Geltungsfundierung*), an originary motivation and intentional justification (*Rechtfertigung*), a constitutive sense-giving (*Sinngebung*). The critical discipline that thematizes science therefore thematizes in the first place science as such, which is formal logic; but it also thematizes the necessary foundation of this science, the *Lebenswelt.* Every logic will therefore comprise a study of the *Lebenswelt.*

From our present point of view, we must first say that the problem of the *Lebenswelt* is only one part of the problem of objective science (*Crisis,* § 33). The problem of the foundation of science cannot, of course, be the problem of science as a whole. In this case the dominant interest is obviously the interest in the "objectively true" world, i.e., in the idealized world of objective science, idealized as an act grounded in the originary

Lebenswelt. The latter interests us only in a secondary way, i.e., to the extent that it contributes to clarifying the sense of the idealization which it grounds (cf. *Crisis*, p. 133 [136]). It is regarded as the domain of forgotten subjective phenomena, as the domain of an anonymously exercised subjectivity, as the subjective foundation of an objective science (cf. *Crisis*, § 29). Hence we have not yet completely overcome the classical opposition between phenomena and objective reality, between secondary and primary qualities.

But we are about to witness a curious reversal. Just as logic first appeared to us as one science among others and in the end showed itself to be the absolutely primary science, so now we are going to see the partial problem of the *Lebenswelt* turn into a universal and primary problem. The *Lebenswelt*, too, can be thematized on its own account, prior to any question concerning its function as intentional motivation of an objective science. When it is thematized, its characteristic and constant sense or intentional being is what interests us (*Crisis*, p. 123 [125]). In this way, rather than remaining within the superficial strata of the constituted (science, idealized nature), we penetrate into the depths of the constituting. We put out of play every scientific attitude, every opinion, every objective intention. We consider only the intuitive *Lebenswelt* in which we all live and which is presupposed by every science. In this way we will see the constituting "engulf" the constituted and bring it back into the constituting itself, disparate as the two may be (*Crisis*, p. 123 [126]). Thus the dimension of the motivating depths of consciousness opens up. The way is free for reduction to the ego (*Crisis*, pp. 118 f. [120 f.]). But to situate ourselves thus "before" every theoretical and scientific interest is not to destroy or suppress idealized (objective) science. Instead, it is to carry out the transcendental reduction of this science. We preserve science as a real fact of the *Lebenswelt* and simply prohibit ourselves from performing its objectifying *Leistung*. We *disinterest* ourselves in its truth value; we suspend and bracket its theoretical interest (*Crisis*, pp. 135 f. [138 f.]). Every interest in the ideal objectivity of science is henceforth set aside. Our investigation is situated at a prior level. If a science can be elaborated in this way, it will obviously be the science of the *Lebenswelt*, a science never yet studied or even constituted, which seeks to establish phenomenologically how the *Lebenswelt* plays its role as foundation of all objectivity and of all objective science. But if this is the case, it is apparent that the science of the *Lebenswelt* cannot be of the same kind as objective sciences. It is of a different order. It does not conform to the universal idea of exact objective science; it is not, in itself, an objective science (*Crisis*, p. 124 [127]).

In fact, the only object of this science is the *Lebenswelt*, and immediate intuition gives the *Lebenswelt* to us as *subjective-relative* (*Crisis*, p. 125 [127]). Hence we can take over what the tradition affirmed concerning the sensible object (*Sinnending*) regarded as merely subjective. Secondary qualities were subjective for the tradition, and the *Lebenswelt* is subjective for Husserl. For the tradition, it is true, this is a subjectivity "caused" by a thing which is in itself external. For Husserl, it is a transcendental and hence constituting subjectivity. But this subjectivity does not preclude truth. A subjective givenness is capable of being expressed in a subjective truth, and precisely this subjective truth is what guarantees its adequate expression. To each object there corresponds a proper evidence and therefore a proper truth and science (*EJ*, p. 20 [12]; *Ideas*, p. 386 [340]; *FTL*, p. 161 [144]). Hence if we undertake to thematize the subjective *Lebenswelt* and still maintain its proper sense, we need a subjective science of this subjective object. This is by no means psychology, which is an objective (positive) science of the subjective. Instead, it is phenomenology, which is the only subjective science of the subjective (*Crisis*, p. 126 [129]; *CM*, p. 30 [68 f.]). This is the radicalism of phenomenology, which cannot be technized or fail to reach its terminus, since it is a constitutive investigation of originary sense. This is one of the arguments that makes it possible to affirm the absoluteness of phenomenology as apodictic science (*Crisis*, pp. 198 f. [202]). This science remains, and can only remain, in the domain of originary evidences, and it is intended only to establish their originary justification. To the extent that it succeeds in this task, phenomenology will have the higher evidences of ideal objectivities grounded in it and legitimized by it (*Crisis*, pp. 127 f. [130 f.]). The experience on which it is itself grounded is not the experience of the objective, which cannot be experienced in itself (*Crisis*, p. 129 [131]); the "objectively true" world is a logical "substructure" which is essentially unintuitive (*Crisis*, § 34d). Originary experience is an evidence which occurs only in the subjective-relative *Lebenswelt*, and the sciences idealize its result as objectivity in itself (*Crisis*, p. 129 [131]). But here the paradox of the *Lebenswelt* appears.

On the one hand, if the *Lebenswelt* is the realm of the subjective-relative, then for just this reason it grounds the objective-ideal domain of science, and the latter is radically different from the former (*Crisis*, p. 130 [133]). On the other hand, the epochē of objective science does not suppress the sciences. It modifies their value and makes them realities of the *Lebenswelt* (*Crisis*, pp. 135 f. [138 f.]). In fact, every scientific operation or theoretical-logical *praxis* belongs by itself to the concreteness of the *Lebenswelt* and is inscribed in it (*Crisis*, § 34e). Thus we have the curious situation that science is at the same time other than the *Lebenswelt* (grounded in it) and an integral part of it (enveloped by it). At a single stroke the problem of the *Lebenswelt* takes on a universality which it did not have when it first presented itself to us. It becomes the universal philosophical problem, since the epochē reduces science and scientific *Leistungen* to being only subjective configurations of the *Lebenswelt*. The problem of "objective" truth immediately becomes secondary, and the reversal is complete (*Crisis*, p. 133 [136]). The traditional opposition between secondary qualities and primary qualities is therefore definitively overcome, since both are thrown back into the subjective.

§ 41. *The thematization of the life-world* (Lebenswelt): *order of the questions*

Now WE ARE ONCE AGAIN at the beginning of beginnings. We can begin the entire philosophical enterprise on new bases. For this *Lebenswelt* is the world of the natural attitude, prior to any reduction. Since no philosophical writer can guide us in our task, we must begin alone in the naïveté which affects every beginning. Our undertaking is by definition—since it is a beginning—devoid of a sound theoretical basis (*bodenlos*). We can, nevertheless, immediately find by ourselves, if not this absolute foundation, at least a point of departure in the immediate intuition of the *Lebenswelt* as such. The natural attitude is therefore a first way, a "natural" and "naïve" way of thematizing the *Lebenswelt*. It even has the advantage of being immediate and first, at least from the chronological point of view. And since the *Lebenswelt* is essentially intuitable (*anschaubar*; *Crisis*, § 34d), we have in intuition the absolute beginning we are looking for. Thus we avoid setting out with a *point of view*. Immediate intuition is the point of departure that by definition gives us the thing as it appears outside of any other determination which might come from a preconception. It is the principle of principles, the beginning of beginnings (*Ideas*, p. 86 [46] and § 24; cf. above, § 16).

Thus the world is given to me; I am surrounded by an ever broadening horizon of determinations. I see in the present actuality of my *cogito*. In the natural attitude, the interest in things is "absolute" and does not allow me to detach myself critically from them. Since no object is isolated but all are surrounded by an infinite horizon of cooperating acts of validation (*Geltungen*; retention and protention) (*Crisis*, p. 149 [152]), the natural attitude really amounts to an *alienation* of the subject in the flow of his naïve perception (*Crisis*, p. 144 [146]). All my acts (perception, memory, volition, creation, etc.) thus necessarily refer to objects of the given world. The continuous actuality of my conscious life prevents me from reflecting on my own subjective operation. The *cogito* never turns back on itself, and the subjective a priori is not in any way explicit. The intentionality here (there is already a certain intentionality in the natural attitude) is a relation of real persons to real objects—of thinking thing to material thing, for example (*Ideas*, §§ 27–28; *Crisis*, pp. 144 [146], 149 [152], 235 [238]). A kind of knowledge is elaborated in this way, an empirical knowledge, a knowledge of the everyday which suffices for everyday "praxis." This is the world of common sense, whose opacity and consistency appear in such a way that they raise no doubt and motivate no process of intentional clarification. From this point of view, the objective sciences themselves come to be inscribed in the world like other objectivities. It is admitted that they are objectivities of higher type, but no more is said. Thus, common sense is satisfied with the naïve assurance that if the objectivity of the sciences is superior to that of the empirical world, this is because the sciences constitute the rigorous and rational knowledge of this world.

Moreover, the natural attitude always involves a practical interest in the object. The subject in the natural attitude is interested in the *Lebenswelt* in a quite concrete way, in the sense that man tries to subjugate the world and dominate it. Such an attitude, which is the natural outcome of everyday naïveté, is, however, scarcely favorable to the birth of a disinterested science of the world. The theoretical interest must therefore discover a *method* which will enable it to develop in a pure and disinterested manner, with an eye to genuinely speculative knowledge.

This is the sense that must be given to the phenomenological epochē and to the transcendental reduction which is its immediate consequence. It would be wrong to interpret the epochē in a context of skeptical subjectivism. The ambition of phenomenology is to understand (*verstehen*) the world and all objectivity in general. This ambition makes it possible to gauge the differences between this attitude and that of Kant, who seeks to guarantee the objectivity of science. Understanding is therefore a genuinely theoretical ambition, and it is realized by way of the transcendental reduction.[5] The latter is for phenomenology a means to theoretical knowledge; it expresses the theoretical interest. Insofar as the natural attitude is above all a practical attitude, it will feel a repugnance to this phenomenological attitude, which seems artificial to it (*Crisis*, p. 248 [251]). Thus the latter attitude is a theoretically pure way of thematizing the *Lebenswelt*, and this new method is inaugurated by the phenomenological epochē. We know what is meant by phenomenological suspension.

Husserl intends to make possible a genuine philosophical knowledge of the *Lebenswelt*. To this end he must rise beyond the world to a *point of view* which makes it possible to judge the world and take one's distance with respect to it. However, we must carefully distinguish between two conceptions Husserl forms of the notion of "point of view." No contradiction with what was said above is implied here. Immediate and originary intuition as an absolute beginning excludes every unjustified a priori. Intuition is thus situated prior to any point of view. By the latter expression Husserl means all the dogmatic positions (*von oben her*) of the *Standpunktsphilosophien* (empiricism, idealism) which settle upon the solution before having even posed the problem—or at least immediately see the solution in the formulation of the problem. "Point of view" is thus to be

5. *Crisis*, p. 189 (193); *FTL*, p. 275 (243). But this comprehension will be perfect only when the reduction has been carried out completely, all the way to the ego. In order to reach the ego, it is necessary to pass through the intermediary thematization of the correlation between world and consciousness. The latter having been discovered historically by skeptical subjectivism, it is therefore correct to say that phenomenology is the descendant of skepticism in this matter. Let us note, however, that in the teleological movement of science and philosophy, skeptical subjectivism is—with respect to the transcendental reduction—the factical example of the ideal exemplar, which is precisely phenomenology (*Crisis*, p. 165 [168]).

understood as "prejudice" in the pejorative sense of the word (cf. *Ideas*, p. 86 [46]). The point of view that phenomenology establishes in the epochē is, to be sure, a position *beyond* the reduced *Lebenswelt*. But it is not a *presupposed* position with respect to the *Lebenswelt* since, on the contrary, the *Lebenswelt* is what is "presupposed" in the point of view that the epochē establishes on it. Here the same phenomenon reappears as in the case of logic and in that of the *Lebenswelt*. The epochē is inscribed at first in the time of the *Lebenswelt;* it has its time of insertion or vocational time (*Berufzeit*) before being defined as a fundamentally new attitude which rises beyond time and makes it possible to gain access to its foundation (*Crisis*, § 35). Here too there is a radicalization of the process, which can only accentuate the reflective character of the epochē. Thus the epochē always presupposes the *Lebenswelt*.[6] In short, since the *Lebenswelt* is immediately intuitive, it is obvious that, if it is presupposed, this cannot be in the pejorative sense but rather in the positive sense, in the sense that every undertaking requires an absolute beginning. Moreover, this point of view is justified by way of the natural attitude itself. The latter leads to the realization of a practical interest rather than a theoretical interest. The theoretical interest is "diametrically" opposed to the practical interest, since it refuses to abandon itself to the real flow of the *Lebenswelt* but, on the contrary, resolutely holds itself apart from this flow and suspends (epochē) the world in its concrete existence. The theoretical interest truly emerges when an appropriate method enables the "pure" scientist to rise beyond the self-forgetfulness of the natural attitude (*FTL*, p. 15 [14]), when the epochē neutralizes the alienation of the subject in the world. Thus the epochē really manifests and expresses the theoretical interest, which could not operate in the state of alienation. The theoretical interest must be freed from this shackle, natural and tenacious as it may be, which Husserl calls the pregivenness of the world (*Vorgegebenheit der Welt*) (*Crisis*, p. 151 [154]). The epochē is what performs this *liberating* function. When the *Lebenswelt* becomes a problem for the theoretical interest, knowledge must choose a point of view external to it in order to judge it (cf. *Crisis*, p. 122 [124]). This choice is essentially free, since the epochē itself is free;[7] but it is

6. From the descriptive-phenomenological point of view.
7. *Ideas*, pp. 107 (64), 109 (65), 110 f. (67); *LI*, p. 537 (II/1, 348); *CM*, p. 25 (64); *Crisis*, p. 237 (239 f.). [A substantial part

not arbitrary. It is required by the very nature of the theoretical interest it expresses. The natural attitude therefore undergoes a profound modification in the exercise of the theoretical interest (the phenomenological epochē). The naïve world changes its value, although it is not devalued (*entwertet*) (*Ideas*, pp. 108 f. [65], 111 [69]; *CM*, pp. 19 f. [59 f.], 25 [64]). A new life of consciousness is required, a reflective life instead of naïve abandonment. The theoretical knowledge interest can express itself in us only in a reflective manner (reduction), since the natural attitude is an alienating abandonment; it requires a conversion comparable to a religious conversion.[8] Instead of letting myself live in and through the natural world, I refuse to perform the existential positing which the natural attitude "forces" out of me (alienation). I do not suppress or cancel the world, but I do not perform the validation of its being (*Seinsgeltung*). I disinterest myself in its being and its appearance (*Sein oder Schein*), in its reality or unreality, in its existence or nonexistence (*Sein, Wirklichsein, oder Nichtsein*) (*Crisis*, pp. 175 [178], 236 [239]; *CM*, pp. 30 [69], 33 f. [72], 36 [75]). I consider only the noematic content of my affirmations regarding it. Thus the world does not disappear for me. The epochē neither suppresses nor loses the world but in a way neutralizes it, leaving in suspense all relativity to real or existential being (*Ideas*, pp. 154 f. [119], 374 [329]; *CM*, pp. 19 f. [59 f.], 36 [75]). My ego is in a way divided in two, and it sets itself up with regard to the world as a *disinterested spectator*.[9] When I observe that the world still subsists despite the suspension of its being value (*Seinsgeltung*), I should not be surprised. If it effectively subsists in a purely noematic form, it is then the immediate correlate of its constitutive noesis. The world reduced to the rank of transcendental phenomenon by the epochē shows itself to be the immediate correlate of consciousness. What the epochē

of the passage on p. 67 of *Ideen I* which the author cites here is omitted in the English translation.—TRANS.]

8. *Crisis*, pp. 137 (140), 150 (153). This conversion is "useless foolishness" from the standpoint of natural human understanding (*Crisis*, p. 200 [204]).

9. *CM*, pp. 35 (73), 37 (75); *Crisis*, pp. 157 (159 f.), 238–40 (241–43), 244 (247), 255 (257). The notions of "point of view" and "disinterested spectator" are obviously correlative and express the same reality in two ways. On "point of view," cf. *Crisis*, pp. 150 (153), 152 (154 f.), 175 (178), 181 (184), 184 (188), 238 f. (241 f.). The Greek word *epochē* itself designates this notion of "point of view from which one withholds oneself."

accomplishes is to bring out this a priori correlation;[10] i.e., it reduces the pregiven world in its naïve being value to the transcendental phenomenon "world," the noema "world" (*Crisis*, p. 152 [155]). The suspension of the natural attitude or phenomenological epochē of the existential validity of the world results in the reduction of the world, now regarded as transcendental phenomenon, to constituting subjectivity.[11] Here we have in summary form that phenomenological operation which has already given rise to such an abundant literature and which is in principle quite simple. The transcendental reduction inaugurated by the epochē is in its full sense the intentional (reflective-constitutive) analysis of the pregiven world and its motivating rootedness in transcendental constituting consciousness. It is intentionality itself in its descriptive-phenomenological dimension. The *Crisis* gives two examples of reduction. One, the more familiar, is that of the pregiven physical world and hence, correlatively, of objective physical science; the other is that of the natural consciousness of the world and hence, correlatively, of psychology as objective science.[12]

The phenomenological suspension immediately brings out the a priori correlation between constitution and constituted, between noesis and noema, between consciousness and the world. It immediately manifests the two-sidedness of transcendental investigation (cf. *CM*, § 17; *FTL*, §§ 8, 55). This is a two-sidedness *within* the transcendental reduction, since transcendental investigation is at the same time noematic and noetic. But we must follow the organic genetic articulation of intentionality and not expect to reach the terminus (telos) of the procedure at a single stroke. Although the epochē leads us in a global and immediate way to subjectivity,[13] we must observe that this subjectivity comprises various strata. It will be necessary first of all to thematize the transcendental phenomenon "world" and

10. *Ideas*, pp. 112 (70), 259 (220); *CM*, p. 37 (75); *Crisis*, pp. 151 f. (154 f.), 181 (184), 238 (241), 243 (246), 244 f. (248). This correlation is clearly intentionality.

11. The epochē and the reduction must be distinguished as two moments of a single operation, and they must be regarded in an efficient ordering of antecedent to consequent.

12. *Crisis*, pp. 103 f. (105 f.), 191 f. (194 f.). The phenomenological-psychological reduction is therefore a type of transcendental reduction (*Crisis*, p. 236 [239]).

13. *Crisis*, pp. 149 f. (152 f.), 239 (242). The epochē neutralizes, and neutralization is immediate. By contrast with imagination, it cannot be repeated (*Ideas*, § 112).

then trace it definitively to its ultimate origin, the pure spontaneity of transcendental consciousness. For although the reduced world is by definition a transcendental phenomenon in consciousness—although, as subjective-relative, it is inscribed in the universal flow of pure experiences of consciousness—it is, nevertheless, a phenomenon, i.e., a noema, the object of a genuine transcendental experience (*CM*, p. 27 [66]; *Crisis*, p. 153 [156]). This new experience sees in it a noematic world whose singularities have an immediate eidetic value and which, like every world in general, has a structure of the known and the unknown, the two mutually influencing each other and changeable according to the same index.[14]

We must never lose sight of the two dimensions of intentionality which we have so often pointed out. In the transcendental-phenomenological dimension, the epoché immediately reveals transcendental constituting consciousness to us, and it is by means of the epoché (hence through the intermediary of the noesis) that progressive analysis reaches the noema. The noema is therefore immediately considered in its value as telos, as intentional unity. This is the line of advance in *Ideas* and, to a lesser extent, in the *Cartesian Meditations*, and it is obviously of Cartesian inspiration. From this point of view, consciousness appears to us at first as the phenomenological *residuum*, as what remains after the epoché of the world and of the natural attitude; and the reduced world appears as a transcendental *nothing* (*Ideas*, §§ 33–34 and p. 172 [137]). Consciousness is a "surplus." However, Husserl cannot stop with this negative definition, essential as it is since it is chronologically first. We soon reach a positive and genuine definition of consciousness: transcendental consciousness, the center and point of departure of transcendental systems of constitutive intentionalities—the ultimate reference and absolute presupposition. Hence, from the transcendental point of view we find in the context of the definition of consciousness a procedure analogous to the one we followed above in order to define logic, the *Lebenswelt*, and the epoché. Just as logic seemed at first to be a particular science,

14. *EJ*, p. 37 (33). Every actual consciousness has a twofold potential horizon, that of retention (*Noch-im-Griff-behalten*) and that of protention (*Vorgreifen*). This dual structure, which is essential to the sense of actual consciousness, is modified correlatively with the same index as the presently actual instant, in its course determining time itself. Cf. *EJ*, pp. 108 (118), 121 (136), 167 (194); *Ideas*, pp. 102 f. (59), 238 (199 f.).

just as the *Lebenswelt* seemed to be a partial problem of the critical thematic and the epochē seemed to be one theoretical occupation among other human interests, so consciousness is presented in *Ideas* first as a residuum and then as an originary and absolute *Leistung*. This is why the exposition of the reduction in *Ideas* presents an abrupt and almost forced procedure, which is not the case in the *Crisis*. The structure of intentionality is *ego—cogito—cogitatum*, and all intentional investigations must be organized following the three elements of this structure. But *in fact*, for us who are at the beginning of our phenomenological procedure, which of these elements is given first if not the *cogitatum?* The *cogitatum* is the constituted; it is what is pregiven to the natural attitude, which always presupposes constituting subjectivity. The epochē reduces the *cogitatum* to the rank of pure phenomenon immediately correlative with subjective constitution. That is, the epochē makes the *cogitatum* appear in itself in its value as constituted, as index of its own constitution, as guiding thread. Thus, from the point of view corresponding to the descriptive-phenomenological dimension, the *cogitatum* or noema appears first as thematic index of constituting intentionalities and not as intentional telos (as is the case from the transcendental-phenomenological point of view).

If the reduction is to be an immediate return from the natural world to the ego (as it is in *Ideas*), the procedure takes on a sudden and abrupt character, without a transition, devoid of a continuous intentional (retrogressive) explication of all the implications contained in the constituted. The world is instantaneously suspended and surpassed; it is even ignored as a transcendental phenomenon. So consciousness can be defined, first of all, only negatively, as "that which remains"; this is the sense of the expression "phenomenological residuum." [15] But from what we have seen, it is clearly possible to take a more "natural" and less "violent" way. If the constituted is in fact given first of all in descriptive or historical experience (immediate intuition before and after the epochē)—and our study gives a prime example of this in Part I, with the case of science—we can, to begin with, consider the constituted in and for itself, but without ever losing sight of the fact that it is constituted, i.e., without technizing it. To this end we suspend the being value which the natural attitude naïvely accords it and thus reduce it to the rank of transcendental phenomenon or pure noematic meaning. But

15. Cf. the very pertinent notes of P. Ricoeur, *Idées*, p. 106, n. 4.

the suspension of the naïve relativity to existence, the bracketing of the naïve *Seinsgeltung,* brings out the transcendental relativity of the noema to the noetic process of its subjective constitution. The a priori of correlation between world and consciousness thus appears by virtue of the transcendental reduction. We have in this reduction the *cogito* strictly speaking (the *cogitatio*). An ultimate reduction is enough to make the ego appear in its purity as originary constitutive act. This procedure, which is that of the *Crisis,* is simpler and more "natural" than that of *Ideas.* Husserl thus prefers it in the end, to the point that he expressly rejects the Cartesian way.

He is aware of the advantage of the Cartesian way, however. It is shorter; the ego is reached at a single stroke (*in einem Sprunge*). The method is therefore immediate. Its shortcoming is that it gives the illusion of the *emptiness* of consciousness (it always implies the definition of consciousness as residuum), since the world is, as it were, suppressed at a single stroke and is recovered only later, by way of the study of constituting intentionality. Since the point of departure in such a phenomenologically immediate way is the ego, the point of view is immediately transcendental; and because of the apparent emptiness (*Inhaltsleere*) of the ego, it runs the risk of being interpreted again in a naïve way—as it was by Descartes, for example, who could not conceive the pure ego except as a real [*réale*] thought (soul) (*Crisis,* p. 155 (157 f.); and cf. pp. 75 f. [76 f.], *CM,* § 10). This real soul would be empty by itself, without the efficient causality exercised from outside it by real things or by God. The Cartesian way therefore runs the risk of ignoring the important fact that the reduced ego is by itself the object of an unlimited transcendental experience and that it can therefore be explicated in itself, as independent of the existence or nonexistence of the world. A genuinely phenomenological position could not fall into the Cartesian trap, and it makes useless the attempt to infer the external reality of the world demonstratively by the dogmatic argument from causality. Hence Husserl wants to avoid any appearances that would lead one to think that phenomenology goes along with historical Cartesianism. What is at stake is the definition of consciousness. Can it be defined immediately as a full consciousness, as a concrete subjectivity? Or must we necessarily pass through the intermediate definition of consciousness as a residual void? In the latter case, it must be recognized that not every danger of historical Cartesianism has been avoided or that, at best, we go from it to a Kantian conception of consciousness. But *Ideas* did not fully resolve the difficulty. The transcendental-phenomenological way, at least as it is treated in *Ideas*, does not avoid all possibility of deviation. The *Cartesian Meditations* have the merit of showing a phenomenological "Cartesian way" that is impeccable from the transcendental point of view itself. To be quite precise, it must be said that the *Cartesian Meditations*, while they are organized strictly according to the transcendental-phenomenological dimension, try to open up a way that is intermediate between the latter dimension and the descriptive-phenomenological. The immediate point of the departure is, to be sure, consciousness itself (transcendental-phenomenological point of view). But this is a concrete consciousness, full of transcendental phenomena playing the role of indices or guiding threads (descriptive-phenomenological point of view) (*CM*, p. 31 [69 f.]). The organization of the investigation is *ego—cogito—cogitatum,* in precisely the order indicated by this proposition. However, the *cogitatum* introduces the *cogito* and then the *ego* (*CM*, p. 50 [87]). In the *Cartesian Meditations* we therefore have an order which is clearly transcendental-phenomenological but in which the *cogitatum* is nevertheless taken—as it is in the descriptive-phenomenological order—as constituted index of its constitution rather than as telos.

This is why, when we say that Husserl departs from the Cartesian way, we mean that he departs principally from the Cartesian way as it is exposited in *Ideas*. Moreover, it is *Ideas* and not the *Cartesian Meditations* that he criticizes (cf. *Crisis,* p. 155 [157]). However, Husserl seems in the end to prefer the way indicated by the *Crisis,* which is exclusively the descriptive-phenomenological way. Perhaps we are to see here a didactic or "existential" preoccupation (the concern to show that the *Wissenschaftslehre,* in spite of its dryness, implies an intentional analysis of human striving and hence, in the end, an analysis of human life—the longing for knowledge and happiness—in all its aspects). It is certain that the *Crisis* gives us a phenomenological way that is easier and less abrupt than *Ideas* and more subjective than the *Logical Investigations.* On the other hand, it is certain that the *Cartesian Meditations*—by undertaking to show a middle way between the two possible dimensions of intentionality—correspond to an ultimate point of view, the last word of phenomenology, the identity of the descriptive-phenomenological and the transcendental-phenomenological dimensions of intentionality (cf. below, "General Conclusion").

But according to the *Crisis* (i.e., in the descriptive order), the first step is a thematization of the *Lebenswelt* (*Crisis*, p. 155 [156 f.]). Of course the headings of the analysis remain, and our investigation is structured according to the three moments of intentionality: *ego—cogito—cogitatum*. These "Cartesian" headings are already announced by Husserl in *Ideas* (p. 112 [70]). But in the *Crisis* he puts them in a new order. He expressly contrasts himself with Descartes and defines his method "in opposition to the Cartesian way" (*Crisis*, § 43). The order he indicates is the reverse of Descartes's: *cogitatum—cogito—ego*. The first descriptive element is the *Lebenswelt*, and hence the *Lebenswelt* is, in a phenomenological perspective, the index or guiding thread that is going to lead us to the ego pole through the intermediary of the subjective modes of givenness. The *cogitatum* is, therefore, the objective at which every intention aims, the objective pole of intentionality (*Gegenstandspol*). The *cogito* is the act of representation (intuition or thought), the originary constitutive and sense-giving act (*Erscheinung von Etwas*). The ego is the subjective pole, the center from which all the constitutive intentionalities emanate (*Richtung auf Etwas*). Intentionality as a whole is thus a *bipolar system* whose actuality is expressed and guaranteed by the *cogito* (*Crisis*, pp. 171 f. [174 f.]).

Thus, here again we will follow the descriptive-phenomenological order by proposing to realize the plan that is only indicated by Husserl in the *Crisis*. The epochē reveals to us the transcendental phenomenon "world." This phenomenon as such, this noema, is what we will study first of all—the *cogitatum* of a constituting *cogito* of the *ego*.

A. THE *Cogitaum*

IF THE REFLECTIVE STUDY of intentionality comprises three headings, the transcendental reduction must be regarded as a total operation in which three stages can be distinguished, three partial reductions in an essential and dynamic continuity. The final sense (*Endsinn*) of the universal reduction is, to be sure, the explication of the ego, the ultimate foundation. But this ego comprises several strata of transcendentality (*Crisis*, pp. 171 f. [174 f.]). The transcendental phenomenon and correlation (the act of the *cogito*) are two examples of these strata which represent in different respects *Leistungen* of the ego. Correlatively, transcendental experience must be seen as a total experience in which several specific levels can be distinguished, corresponding to the various headings of intentionality. And since this transcendental experience can only be reflective, we will have three levels of reductive experiences, three increasingly radical stages of reflection, which bring us from the immediate evidence of the object to noematic reflection strictly speaking on the *cogitatum*, to noetic reflection on the *cogito*, then at last to the ultimate reflection on the *ego* (*Ideas*, p. 409 [362]). These three stages are in a univocal continuity and mutually continue one another following the schema of the shifting of intentionality. They may seem to be three distinct reductions, and this may lead us to believe that the transcendental reduction is not unique but multiple. This is clearly not the case. The reduction is one and universal, but it is an intentional analysis tracing the chain of motivating implications up to the absolute foundation.

The first reflection inscribed in the unitary and universal movement of the transcendental reduction is therefore noematic reflection on the natural experience of the world. The natural attitude gives us the world immediately. By suspending for a first time the natural thesis of the world, the epoché brings us back from the naïve self-forgetfulness of natural evidence and manages to grasp what is intended as such in this natural experience. This first reflective evidence therefore gives us a *new world*.[16] Noematic reflection is indeed reflective; but within reflection it possesses a certain immediacy, coming from the fact that it is directed exclusively on the noema. The subjectivity of the noema is what accounts for the ambiguity of noematic reflection.

§ 42. *Pure description and phenomenological naïveté*

THIS WORLD IS NOT, strictly speaking, new. It is really the same world as before, but reduced to its noematic meaning (*Vermeintes als solches*). The epoché neither destroys nor suppresses the natural world; the natural attitude simply changes

16. Cf. the analogous noematic reflection in the case of the judgment *schlechthin* and the judgment at a second level (*FTL*, p. 132 [117]).

its sign. The reduced world is a world whose existence or non-existence the phenomenologist does not take into consideration. The reduced attitude is a new attitude, one which keeps the same theoretical content as the natural attitude but assigns it a new sign. The matter remains, but the thetic character is modified. From now on the world presents itself to phenomenological investigation with a new ingenuousness. The world is what is given solely as such. It is what it is, and in an evident originariness. The reduced world, being a mere "intended," is in effect transparent and essentially intuitive. The glance penetrates it throughout and is not stopped in its immediate grasp by the opacity of an unjustified presupposition. The question of being value (*Seinsgeltung*) and truth value is suspended. In accepting a pure noematic intention in an immediate evidence, the phenomenologist does not run the risk of accepting a positional and existential character that has not been clarified. The epochē allows to remain of the world only what is intended (*vermeint*) in our affirmations. It brings us to an essentially intuitive world, an immediate transcendental experience which justifies itself by virtue of its very immediacy and which sets aside all the opaque presuppositions of the natural attitude—i.e., all the value judgments the natural attitude brings to the originary *Lebenswelt*.

But if, on the one hand, the world as intended is immediately intuitive, and, on the other hand, all mundane prejudices are suspended in it (contrary to the natural attitude), the phenomenologist can let himself be led by the stream of his immediate transcendental experience. The reduced world appears as a diverse and changing multiplicity. All these phenomena can be described in a purely phenomenological manner if the phenomenologist applies himself to following step by step the noematic manifold of his experience, if he lives in the continuous flow of his transcendental experience. For if the epochē (or rather its first stage, noematic reflection) immediately gives us a "new" world, this new world must be "lived." We came across this process of living an intentional structure (*hineinleben, dahinleben*) in the intentional analysis of science. The phenomenologist reduces science and lives its noematic tendency (*CM*, § 4; *FTL*, pp. 8 f. [8]; *Crisis*, pp. 70 f. [72], 98 [101]). So too, in considering the reduction of the psychological ego as it is given in the *Crisis*, we end with a field of transcendental experiences of the reduced ego which we can live subjectively as disinterested spectators in order to discern its noematic sense. We then have before us an infinite horizon of pure intentional life taken in its primary originariness, prior to every prejudice that is constituted and admitted in itself without clarification (*Crisis,* pp. 239 f. [242 f.]). Whether we consider the transcendental reduction primarily as the reduction of the natural world, of the psychological consciousness of the ego, or of objective science, our first phenomenological step is always a pure description which goes through the domain of transcendental experience of the reduced object, the domain of the ego's self-experience as bearer of its transcendental phenomena, and devotes itself to the inherent evidence of this domain.[17] There is a sort of naïveté here, to be sure, since the phenomenologist abandons himself to the flow of his experience and thus lives in the reduced world as he lived, before the epochē, naturally in the natural world. All the descriptions of the natural attitude, whether these describe the naïve experience of the world or that of the ego, can be taken up again here. But it must be understood that the epochē and the transcendental reduction are meant to establish a certain theoretical *ingenuousness* which does not have the drawbacks of the naïve natural attitude. In the epochē, the natural world must be lived naturally.[18] If there is naïveté here, is it not the naïveté of fidelity to the principle of principles? Does the firm resolve to admit only what is immediately intuitive not imply a certain abandonment to what is immediately given? In this sense, intuition is itself naïve. But a phenomenological intuition does not run the risk of alienating the subject from himself. Worldly interests are suspended; phenomenological naïveté is nothing but the originariness of the intuition of the transcendental phenomenon. It is therefore a naïveté within the epochē, a phenomenological and legitimate naïveté. It consists in grasp-

17. Husserl distinguishes two stages in the work of transcendental phenomenology (*CM,* p. 29 [68]; *FTL,* p. 286 [252]). Here we are concerned with description of the reduced ego.

18. *Crisis,* p. 176 (180). Thus life in the reduced world is the same life as that in the natural attitude, but *in an exemplary mode.* This corroborates what we have often seen, that the reduction has an eidetic value (or, more precisely, that reduced objects have an eidetic value) and that, since the eidos is an exemplar, this eidetic value is in reality an exemplary value. (On the other hand, the epochē obviously modifies profoundly the sense of life in the reduced world. It initiates a constitutive reflection, as the passage following the one we cited indicates.) This is also why language is the only object that is not submitted to reduction. By itself it is already the reduced world. Cf. above, § 22; *Ideas,* p. 189 (151); *EJ,* pp. 57 f. (58 f.).

ing the object only as what it is, as it is immediately given in itself.[19]

Granted all this, it must still be said that this naïveté of transcendental experience of the "world" involves certain obscurities.

To try to describe the *cogitatum* in itself is evidently to detach it from the whole intentional dynamism of consciousness. It is to thematize something constituted (which can be grasped only as constituted, i.e., in the constituting correlation) independently of the process of its constitution. The constituted—in this case the reduced world—is therefore not absolutely clarified; and since it is not fully intuitive (evident), it necessarily involves a certain opacity. Consequently, admitting it as immediately intuitive in transcendental experience is a "naïve" procedure, similar to the naïveté of the natural and dogmatic attitude, which admits in itself and from the first the existence and truth, although unclarified, of its object. Phenomenological naïveté seems to be tainted with the same pejorative note as natural (precritical) naïveté.

However, there is a great difference between the two naïvetés. That of the transcendental experience of the reduced world is necessary. We are at the beginning of the transcendental reduction. In the epoché we have no prejudice, no dogmatic point of view; we can no longer prejudge the end of our undertaking. In a word, we can build upon nothing (*bodenlos; Crisis*, p. 181 [185]). This situation cannot be permanent. The phenomenologist must construct for himself an evident point of departure (*Crisis*, p. 181 [185]; *CM*, pp. 8 [49], 13 [53]). This is an essential necessity, since every procedure must obviously begin somewhere.

So, even though the epoché is in itself absolute, definitive, and immediate, it must "begin" by taking its place in the everyday activities of the knowing subject. The phenomenological procedure cannot, however, *proceed as* the natural attitude and the dogmatism which is the systemization of this attitude proceed. But it cannot avoid *setting out from* the natural attitude. The latter is obviously only a starting point. The phenomenological procedure immediately takes its distance with respect to the natural attitude and rejects the alienation this attitude entails.

19. Phenomenological intuition is eidetic (i.e., exemplary), the in-itself being an extrinsic formality in phenomenology. This resolves the difficulty of a science which is both eidetic and descriptive; cf. *Ideas*, §§ 71–75, esp. § 74.

The negation involved in the epochē is therefore only a first aspect of the more fundamental operation designed to give us a new field of evidences, those of the transcendental experience of the reduced world. The thematization of the world as *cogitatum* does indeed leave in anonymity the intentionality constituting this world (*CM*, p. 46 [84]), but, in contrast to the natural attitude, it does not deliberately ignore this intentionality. This is phenomenological naïveté, the naïveté of a beginning of phenomenology, which shows that a point of departure as such cannot by itself be absolutely clarified (which would suppose the solution to be given before, or at least with the beginning of, the procedure). It is the naïveté of a method seeking its starting point and to this end "groping" while waiting to submit itself to its own criticism. It is a legitimate and even inevitable naïveté (*Crisis*, pp. 155 f. [158]). The naïveté of the natural attitude induces us, by the apparent solidness of its opacity, to "build on it" and take it as a foundation that is evident and immediately justified in itself. Phenomenological naïveté, on the contrary, induces us to criticize it (to "build *under* it") and motivate it by a return to the originary system of intentionality which constituted it. The former therefore claims to play the role of foundation, the role of logical "first" or *de jure* point of departure. The latter is an appeal for intentional clarification. It is a point of departure, to be sure; this is its "naïve" immediacy. But it is a *de facto* point of departure, a chronological first, in the descriptive-phenomenological dimension of intentionality. Therefore we need have no fear. It is legitimate to begin transcendental experience in a phenomenological naïveté of sorts. We need a certain confidence in the transcendental procedure and its free initiative. This confidence does not abandon the requirement for an ultimate and definitive transcendental constitution but assumes it. It delimits a first descriptive and noematic phenomenology, which is affected with a cerain apodictic naïveté (*CM*, p. 151 [177 f.]). It is in virtue of this confidence that we can live the natural world naturally in the epochē and can naïvely describe the phenomenological field of transcendental experience.

The goal sought by the epochē has therefore been reached. Pure description of the reduced *Lebenswelt* is nothing but the originary "seeing" of what is given to us in this new phenomenological attitude. Description pursues no interest other than the theoretical, pure speculative, and disinterested interest. According to Husserl, it realizes a sort of pure contemplation; it realizes the pure theoretical interest in a "consistent" fashion

(*Crisis,* p. 155 [158]) and involves no alienation of any kind—whether in the theoretical mode, in the sense that the natural attitude wrests from us an acquiescence in the natural world, or in the practical mode, in the sense that the natural theoretical interest continues in a realizing activity or simply in a voluntary love. Husserlian "contemplation" is pure; the disinterestedness of the Husserlian "contemplative" excludes all love, since love itself is an alienation.[20]

§ 43. *Pure description of the* Lebenswelt *and noematic morphology*

IN THIS NEW ATTITUDE, which suspends the natural attitude and thereby reveals its profound sense, a pure and disinterested interest in the *Lebenswelt* comes to light. The study of the *Lebenswelt* is thus raised to the level of a pure science. The *Lebenswelt* shows itself as what it is: the world of life, of the actuality of consciousness, with its structures of the known and the unknown; the world of empirical things and of man as psychophysical being, structured according to a dual "spatiality" —space and time (*Raumzeitlichkeit; Crisis,* p. 142 [145]; *CM,* p. 36 [75]); the *manifest* world, i.e., from a more profound point of view, the world manifesting transcendental subjectivity (index); the immediate world of empirical experience and of the positive sciences. What obtains in the natural attitude, insofar as this attitude already represents a certain natural theoretical interest, is taken up by the phenomenological attitude. The *Lebenswelt* is lived naturally in the epochē so that its sense, its eidos or ideal telos, will appear. The description of the *Lebenswelt* immediately takes on an exemplary value, as we have seen (cf. above, p. 262, n. 18). The epochē is a theoretical attitude which allows the object to appear in itself, in its essential "itself," without the interested participation of the scientist. This is the noematic aspect of the disinterested attitude the ego has in the phenomenological attitude. On the one side (the noetic), the subject must be disinterested in its object and describe it simply as it appears; on the other side (the noematic), the object must be left "free" to exhibit itself in its genuineness, without any interference on the part of the subject in the experience of the object's "itself." No question is to be posed by the

20. Cf. below, p. 273, n. 30. Cf., especially, Sartre's thought.

phenomenologist to the object. This absence of questioning addressed to the object expresses the phenomenologist's disinterestedness and guarantees the object's freedom in its genuineness; it guarantees the originary givenness of the object, the originariness of what is given (*Ideas*, p. 262 [224]). But it must not be inferred that phenomenology involves no question to the object or that the object gives no answer to the phenomenological interest. The question must arise of itself in the thing itself. Even though the subject poses no question, the object is nevertheless put in question. It is not the subject that questions; it is the object itself that *becomes* a question. This is why the attitude of suspension is so important. The subject must not disturb the originary appearing of the thing; the purity of the originary givenness of the thing must not be tainted. The thing must be left to speak for itself. The subject must therefore be disinterested in the highest degree; he must abstain from any interest (which is always more or less inopportune). This obviously represents an extraordinary *tension* for the subject. The subject suspends his natural theoretical interest but still wants to know the object philosophically. This is a reflective tension, a contemplation which seeks to be silent in itself in order to let the object speak. It is a tension contrary to nature, since the natural reaction would be precisely to go toward the object and ask it what it is (to "embrace" it, in Sartre's words). It is a phenomenological tension in the strict sense, since the natural attitude is suspended but a theoretical interest remains. In the epochē, one must live a theoretical interest that already emerged in the natural attitude. In the epochē, one must live the natural theoretical interest. This is the sense of Husserl's admirable words, "In gewisser Weise muss also der Philosoph in der Epochē das natürliche Leben 'natürlich durchleben,'" ("Thus in a certain sense the philosopher must also 'naturally live through' the natural life"; *Crisis*, p. 176 [180]). The only purpose of this disinterestedness, this "self-domination" or self-suspension, is to preserve the ingenuousness of originary intuition. The object must give itself; and if it is by itself apodictic, the putting it in question will be at the same time an apodictic answer. If it shows itself not to be absolute, it will show itself to be a question or pro-blem,[21] i.e., the theme of a constitutive investigation. The epochē is thus intended to bring out the intentionality in the object by showing its necessary reference to the noesis, to tran-

21. [Cf. above, Translator's Introduction, p. xxii.—TRANS.]

scendental consciousness; it regards the object as an index. This conception of the epochē explains why it is legitimate to begin with a noematic description of the objective world of the natural attitude. Thus the way is first opened to an *ontology of the natural world*. This will be a material ontology—since it has to do with the concrete region of the world—and an ontology which is already possible outside any transcendental interest but which is taken up by the reduced transcendental attitude.[22]

The description of the *Lebenswelt* therefore needs to be elaborated in a veritable *morphology of noemata*. In fact, we have the possibility of going beyond the level of the material ontology of the *Lebenswelt* in order to rise to a formal ontology grounded in the immediate experience of the noema "world" and in the formalization of this as the noema in general. The rubric *"cogitatum"* that Husserl proposes thus turns out to be the heading for a fruitful phenomenological investigation, which Husserl enjoins us to undertake despite its essential relativity (*Ideas*, p. 287 [247]). Up to now we have seen the thematization of the *Lebenswelt* and the "naïve" attitude it assumes; now we are going to see an analysis of the formal structure of the noema open up.

The *Lebenswelt* is regarded as a noema, but it is a composite, total, infinite noema. It comprises an infinity of noemata which are ordered and organized unitarily in an infinite (teleological) unity represented by the noema "world" (*CM*, p. 54 [90]). These particular noemata are extremely diverse. Pure description of the *Lebenswelt* begins by grasping the objects in the total complex of their objective determinations (*EJ*, p. 212 [251]) and goes on to assign these determinations to their respective objects.

Noematic description cannot be satisfied with this elementary view, however, nor *a fortiori* with a morphology of noemata. It must see into the unity of the noema, a unity which underlies the manifest multiplicity of noemata; there is a genuine science only when there is a unity of its object. Our description has shown the multiplicity of individual objects, and formalization simply purifies for itself this structural diversity of the noema in general. Although the noemata are multiple, they are nevertheless noemata. There must therefore be both variable elements

22. *Crisis*, pp. 142 (145), 173 (176). *FTL* also speaks of a mundane ontology to be established with the "naïveté of a transcendental positivity"; cf. p. 291 (256). In this way phenomenology takes up the "pure description prior to all theory" which *Ideas* gives as the beginning of a natural knowledge (p. 105 [62]).

and constant elements in the formal structures of the noema in general. Formalization of noemata as the noema in general manifests the essential unity in all noemata while respecting their diversity. We must also keep in mind that the noema is the correlate or intentional result of a noesis. As such it has a sense; it is the meaning of an object reduced to the rank of transcendental phenomenon; and this sense is its content (*Ideas*, pp. 261 f. [223], 361 [316]). Thus we discover a first central stratum within the noema, a first constitutive core which essentially defines the noema as this or that sense. This core is stable and permanent; it supports "peripheral" (accidental) determinations, which are the variable elements of the noema.

§ 44. Qualities and characters of the noema

THE VARIABLE ELEMENTS of the noema form part of the noema strictly speaking, but they do not determine it intrinsically in its *sense*. This is why they are secondary. It is obvious that a noema will be different, depending on whether it is perceived, remembered, imagined, etc.; but it does not thereby change its meaning content (*Ideas*, pp. 265 f. [226]). The characters of being perceived, remembered, etc., are modes of *presentation* of the noema.[23] So when analysis finds that the noema is presented as real, possible, probable, doubtful, it grasps in these determinations *being characters* (*Seinscharaktere*) which do not intrinsically affect its sense (*Ideas*, § 103). A meaning content is real or imaginary; these are characters which modify it, to be sure, but which for just this reason insure the permanence of its sense as sense under a variety of secondary determinations. Finally, the noema can be either affirmative (positive) or negative. Here analysis find characters of a special kind; since they extend universally to all the characters mentioned above, they are universal being characters (*Ideas*, § 106). Whereas the real is not the possible or the probable, and the perceived is not the imagined, the affirmed can be either real or possible, either perceived or imagined. Affirmation and negation are therefore characters applying universally to the sphere of noemata and, by correlation, to the sphere of noeses themselves.

23. *Ideas*, § 99. We must add here the founded characters: judgment, volition, desire.

However diverse the characters mentioned here may be, there is, nevertheless, one fundamental determination common to them all. The noema is in and through them *positional*. Presentation characters and being characters are, both of them, positional or thetic characters. They are correlates of noetic acts which are called thetic acts, since they posit being in this or that particular mode (*Ideas*, p. 297 [256]). The noema can thus be analyzed into a *sense* and a *positional character*—a "matter" and a "quality," to take up the language of the *Logical Investigations*. In this way, Husserl can make precise the notion of quality, which was scarcely clear enough in the *Logical Investigations*. There it seemed to include presentation characters as well as being characters, but from the noetic point of view alone. But the noesis-noema correlation makes it possible to go beyond this one-sidedness. Appearances to the contrary, the characters of being perceived, imagined, etc., are not subjective modes of givenness of the noema. A noema is "perceived," "imagined," etc., when it bears in itself the specific character which results from the fact that its originary constitution is a perceptual or an imaginative act. This is an objective character which attaches specifically to the noema qua correlate of a perception or of an imagination. This character is therefore objective or, more precisely, noematic. It forms an integral part of the noema, as one of the variable elements based on its constant element, the sense.[24] The same is true for the character of reality, which is the correlate of the noetic act of certainty (originary doxa); for the character of possibility, which is the correlate of the noetic act of presumption; and for the other characters, including the affirmative and negative.[25] The notion of quality explicitly takes on a noematic extension, and it legitimately counts as a constitutive concept in the morphology of noemata by the same right as the notion of character.

Although only the universal characters can apply to all other characters indiscriminately, it must be added that the characters belonging to the first series (presentation characters) can modify the being characters of the second series, and vice versa; a "real" can be "perceived" or "imagined," and a "remembered" can be

24. *Ideas*, pp. 290 f. (250). In *Ideas* (p. 362 [316]), Husserl explicitly criticizes the exclusively noetic conception of quality given in *LI* and attributes to quality a noematic significance as well.

25. Cf. *Idées*, p. 354, n. 1, where Ricoeur gives an excellent table of the correlation between being characters and belief characters.

"probable." But each series implies an originary character or "proto-quality," of which all other qualities are secondary modifications. Thus the presentation character "perceived" is originary with respect to the characters "remembered" and "imagined." The latter are therefore only presentifications (*Vergegenwärtigungen*) (*Ideas*, § 99). The remembered is a perceived in the past, a modification of an originary perceived. The same is true for the other series of characters. The proto-quality of the being characters is the real (*Ideas*, p. 298 [258]); the possible and the probable are only its secondary modes. Similarly, negation is a mode of affirmation; this is the essential phenomenological thesis that nonbeing is (a mode of being) (cf. *Ideas*, p. 306 [265]). In each series of characters of the noema, then, there appears an exemplary "first" which extrinsically defines its modes as secondary derivations. Here again we find the exemplarist structure of phenomenology. Every mode is a derivation from an originary first mode which defines it relatively (by anticipation) and which is defined in itself.[26] Taking into account the possibility on the part of the characters of mutually determining one another, we thus obtain the positional character "perceived-real-affirmative" as originary character and universal exemplar defining the idea of true perfect knowledge, i.e., ideally determining the noematic sense as objective truth.[27] In a derived (exemplary) manner we obtain an infinite number of modifications of characters representing all possible forms of positional characters (*Ideas*, § 107). To this possibility of being modified ad infinitum is added the converse property which is essential to every mode, the property of referring to its unmodified "first" (which is, in exemplarist terms, its in-itself). Thus the genesis which governed the noema's constitution appears phenomenologically in the noema, or at least in its character (*Ideas*, p. 304 [263]).

These analyses obviously remain incomplete as long as the noemata are not explicitly ascribed to their correlative noeses. However, they make it possible to account for the richness and the precision of the phenomenological descriptions undertaken

26. We must add the essential possibility of making each modification of character into a primary character, which involves us in an infinite process of iteration. Cf. *Ideas*, § 105.

27. According to *EJ*, this is the specific characteristic of a normal (uninhibited) explication of the originary experience of the *Gegenstand*—or, more precisely, the specific character of the correlate of this explication.

by Husserl. They show the essential multiplicity inherent in the noema, a multiplicity proceeding above all from the diversity of its variable and secondary elements.

Although a certain unity already appears in this finding that all characters, however diverse they may be, are positional, we must still reach the constant basis of the noema which alone insures its unity in principle. We must therefore study the noematic sense in itself, after having seen the various qualities which affect it and diversify it. The question promptly arises of how we can make this noematic basis itself appear. How is the noematic sense to be phenomenologically (intuitively) justified? What is the originary dator experience of the pure noematic sense? The complete noema is composed of the noematic core (the sense) and thetic characters. The noema is therefore always given with this or that quality. What we have seen up to now has shown us the necessity of a noematic core but not its originary givenness. Now, characters are modes in which the noematic core is given as a noema qualitatively determined in this or that manner. Thus the question arises: is there a suitable modification or appropriate character of the noema which gives us the noema in its pure sense? This amounts to the question whether an originary experience exists which makes it possible to give the noematic sense "as if" it were absolutely independent of every thetic character.

Now, after the universal being characters (affirmation and negation), Husserl introduces one last character—a character he regards as absolutely unique in the whole sphere of noematico-noetic structures. Its status completely isolates it from all the others, and it is of the greatest phenomenological significance. The qualities or modifications of the noema have the property of being able to apply to all noemata (under certain restrictions, since only the affirmative and negative modifications are universal). The new modification that Husserl introduces here has in common with the universal characters the fact that it too can apply to all the other characters. But, instead of being *added* to them, instead of bringing a supplementary modification to the noematic core, it has as its specific effect the removal of all determining effectiveness from characters already existing. It suspends them but does not cancel or destroy them; they subsist and can be found again subsequently as superstructures of the noematic sense. In a word, it *neutralizes* the characters. The third modification (universal being character) is thus the neutrality character (*Ideas*, §§ 109–10). This word is to be taken in its strict sense (*"ne-uter"*). The noematic core "affected" with this new character has neither presentation character nor being character. It is given as neutral, "as if" it had no character, "as if" every quality had disappeared from it. The noetic operation of neutralization attains as its immediate noematic correlate the noema "stripped" of its customary characters; it attains the pure noematic sense, the pure meaning content of the noema.

It is evident that Husserl here wants to situate the transcendental operation of the epoché and its correlate among the various noetico-noematic structures of consciousness. Neutralization is the proper effect of phenomenological suspension. The world or the object in general is reduced to its pure essence by the epoché, and the transcendental experience made possible by the epoché is eidetic, i.e., exemplary (cf. *Crisis*, p. 176 [180]). The world is reduced to its pure meaning, independent of every character—since a character can be the expression of a worldly interest (in particular, the interest in reality) and since it "veils" the inner nature of the object in itself (*selbst*). The epoché has as its effect the revealing of the object to itself before a disinterested spectator. Husserl describes the substance of this operation under the name "neutralization." The epoché is thus a *neutralizing noesis*, which, like every noesis, necessarily has a noematic correlate. The correlate in this case is a *neutralized noema;* the epoché yields the reduced object. Hence we have here a modification of a unique kind, one which is definitive and not iterable and which is therefore absolute (as opposed to imagination). It is an operation which abstains from all positing, which therefore suspends every positional character (*Ideas*, pp. 306 [264], 312 [270]). It yields the object (the noema) in the form of the "merely thought," in the form of a "mere representation." [28] Neutralization divides consciousness in two in an absolutely universal way,[29] so that the neutrality character cannot in the strict sense be regarded as a derived mode of the

28. *Ideas*, p. 307 (266). This is the *blosse Vorstellung* of *LI*.
29. *Ideas*, p. 319 (277). Cf. the text of *CM*, § 25, which seems parallel to the passage cited but which differs in that the counter-noema seems to be ascribed to "imagination." The text in *CM* can be cited, nevertheless, because Husserl himself observes that the word "imagination" is too imprecise. In any case, the reader will recognize here the absolute distinction between object (*Gegenstand*) and sense (*Sinn*), a distinction which has already been noted several times.

character of positionality (*Ideas*, pp. 318 [276 f.], 322 [280]). Whereas all the characters we have encountered hitherto are positional characters and refer to an originary positional mode (the *Ur-modus*, "perceived," "real," "affirmative"), the neutral character is the only one of its kind. Like the epochē, whose noetic performance and noematic correlate it explicates, it defines and sets up a new theoretical attitude, one which is irreducible to any other interest of knowledge.

The neutralized noema is a noema reduced to its noematic sense, just as the world suspended by the epochē is reduced to the transcendental phenomenon or meaning "world." Everything happens in each case "as if" the character and the real world were suppressed, whereas they are only suspended, having lost all positional "force." In the epochē—that is, in neutralization—we again find the phenomenological fiction deliberately willed (the epochē is free) in view of the theoretical interest of pure phenomenology. The *Als-ob* or *Phantasieren* of the suspension is what originarily admits an ideality or meaning that is in fact a quasi-reality, a reality suspended in whatever "force" of reality it has.[30]

§ 45. *The object = determinable* X *in the noematic sense. Noematic* quid *and* quomodo

NEUTRALIZATION is therefore the originary "character" of the noematic sense. In this way we reach the core stratum

30. Cf. *CM*, pp. 58 f. (94). We could go into more detail concerning the connection of neutralization with aesthetic contemplation. When Husserl discusses the relationship between imagination and neutralization, doesn't he take as his example the aesthetic contemplation of Dürer's famous engraving, "The Knight, Death, and the Devil" (*Ideas*, § 111)? The object of aesthetic contemplation is an object which gives itself neither as being nor as not being, nor in any other positional modality, but as quasi-being (*gleichsam seiend*). It is a *neutralized object* (*Ideas*, pp. 311 [269], 327 [285], 340 [298]; *LI*, p. 645 [II/1, 490]). This "neutral" aesthetic contemplation corresponds to the phenomenologist's pure and disinterested contemplation. Here we would have to extend this line of thought with a study of phenomenological aesthetics in the manner of M. Dufrenne. It remains true, however, that in sound phenomenology—even if the pure contemplation of the disinterested phenomenologist has an aesthetic mode—true aesthetic contemplation is a factical example illustrating the modification which neutralizes positional perception (*Ideas*, p. 311 [269]).

which supports the noematic characters. But our inquiry immediately begins again: Are we not in a movement of intentional shifting? For what is a sense but an ideal relation, an intention of an object? Hence we must penetrate still more deeply into the structure of the noema. Our line of advance thus discovers the most fundamental dimension in the composition of the noema: its *object*.

Let us again take up the point of view of the *Logical Investigations:* the important distinction between content and object (*LI,* p. 535 [II/1, 345 f.]). The noema has a content which, being precisely the sense, refers to the intentional object. Noematic description reveals an internal teleology which is simply the *Gegenständlichkeit* of the noema. But in order to describe this in a purely descriptive way, description does not cease to be noematic; it does nothing but follow the object according to the rules of intuitive adequation. Phenomenological disinterestedness and the epochē are strictly maintained, and what is attained is precisely the intended as such (*Ideas*, p. 266 [227]; cf. pp. 365 [320], 306 [264]). This is why the description uses expressions taken from formal and material ontology (such as "object," "property," "meaning," "determinations," etc.) and excludes any expression pertaining to noetic description (*Ideas*, p. 364 [318 f.]). Noematic description is ranged under formal ontology, since it unfolds in an analysis of the formal structure of the noema in general, in a morphology of the noema.

But the nature of content and object must be delimited. The noema, insofar as it signifies, shows itself as determined in this or that way. It comprises a bundle of objective determinations unified in a meaning of an object. It therefore immediately appears that the sense of the noema represents a certain multiplicity of objective determinations unified by an intentional reference to an object (*Ideas*, pp. 364 f. [319 f.]). Here too Husserl takes up the important theme of *intentional unity.* Multiplicity is intelligible only through unity; and since by definition the multiplicity is not one in itself, it must necessarily be unified by reference to the unity. The unity in the multiplicity must therefore be a teleological unity, a unity by dynamic participation in a unitary pole. (The theory of intentional unity is in fact a particular formulation of Husserlian exemplarism.) If the noematic sense (content, matter) set forth by way of the epochē as neutralized noema is a multiplicity of determinations, then, there must necessarily be a unique substrate for these various determinations, a unique subject of the sense. As Husserl himself says, if the noematic sense is a closed system of predicates, then these predicates must receive their unity through their intentional reference to an object, which is thus their center of unity or reference point. In short, there must be a unique object for these multiple objective determinations (*Ideas*, p. 365 [320]). In this way noematic analysis gains access, through the matter, to a central noematic moment which is the object pure and simple (*Gegenstand schlechthin*), the ultimate support of every objective determination and ultimate subject of every objective predicate. But this support does not assert its unity as any complex at all, as an incoherent connection of determinations. It is identical and is given in variable objective predicates. It is "= X" (undetermined), since it cannot be "determined" apart from its particular objective determinations (*Ideas*, pp. 365 f. [320 f.]).

Thus we must distinguish two levels in the formal structure of the noema: the level of multiplicity (determinations or objective predicates constituting the content or noematic sense) and the level of unity (object pure and simple, "= X"). These two levels are inseparable from each other; neither is given in isolation. The objective determinations cannot subsist as such; they are necessarily determinations of an originary objectivity, of a substrate. Conversely, the substrate object is given only in its objective predicates (*Ideas*, p. 365 [320]). Both pure multiplicity and pure indeterminacy are unintelligible in themselves; objective determinations cannot be without an object, and vice versa. Only the object pure and simple is an object in the strict sense, however. It alone insures the objectivity of the noema and of its sense, as well as the unity of their multiple determinations. If there is reciprocity between the objective determinations and the object, this is an "oriented" reciprocity, a reciprocity within intentionality. The object is what makes the intentionality of consciousness operative, since it is the correlate or intentional unity pole of consciousness. If this object is given only with its objective determinations expressed in the noematic sense, then the noema has a relation to its object only by means of its sense or content (*Ideas*, pp. 363 [318], 360 [315]). Hence the content of the noema must not be confused with its object. The sense (*Sinn*) is not the object (*Gegenstand*), although it is an *Objektivität*, as we know. The noema can have only one object, since the object is the unifying function.[31] This object can be only the

31. *Ideas*, pp. 366 f. (321 f.). The concept of function is therefore parallel with that of intentional constitution. Cf. *Ideas*, § 86.

ideal telos of its intentional aiming. It can only be ultimate, and as such it is presently undetermined. The noematic sense is intercalated between noema and object. It is what manifests the object and progressively realizes it to the extent that experience allows knowledge of the object to be perfected. There can therefore be many noematic senses for the same object (*Ideas*, p. 367 [322]).

The noema has one object and can have many senses. The noematic content is therefore variable or multiple. If we want to attain something stable and identical, we will evidently have to proceed to the object pure and simple, the ultimate substrate of every determination. But this is the outcome of an infinite investigation. Just as there is only one idea of science but numerous theoretical systems which try to realize it historically, so here the intentional object is unique, but the effective content of its corresponding noema is multiple and variable. On the other hand, the very progress of science realizes the idea of science. With respect to its effective realization, the idea is indeterminate, a merely potential telos (this is the descriptive-phenomenological or existence-act point of view). But in itself it is absolutely and fully determinate, it is the eidos and motive of every realization (this is the transcendental-phenomenological or value-act point of view). Similarly, variations of the noematic content are directed to determining the object fully in itself. From the point of view of the present, then, the object is indeterminate. But in itself it is fully determinate; with it we have knowledge of the object in its *Selbst,* the motive of every progress of experience directed to its total explication.

In short, the situation is this. On the one hand, the object pure and simple is actually indeterminate and potentially determinate (existence-act point of view). On the other hand, the noematic content (sense) is actually inadequate and potentially adequate to the object (value-act point of view). In this intentional dynamism, the noematic content or meaning content of the noema tends ad infinitum to reach the object pure and simple. If there are actually *many* noematic senses for a single object, this is because there is in itself *one* noematic sense that is adequate to the object. This coincidence—like adequate knowledge, which it is another way of expressing—is an idea. That is, it is an ideal end or norm pre-scribing an infinite process of realization. The idea, regarded alternately as potency and as pure act, brings us back to the exemplarist dialectic of act and potency or, more radically, to the dialectic of fact and idea. But we know that fact and eidos differ not in nature but in degree, the latter being the idealized totality of the former. There is therefore only a single object in the course of being realized teleologically in and through the various noematic senses. This is why we must distinguish between two concepts of "object" for this unique object. One concept defines the object in itself as the pure intentional center of the objective determinations comprised in the noematic sense. The other concept defines the object in its determinations, as the object pure and simple in the "how" of its objective determinations. On the one hand we have the object pure and simple; on the other we have the noematic sense (material core without qualities), which is simply the object pure and simple in the "how" of its noematic objective determinations.[32] What we have is really one and the same teleological object. The two strata in the formal structure of the noema, although they are distinct, are not absolutely distinct but are, on the contrary, in dynamic (intentional) continuity. The words themselves express this admirably: the noema has a sense which orients it toward its object; sense (*Sinn*) is always a direction (*Richtung*) or intentional orientation.

In sum, we must distinguish a *quid* and a *quomodo*. The noema has in the first place an objective determination, which is the sense. This is the noematic *quid* (*noematisches Was*) in a first sense of the word. But this *quid* is relative to an originary *quid*, which is the object pure and simple. When the terminus of intentionality is really [*réellement*] attained or at least anticipated in an idea, we realize that the noematic *quid* (i.e., the content [*contenu, Inhalt*] of the noema) is precisely the presently actual content [*statut, Gehalt*] in which the originary *quid* is noematically determined. We find, that is, that the noematic *quid* is the originary *quid* in its noematic *quomodo*. This is a *noematic quomodo* which must be carefully distinguished from the *noetic quomodo*, which is the "how" of the subjective modes of givenness (*Ideas*, § 132). It seems that we have before us the fact-eidos dialectic; the essential determination is the same

32. *Ideas*, pp. 366 f. (321 f.). Thus we can see why the object is a "determinable X in the noematic sense" (*Ideas*, § 131). The French translation [as well as the English—Trans.] is weaker than the German phrase. This conceptual duality is more radical than that which Husserl introduces between simple act and founded act. Here we are distinguishing within the simple act between the object pure and simple and the object in its noematic "how" (*Ideas*, p. 123 [83]).

between the noematic quid and the originary *quid*, between the object in its *de facto* actuality and the object in its ideal actuality. Formal univocity and difference in degrees of perfection (of ideality): this is indeed the dynamic dialectic of exemplarism or, alternatively, of participation.

The various strata we have brought to light in the noema in general are strata of the formal structure of the noema: quality or character; sense, content, or matter; object (= X). These three terms—noema, noematic sense, and object—are in intentional continuity. But intentionality is considered here from the noematic point of view, in its results rather than in its constitutive *Leistung*. This is all the more true since the noema as such is a constituted. This is why noematic description is a static analysis and succeeds only in discovering relations of noemata to sense and of sense to object, without bringing into play the dynamic *Leistung* that constitutes them. Synthetic intentionality is sedimented in its products (*Erzeugnisse*), and these are what noematic morphology describes.

But the reader will notice the ambiguity of our situation. We have explicated the analytic positions of *Ideas* on the topic of noema and object by express reference to the intentionality of science as we know it from Part I. We have shown in outline how the intentional products analyzed by noematic description are grounded in an originary constitutive movement. However, we do not claim to have gone beyond the noematic framework which pre-scribes to us the noematic description of the *cogitatum* as such. If our advance seems somewhat "wobbly," this is not simply appearance but reality. Every study of the noema reveals the necessary constitutive dependence of the noema with respect to its corresponding noesis. The morphology of noemata requires a necessary complement, the morphology of the corresponding noeses. Similarly, the "formal ontology of the noema" requires as its complement the "formal ontology of the noesis" (*Ideas*, p. 287 [246 f.]). But it is to be noted that the object itself is what manifests this requirement. In the spirit of the transcendental reduction, the noema itself is what is in question. The noema itself reveals its insufficiency in itself. The object turns out to be the index of a subjective and constitutive investigation. The ego of the phenomenologist is disinterested. His description follows the organization of the various strata of the *cogitatum;* and if it is extended in a transcendental direction, its first noematic progress is continued in an intentional elucidation. As it was for Plato's cook, it is here a matter of cutting the chicken according to its articulations. The sole concern of the phenomenologist is adequation, fidelity to intuition. Intentionality, whose distinctive characteristic is self-transcendence, is charged with leading the phenomenologist, by itself, to the terminus of his investigation. It is enough to begin well and the procedure infallibly reaches its goal.

Noematic description discovers the object pure and simple, the ultimate substrate, at the terminus of its advance. It cannot determine the object in itself, however, but makes it an indeterminate X—albeit from one of the possible intentional points of view. But if from the transcendental-phenomenological point of view the phenomenologist can assert that the object is fully determined, there is no reason to see in this ultimate X an individual rather than the totality of the world or, alternatively, the totality of being. In fact, the only determinations we have of this object, X, are those given to us in the sense of its correlative noema (cf. *Ideas*, p. 377 [332]). These determinations are variable; only the object is identical. The object is the principle of unity of the noematic multiplicity. But, according to Husserl, a substrate is necessarily individual. It seems that the object pure and simple is therefore this or that individual. Thus we will have a multiplicity of noemata corresponding to a real multiplicity of individual objects. And what we have just shown will therefore be simply the formalization or visualization as ideal example (ideation) of one particular case among many.

However, in virtue of the doctrine of *horizons*, the difference between the individual object and the totality of being (world) is entirely relative. Each individual object has an internal horizon, of course—a series of determinations which define it in its own nature (intrinsically). But there is also an external horizon, the infinite field of its relations with other objects, which defines it relatively (extrinsically) (*EJ*, pp. 32–34 [28 f.]). But the external horizon of the individual object is in fact the internal horizon of the totality of being. In the final analysis, then, the external horizon of the individual object is the internal horizon of this very totality. Thus there is a univocal continuity between the determinations of the individual object and those of the universal object. One is the part, the other is the whole. There is but one reality, which is the single and unique substrate of all possible determinations, the world, the *Weltall*, the concrete universe (cf. *EJ*, p. 139 [159], par. 1). The object pure and simple (= X) can therefore just as well be conceived either as an individual or as the universe itself. In the latter case we find the nominalist principle *determinatio negatio*, since the objective determinations expressed by the predicates of the noematic sense "shrink" or "narrow" the concrete universe in such a fashion as to give it only in the form of one of its parts. This is indeed a temporary limitation, one which is destined to be immediately surpassed, since the progress of knowledge is precisely a matter of surpassing the particularity of the individual object in order to reach the concrete universality of being in its totality. But now the world or universe is an individual, and even the unique concrete individual (*EJ*, pp. 139 [159], 363 [441]). And the universal structure of the object in general expresses this world formally, since it is, above all, the formal structure of the individual as such. To be sure, the indeterminacy of the object pure and simple makes it difficult to use the term "individual." Let us speak instead of "something" in general (*Etwas*), of "everything and anything" (*alles und jedes; Ideas*, pp. 67 [27], 88 [48]), the universality of being (*All-seiendes; EJ*, p. 137 [157])—or, more concretely, of the world, the *Lebenswelt*.

The "something" to which we gain access is therefore the universal substrate of all determinations, the totality of being. This totality is conceived in three ways: (1) from the descriptive-phenomenological point of view, it is conceived as an indeterminate X, the telos of an infinite advance of approximations; (2) from the transcendental-phenomenological point of view, it is conceived as a fully determined objectivity, the transcendental motive of the realization of knowledge; (3) formally, from the standpoint of formal ontology, it is conceived as the object in general, the universal essential objective form.

B. THE *Cogito*

§ 46. *Noetic reflection gives the noetic* quomodo *of the life-world* (Lebenswelt)

ANALYSIS NOW TAKES a more straightforwardly critical (reflective) turn. Noematic description comes first "naturally," since the theoretical interest is directed first of all to the object.[33]

33. In fact, the noematic characters are not given by reflection; cf. *Ideas*, § 108.

Husserl then enjoins a constitutive turn situated at what he calls a "first level of reflection." This must, of course, be understood in relation to the phenomenological attitude of suspension, in which the transcendental experience of the reduced world takes place. In relation to the world of the natural attitude, noematic description is already a reflection (*Ideas*, pp. 409 [362], 416 [309]). This is a noematic reflection, which suspends the naïve being value and truth value of worldly affirmations and seeks to see into their identical sense (eidos). But if we undertake to give an exhaustive analytical treatment of the epochē, as Husserl does in the *Crisis* (§§ 35–36), we may well think of it as a universal medium in which noematic description corresponds to a first direct (*geradehin*) movement of experience— a movement that is therefore in a sense naïve and in which only a critical procedure other than noematic description can be called "reflection" in the strict sense. Husserl's words—which may at first sight seem surprising, if not contradictory—are thereby justified. The first degree of reflection must be understood from within the reduced attitude; it is reflection on the noema. From the noema we shall proceed to the noesis and then, in a second degree of reflection, to the ego itself (*Crisis*, pp. 172 [175], 182 [185]). This first reflection in the epochē thus establishes a second way of thematizing the *Lebenswelt*, one which is quite distinct from noematic description and which breaks through the normal course of experience of the world (*Crisis*, p. 144 [147]).

But if noematic description is the inauguration of transcendental experience, a complete analysis cannot ignore the important fact that the phenomenon under consideration is a transcendental phenomenon. It is a phenomenon which is proper, not to a natural empirical consciousness, subject to the effective influence of things which are in themselves problematic, but to a consciousness reduced to its originary purity as a constitutive *Leistung*. The transcendental phenomenon is the phenomenon proper to transcendental subjectivity. Its very sense is to be constituted by the transcendental ego, and by this it shows its essential relativity to constitutive consciousness. In this way, the change of value (*Umwertung*) of the natural object is concretely realized. The natural object is originally relative to a natural external world and, in this world, to a particular called empirical consciousness. This relativity to natural existence is bracketed, which does not mean that the reduced object is now taken as an absolute; an absolute reality (*Realität* or *Wirklich-*

keit) is in general as absurd as a round square.[34] On the contrary, another relativity makes its appearance, this time a transcendental relativity. The natural object reduced to its pure sense turns out to be intentionally relative to transcendental subjectivity. The transcendental relativity grounds and even constitutes the natural relativity. Suddenly the objective, which the natural attitude took as an absolute, becomes a subjective-relative. The most persistent of alienations, the natural belief in the absolute existence of the given world, is suspended. The epochē frees the genuine sense of the world by linking it constitutively to the ego. This is a veritable *freeing,* since it is a matter of passing from an alienation (*Bindung*) to a supremely sense-given autonomy (*Crisis,* p. 151 [154]; cf. below, p. 336).

But this means that the given world, the immediately perceived noema, is no longer regarded as world or as noema but is questioned in its value as pregiven or as immediately perceived. Reflection thus becomes explicitly and "purely" subjective. It is no longer the constituted or the given that is under consideration but the givenness or constitution itself (*Crisis,* p. 156 [158 f.]). The epochē explicitly reveals that the reduced object or transcendental phenomenon is a constituted object, by freeing the pure sense of this object. Reduced transcendence plays the role of index or guiding thread for phenomenological analysis (*Crisis,* § 48; *CM,* § 21; *FTL,* p. 268 [237]), which is in this way guided toward constitution and then finally (teleologically) toward the ego. These observations make it more understandable why the first effect of the transcendental epochē is to bring out the constitutive correlation between object and consciousness, between constituted and constitution—in a word,

---

34. *Ideas,* p. 168 (134). In *Ideas,* p. 397 (351), Husserl explicitly appeals to the principle of noncontradiction. This may seem surprising, since one of the fruits of intentional teleology is precisely to demonstrate dialectically the absolute invalidity of this principle; since nonbeing is a mode of being (i.e., since nonbeing is), contradiction no longer functions as it did in classical thought. And in fact this relativity or "relativization" of nonbeing must be understood in an "absolute" manner. It is not to be taken as Plato used it in *Sophist,* 259a, where not to be is to be other, i.e., to participate. Plato does not settle the question of absolute nonbeing; he does not inquire whether "nonbeing is not" absolutely—which would plunge us dialectically into an infinite regress. Only relative nonbeing interests Plato, and it is conflated with the being of participation. For Husserl there is only constituted being. Even the sense of nonbeing needs to be constituted in consciousness, and *as being.*

to bring out intentionality itself in its more actual aspect, the *cogito* (*Crisis*, § 41). The line of advance is as follows. The epochē brings out the transcendental relativity of the object reduced to the pure sense, i.e., it brings out the a priori of the constitutive correlation between noema and noesis (*Crisis*, § 46: "Das universale Korrelationsapriori"). Then the constituted object is the index of its subjective constitution, and we find intentionality (*Crisis*, p. 169 [172]). Analysis seems to distinguish several stages, but it is a single intentional movement, a single intentional shifting which we go through reflectively (*Nachverstehen*), i.e., counter to its originary historicity.

The *appearing* of the object or transcendental phenomenon is now put in question by a reflection on the transcendental phenomenon—a reflection which for this reason sets out from the object itself. The subjective mode of givenness is what interests the phenomenologist, the subjective multiplicity in which the object appears to consciousness and, as such, is constituted (*Crisis*, p. 144 [147]). After the noematic description of the constituted, Husserl therefore summons us to an explicit reflection on transcendental constitution: after the *cogitatum*, the *cogito*. This is the second way of thematizing the *Lebenswelt*. Theoretical attention turns away from the noematically given object "world" to direct itself on the experience of this object, the subjective modes of appearance of this same world (*Crisis*, § 38). This is noetic reflection (*Ideas*, pp. 409 [362], 416 [369]), which necessitates a complete conversion of interest and a completely new voluntary initiative in order for us to become reflectively aware that our world—so natural that it seems to be absolute in itself—is originarily constituted in the universal intentional life of consciousness through a multiplicity of subjective configurations which are sometimes concordant and sometimes discordant but which, in the latter case, are immediately corrected in the synthetic sense of a unique intentional unity, the ideal telos of all subjective (noetic) experiences and the ideal exemplar of all their correlative noemata (*Crisis*, p. 145 [147 f.]). This intentional life is nothing but transcendental constitution, i.e., the universal and infinite *cogito* synthetically constituting its universal and infinite *cogitatum* (*CM*, p. 42 [80]). This *cogito* can and must be explicated in the originary intuitive mode, and this is precisely why it can be adequate only ideally and at infinity (*Ideas*, p. 418 [371]).

Along with the many objective determinations of the object as such, or, more exactly, beneath them as their constitutive foundation, intentional analysis therefore grasps the multiple subjective "how" (*quomodo*) of the modes of givenness of the objective—the subjective a priori, the transcendental system of intentionality which is constitutive of the object. Reflection becomes the science of the "how" of the world's pregivenness. It elucidates the ultimate subjective foundation that insures every objectivity its genuine "force." This science is therefore an integral part of transcendental phenomenology, which is the ultimate apodictic and universal science and the source of all scientific validity (*Crisis*, pp. 146 f. [149]). So we must see a second object in the "how." We saw above that the noema comprises a noematic multiplicity. The sense is in fact made up of several objective predicates which determine the one subject of the sense: the object (= X), which is a priori noematically determinable. At this point we have therefore discerned a first object in the "how": the noematic *quomodo* of the originary *quid* (variable and multiple sense of the object or identical substrate; *Ideas*, p. 366 [321]). But this *quomodo* or noematic sense is an abstract essence; it is a moment of the complete noema. The latter must therefore—in order to be able to completely justify its sense—comprise, in addition, the subjective modes of its originary givenness, i.e., what may be called, correlatively, the noetic *quomodo* (*Ideas*, p. 368 [323]). Correlatively with this *quomodo* of subjective modes of givenness, a character of greater or lesser intuitive fullness accrues to the noema, depending on whether the noetic *quomodo* is brought out in its synthetic totality or only partially; the noema is grasped in a more or less clear consciousness, to the limit of blind obscurity (cf. *Ideas*, p. 368 [323]). The problem of the noetic *quomodo* leads us toward the problem of *clear rational consciousness* (according to *Ideas*, §§ 136–37), i.e., the problem of *evidence* (according to *FTL*, §§ 59–60); and it leads us correlatively toward the problems of intentional and cognitive essences (according to *LI*, Fifth Investigation, §§ 20–21, and Sixth Investigation, §§ 25–26).

The complete noema thus appears as in itself intentionally implying the corresponding noesis, the complete constituted as implying its constitution, the *cogitatum* as implying the *cogito*. The genuine sense of the noema necessarily requires this implication, without which the noema is not transcendentally understood. This amounts to saying that only the explicit correlation between noema and noesis is a concrete essence, a phenomenologically self-sufficient intentional experience. Noesis and noema are, respectively, the real [*réel*] and intentional components of consciousness. Their synthesis in the living *cogito* is the unique phenomenological "absolute." Every actual *cogito* is an *object*-consciousness, an object-constituting consciousness whose object is transcendentally legitimized.

There is no reason not to infer immediately the correlative proposition that the noesis as such is also an abstractum, a partial moment of a complete intentional experience (cf. *Ideas,* p. 249 [210]). Its sense necessarily implies the noema as its intentional pole. And since the sense of the noesis is simply the noema, the only concretum is the complete noesis, the noesis intentionally implying its noema. Thus it must be said both that the complete noema intentionally implies the noesis and that the noesis intentionally implies the noema, that constitution implies the constituted and that the constituted implies constitution. This expresses the necessary and a priori correlation between noema and noesis, a correlation which is a mutual relativity. Only this correlation insures the concreteness of consciousness. In the end, then, this means that intentionality alone constitutes concrete consciousness, since correlation is nothing but intentionality itself. And this concrete consciousness can be defined reciprocally as complete noema or as complete noesis. Thus we are dealing with a single problem, the functional center of all of phenomenology. The problems of noematic and noetic concreteness, of the concrete consciousness, of the a priori correlation between noema and noesis, of transcendental constitution, and even the problem of intentionality form only one problem and come together under the single heading of the *cogito.*

Our present point of view obviously does not bring us immediately to correlation in its pure form. After the reduction of objective science, we considered only the *Lebenswelt.* The latter, as constituted, refers us to the manifold of its subjective appearing (noetic *quomodo*). Correlation first takes the particular form of the correlation between world and consciousness. Idealization of this particular correlation provides us with correlation in its eidetic form, the noetico-noematic correlation between consciousness in general and being in general. In fact, we need only take the factual correlation between world and consciousness as factical example to infer from it by the method of idealizing visualization (ideation) the universal eidetic structure of the correlation between all being and consciousness. Thus it can be affirmed that all being is the index of its systematic constitutive multiplicity. Transcendental phenomenology itself is (synthetically) normative, since it elucidates a universal intentional structure in which every particular consciousness participates. We have here a (synthetic) formulation of Husserlian exemplarism.[35]

Just as world and concrete consciousness are mutually correlative on the level of the factical example, so the eidos noema and the eidos noesis are mutually correlative on the ideal level. If there is a morphology of noemata, there is also a morphology of noeses (*Ideas*, p. 287 [247]). There is therefore a parallelism of noema and noesis, although this expression places serious difficulties before us. First, this cannot be a parallelism strictly speaking. It is not enough to say that to every noema A corresponds a noesis A (*Ideas*, p. 287 [247]). The correlation here is a dynamic and realizing participation. The parallelism is oriented, and this orientation is, precisely, intentionality. But the notion of orientation is quite foreign to the notion of parallelism taken in itself. Moreover, this cannot be single parallelism but rather several. We will see that there are at least two parallelisms, since the noema is composed of two essential strata, the sense and the noematic character (*Ideas*, p. 289 [248]). These two elements must both be constituted, and they refer respectively to a noetic act character (*Aktcharakter*) and to an originary objectifying constitution. Thus we must clearly distinguish between two correlations, the better to understand their unity in principle. On the one hand we have the correlation between the object as it appears in a certain noematic sense and its noetic constitution, and on the other we have the correlation between noematic and noetic characters (*Ideas*, p. 290 [249]).

To grasp the question in its full extent, we must begin with intentional experience.

§ 47. Actuality and potentiality of the life of consciousness. The ideal temporality of consciousness

INTENTIONAL LIFE is an "objectifying" life; the ego is conscious of its objects, and it is in this consciousness that it

35. As we will see, eidetic phenomenology is transcendental logic. Cf. *Crisis*, p. 166 (169). *Ideas*, p. 287 (246), also speaks of the correlation between the eidos "noema" and the eidos "noesis."

actually lives. The object (noema) must therefore always be distinguished from the consciousness of the object (noesis). The ego does not live in the object, of course, but in its "consciousnesses of" the object.[36] This consciousness is simply intentional experience [*vécu*] in the broadest sense, which coincides with the concept of consciousness itself (cf. *Ideas*, p. 126 [87]). The ego is mere relatedness to the object, and hence it can "live" only in this relatedness, in and by its *cogito* (*Ideas*, pp. 232 [194], 270 [231]). We thereby avoid reducing the object to a real component of consciousness (empiricist or subjectivist idealism, psychologism). But even though intentional experience is the very life of the ego, it is not immediately present to consciousness; it is not the first object grasped by the ego. On the contrary, a reflection is needed in order to grasp it (*Ideas*, pp. 142 [105], 222 [184]). What is lived is not seen insofar as it is lived but insofar as it is reflected (*Ideas*, p. 416 [369]). Reflection necessarily modifies its object and in it grasps an object of second degree rather than the originary object. Lived experience is not grasped as lived; rather, it can be grasped only as object, and this necessarily alters its originary sense. The experience as presently lived by the ego in its originary *cogito* cannot presently be grasped as such. Reflection can grasp it only in a reflex or secondary mode, a mode which is not originary but modified (*CM*, p. 34 [72]). This is the reason for the disparity in principle (the essential inadequation) between intentional analysis and its object, the infinite teleology of consciousness. Husserl pointed out that the goal of reflection is not to "repeat" the object. If the object can be grasped only reflectively (as is the case with experience), knowledge can only be inadequate and hence subject to the process of *Nachverstehen*, which is so typical of phenomenology. Even though reflection is necessarily inadequate, adequation nevertheless remains the ideal it pursues. Intentional analysis tends to "make up" ad infinitum its initial "lag." Factual inadequation anticipates ideal adequation, and the latter is the transcendental motive of the intentional teleology of consciousness.

This is why the experience [*le vécu*] turns out to be an idea. Let us take a simple example, the perception of a table. In noematic terms, the table is immediately "given there." The

36. It will be necessary, however, to introduce an important distinction between the "real" [*réelle*] and the "intentional" life of consciousness, parallel with the distinction between the real and intentional components of the experience [*vécu*].

correlative perception proves to be multiple, however. The noema is one, but the constitutive experience goes through a series of different stages in essential and teleological continuity. At first I perceive the table top and two legs; but the other side of the table, the drawer and the other two legs, escape me for the moment; a new phase of experience will give them to me. This succession of continuous and convergent stages is grasped reflectively as a multitude of different intentional experiences. But, by definition, one noetic reflection can grasp only one experience. The entire series of experiences is therefore inscribed in time; or better, it plays a part in constituting time, i.e., in constituting the pure ego. *One* act of reflection can therefore grasp only *one* moment of this series, the moment corresponding to the present moment [*l'actualité*] of the life of the ego. The intentional experience in its isolated state cannot be a concrete essence any more than the present "now" that it defines.[37] It is inscribed in the continuous flow of the ego's intentional life, and only this flow is the absolutely concrete and independent intentional experience. Here again we find a characteristically phenomenological position: only the totality is concrete. Since the flow of experience (i.e., the intentional life of the ego) cannot presently be grasped in its totality[38] except in the form of an *idea*, only the idea of the lived flow is concrete—that is, the idealized totality of particular factual experiences (*Ideas*, pp. 239 f. [201 f.]). This conclusion is further confirmed by the fact that there is no originary or determinate standard unity of time. How could it be determined that a certain fraction of time is the simple and originary unity? Even a noetic reflection that grasps an intentional experience at the moment it occurs is not absolutely assured of finding in it a simple and originary experience. The intentional experience, too, is composed of several partial experiences. Therefore, the intentional experience is likewise a flow, and its determination is an idea (*Ideas*, p. 220 [182]). The unity (measure) of intentional experience or phenomenological time is therefore not the "now" (cf. Descartes's "instant"). The unity of intentional experience is its totality, the

37. *Ideas*, pp. 240 f. (202). A concretum that is not independent is not really concrete in the strict sense of the word, according to *Ideas*, p. 76 (36).

38. *Ideas*, pp. 118 f. (79). The flow of intentional life is therefore a possible totality, and it is thematized as such in and by an *idea* (which is itself possible from the descriptive-phenomenological point of view).

idea of the universal flow of the ego's life, the infinite *cogito* itself.

However, even if the present "now" is a moment (which cannot presently be grasped) of the totality of intentional life, it is the necessary formal structure of this totality. In fact, it is a priori evident that the whole intentional flow passes "through" the "now." This passing is not conscious in an actual way but only in a reflective, hence intentional and potential, way. Although it is presently actual, it is not attentional (*Ideas*, §§ 92, 113). If reflection directs the attention of consciousness on the "now," it grasps it only as "what just now was" (*soeben Gewesenes*). The "now" is never grasped adequately in its value as living "now"; reflection grasps it as *lived* (already past). The originariness of the "now" thus remains a zero point and hence an idea (*Ideas*, p. 237 [199]). The ideal "now" is therefore the necessary a priori form of consciousness itself. The successive and changing present moment [*actualité*] of intentional experiences is subject to a permanent and identical form; it is perpetual relation of past to future. This necessary relation is eidetically formalized in the ideal structure of the "now," the present moment of time (*Ideas*, p. 237 [199]). In itself an empty and identical form, the "now" is filled by a flowing matter and thus constitutes an originary present intentional experience, the zero point or limit idea of an indefinite series of prior and future experiences (*Ideas*, p. 238 [199 f.]; *EJ*, p. 385 [465]). All past experiences are in principle ordered to originary experience in the mode of the filled "now," and, similarly, all future experiences are anticipated and pre-scribed by the originary experience of the "now." The filled "now"—the present originary experience—therefore determines a two-dimensional system of consciousness, two correlative horizons of potentialities of consciousness. The first, that of the past, is reactivatable by memory (*Wiedererinnerung*), the second, that of the future, by "pre-memory" [*pro-souvenir*] (a translation of *Vorerinnerung*, "anticipating interiorization"). These two experiences are in themselves present experiences, although, at the same time, they are essential modifications of originary experience (perception). They are preconstituted by and in a correlative class of phenomenological configurations which are lived in an unreflective manner: *retentions* and *protentions*. These are unreflected (unseen) experiences of consciousness which constitute the hyletic substructures of present memories and anticipations and which thereby play a role in constituting the complete sense of originary experiences (perceptions) by surrounding them with their necessarily pre-scribed temporal and potential horizons.[39] The originary experience in the mode of the filled "now" is thus surrounded by two temporal horizons of potentialities of consciousness which it mediates in its present development, thereby assuring the permanence and continuously present actuality of consciousness (*Ideas,* p. 220 [182]).

Experience [*le vécu*] is therefore *actual* from the point of view of its effective existence. In this respect it is surrounded by potential horizons of consciousness. On the other hand, it is *potential* from the point of view of its total determination (*CM,* § 19). These mutual relativities determine its teleology, its intentional tendency toward ideal and concrete totality. Consciousness itself is thus both actual and potential, in the two possible reciprocal senses defined by two dimensions of intentionality. It is essentially an intentional life, the infinite teleology of the *cogito,* defined ideally by the idea of the infinite flow of experience. It is essentially a passing from potency to act, from *dynamis* to *entelecheia,* or from act to potency, from partial fact to ideal and exemplary whole (cf. above, § 10). This passing, which describes the very history of consciousness, is concretized in a passing from past to future. The structure of the latter passage is therefore precisely that of time (*CM,* p. 43 [81]), which is subject to the identical form of succession: the "now."

39. Retention is a passive or potential memory (*EJ,* pp. 109 f. [120 f.]), a primary unreflected recollection (*Ideas,* p. 216 [178]; cf. *Idées,* p. 248, n. 1) which is essentially implied in perception and which contributes to the constitution of the sense of perception (*LI,* p. 544 [II/1, 357]; *Crisis,* p. 160 [163]). It is therefore an originary and necessary modification (by way of development), inseparable from originary consciousness (*FTL,* p. 318 [279]). Recollection is a reflected memory (cf. *Idées,* p. 248, n. 1), a clear evidence of the experience of the past (*FTL,* p. 328 [288]), and therefore a presently actual experience in its own right (*Crisis,* loc. cit.). But it participates in the originary rationality (clarity) of perception (*Ideas,* pp. 393 f. [347]) and is therefore an essentially modified experience, even though it is separate and autonomous. The case of protention and *Vorerinnerung* is exactly parallel. Protention is an unreflected anticipation, implied in the sense of the presently actual perception and therefore inseparable from it. *Vorerinnerung* is a reflected anticipation—an essential modification of perception which is originarily constitutive of the future (*Crisis,* p. 169 [172])—and is also autonomous.

§ 48. *Qualities and characters of the noesis*

THE EGO THEREFORE LIVES in its *cogitationes* in an essentially diverse manner; intentional experiences have a multiplicity of different modes. We have seen principally the actual mode and the potential mode, which correspond to attention and inattention. Actuality and potentiality are universal modes of consciousness expressing a universal formal structure of consciousness which determines its two-dimensional character. The "now" is the actual; the past and the future are both ordered to it. But even in the "now" the ego can live in different ways. Consciousness can perceive, remember, presently anticipate. These are in the strict sense acts of the ego (*Ichakte*). These acts of the ego must now become our theme. They constitute the *cogito* and define consciousness or intentional life as actual.

Hence we find here the noetic correlates of presentation characters. Just as the object presents itself to the reflecting ego noematically as "perceived," "remembered," or "imagined," so the corresponding constitutive noesis proves to be perception, memory, or imagination. The noesis as pure noetic experience is thereby qualitatively characterized. The noetic characters are precisely what bring it about that we have to do with a perception or a memory. But the "remembered," like the "imagined," was shown to be a modification of the noematic character "perceived." The latter is therefore the originary character on which the others depend in a relative way; it is the "first," extrinsically defining its own secondary modifications. There is therefore a noematic "intentionality" in noemata. However, this cannot be a true constituting intentionality but only its constituted correlate. We must therefore proceed to an intentionality strictly speaking, which must be noetic.[40] This is what, "parallel" to noematic intentionality, manifests the exemplary dependence of the modes of consciousness among themselves. Thus memory refers to perception. Memory is a "having perceived," a past perception;

---

40. The exemplary reference of the modified noematic characters to the originary character is an "improper" noematic intentionality, an intentionality that represents the quasi-analytic relation of constituted objectivities independently of their constitution—hence an intentionality that "reflects" intentionality strictly speaking (*Ideas*, pp. 294 [254], 298 f. [258]). The relativity of the noematic sense to the object (= X) is also a noematic intentionality.

consequently, the perception enters consciousness along with the memory. However, this is not a matter of real inclusion of the perception in the memory; the former is not contained in the latter. But the memory intentionally refers to the perception, since it is a secondary modification of perception. If there is inclusion, this is *intentional inclusion* of the perception in the memory (*Ideas*, p. 291 [250]). The same observations hold for anticipation (*Vorerinnerung*). It is a perception in the future, and the anticipation therefore intentionally implies the perception. Similarly the imagination is a perception in the mode of the "quasi." There is therefore intentional inclusion of the unmodified consciousness in the modified consciousness, and this inclusion means an immanence as well as a transcendence. Husserl speaks of "inclusion" because in each case we have to do with perceptions; and this inclusion is "intentional" because we have to do with various modes of perceptions. "Intentionality" here expresses the exemplary relation of the originary consciousness to the modified consciousness or, conversely, the exemplary relation of the fact or factical example to the idea or ideal exemplar, of the derived "second" to the defining "first." This intentionality must be understood in the strict sense as a constituting relation, every experience being a "grasp" of an object or "consciousness of . . . ," and the "consciousness of . . ." being realized in an optimum and normative mode in perception.

In general, then, every experience qualified by a secondary character, every modified experience, necessarily refers to an unmodified and originary experience, to an exemplary experience (*Urerlebnis*). Thus, in the present case, the modified experience of memory or anticipation intentionally refers to the originary experience of perception (*Ideas*, p. 221 [183]). Only the latter is an originary presentation—memory and anticipation, which are modes of perception, being *presentifications* (cf. *Ideas*, § 99). Although both presentations and presentifications can be actual and presently posited in the "now" of consciousness, Husserl attaches much weight to the affirmation that modified consciousness and unmodified consciousness, derived experience and originary experience, are linked by an intentional reference.[41] Here Husserlian exemplarism is exhibited in a new and different way. We must not in any case regard the experience in general as a genus whose species are originary and

41. This shows that there is nothing temporal about intentionality by itself.

modified experiences. This view would lead us to hold that there is a real inclusion of the modified experiences in the originary experience, the species forming part of the genus and the genus intrinsically determining the species. Genus and specific difference stand in the relation of matter to form. The species is therefore really composed of the genus and the specific difference, and together with them it necessarily constitutes a single individual. But the modified experience (in this case the memory), and in general every modification, is extrinsically determined by the originary experience. It is therefore defined by its reference (its intentionality) to the latter. It does not form a single individual with the originary experience. On the contrary, the modified experience and the unmodified experience are *two*, and the intentional reference (the exemplarity) uniting them is necessarily *dialectical*. The originary experience does not form an integral part of the modified experience, but it makes possible in an exemplary way the derived constitution of the modified experience. Thus there is for Husserl no doubt on this subject: to noematic intentionality there corresponds intentionality strictly speaking, noetic intentionality. In each case the mode intentionally refers to its exemplar. If the originary experience is a genus, it is a *genos* in Plato's ideal sense of the word. That is, it is a normative "first" and extrinsic principle of definition (cf. *Ideas*, p. 300 [259] and above, § 17).

But the multiplicity of actual experiences is not exhausted with the delimitation of the noetic presentation characters. Every noema that is perceived, remembered, etc., appears also in the characters defining its being value: a certain object is real, possible, probable, etc. Here too we will find the characters of certainty, supposition, conjecture, etc., in the corresponding constitutive noesis. To the being characters of the noema, then, there correspond *belief characters* of the noesis. These characters are doxic or thetic in the sense that they posit being in this or that mode (cf. *Ideas*, § 103). Here again there is an intentional reference of doxic characters among themselves. An order is established, beginning with the originary belief (*Urdoxa*), which is certainty (*Ideas*, pp. 299 f. [259]). The latter can therefore be intentionally transformed into supposition, conjecture, question, doubt, just as, correlatively, the originary constituted character of reality is modified into the characters "possible," "probable," "problematic," "doubtful." [42] There must, then, be a

42. Cf. *Idées*, p. 354, n. 1.

"proto-form" (*Urform*) that makes it possible to unify and order the essential multiplicity of doxic characters. Certainty of belief, the originary doxic character, plays this role and is in fact intentionally included in the derived modifications (*Ideas*, p. 298 [257 f.]). The same observations we made regarding the noetic presentation characters are true here as well. Moreover, it is in connection with the doxic modes of noetic consciousness that Husserl introduces the distinction between genus and species, on the one hand, and originary experience and modified experience, on the other.[43] The multiplicity of noetic experiences is therefore ordered according to an intentional unity in virtue of this exemplary principle, the *Urdoxa*—which is an ideal principle, since it is the telos of an infinite noetic intentionality.

But a derived multiplicity (and hence a unity) immediately reappears. Every secondary mode is intentionally relative to the primary mode, but it may happen that the secondary mode as such is considered by reflection. It is then presented to consciousness as an originary being, and its modified doxic character undergoes a second modification of sense so that it is subsequently considered as a simple doxa in the unmodified sense (*Ideas*, pp. 300 f. [259 f.]). In other words, phenomenological analysis here reveals the essential possibility on the part of every modified experience of being considered as an originary experience in the manner of a simple and underived belief. Every mode of belief can be regarded as a belief, and every mode of being as a being (*Ideas*, § 105). The addition of new noetico-noematic characters gives rise to the appearance in consciousness of new objects, which are in turn grasped as originary objects in an originary mode of belief (*Ideas*, p. 301 [260]). This is why the difference between mode and nonmode or between modified consciousness and originary consciousness is entirely relative. It would be better to speak of every manifestation of consciousness as a "mode of consciousness." Thus, originary experience as well as derived experience is a mode. "Mode," then,

43. *Ideas*, p. 300 (259). Husserl thereby shows that he rejects the interpretation which might be called that of classical logic (the logic of genus and species) because it destroys precisely the logical exemplarism that he wishes to establish. If there were a genus "doxa," the universal principle of intrinsic determination for all its species, then all the modes of doxa would be of the same value and would be on the same level; there would no longer be a teleological ordering between the secondary derivations and an examplary first. In a word, there would no longer be any intentionality.

includes being and belief in the unmodified sense (*Ideas*, p. 299 [258]). To indicate the intentional reference, we will therefore use the term "originary mode" to designate the exemplary form. So perception and the originary doxa are originary modes of consciousness. But this is not just a terminological device, adopted with a view to simplifying the analysis. Husserl wants to make it clear that the mutual relativity of the modes of consciousness is infinite (in fact, the possibility of intentional transformation of modified doxa into originary doxa sets up a *processus ad infinitum*, thematized in the eidetic form of the "and so forth," and makes it possible to infringe the principle of noncontradiction), and that the originary mode or originary unmodified consciousness remains an idea, an ideal norm. This will appear still more clearly with the third series of doxic modifications, affirmation and negation.

It is unnecessary to go through the particulars of the noematic "yes" and "no." Let us simply recall that the exemplarist structure is to be found here. Affirmation is the originary mode (the unmodified consciousness) of which negation is the secondary mode. Negation is the negation of something, which does not mean that negation is immediately and necessarily the negation of an affirmation. We must introduce here a distinction between affirmation and positing (*Bejahung und Setzung*). This is a crucial distinction (*Ideas*, pp. 301 f. [260]). It appears that affirmation is already a modification, hence a secondary consciousness. Only positing is an originary consciousness (*Urmodus*). To understand this, we must bring in the doctrine of *Experience and Judgment*. Experience normally unfolds in a continuous and uniform manner. The object's predicates are progressively explicated (*Explikation*), and the sense which is originarily anticipated and which exemplarily orients the presumed course of experience is synthetically fulfilled in a concordant manner (*einstimmige Erfüllung*). But perceptual experience may be subject to essential modifications—doubt, for example, which is the first step of negation pure and simple. If experience issues in the modalization of doubt, for example, it obviously cannot remain there. The doubt must be overcome, either in a new positing or in a negation. Therefore, neither this affirmation nor this negation is originary. On the contrary, they are constituted in a reflective reconsideration of an inhibited experience, a reconsideration intended to bring out of this experience its genuine sense. These affirmative and negative qualities are therefore secondary characters of experience. In predicative terms, they are secondary characters of the predicative doxa. They refer to an originary and immediate character, the primary affirmation or originary positing (*Setzung*), which is simply experience pure and simple (*schlichte Erfahrung*). Hence, if negation cancels, affirmation confirms; it gives its assent to a corrected experience (*Ideas,* p. 302 [261]). Of course, it is still true that negation is a mode of affirmation. But it must be added that affirmation itself is relative to an originary positing. Affirmation and negation are both relative to a primitive *Ur-doxa* (*Ideas,* p. 301 [260]). Hence we have here an interlocking of intentionalities which delimit successive levels of originariness. Negation, as the modified doxic experience, can in turn be regarded as an affirmation. Instead of being considered a qualitatively modified object, what is cancelled is considered a new object in a doxa which is in turn originary. Nonbeing (the negated) is thus taken as being, as unmodified (affirmed) being; negation is taken as affirmation, as the positing of nonbeing (*Ideas,* p. 303 [261]). This shows that, although "originary consciousness" is an eminently relative concept, negation is in any case not an originary concept. The "no" is never originary, and the negative judgment is not a fundamental form (*EJ,* § 72).

Only the primary positing (*Setzung*) is originary. It is the normal telos of uninhibited (concordant and continuous) experience and consequently of the predicative judgment that is immediately grounded in this experience. But this uninhibited experience, concordant in its full extent, is an idea or ideal norm (cf. *EJ,* p. 287 [346]). In fact, experience almost necessarily has modalizations. So originariness is in fact always secondary for us (descriptive-phenomenological point of view), and Husserl introduces a *processus ad infinitum* that is designed to justify the relative originariness of modified experiences. Modalized experience needs to be "reflected" and criticized, i.e., corrected. The doxic characters which then qualify it cannot be originary in the strict sense of the word. They are already derived, intentionally referring to an ideal of immediate concordance at which all knowledge in general aims.

Finally, we must keep in mind that, just as all noematic characters are positional, the noetic characters distinguished here are thetic characters. They intentionally refer to an exemplary first, and the entire sphere of noeses is a priori under the dominion of this universal norm: *certain affirmative perception.* It must be added that our description of noetic characters is universal in scope. Every noesis comprises a qualitative characterization and what might be called a noetic "core," two structural strata which correspond in the noesis to the noematic character and core studied above. Whatever phenomenological order of "representation" may be under consideration, each noesis (judication, volition, etc.) includes its own modes of originariness and secondariness, its own modes of doxa, of affirmation and negation. The noetico-noematic structures may be more complicated, but the basic principle remains the same (cf. *Ideas*, p. 296 [255]).

The affirmative and negative series of characters most clearly exhibits the univocal ideality of the originary consciousness, an ideal status which consists in two things: (1) the value of this consciousness as exemplary norm, never really reached or presently realized, and (2) the intentional reference of every mode to this originary first, which is the intentional pole of every mode of lived consciousness. The latter point must be understood in the sense of intentional shifting. From an analytic point of view, formal logic includes several specifically different concepts of the judgment. From the synthetic point of view, there correspond to these various concepts of the judgment various intentionalities which interlock with one another in such a way as to form a single intentionality. We find a similar situation here. We have brought to light three series of noematic and noetic characters. They seem to be irreducible to one another, but we have just seen that, for the third series (affirmation and negation), Husserl explicitly refers us to an originary doxa. In fact, it must be said that doxic characters as well as affirmative and negative characters intentionally refer to an originary primitive grasp. An affirmation is an affirmative or confirmative grasp (consciousness) of something, just as a certainty is a real [*réelle*] grasp (consciousness) of something. We have here noetic characters, i.e., in the strict sense, characters of an originary noesis. But the reductions we carried out above have brought us to the lived world. The originary grasp of this world, the originary noesis, is therefore *perception*.

Belief characters and universal characters of affirmation and negation therefore refer to perception, the originary *Setzung* which they qualify in different ways. We must therefore distinguish, on the one hand, between the originary noesis (perception) and the secondary noeses (imagination, memory) which are their immediately derived modes, and, on the other hand, between the originary noetic characters strictly speaking, which come to qualify the originary and derived noeses (certainty, affirmation) and the modes of these characters (doubt, etc., and negation).

From the letter of Husserl's text, of course, it appears that perception itself is to be counted among the noetic characters. Serious difficulties present themselves here, which can nevertheless be overcome dialectically. It can, in fact, be shown that just as an originary consciousness is an originary *mode* of consciousness insofar as it is a *nonmode* of consciousness, so perception is an originary noetic *character* insofar as it is a *noncharacter*— since it is the support (substrate) of secondary characters. The notion of character (quality) implies something "accidental." The character can vary without the identical core that plays the role of substrate being affected. The noematic character is variable, while the noematic core is identical. Similarly, the noetic quality is variable, as we will see, while the material datum (hylē) may be identical. But the hyletic datum is not constitutive by itself. Outside its function in the noesis, the hyletic datum is blind. If perception is, then, only an "accidental" character of the noesis, how can we explain the hyletic content [*teneur*] of the perceptual experience? There must necessarily be an originary noesis, an originary noetic "core"; and we have just seen that perception is this originary noesis for the *Lebenswelt*. We must now regard perception as a primitive experience (i.e., as a hyletic datum which is by itself immediately endowed with a noetic function), as an "absolute" experience (absolute in that it is not noetically qualified by a character), as an experience whose hylē is by itself a noesis. This "pure" noesis or "constitutive" hylē is an infinite idea, never realized and factually unrealizable. It can be idealized or anticipated in itself (exemplarily).[44] If, then, the originary noesis is an originary noetic "character," it is so in the same sense in which we say that the originary consciousness is a mode of consciousness. We have here an aspect of the phenomenological surpassing of the principle of noncontradiction by the dialectical principle of the "and so forth" ad infinitum. Nonbeing is a mode of being (first moment); nonbeing is (second moment).

Husserl can thus assert, correlatively, either that perception is a noetic "character" or that it is the originary noesis strictly speaking which is accidentally qualified with a certain noetic

44. Cf. *EJ*, p. 287 (346). Cf. the same problem in the case of the judgment, § 35 above.

character. Both formulations are correct. (1) Noetic reflection reveals a series of distinct characters which refer to an originary character, the perceptual noesis. (2) The originary noesis is perception, which alone is the noesis strictly speaking and which is secondarily qualified by noetic characters. In the first case we are saying that what we have here is the first parallelism brought to light between noesis and noema, applied exclusively to the noetico-noematic characters. In the second case we are saying that a new parallelism of noema and noesis comes into play, that between the noematic core and the noetic "core." For after the variable character we reach the stable core, the substrate. Both formulations are doubtless correct, but they do not have the same sense. The one is static; the parallelism it expresses is strict and analytic—between character and character. The other is intentional; there is explicit reference to the "core," the foundation of the character. If the first parallelism were rigorously applied, we would end by affirming that the noetic "core" is a noetic operation without characters, and we would have neutralization. Taken to its extreme, this position would be absurd, since it would end by identifying hylē and neutralization and would thereby destroy intentionality. In the second case, we end with an originary thetic consciousness which is a noesis strictly speaking, the perception in which the sense of our world is legitimized.

Finally, let us note that if both formulations are correct, if the originary perception is both an originary noesis and an originary noetic character, this is so in virtue of this law of exemplarism: the unity, being the measure of the multiplicity, is at the same time an integral part of the multiplicity and external to it. We have perception in the first case as originary character, in the second as originary noesis. This can be expressed in a unique way thus: perception is a noncharacter, i.e., a nonmode.

§ 49. *Hyletic manifold and intentional functions*

WE HAVE THUS ALREADY MANAGED to determine in part the *content* of the intentional experience. With the noesis, now considered as implying its derived modes, we have reached an element that defines the present life of the ego. The ego lives in the present consciousness, in the *cogito;* and by *cogito* we mean noetic experience in general, the noesis in general. But the present life of the ego is a real [*réelle*] life of consciousness; the ego lives really in its *cogitationes*. The noesis is a real moment of the total experience.[45] The experience is consequently composed of various moments which are intentionally correlative. We must not forget the essential principle that the noesis is always consciousness of something and that it therefore *includes* its object in a certain way—or, conversely, that the object is one of its moments. But the object is the intentional telos of consciousness, not a real, integral part of it. The ego is conscious of its objects but does not really live in them. The object is therefore an intentional moment of the experience, the moment which, strictly speaking, defines the (teleological) movement of intentional transcendence of every experience. We must therefore distinguish between descriptive content and intentional content of the experience[46] or between a real content and an intentional content (*Ideas*, §§ 41, 88, 97). The ego really lives in its noeses, but it is immediately conscious only of its noemata. The noetic life of the ego is real; the noematic consciousness is intentional.

However, the noesis, or the experience strictly speaking, can in turn be intentionally present to consciousness. When it is,

45. This is a point on which Husserl's terminology becomes more precise between *LI* and *Ideas*. *LI* speaks of the noesis as a really [*réellement*] conscious moment, which it cannot be. Consciousness being necessarily intentional, the ego can be conscious only intentionally; whereas the ego can really live in its experiences [*vécus*] without being conscious of them. Cf. *LI*, p. 565 (II/1, 382).

46. *LI*, pp. 576 (II/1, 397 f.), 578 (399). We can see here the ambiguity of the distinction between real analysis and intentional analysis. Matter and quality are real moments of the experience; they are the hylē that we are about to see and the character we have already seen. Description of these elements taken by themselves is actually a real psychological analysis. But can we abstract from intentionality elements whose entire sense is to intentionally constitute the object? Moreover, Husserl shows here that the real moments of the experience are already intentional moments. It is best, however, to maintain the distinction between real component and intentional component, while tempering it with the phenomenological thesis of their univocal intentional continuity. The same holds for formal logic and transcendental logic. Transcendental logic elucidates the sense of formal logic. The latter must therefore be in a way transcendental. And the same holds for every object in general in relation to its subjective a priori. This is an aspect of intentional shifting, which is simply the dynamism of self-transcendence characteristic of phenomenology.

the ideal infinity of the constitutive intentionality attaches to it. The intuitive glance is then directed toward the noesis as the new noema of a teleological multiplicity of new noeses, which are in turn really experienced but not immediately conscious. The intuitive glance must then in turn be grasped by a new intuitive glance, and so on ad infinitum. A perfect transparency on the part of consciousness, a perfect consciousness of consciousness, is thus an infinite idea—precisely because every consciousness in general is necessarily intentional, i.e., teleological, and not immediate (not real) (*FTL,* pp. 158 f. [142]). This infinite ideality, which is eidetically structured by the "and so forth," is for Husserl the only means of avoiding empiricist psychologism. Empiricism does not acknowledge the *processus ad infinitum,* because it will not recognize intentionality and because it confuses the intentional content with the real content of the experience.

But the noema is multiple. It includes a sense, and this sense must also have a counterpart in the noesis. Just as the noematic character is an intentional moment, as opposed to the real moment of the noesis which corresponds to it, so to the noematic sense there must apparently correspond a real moment of the total experience. We are thus brought to the *hyletic datum* (cf. *Ideas,* § 85). This is the counterpart we are seeking for the noematic sense—or, alternatively, the counterpart of the object, although, as we will see later, the ego itself is the express correlate of the object. The hyletic datum in general is constituted by the real multiplicity of the data of sensation in which the noematic sense is adumbrated.[47] It therefore appears immediately as a real manifold by contrast with the intentional unity (*Ideas,* pp. 131 f. [94]); it is of another order than the object. The hyletic datum (in eidetic terms, the hylē) is a real part of the experience. The object adumbrated in it is an intentional moment of this same experience (*Ideas,* pp. 132 [94 f.], 284 [244]; *LI,* p. 565 [II/1, 382]). The first is really lived and mediately (reflectively) conscious; the second is not really lived but is intentionally conscious. The latter is the ideal (irreal) transcendence of consciousness; the former forms an integral part of the real immanence of consciousness. The hylē thus gives the object in a certain way. It gives the various sensible determinations of the object, but it is not these sensible determinations

47. The data of sensation (*Empfindungsdaten*) are what are called "primary contents" in *LI,* p. 815 (II/2, 180).

themselves (*LI*, p. 356 [II/1, 129]; *Ideas*, pp. 246 f. [208]; *FTL*, p. 165 [147]). Only for the hyletic manifold is Berkeley's maxim valid: *esse est percipi*, its being is its being perceived.[48] Its being is its being really (subjectively) lived. It is not the first object of consciousness, and (in opposition to psychological empiricism) it can be grasped only reflectively (*LI*, p. 429 [II/1, 220]; cf. *Crisis*, pp. 86 [89], 93 f. [96]). Correlatively, the *esse* of the noema may be said to be its *percipi* if we keep in mind the difference between real inclusion in consciousness and intentional inclusion (*Ideas*, p. 287 [246]).

The error of the empiricist psychologists—and even of Descartes, when he wanted to proceed demonstratively from the picture idea (an object immanent in consciousness) to external reality—was precisely to take the necessary inclusion of the object in consciousness, which is precisely intentionality, to be a real inclusion. This reduced the object to the hyletic datum of sensation, the adumbrated to the adumbration, intentional consciousness to real experience, the irreal transcendent to the immediate immanent. The phenomenological principle involved here is that there is only a single intentional object, a single intentional unity of consciousness (*Ideas*, p. 263 [224]). Descartes and the empiricism to which he gave rise conceived two intentional unities, which is absurd in phenomenological terms. They assume a problematic relationship between an internal subjective unity and an external real unity which is, for just this reason, not constitutively experienced. Dogmatism takes root in this contradiction, which is only a phenomenological expression for the aporia of the Kantian in-itself.[49] Reducing the in-itself to intentional immanence, on the other hand, makes it possible definitively to overcome all dogmatism, even the naïveté of noematic description, since doing so immediately links the in-itself to its constitutive a priori.

However, there is no immediate continuity between the hyletic datum and the noema, in any case no real continuity, since we are dealing with two distinct but no longer constitutive orders of reality. The hyletic manifold gives or adumbrates the object (*Ideas*, pp. 131 [94], 139 f. [102 f.], 283 [242 f.]), but not

48. Its time of givenness is its time of being; cf. *EJ*, p. 255 (306).

49. Concerning Kant's thing in itself, Jacobi said: ". . . without this supposition, I cannot enter into the system; with it, I cannot remain there" (quoted by H. Vaihinger, *Kommentar der "Kritik der reinen Vernunft"* [Stuttgart, 1881–82], II, 37).

by itself. In itself the hyletic manifold is a matter (as the word "hylē" signifies), and matter by itself is not intentional (*Ideas*, pp. 120 [81], 247 [208]; *LI*, p. 559 [II/1, 374]). In order for there actually to be a constituted noema, the hyletic manifold must take on a constitutive function strictly speaking, an intentional function which confers intentional form on it. In other words, a noesis is required. The intentional experience therefore analyzes into a sensory matter (sensory hylē) and a noetic form (intentional morphē), but it subsists only in and by the unity of its material and formal elements.[50] We can here take up Kantian language; the matter (hylē) without intentional form is blind, and the noesis without the hyletic datum is empty (*Ideas*, p. 247 [209]). The union of the two is what really [*réellement*] makes up the individual experience. Sensory hylē and intentional morphē are explicitly taken in the classical relationship of matter and form. The determining element, the one which specifically introduces intentionality into the matter which is by itself blind, is intentional form, i.e., the noesis (*Ideas*, p. 249 [210]). The latter realizes intentional sense-giving; it is what "gives a sense" to the informed matter.[51] The experience is therefore noetic when the hylē is actually informed by a noetic moment and when, by virtue of this moment, it has a sense (*Ideas*, pp. 261 f. [223]).

The noesis therefore performs a transcendental constitutive function. It is what eidetically expresses the consciousness of something (*Ideas*, p. 251 [212 f.]). Having a sense, consciousness is necessarily a teleology, i.e., the order constituting a synthetic unity out of a hyletic manifold. The intentional function of the noesis therefore establishes a transcendental relation of constitution between hyletic experiences (real material moments of consciousness) and the noema (intentional moment of consciousness). It reveals (gives) to the hyletic manifold its teleological objective sense (*Ideas*, p. 252 [213]). The pure study of the hylē (hyletics) has significance, not in itself, but in connection with the phenomenology of transcendental consciousness. The hylē has sense only functionally, insofar as it provides

50. *Ideas*, p. 247 (208 f.). The *Sinngebung* mentioned in this passage is not yet constitution of the object but is rather "information" of the material manifold by a morphē for the purpose of constitution. Here the intentional is therefore really (noetically) lived. Cf. below on the concept of *Auffassungssinn*.

51. Cf., in the preceding footnote, the observation based on *Ideas*, p. 249 (210).

a material substructure to an intentional constitution (*Ideas*, pp. 253 f. [215]).

To be more precise, we must distinguish between noesis and function. Information of the hylē by the noesis is what gives the hylē an intentional function. The function is therefore the constituting operative unity of noesis and hyletic manifold, to which the intentional synthetic unity of the constituted noema corresponds. The hylē performs a function, to be sure, but this function is grounded in the essence of the noesis (*Ideas*, p. 251 [212]). Conversely, the function of the noesis would be ineffective if it were to find no hyletic manifold to inform, to intentionally order in a synthetic unity. The intentional function is therefore the unifying and constitutive *Leistung* of consciousness; it designates the teleological transcendental exercise of consciousness itself, its intentional life. And so Husserl affirms that the problem of the function is central in phenomenology (*Ideas*, p. 252 [213]). It is the crux of transcendental constitution, here considered in its originary mode, the originary constitution of the empirical object (perception). The intentional function defines the *Leistung* of consciousness and implies all its elements: hylē, noesis, noema. It manifests the essential dynamic continuity of these elements and therefore makes the expression "noetico-noematic parallelism" obsolete (cf. *FTL*, p. 285 [252 f.]).

The noetic function can take a variety of forms. Here, in the privileged case of perception, it takes the form of animation by perceptual apprehension (*Beseelung durch Auffassung*). The data of sensation are in themselves blind; they must be "animated" by signifying apprehensions. They then explicitly become "presentations" or "figurations" (*Darstellungen*) of the noematic object (*Ideas*, p. 132 [94]). Relations parallel to those which obtain between noetico-noematic qualities and matters are therefore found to obtain between hylē and intentional morphē. An identical noesis exercising the same function can thus have several different matters. The same perception can give different perceived objects if the hyletic manifold is modified; a variation in the hyletic "texture" brings with it a noematic modification of the perception (*Ideas*, p. 284 [243 f.]). Conversely, the hyletic manifold can remain identical even if its meaning is modified by variation of its noetic quality (intentional function). Thus different noetic qualities, and hence different constituted objects, can correspond to the same sensory matter.[52] But the noesis is what necessarily informs the hylē, it is what essentially determines *what* (quality) the constituted object will be and, more radically, whether or not there will even be a constituted object (whether or not there will be a concordant constitution).

Thus it appears that the noetic moment of the experience is what provides the apprehension sense (*Auffassungssinn*) of the hyletic manifold and insures the fundamental meaning (*Sinngebung*) we mentioned above (p. 303, n. 50). This notion of apprehension (*Auffassung*) is subtle. It designates the manner in which the hyletic manifold is taken up[53] in the noetic act, the way in which it is "ap-perceived," which will be determinative for the sense of the noema adumbrated in the hylē. But this apprehension, which shows itself to be an initial moment of the intentionality to the object, is diverse in nature. It may in the first place be perception, imagination, reflection, etc. It is then an intentional act strictly speaking. But it may also be constituted from derived and less essential operations of the ego: explicating, putting in relation, global grasp, retaining a certain part of the object in grasp, secondary position-taking, conjecture, etc. At this point we might define apprehension (*Auffassung*) as an act character (*Aktcharakter*) in the strict sense (cf. *Ideas*, pp. 257 f. [218 f.]). Finally, it may be a mere kinesthesia.[54] Thus, for example, in the perception of certain ambiguous figures the perceived shape can become completely different by a mere conversion of visual attention. The hyletic matter remains identical; the noesis, too, remains essentially identical. Only the attention, the orientation of the glance, varies. This example shows perfectly how apprehensions can be a small but nevertheless

52. *Ideas*, p. 288 (247); *LI*, p. 565 (II/1, 381). We will see that this difference in sense-giving is a consequence of the difference in the initial *Auffassungen*. The latter are necessarily different, according to *Ideas*, p. 288.

53. Note the etymology of the German *Auf-fassen* and the French *as-sumer*. [And, we might add, of the English "ap-prehend."—TRANS.]

54. *Kinestheses* are functional movements of the lived body (*Leib; corps propre*). On this point cf. *CM*, pp. 97 (128), 116 (145); *Crisis*, p. 106 (108 f.). They modify the intentional horizon of experience (*CM*, p. 44 [82]) and determine the multiplicity of appearings of the perceived object (*Crisis*, p. 161 [164]) while making possible the continuity of experience (*EJ*, p. 83 [89]). An example of this is different points of view and angles of view (*Ideas*, pp. 282 [242], 289 [249]).

very important moment in the constitution of the sense of the object. In our example, what is involved is not even a physical movement of one's body but simply a different distribution of the weight of attention on the same hylē and in the same perception. This modification is possible even in complete physical immobility.[55]

It is this noetic moment, however, which insures transcendental constitution. Noetic apprehension—the noetic act in the broadest sense—teleologically orients the hyletic manifold of sensations, which is blind by itself, and transcendentally constitutes an objective noema on the basis of animated figurations. The transcendental constitution of the object (intentional unity) in the hyletic multiplicity by means of noetic functions is an aspect of the fundamental problem of the one and the many— i.e., of exemplarism—as we will see again in the conclusion.[56] In short, if we remember that the hyletic manifold animated in figurations is, strictly speaking, the appearing of the object, we can say that the object is constituted in its appearing.[57] Thus, with the *cogito*—more precisely, with the explication of intentional functions of constitution—we have realized the program pre-scribed by the *Crisis:* the second thematization of the *Lebenswelt* in the noetic *quomodo* of its givenness (*Crisis,* § 38). With the synthetic-constitutive a priori of the function, we have reached the subjective structure which transcendental logic called for (cf. *FTL,* p. 191 [169]). Let us note, finally, that even though our account has been limited to the "hylomorphic" composition of perception, it has an exemplary value. All objective constitution necessarily comprises a hylē and an intentional morphē. We are dealing only with perception, as Husserl does, because it is the originary givenness of the originary object (*Ideas,* pp. 375 f. [330]).

55. Cf. *LI,* p. 566 (II/1, 384). Physical immobility is in fact a true kinesthesis, since (by reason of the dialectical principle discovered above) even rest is a mode of movement. Cf. *Crisis,* p. 106 (108).

56. *Ideas,* p. 284 (244). The unity is transcendent to the many. Of course the constituted is a datum, but it is irreally included in the intentional experience; *Ideas,* pp. 285 (244 f.), 375 (330). This is the transcendence of irreal inclusion (*Transzendenz irreellen Beschlossenseins*); *CM,* p. 26 (65).

57. The hyletic manifold informed by the intentional function of the noetic moment constitutes the "representation," the "figuration," the "adumbration" or "perspective variation"—i.e., in sum, the appearing of the object (*Ideas,* pp. 132 [94], 284 [244]).

Therefore, the noesis, the noetic moment, is what bears responsibility for intentional constitution; the *cogito* is what exercises the intentional function of the ego. (This will be confirmed in more detail when we have seen that the ego is a pure subject [= X].) The noesis is what gives the ego its object. And it is in the *cogito* that the object is constituted; the *cogito* is what insures the intentional continuity between sensory hylē and constituted noema. In a word, the *cogito* is what insures the concordant sequence of transcendental motivation, the link between the intentional transcendence of the object and the ego (*Ideas*, p. 143 [106]).

If, in addition to the first parallelism, we can speak of a second parallelism between hyletic datum and constituted noematic sense, it will immediately be seen that this expression raises great difficulties. Is this really a matter of a parallelism? No; on the contrary, there is an intentional continuity between hyletic datum and objective noema. We must not let ourselves be misled by the difference in being between the lived hylē and the intended object. The first is *ordered* to the second by the noetic function of constitution. The really lived aspect of consciousness is what teleologically constitutes the irreally (intentionally) lived; the immanent is what constitutes the transcendent. In *Ideas*, several parallelisms are spoken of. Three, in fact, are to be distinguished: (1) the parallelism of noetico-noematic characters; (2) the parallelism between the hyletic manifold and the noematic objective core (sense); and (3) the parallelism between the complete noetic experience (hylē + noesis) and the complete noema. All these parallelisms are in fact "constitutive parallelisms"—an improvised expression, which the "analytic" distinction between characters and noetico-noematic "cores" legitimizes to some extent. The last parallelism, however, is the customary expression for intentionality. This is an "oriented" parallelism, as the expression suggests. In the strict sense, then, there cannot be a parallelism but only an intentional teleology. This is so true that we should not even speak separately of the noetic experience and its noematic counterpart, as if the latter were external to the former. The complete intentional experience comprises two constitutive parts. One is the noetic experience, composed of hylē and intentional morphē; the other is the noematic experience, an intentional moment of the *cogito*.

§ 50. *Rational consciousness: evidence and truth*

THE NOETIC *quomodo* of the *Lebenswelt* thus proves to be in fact the constitutive *quomodo* of the *Lebenswelt*. It is the teleologically ordered manifold of consciousness in which the *Lebenswelt,* the natural empirical object of immediate perception, comes to be constituted. Thus we have reached the originary givenness of the world (*Selbstgebung*) or, at the level of the empirical object, originary evidence. This is what will enable us to explicate the final phenomenological character which attaches correlatively to the constituted noema and the constituting noesis: rationality (*Vernünftigkeit*).

The object must in general be able to legitimize its sense; and, as we know, validity is originary only in and by intuition (*LI,* pp. 235 [I, 241], 238 f. [I, 244]; *Ideas,* pp. 51 f. [10 f.], 81 [41], 92 f. [52], 223 [185], 230 [192]; and cf. above, p. 84). Only *seeing* in general, or *evidence,* can insure the rationality of a noesis and a corresponding noema (*Ideas,* § 136). The legitimacy of a cognition is therefore a problem of rational validity or transcendental lawfulness. Evidence, seeing in general, is the guarantee of transcendental lawfulness, and it decides the *Rechtsfrage.*[58] There is a clear analogy with law (*jus*): an evident cognition must justify its claim. Evidence is a "trial" in justification, and the chief witness is the evident synthetic experience which originarily constitutes transcendental lawfulness (*FTL,* p. 164 [146 f.]). The problems of evidence, of truth, of validity, of lawfulness of knowledge, are therefore problems of reason and are to be elucidated within the framework of a phenomenology of reason.[59]

But to speak of evidence is immediately to speak of intention

58. *Ideas,* p. 84 (44); *FTL,* p. 335 (208). Lawfulness (*Recht*) is the intentional telos of a justification (*Rechtfertigung*) and hence resolves the question of justification or truth (*Rechtfertigungsfrage, Wahrheitsfrage*) (*EJ,* p. 311 [377]). We will necessarily end in the thematic of truth.

59. *Ideas,* pp. 360 f. (315). Cf. especially *Ideas,* Fourth Section, Second Chapter. "Rational validity" renders the German words *Rechtheit, Gültigkeit, Triftigkeit;* cf., for example, *Ideas,* pp. 387 (341), 404 (357), 360 (315). As we might expect, the juridical aspect of evidence expresses phenomenological exemplarism in a way. Originary lawfulness [*droit*] or evidence is in fact the ideal norm or rule of all *de facto* constitution.

and fulfillment, of concrete and realized intentionality.[60] In fact, in the originary constitutive experience of the transcendent object (*Lebenswelt*) we have an anticipating intention and a subsequent fulfillment. Every perception begins with an initial apprehension (*Auffassung*). We know that this is the crucial initial moment of originary experience, since it is what determines—in an ideal and still empty (possible) manner—the sense of the object, i.e., the presumed direction of experience. This apprehension can be extremely diverse in nature, as we know. It can even be a global grasp (*Erfassung*) of the object, in which the object is grasped from the first in its undetermined totality (cf. *EJ*, p. 117 [131])—which clearly assumes past experiences of the same object, experiences sedimented in retention and awakened by a new similar experience. When this occurs, a consciousness of analogy is originarily constituted which makes it possible to foresee the further course of the experience in a quasi-empirical manner and in a way to grasp the totality of the object itself. Apprehension strictly speaking does not necessarily include this empirical note. It is only the primitive awakening of the originary consciousness and the originary "pre-sumption" of the course of constitutive experience.[61] It determines a priori the teleology of possible experience and normatively anticipates an ideal process of fulfillment. Apprehension is the initial moment of the experience, the very beginning of the experience. Like every beginning, it anticipates its terminus (telos) by pre-scribing the intentional horizon of possible consciousness (*EJ*, p. 81 [85]). Apprehension is therefore originary intention (*Abzielung*), on the one hand, and, on the other hand, beginning of realizing fulfillment (*Erzielung*) or idea(liza)tion of the completed fulfillment. In a word, in explicating the intention, apprehension needs to be fulfilled in the realizing process of the intention (cf. *EJ*, pp. 83 [88], 200–202 [236–38]; *LI*, p. 563 [II/1, 378 f.]). It is therefore immediately followed by further moments, i.e., by a determining

60. Cf. Husserl's expression "*Bedeuten* in concreto" (*LI*, p. 593 [II/1, 421]).

61. The exact relationship between *Auffassung* and *Erfassung* is difficult to establish. In *EJ*, these two concepts are very close if not identical. What distinguishes them, it seems, is that one is an initial grasp and the other a global grasp of the object. Each is teleologically oriented toward a more perfect determination of the object, and they are therefore anticipative (potential) states of consciousness. In *Ideen II* (pp. 22 f.) another difference is added to this: *Erfassung* becomes an explicit *Auffassung*.

explication; the object that is immediately anticipated as to its sense continues to appear originarily in all or part of its determinations.[62]

Two cases now present themselves. Either the objective explication follows a concordant course, and the sense ideally anticipated by the apprehension is fulfilled in a synthetic and originary manner; or else the explication (i.e., the experience itself in its totality) undergoes modalizations or inhibitions which make it deviate from the continuous course pre-scribed a priori by the apprehension. In the latter case the experience needs to be taken up again, criticized, and corrected in order to recover the essential concordant unity. The intention is fulfilled in either case, directly in the one case and indirectly in the other. The telos of this process is therefore necessarily a state of perfect fulfillment of the intention, to which there corresponds, on the one hand, perfect rationality of the noesis (perception) and, on the other hand, perfect intuitive fullness of the noema (the perceived). This is where the "second object in the 'how'" is to be situated, conforming to this second concept introduced by Husserl: the noema in its mode of fullness (*Ideas*, § 132; cf. above, p. 284). To be fully constituted in itself, the sense can be given in a more or less originary manner, in an intuitive or an unintuitive mode. Not only the fullness of the sense counts; the "how" of its fulfillment is equally important (*Ideas*, p. 380 [334]). Perception is precisely the intuitive mode of this "how" at the level of the natural empirical object. It gives the bodily presence of the object (*Leibhaftigkeit*); and in it, the perceptual intention is at its maximum degree of objective fulfillment (*Erfülltheit*) (*Ideas*, p. 380 [334 f.]). The perceptual noesis now merits the title "rational consciousness," and the perceptual positing of the object is rationally legitimized.

We have here the criticism of the positional character, whose originary and derived modes we saw above. The positional character is valid only on the foundation of an intuitively fulfilled sense, and the rational character thus attaching to an originarily given sense definitively ratifies the object's intuitive mode of fullness. Intuition motivates and rationally legitimizes the belief characters and being characters (*Ideas*, pp. 380 f. [335]; *CM*, § 26; *Ideen II*, § 56 [a]). Evidence is thus a noetic process of

62. *Erfassung* is a lower level of objectifying activity, and explication (*Explikation*) is a higher level. It rests with the latter to fulfill the initial intention, to confirm or disconfirm it. Cf. *EJ*, p. 104 (114) and all of §§ 22–23.

intentional motivation of a fully intuitive sense (*Ideas*, p. 381 [335 f.]), and this evidence alone is truly transcendental constitution.

But when the noesis is evident legitimately, the noema merits the character of *truth*. It is in the originary process of the noesis that the truth of the noema is constituted. In fact, to a noesis or evident *cogito* there necessarily corresponds a noema all of whose characters (in particular, the originary being characters, certainty and doxa) are rationally motivated.⁶³ The intention which a priori pre-scribes the sense of the object in the apprehension (*Auffassung*) undergoes a process of verification (*Bewährung*) in the course of fulfillment. Depending on whether the course of experience is concordant or discordant, this intention is confirmed or disconfirmed. In other words, the subject accompanies his experience with judgments such as "The object is indeed such as the intention anticipated it," "It is not such," and so on. In the process of fulfillment, a constant confrontation between the intention and its fulfillment takes place. This is a result of the synthesis in virtue of which a "consciousness of the same" is constituted in the flowing manifold of noetic experiences. (1) In the multiple appearing of adumbrations, an objective ideality is synthetically constituted, an intentional unity to which we order this constitutive multiplicity. (2) What is true of sensible intuition (perception) is also true of categorial intuition (judication). In the passing of the judgment from distinctness to clarity, the consciousness of the ideal identity of the judgment as such is constituted, i.e., the anticipation of the pure predicative meaning is confronted with the originary givenness of the categorial objectivities which are meant. Evidence in general is therefore the constituting grasp or originary seeing of an identity (not only qualitative but numerical) in and through a multiplicity of noetic "appearings" (*FTL*, pp. 162 f. [145]). Synthesis is thus the original form of consciousness, and it links one noetic experience to another by an intentional ordering to one identical noema which is constituted in it. It consists in a process of identification of the intentional unity, a process of "recognition" of the object as identical (synthesis of recognition).⁶⁴ Intuitive intention and intuited object are therefore

63. Truth is the correlate of perfect evidence (*CM*, p. 11 [52]). Evidence is constitutive of truth (*FTL*, p. 266 [235]).

64. *FTL*, p. 160 (143); *CM*, pp. 39 (77), 41 (79 f.). This synthesis, being structured by the universal form of time and concretely manifesting this form, is therefore the primal form belonging

closely linked—in a manner that is not real, to be sure, but intentional and ideal, i.e., synthetic (*Ideas*, p. 130 [92]). Their unity is a constant correlation. Specifically, it is a constant verifying confrontation in the very process of fulfillment. This confrontation tends toward the adequation of the intention and its originary fulfillment. Perfect adequation alone genuinely guarantees transcendental lawfulness, i.e., truth itself.

Verification is thus an adequation of the meaning intention to the originary givenness of the object meant (cf. *EJ*, § 68). Truth is the terminus (telos) of this adequation; it expresses the final and definitive coincidence (*Deckung*) of the a priori intention with the originarily given object in all its determinations. Truth, the telos of verification, can therefore only be *critical*.[65] This doctrine of truth is absolutely original with Husserl; and even if it seems to take up a classical notion (truth as adequation), it marks this notion with a specifically intentional (i.e., ideal) nuance—as we are about to see. The doctrine is verified at all the objective levels, prepredicative as well as predicative. Here we are considering it at the perceptual level. At this level, we must be clear as to the notion of "critical truth." (1) Truth is fully explicated at the judicative level; truth is a predicate of the judgment. But it is *preconstituted* in originary experience. (2) It takes on a "critical" mode because it is the result of a confrontation (putting in relation) between a sense anticipated a priori and the fulfillment of this sense. This verifying relation makes it possible to define the truth that is preconstituted in experience as critical. Thus it is *ready* to be genuinely expressed in the judgment; preconstitution is always a *Bereitschaft* (*Ideas*, p. 195 [157]).

We have encountered this intentional schema at the judicative level as well. The evidence of distinctness—that is, the very sense of the judgment regarded as originarily given in its ideal "itself"—is fulfilled in the evidence of clarity, in adequation to categorial objectivities in their originary mode of givenness. Here, too, evidence is defined as the intuitive fulfillment of an intentional anticipation (just as the evidence of distinctness is the pure fulfillment of meanings confusedly anticipated in

---

to consciousness (*CM*, §§ 17–18). The synthetic constitution of the intentional unity is therefore infinite, since the noetic manifold —like time and consciousness—is infinite (*FTL*, pp. 162 f. [145]).

65. *FTL*, p. 127 (113). Similarly, lawfulness is the telos of justification.

verbal articulations). Even if it is no longer a matter of strictly perceptual intuition, it is always a matter of an intuition, an evident consciousness or originary and constituting *cogito*, although here it is properly called categorial intuition. (On this question in its entirety see *LI*, Sixth Investigation.) Furthermore, here, too, we must be clear about the sense of "critical truth." Truth takes on two specific modes corresponding to the two dimensions of intentionality. Apophantically, truth is necessarily critical. "Critical" is taken here in the strong and primary sense of a reflective turning from the distinct judgment to the originary givenness of the categorial objectivities which are merely intended in it. This "turning" is a reflective adequation, and it defines truth as consciousness of the judgment's correctness (*Richtigkeitsbewusstsein*). Here, truth is the truth of the judgment as such. Ontologically, truth is a truth of being (*Seinswahrheit*), i.e., the doxic positing of an object that is fully intuitive and hence rationally motivated. This truth is the explicit expression of the preconstituted truth of experience. It implies the same immediacy and assumes the same originarily fulfilling adequation of the intention by a concordant experience, and it is therefore critical in the same sense.[66]

There are therefore several types of evidences (rational intuitions). *Categorial intuition* is the constitutive evidence proper to categorial objectivities, i.e., to ideal-objective logical configurations. *Eidetic intuition* or *ideation* (which we also call "idealization") is the constitutive intuition of the eidos. *Empirical* or *sensible* intuition is perception, the constitutive intuition of natural or empirical objects. It is what we are considering as an example in this study of the *cogito*. It must not be thought, however, that we have to do here with irreducible types of intuition. The first two intuitions are founded on the third; this is what we have tried to show by means of the transcendental reduction. The reduction of objective science in general—which is adequately expressed in the judgment—to the *Lebenswelt* shows in fact that the judgment in general, and likewise every essence in general, assumes the originary givenness of the perceptual thing. Categorial intuition and eidetic intuition are therefore founded acts which refer to a simple and originary act. This is

66. Cf. above, § 32; *EJ*, §§ 68, 73, 74, 75, where Husserl says that the judgment of existence and the judgment of actuality are essentially critical, because neither existence nor actuality is an intrinsically determinative predicate of the object but rather qualifies the object critically.

314 / TRANSCENDENTAL LOGIC

the reason for the constant privilege given to perception in Husserlian phenomenology, and it is the "realistic" aspect in this thought. Before the ideal objectivities of science and the eidē of philosophy, there are the natural objectivities of the *Lebenswelt,* which are immediately constituted (i.e., rationally legitimized) in and by perception.[67]

But this essential intentional relativity of every intuition to originary intuition implies no depreciation of the founded intuitions. Each has its own specific structure and its own type of truth. Thus truth at the level of logical configurations resides in the clarity constituted by the dator evidence of categorial meanings—i.e., by fulfillment of distinct meanings by the originarily present categorial meanings. Likewise, the truth of eidē (ideas) is the result of ideal fulfillment of the corresponding intention. Actually, in this case it is not a matter of real presence but only of an ideal presentification of the fulfillment of the eidetic positing. The constitutive originary experience of the idea is an ideal a priori anticipation. Husserl even emphasizes that the constitutive evidence of an ideal truth is an "imaginative presentification," which confirms our reflections on idealization of the total development as an idea and on the phenomenological fiction of the *Als-ob* (cf. above, § 11). On the other hand, the truth of a real positing rationally requires an actual fulfillment. In order for experience to result in an objective truth, it must actually fulfill the a priori intention of the apprehension (*Auffassung*); it cannot stop with an unfolding of possible perceptions.[68]

It follows from these observations that (1) to each region of being there corresponds an appropriate originary evidence (dator consciousness) (*Ideas,* p. 386 [340]; *FTL,* p. 161 [144]; *EJ,* p. 20 [12]); (2) for each object there is an a priori possible

---

67. Perception is the *Urmodus* of intuition (*Crisis,* p. 105 [107]), the *Urmodus* of *Selbstgebung* (*FTL,* p. 157 [141]; *Ideas,* p. 198 [161]). It is a simple noetic act made up of a single intentional stratum (*Ideas,* pp. 268 [229], 282 [241]). Hence it will be the exemplar extrinsically determining all derived constitutive acts (*Ideas,* pp. 265 [226], 375 f. [330]). This explains the intentional inclusion of perception in the derived modes of consciousness. It is also to be noted that the phenomenology of the material thing is likewise primary (*Ideas,* p. 422 [375]; *FTL,* § 64; *Crisis,* p. 160 [162]).

68. *Ideas,* p. 391 (345). Actually, no rational legitimation can be completely effective. Reason is an idea, as we will see; and no fulfillment can be total if it is not in some way ideal—i.e., if it is not ideally thematized (anticipated) or presentified.

rational evidence (*Ideas,* pp. 379 [333], 395 [349], 398 [351 f.])
—i.e., every object derives its sense and its being from a subjective constitution, from an originary *Sinngebung* (*Ideas,* § 55;
FTL, § 94 and p. 244 [216]); and (3) each constituted object is
the index of its necessary subjective constitution, each object
refers to a noetic multiplicity in which it is constituted. Each
object must be capable of being rationally legitimized in an
evidence, in an appropriate seeing. The object is thus the guiding
thread (*Leitfaden*) of the intentional analysis that will enable us
to bring to light the noetic *quomodo* of its constitution (*Ideas,*
§ 150; *CM,* §§ 21, 29; *FTL,* pp. 268 [237], 276 [244]; *Crisis,*
§ 48). The constitution that is "indicated" must therefore be capable of being methodically revealed in an intuitive mode; intentional consciousness is essentially intuitive and transparent,
albeit ad infinitum (*Ideas,* p. 418 [371]; *FTL,* pp. 244 f. [216];
and cf. above, p. 301). Intentional (not real) analysis is what
manifests this intuitivity. We have an example of this analysis
in the reflective line of advance (descriptive-phenomenological
point of view) we followed in transcendentally reducing the
Lebenswelt to its motivating origins.

§ 51. *Reason: idea(liza)tion of the intentional infinity.
Eidetic phenomenology*

However, we must not ignore an essential point
which affects the entire doctrine of evidence and truth. Yes,
the intention that is anticipated in experience by the *Auffassung*
is fulfilled by and in the continuous synthetic progress of experience. But this progress is indefinite. It can never be said that
the last determination has been reached and, with it, the totality
of the object's determinations. No determination is the last one;
every determination is relative and intermediary, none is absolute (*EJ,* pp. 32 [27], 80 f. [85]; *FTL,* p. 115 [102]). Being
itself is becoming (*EJ,* p. 386 [467]; cf. below, "General Conclusion"). No totality is final and definitive, so every totality is
necessarily infinite; the idea implies totality and infinity at the
same time.[69] With each determination of the object a new one

69. This is shown clearly by the exposition of *Wesensforschung*
(ideation); cf., for example, *FTL,* pp. 246 f. (218 f.). Perfect evidence itself involves originary givenness of all the object's determinations; cf. *CM,* p. 63 (98).

turns up, and this is not merely an earlier one repeated or regarded from a new angle (*Ideas*, pp. 137 f. [100]). The flow of
experience is therefore infinite by definition, and the givenness
of the object is never adequate. Perceptual consciousness can
never absolutely justify its value as rational. Perception is an
infinite noesis (*Ideas*, pp. 413 f. [366 f.]) which cannot be a
rational consciousness in the original sense of the word. At most
it tends to be rational. Rationality remains an ideal which is
asymptotically realized ad infinitum by perception. Likewise,
the truth of the perceived object (like that of any other object,
e.g., categorial) is never absolutely legitimized. Here too it must
be said that truth is a limit term toward which all knowledge of
the noema tends without actually arriving at it. Truth and
evidence are two correlative *motives* of realization rather than
actual present realizations. This implies two affirmations which
are essential in phenomenology: (1) It must not be concluded
that the noesis is never rational or that the *cogito* is never evident but rather that they are so only in a derived and secondary
manner. For just this reason they refer to an originary mode of
rationality, rational consciousness in the strict sense, which is
their telos or exemplary idea, the norm which defines them and
measures them extrinsically and intentionally. This rational
consciousness is not really included in the derived mode of
rationality, but it is the hidden source of their validity. It intentionally motivates them by this very relation of mensuration
or normation. (2) Even though it is never really or presently
attained, this originary rational consciousness is nevertheless
a priori idealizable (ideatable). It is eidetically possible, and it
enjoys an ideal existence which is precisely that of the idea
(ideal objectivity).

Thus the adequate givenness (evidence) of the thing is intentionally thematized in the form of an idea, and, correlatively,
truth is an idea lying at infinity (*Ideas*, p. 397 [351]; *FTL*, 277
[245]). "Idea" is to be understood here in the sense it usually has
in phenomenology, the sense of definite thematization of an
absence of limit in a process.[70] Evident and rational consciousness is the idealization of the infinite noesis which ideally realizes
the possible perfect constitution of the object. But we know only
a narrowly limited part of this possible constitution (evidence);
here too the idea thematizes an "and so forth" ad infinitum.

70. This thematization is essentially intuitive and therefore
ideally originary. Cf. *Ideas*, pp. 239 (201), 414 (367).

Likewise, truth is the idealization of the rational character of the noema constituted in the intuitive fullness of all its determinations. Here, once again, the idea of truth thematizes an "and so forth," a process of which we presently possess only a limited part (*Ideas*, p. 414 [367]). Evidence and truth are therefore two correlative ideas, one pertaining to the noesis (*cogito*), the other to the noema (*cogitatum*). This idealizing note, which only expresses in a particular (definite) mode the intentional infinity of consciousness, gives the doctrine of truth its specifically phenomenological character. Truth is, of course, the constituted result of an adequation, i.e., of a constitutive criticism. But this adequation is infinite. Fulfillment never really reaches its telos; the intention necessarily transcends the process of its confirmation (verification). Truth is the infinite task of an infinite constitution (evidence).

Of course, Husserl strictly distinguishes (in *Ideas*, at least) between immanent perception and transcendent perception (*Ideas*, § 38). The latter is the perception of the transcendent object, which, being given in adumbrations, is by definition an ideality transcending consciousness. Hence its givenness cannot be adequate; rather, it motivates a perceptual constitutive surpassing on the part of consciousness.[71] By contrast with the transcendent thing, the intentional experience [*vécu*], because it is immanent, is given in an absolute manner. It is not given in and by adumbrations; it is therefore grasped (constituted) absolutely by present noetic reflection (without a *processus ad infinitum*).[72] But this is a position that Husserl himself cannot maintain in all its rigor. The experience seems not to be subject to the constitutive schema of intentionality. It seems to escape from the consciousness which it nevertheless really composes. But it must be understood that the "absoluteness" of the experience is relative. The intentional experience is not in fact an absolute unity of the temporality of consciousness. It too, precisely qua particular experience, is a flow of consciousness (*Ideas*, p. 140 [103]; cf. above, § 47). The difference is one of

71. *Ideas*, pp. 137 (100), 139 (102), 384 (338 f.), 397 (351). It follows from this that the determination and adequation of perception, which are really and actually "inadequate," are ideally and potentially adequate; reason, being a pure idea, is infinite. Cf. *Ideas*, p. 413 (366); *CM*, p. 122 (151); *Crisis*, pp. 157 f. (160).

72. *Ideas*, pp. 139 f. (101 f.). The experience qua objectivity seems not to be constituted as the object in general is constituted, i.e., as the noematic unity of a noetic multiplicity.

magnitude; not only is consciousness in its totality an infinite lived flow, but the particular intentional experience as well (*Ideas*, p. 220 [182]). The experience is necessarily an experience which lasts. As such, it is inscribed in an infinite continuous duration of intentional experiences, i.e., in the flow of consciousness in general. Affirming the duration of the singular experience is another way of expressing the essential univocity of consciousness. The singular experience is not a unity which makes it possible to analyze the temporality of consciousness (like Descartes's "instant"); it is only an abstract moment of consciousness itself.[73] Hence, what is true of the infinite flow of the intentional life of the ego in general is univocally true of the singular experience as well. The infinite lived flow is unitarily thematized in the form of an idea. It is the anticipating idealization of the totality of intentional experiences, thematizing the in-finity of this flow by means of the eidetic structure of "and so forth" (*Ideas*, p. 240 [202]). This ideal (idealized) flow alone is concrete and adequately grasped. Its finite parts are by definition "abstract" (dependent) and inadequately grasped (*Ideas*, pp. 240 f. [202]; cf. above, § 47). Immanent perception is no more really adequate than transcendent perception. Its adequation, too, is ideal and potential, and so it may be said that the in-finite flow of the singular experience is a priori thematizable in the form of an idea. But because immanent perception is inadequate, it is subject to the structure of the intentional infinity. The singular experience, too, must be constituted in a continuous flow of modes of givenness which it teleologically orders (*Ideas*, p. 237 [198 f.]).

Noetic reflection thus proves in a general way that all constitution is necessarily intentional, that all constitution involves a constitutive noetic infinity teleologically ordered to an intentional and noematic unity. In a word, every object of consciousness, whatever it may be, is an ideality necessarily transcending the real consciousness in which it is intentionally constituted (*FTL*, p. 165 [148]). Every object is the intentional unity of

---

73. *Ideas*, p. 236 (198). This situation is always to be regarded in terms of the problematic of parts and wholes. The universal flow of consciousness is the whole of the experience, with respect to which the singular experience is a part. But we are in a perpetual development; the part is not absolute. The part, too, is a whole with respect to its own parts, and so on ad infinitum. The "division" of the experience into parts is, like the experience in its totality, infinite. Cf. the same situation in the correlative noema; *Ideas*, p. 415 (368).

the noetic manifold which rationally motivates it. Evidence is an intentional function of constitution, which means that it is by definition a presently inadequate constitution and that this inadequacy necessarily motivates an infinite process whose telos is unitarily thematized in the form of an idea. And this agrees perfectly with our earlier conclusions, which held that truth is the telos of an infinite adequation.

It therefore remains that all legitimizing intuition (hence all reason) is infinite, that all evidence and all truth are actually inadequate but nevertheless tend in each case toward a telos—potentially realizable ad infinitum—which is, respectively, ideal (originary) reason, evidence, and truth. Reason and truth are actually inadequate but potentially adequate. This is our result, expressed from the descriptive-phenomenological point of view. Reason and truth are ideally adequate, and, from the transcendental-phenomenological point of view, all reason and all factual (factical) truth can necessarily be only potential reason and truth. Truth and reason (evidence) are therefore, respectively, the totality of rationally motivated determinations of the object and the totality of the rational motivation of these determinations. Reason is transcendental constitution, total and infinite evidence, and truth is its total and infinite rational correlate. But this infinity is necessarily ideal. Truth and reason are ideas. Truth is the idea of the rationally motivated noema; reason is the idea of transcendental constitution, of intentionality itself—i.e., of the one and infinite consciousness. The thematization of consciousness or transcendental subjectivity as reason is thus the last word of eidetic phenomenology, the phenomenology of ideal "essences" or ideas, which considers all the intentional structures of consciousness in their constituting relation to their exemplary eidos, i.e., in their originary and ideal "primal" realization.[74] Since the intentional distinction between noesis and noema can never be ignored, it must be said that the thematization of reason is the telos of noetic eidetics (phenomenology of the *cogito*)

74. This eidetic phenomenology is the only possible form of a philosophy that would avoid the naïve errors of metaphysics (*CM*, p. 72 [106]). Cf. *CM*, pp. 77 (110), 155 (181). These passages refer more precisely to the pure ego; but, as we shall see, the ego is nothing apart from its *cogito*, and the latter is the true concrete transcendental subjectivity. Cf. *Ideas*, §§ 56–62, passages which deal with the reduction of the eidetic and which define phenomenology (in a still inadequate way) as an intuitive eidetics of the region "consciousness."

and that the thematization of truth is the telos of noematic eidetics (phenomenology of the *cogitatum*).

But if reason is an idea, it is also the case that the idea is essentially rational. Every idea is reason; this is why the phenomenology of ideas is a phenomenology of reason. And the idea is necessarily reason because its intentional constitution is precisely the idealization of the infinite totality of its possible constitutive experience[75] and because it is not tied to a real and necessarily inadequate fulfillment.[76] It follows from this that the idea is necessarily evident, whereas the singular fact (even perceptual) is not, and that eidetic phenomenology is also necessarily intuitive—although at first sight this may seem to be impossible or even contradictory, since intuition is realized in an exemplary way in and by sensible perception (cf. *Ideas,* §§ 71–75). Conversely and correlatively, the fact is not rational on its own account. It is irrational, and its rationality consists solely in its idea. This suffices to prove in a manifest way the "exemplarity" of rationality. Rationality is an extrinsic form (norm) which determines the irrational fact relatively (intentionally, hence dialectically) (*CM,* pp. 81 [114], 155 [181]). But it should be added that this "irrationality" of the fact cannot be absolute. The absolute in phenomenology is a mere limit idea. The fact, insofar as it *is,* is necessarily rational in some way, however minimal. The very possibility of the fact resides in its normative relation to the a priori idea, i.e., in this a priori (this in-itself) itself. The idea is in the strict sense the possibility of the fact. The same is true of all ideas: reason is the possibility of unreason, adequation is the possibility of inadequation, and so on. Each fact implies in itself the essential possibility of ideally surpassing itself and reaching its essential state of perfection, the possibility of fully realizing its in-itself. We have here an aspect of the self-transcendence of consciousness (*Ideas,* p. 413 [366]).

This ideality of reason manifests itself in yet another way. Every act of consciousness is rational to some extent. Thus

75. *FTL,* p. 247 (219). Constitution of the eidos (ideation) is therefore simply rational consciousness (evidence) of the factical object. Once again the univocity of consciousness appears to us in the form of the univocity of fact and idea.

76. Compare the texts of *Ideas,* cited above on p. 317 (n. 71), with that cited on p. 314 (n. 68). Imagination of the real fulfillment—i.e., ideal(ized) fulfillment—is necessarily adequate, since it is thematized in a definite manner (in the ideal-infinite mode of the "and so forth").

memory and anticipation (*Vor-erinnerung*) are genuine acts of consciousness. They have their own rational force, which suffices to legitimize the remembered or the anticipated as such (*Ideas,* p. 392 [346]). But here again we find a latent relativity. The rational force of memory is secretly borrowed from that of perception, and the same is true of anticipation (*Ideas,* p. 393 [347]). This is not to say that the reason of memory is the reason of perception; rather, the first intentionally includes the second. It *is* not, but it *has,* a rationality of the perceptual type. There is no real inclusion but rather an intentional and motivating reference. So also, the truth which is correlative with each more or less rational act of consciousness refers to the correlative truth of the originary rational act. Every truth thus has an intentional reference to an originary truth, which is the truth of originary intuition. Indeed, Husserl affirms that originary reason is truth in the absolute sense (*Ideas,* p. 388 [342]). He thereby connects truth with the noesis proper. In *Formal and Transcendental Logic,* on the other hand, truth is explicitly situated on the noematic side (cf. *FTL,* p. 43 [38]). This is only a manifestation of the ambivalence of phenomenological terms, a manifestation of the fact of correlation between noesis and noema (*Ideas,* p. 387 [341]).

Thus, in the order of the objective reality of the *Lebenswelt,* the ideality of truth and evidence is complicated by an intentional relativity of the modes of constitutive consciousness proper to this domain. Here there are two exemplarist structures interlocking with each other: evidence or perfect *Selbstgebung* being the ideal norm of every actual *Selbstgebung,* and perception being the originary mode of consciousness of the *Lebenswelt.* Such complications obviously cannot occur in the pure eidetic world, since the idea is by definition the univocal ("absolute") idealization of an actual *de facto* givenness.

With this final thematization of rational consciousness, we have not really discovered new notions, but we have prepared the framework for a formal (eidetic) broadening of the study of perceptual constitution into a study of universal seeing or evidence. The phenomenology of perception becomes the eidetic phenomenology of evidence in general (*cogito*). Evidence is intentionality; it is the constitutive noesis in its perfect and fundamental mode. As such, it is identical with reason. It is not, however, an accidental faculty of intelligence. It is precisely the idea of constituting consciousness, its act (*Leistung*) considered in its formal (eidetic) and exemplary (since it is

322 / TRANSCENDENTAL LOGIC

normative of every actual act) realization.[77] As *Leistung*, it is the teleological function of intentionality in general (*FTL*, p. 244 [216]), i.e., the function of synthetic ordering of a noetic multiplicity to an intentional (noematic) unity, considered in its primary and originary mode.

Perception is the constitutive seeing of the lived world. The evidence of clarity is, similarly, the constitutive categorial seeing of the evident fulfilled judgment. By ideally formalizing these diverse factical "seeings" we obtain the eidos "evidence." The latter is therefore defined as the intentional *Leistung* in general, the perfect form of intentionality, expressed eidetically (independently of the concrete modes in which it is factually realized) as the a priori structure of consciousness (*FTL*, pp. 157 f. [141], 288 f. [255]). It is thus that Husserl can describe constitution in a universal and "formal" (eidetic) manner as an evidence which is originarily creative of all transcendental lawfulness (*FTL*, p. 159 [142]), as a universal intentional structure whose extension takes in the totality of the intentional life and whose telos is reason itself (*FTL*, p. 160 [143]), as the function constitutive of every objectivity in general, regarded as synthetic and intentional unity[78]—all of these expressions rendering formally what we have seen in concrete detail with regard to the noetic functions of perception.

But eidetic universality does not preclude the explication of the various modes of evidence. Evidence in general is the exemplary ideal and the eidetic structure of all effective givenness. Its originary mode is perception (*FTL*, p. 158 [141]), the *Selbstgebung* of the real object of the *Lebenswelt*. A secondary mode of perception is clear memory (*FTL*, p. 158 [141]). Explication of the various objective regions to which the originary modes of evidence correspond unfolds in a parallel fashion (*FTL*, p. 160 [143]). In this way the primacy of perception is

77. "Reason itself . . . is a form-concept" (*FTL*, p. 29 [25]). Cf. *CM*, p. 57 (92). Husserl thereby takes up the legacy of nominalist thought, one of whose modern representatives is Spinoza (cf. esp. *Ethics*, Part II, Proposition 48, scholium).

78. *FTL*, § 61. Cf. the following definition of the objective as synthetic unity of intentionality: "Something Objective is nothing other than a synthetic unity of actual and potential intentionality, a unity belonging to the proper essence of transcendental subjectivity" (*FTL*, p. 274 [242]). This excellent definition of the object is complete. It both insists on the "synthetic fixation" which evidence realizes and accounts for the essential potentiality of every object in general by exhibiting the object's necessary horizons.

affirmed; that is, noetically, the primacy of the lived processes of originary experience (*FTL*, pp. 164 f.) and, noematically, the primacy of real objectivities as opposed to irreal (ideal) objectivities (*FTL*, § 64).

Reduction of objective science to the *Lebenswelt*, which we defined as a particular case of the reduction of logic (science in general) to experience in general, therefore leads us to the eidetic level it exemplifies.

But let us not forget that the reduction of the judgment to experience or of science to the *Lebenswelt* has a logical value. It represents the reflective turning from objective formal logic to its intentional and motivating origins (which are explicated in transcendental logic). In general, the reduction we have carried out in its two modes, eidetic and factical, is a constitutive criticism of objectivity in general by reflection on the actual *cogito* of the pure ego. If the turning to experience has a transcendental-logical value, this is because eidetic phenomenology —the phenomenology of reason, which thematizes constitution, i.e., evidence and truth correlatively in their originary mode— is the last word, the telos of objective formal logic. Eidetic phenomenology is identical with transcendental logic.

Formal logic by no means loses its formal character by being continued in transcendental logic. More precisely, transcendental logic is itself a formal logic insofar as it is an eidetic phenomenology. Indeed, we should speak instead of an objective formal logic and a subjective formal logic.[79] The first explicates the formal structures of the constituted objectivity (categorial objectivity); the second explicates the formal structures of the constitution of the object in general. The *cogito*—that is, intentionality—is thus the subjective form of the object in general. And precisely by reason of its infinity and because it is possible to thematize it only in the form of the "and so forth," intentionality is an idea and therefore a proper object of eidetic phenomenology. Evidence and reason are formal concepts, and the "formal" here is clearly the subjective formal (*FTL*, p. 28 [25]). It is identical with the subjective a priori, and this term can now be understood in its full eidetic sense as subjective form. The a priori of correlation is the universal form of transcendental constitution in general.

Transcendental logic thus affirms its normative and

79. To the objective- or analytic-formal there intentionally corresponds a subjective-formal, according to *FTL*, p. 212 (188).

exemplary character insofar as it explicates reason—i.e., the idea, the subjective form, the exemplary constitution of the object in general. The normation in this case is simply no longer analytic but synthetic. This subjective form is the eidos. The transcendental-formal is the eidetic, and transcendental logic is eidetic phenomenology. This insight is the ultimate fruit of our method and of our exemplarist interpretation of Husserlian phenomenology.

C. THE EGO

§ 52. *The pure ego as indeterminate subject* (= X)

BUT ONCE AGAIN OUR SEARCH GOES BACK to the beginning. A second degree of reflection will thematize the transcendental ego itself. The noema is constituted by means of intentional functions of a subject; every *cogito* is the *cogito* of an ego. The first thematization of the *Lebenswelt* consisted simply in noematic description. A first reflection oriented us toward the originary subjective mode of givenness of the *Lebenswelt,* i.e., the object in general. We are now undertaking a second and final reflection, which will reveal the pure ego to us (*Crisis*, pp. 172 [175], 182 [186]). Once more our undertaking is radicalized. It brings us to the primordial fact, to the ultimate intentional ground, the only absolute foundation: the transcendental ego, the pure I—in a word, transcendental subjectivity, to which all being in every possible sense is relative (*FTL*, pp. 236 [209], 273 [241]). This is a necessary outcome, which I can avoid only if I cease to be a philosopher. And so the explication of transcendental subjectivity is the deed of first philosophy (*FTL*, p. 237 [209 f.]). But, as we have seen, the *Lebenswelt* is the constitutive presupposition of logic. Its ultimate thematization in and by the analysis of the ego is therefore the final and definitive calling of logic in its transcendental mode. The turning to reason, to the originary and absolute constitution of the object in general in transcendental subjectivity, is thus the turning to *logical reason* (*FTL*, p. 267 [236]; cf. p. 231 [205]). All reason is thus necessarily logical, because it expresses (actually or potentially) the idea of constituting consciousness.[80] Phenomenology itself,

80. The idea, being "genuine" because it is originary, is necessarily logical (*FTL*, p. 28 [25]).

insofar as it is science of the idea or of reason, is a transcendental logic. This is its profound sense; it is the synthetically normative science par excellence—science in general, the exemplary eidos of science, genuine science, universal science, first philosophy—which, by thematizing transcendental subjectivity as phenomenological foundation of all reality, originarily grounds all human sciences and gives the multiplicity of human wisdom the consciousness of its intentional sense and its unity in principle. Therefore, only the explication of transcendental subjectivity enables Husserl to realize his critical project (*FTL*, § 103; p. 4 [4], 272 [240]).

There is therefore objectifying constitution in the *cogito*, constitution of an object by a subject. Every act and every evidence necessarily involves two poles: the object and the pure ego (*Ideen II*, § 25). Intentional experience (i.e., the *cogito*) is the actual relatedness of ego and object. Every relation implies two terms, and this essential duality determines the duality of the phenomenological points of view. Depending on the direction in which we consider the intentional relation, we obtain the descriptive-phenomenological point of view (the direction from object to ego) or the transcendental-phenomenological point of view (the direction from ego to object). We have seen the object pole, and we have also seen the actual relation. Our reflection will now be perfectly complete only with the evident thematization of the ego (ego pole). We gain access to the latter if we reflect one last time on the noesis, on intentional experience.

Experience [*le vécu*] in fact involves an essential ambiguity. Up to now we considered it as the noetic *quomodo* of the originary givenness of the object. This is a first aspect of the noesis; we can call it the objective aspect. But the noesis is an experience. It is a moment of an intentional life; and every life implies something living, a necessary substrate which lives precisely in this life. Thus the intentional experience is essentially twofold (as might be suspected, since it realizes the effective unity of the object and the ego). It includes a second aspect, which is called the subjective aspect and which manifests the belonging of the experience to a subject. This aspect is what makes it possible to grasp the intentional experience explicitly as a particular mode of the life of the pure ego (*Ideas*, p. 234 [195 f.]; *Ideen II*, p. 105). The intentional experience is therefore a *quomodo* in two ways. It is the "how" of the object's subjective givenness (constitution), and it is the "how" of the ego's life. In the noesis, noema and ego "appear" at the same time.

In fact, noetic experience is not the ego itself but a mode of its life or, more specifically, of its intentional life. This life is obviously multiple, and in our study of the *cogito* we have just seen the essential multiplicity of experiences. But here too the phenomenological thesis of intentional unity applies: every multiplicity necessarily implies a unity which orders it. This ordering is what guarantees the rationality of the multiplicity. Now, the noetic multiplicity, regarded as the constituting appearing of the object, is intentionally related to the constituted object. But if we regard experience, in virtue of its essential ambivalence, as the "how" of the ego's intentional life, it is precisely to this ego that the multiplicity of its intentional life must be ordered. Like the object, the ego thus shows itself to be a type of transcendence synthesizing a multiplicity of intentional experiences. It pre-scribes a second polarization of consciousness, that of the various experiences which are intentionally unified by their common quality of being *cogitationes* of a single pure ego (*CM*, p. 66 [100]). But if the ego in a way transcends the ordered manifold of the manifestations of its own life, this is a peculiar sort of transcendence—a transcendence that is not constituted since, on the contrary, it is constituting (*Ideas*, p. 173 [138]). The ego "appears" in the *cogito*, of course, and, like any other object, it is not a real moment of experience. But here the "experience" is not like other experiences (*Ideas*, p. 172 [137]). The ego is not constituted in the *cogito* in the sense that it is adumbrated in experience, so Husserl can even say that it does not appear (*Ideen II*, pp. 104 f.). This is the ambivalence of experience, which at the same time *manifests* the ego and *constitutes* the object. There is both unity and distinction. Object and ego are intentionally included in the actual *cogito;* that is, they are immanent in consciousness. They represent two transcendences in two "diametrically" opposed directions.[81] On the one hand we have the *transcendent* properly so-called, and on the other the *transcendental*—to use a term which expresses both the "transcendent" and the constituting character of the unity of the pure ego. These two poles are obviously correlates within the immanence of universal consciousness. Their correlation expresses intentionality and defines

81. Husserl further insists on the fact that the poles (object and ego) are not analogous (*Ideas*, p. 234 [196]) and that they differ in kind and in origin (*Ideen II*, p. 105).

the exact framework in which transcendental constitution moves (*CM*, p. 26 [65]).

Noesis-noema parallelism is found again here, in a still more radical form, although the critical remarks addressed to the notion of parallelism still hold. It is no longer really a matter of noesis-noema parallelism but of ego-object or transcendental-transcendent parallelism. The intentionality involved remains the same, but here it discloses its ultimate teleological poles in a definitive way. We saw that the noema itself refers to an object pure and simple which is undetermined in itself (= X). This X is what defines the "noematic" intentionality of the sense and ideally insures the objectivity of the noema. For this X is actually the idea of the object which the successive noematic senses progressively attempt to realize; it is the substrate of the objective determinations of the noematic sense, the *quid* of the noematic *quomodo*. We find an exact copy of this structure in our reflection on the ego. If the lived intentional flow is the multiple "how" of the intentional life, it necessarily implies a substrate, which is the pure ego (*Ideen II*, p. 97). Thus we can call the intentional experiences in their diversity a vital *quomodo* which as such requires a living *quid,* the pure ego. We can see immediately the intimate unity which *quomodo* and *quid* constitute here. Just as the complete noema comprises noematic sense and object, here the intentional experience comprises vital *quomodo* and living *quid* (pure ego). The vital unity that is the experience is one moment of the life of the ego; it is the phenomenological *concretum* in the strict sense. It must be added that this *concretum* is the intentional life of the ego in its totality, the idea of the infinite flow of consciousness. In other words, every noetic act necessarily implies the ego; the ego is necessarily present in and fundamentally accompanies every experience. Husserl can take over the famous formula of Kant's Transcendental Deduction: "The 'I think' must be able to accompany every representation" (cf. *Ideas*, pp. 172 f. [138]; *Ideen II*, p. 108). We know that for Kant the "I think" is the pure transcendental subject. The ego accompanies every experience. It is permanent (it is "always there") (*Ideen II*, pp. 103 f.). Moreover, it accompanies every experience fundamentally. It is the foundation, the subject or ultimate substrate. The subject lives its intentional life and remains identical in itself even though the intentional life is diverse. Finally, since every determination supposes a substrate, the subject is necessary (*Ideas*, p. 172 [137 f.]; *Ideen II*, p. 100). Experience is possible only on the foundation of a permanent, identical, and necessary subject. This subject is the only originary foundation, the only transcendental absolute (*FTL*, p. 236 [209]; *Ideas*, p. 236 [198]).

Now, precisely this pure, identical, necessary ego lives "in" its intentional life. It "functions" (*fungiert*) in the *cogito* (*Ideen II*, p. 99), and its life consists in transcendental systems of intentional constitutions (*CM*, p. 65 [100]). Hence it forms a concrete unity with experience. Only analysis can try to consider the ego in its purity (as pure ego), but this will be a manifest "abstraction." The ego can subsist only in and through experience (*Ideen II*, pp. 99, 111; *CM*, p. 67 [102]). This is why it is so difficult to give determinations of the ego other than to say that it is permanent, identical, and necessary. The pure ego in itself is indescribable. One affirmation alone is possible with regard to it: it is the transcendental subject of its intentional life, the "identical" of the multiplicity constituting the object. Husserl even goes so far as to claim that the pure ego cannot be considered on its own account—in other words, that it cannot be the proper theme of a study. In phenomenology this is a surprising result, to say the least. This assertion must be understood in relation to the theory of the abstract and the concrete. The absolute concretum is the solitary intentional life; the pure ego is in itself an abstractum. The determination perfectly suited to it is that of "subject," and this notion implies identity and permanence. The pure ego is therefore the subject of transcendental constitution, the ego pole of intentionality, the center and point of departure of every intentional function, the point of departure of every constituting teleology (*LI*, p. 548 [II/1, 359]; *Ideen II*, p. 105; *Crisis*, p. 186 [190]). It is only pure opening onto the object, pure origin (*reiner Ursprung*),[82] which is another way of expressing the fact that it is the term of a relation. But this subject, this opening onto the object, remains in itself simple and "poor." Husserl speaks felicitously of the ego's "richness," which resides entirely in the *cogito*, in the actual intentional function. The richness of the ego is its concretion and hence its very intentional life. In itself it is simple, undivided, numerically identical, and empty of determinations.[83] It is originary in the

82. Cf. the phrase in *Crisis*, p. 171 (174), "Richtung auf Etwas" ("direction toward something") and those in *FTL*, pp. 236 f. (209), "intentionale Urgrund für meine Welt," "Urtatsache" ("primitive intentional basis for my world," "primal matter-of-fact").

83. *Ideen II*, pp. 105, 97 f. The pure ego, being "poor" and having nothing to hide, in a way realizes the perfect "transparency" of consciousness to which phenomenology aspires. Cf. above, p. 301.

strict sense of the word. It is the absolute beginning which phenomenology requires, and as such it is absolutely undetermined. It provides no "handle" for description (it is indescribable), and the only way to thematize it is to describe it in the "how" of its intentional life. It does not lend itself to the question *quid est* but only to the question *quomodo est*. In fact, if we could describe it, we would have a representation (*Vorstellung*) of it, which would make it an object (*Gegenstand*). But the ego essentially refuses to be an object; it is pure subject. To make it an object would be to destroy intentionality and hence to destroy the very notion of objectivity. The ego is why there is an object; it is the necessary subjective presupposition of the object in general. The principal complaint Husserl draws up against logical psychologism is that it is not a properly subjective science, as we have seen (*LI*, p. 549 [II/1, 360]; *Crisis*, p. 126 [129]; *CM*, p. 30 [68 f.]). But if the ego can be grasped and described only in the "how" of its concrete life, we have only to refer here to our study of the *cogito*, in which we have given the essential points.[84]

It follows from the above observations that even if Husserl himself does not affirm that the pure ego = X (and in fact we know of no texts to this effect), it is nevertheless legitimate to claim that this is the case. The ego—pure origin subject of intentionality and absolute beginning of the teleology of consciousness—is an X. Subject-object "parallelism" is set up here in all its rigor. The noematic sense requires a subject X (this is the substrate object of noematic predicates, the *Gegenstand schlechthin*), just as noetic experience—expressing the intentional life of the ego—requires a pure subject X (*Ideen II*, p. 311). The two ultimate and correlative teloi of intentionality, the transcendental and the transcendent, are thus indeterminate terms (= X).

Let us make this important result clear from the two phenomenological points of view. We know that the noematic sense tends ad infinitum to reach the objective X. Similarly, it must

---

84. *Ideas*, p. 233 (195); cf. *Idées*, p. 271, n. 1. "It cannot itself be a content, and resembles nothing that could be a content of consciousness. For this reason, it can be no further described" (*LI*, p. 549 [II/1, 359]). In *Ideen II*, p. 101, however, Husserl says that the pure ego is grasped in *what* it is (*als das, was es ist*) and *how* it "functions" (*und wie es fungiert*). In *CM*, p. 66 (100), the pure ego is grasped as identical and not as a flowing life—i.e., according to *Ideen II*, p. 97, as absolute.

be said here that intentional life tends ad infinitum to determine the X that is the pure ego. Like the object, the transcendental ego is an *idea*. The teleology is here considered from the descriptive-phenomenological point of view of the existence act, according to which the fact is really existent and actual and the idea (telos) is merely possible (hence actually indeterminate). But from the transcendental-phenomenological point of view of the value act, the idea is fully defined; it is simply "narrowed," for the present, to the data of immediate experience. But the latter gives only this or that particular experience (cf. above, § 45).

§ 53. *The concrete subject is intentionality itself*

HOWEVER, even if the ego is indeterminate, even if in some sense it *is* nothing, we would be wrong to think that it *has* nothing. On the contrary, it is the substrate of its habitualities. To it is connected what Husserl calls the "sphere of ownness." Here we must bring in the power which every act possesses of *sedimenting* on its subject. Each act leaves a "trace" on the ego, a determination which contributes to the concretion of the ego. It is in this way that the ego which has perceived a certain object is other than the ego which has perceived a certain other object. All position-taking likewise sediments on the ego (*CM*, § 32). Thus the ego gradually emerges as pure ego of constant style, since these sedimented determinations are stable unless new determinations explicitly come to erase them. These intentional sediments thus constitute stable acquisitions of the ego, which Husserl expresses by the word *Habitualitäten* (in French, *habitus*, a Latin word rendering the Greek word *hexis*). These are determinations which the ego possesses (*habitus* comes from the Latin *habere*) and which contribute to giving the pure ego a personal physiognomy. The total collection of habitualities sedimented on the pure ego and thus determining it makes possible a first definition of the "person." [85] Husserl distinguishes sharply between a pure ego subject, a concrete ego constituted by the habitual sediments of its own acts, and intentional life properly speaking (*CM*, pp. 67 f. [102]). The ego is manifested in the intentional life; this is where the ego "comes and goes" [il entre

85. *CM*, end of § 32. This is yet another quantitative definition. A more extended study of the person in Husserl would show that the person is an idea.

en fonctions et sort de fonctions; es in seiner Art "auftritt" und wieder "abtritt"; *Ideen II*, p. 103]. But what persists of these intentional acts constitutes the proper domain of the concrete ego or monad, its sphere of ownness.[86] In order to bring this sphere to light, we must therefore first pass through a thematization of the pure ego as such. That is, a second reflection or reduction is necessary, which leads us from the noesis to the ego (*CM*, § 44).

This doctrine of the pure ego is, to be sure, static, and we saw above that the notion of noesis-noema parallelism was a static notion. To say that the ego = X, however, amounts to saying that the ego is the absolute beginning of intentionality. To say this is therefore to make the ego the originary foundation or point of departure of intentionality and hence already to insert it in some way into intentionality. The distinction between intentional life and pure ego is the result of an abstraction. As such it can only be static, since the concretum is the flow of experience. The ego is of course transcendent with respect to the manifold of its concrete life. But, as we know, this transcendence is an *immanent transcendence*. The ego forms part of the flow of consciousness; it is the first moment of this flow, its origin or exemplary beginning. So we should not be surprised at the tendency that immediately shapes Husserlian phenomenology, the tendency to understand the pure ego as intentional life itself and to see in the latter the genuine transcendental foundation. The pure ego is considered as actual *cogito*, foundation of all constitution. This is really the sense of the "I think" or the "I am," which can be called either an originary egological act or an originary actual ego. The dynamic and genuinely phenomenological notion of intentional *Leistung* thus replaces the static notion of the pure ego as X, and the notion of transcendental subjectivity replaces that of pure subject. The pure ego, considered essentially as act and not as "faculty" of act (potency), is identical with transcendental constitution. This is one aspect of Husserl's nominalism, of which we have already spoken.[87]

The nuance between transcendental subjectivity and subject may seem minimal, but the difference is nevertheless important.

86. Cf. *CM*, § 33: "The full concretion of the Ego as monad and the problem of his self-constitution."

87. Cf. above, p. 322, n. 77. This nominalism gives us a new way of expressing the actuality in principle or ideal actuality of consciousness.

The ego is a conscious subjectivity, an actual or potential operation of consciousness, a constitutive (i.e., living) intentionality;
it is absolute being in the form of an intentional life.[88] The ego
thus defines the universe of possible forms of experience; and
since this universe is infinite, the ego represents it in its exemplary and excellent form, the form of evidence (*CM*, §§ 36,
39; *FTL*, pp. 157 f. [141]). The ego is the ultimately constituting
and therefore necessarily apodictic subjectivity (*FTL*, p. 251
[222]). The ego now coincides with the very exercise of intentionality in its excellent mode, the mode of evidence. The ego
itself is reason,[89] i.e., subjective form of the object in general.
This confirms our preceding analysis, which showed that reason
is the ideal thematization of completed constitution. Thus, just
as reason and evidence are transcendental constitution considered in its completed (i.e., exemplary and normative) form
(*Urstiftung*), the transcendental ego is the originary ego, the
Ur-ich (cf. *Crisis*, p. 185 [188]), intentionality itself in its living
typical exercise by a subject inseparable from it. The two expressions are equivalent.

Thus it appears that the ego is constituted in the very flow
of its intentional life. The pure ego ($= X$) is not yet rationally
justified, in fact, if we are satisfied to reveal it by means of a
static (objective-logical) analysis—since by an essential necessity every predicate necessarily assumes an identical subject.
Although the pure ego ($= X$) is indeed the transcendental
"absolute," it is not the last word. Every object must be intuitively justified, and the ego cannot escape this fundamental
rule.[90] The pure and transcendental ego, too, must be intuitively
justified in a rational evidence. But it is given in and by the flow
of its experience [*le flux de son vécu*]. The only rational justifica-

88. *FTL*, § 94 ("leistende Intentionalität," "lebendige Intentionalität"), and p. 273 (241) ("Absolut Seiendes . . . in Form eines in-
tentionalen Lebens"). In an ideal thematization we can speak of
the ideal actuality of consciousness or of the ego, since the ideal is,
by definition, the possible.

89. The nominalism is radical; the "faculty" (in this case,
reason) takes the place of the subject and is itself radically excluded
in favor of the mere act (*Leistung*)—in its infinite ideal totality, of
course.

90. *Ideas*, p. 236 (198). This brings us back to the problem of
the self-constitution of the ego, which is the ultimate—although infinite—instance in phenomenology. [The hyphenated *in-finie* suggests, in French, the notion "unfinished" or "not yet completed,"
a suggestion that does not come through in the English—TRANS.]

tion of the ego will therefore be that which secures for us the idea of the infinite totality of the lived flow [*du flux vécu*]. Only the idea is rational, as we know; it alone expresses the completed constitution of its ideatum. In other words, it is in the *cogito* that the pure ego is constituted. We have just seen that the *cogito* is defined essentially as an intentionality between two poles, each of which = X (the pure ego and the object). Each pole is an idea which is concretely realized progressively and correlatively (by virtue of noesis-noema correlation). The successive noematic senses are directed to realizing the mode of fullness of the object pure and simple. Correlatively, the various constitutive noeses are directed to realizing the mode of fullness of the pure ego, the personal monadological ego. If, on the one hand, the intuitive fullness of the object is *truth,* the concrete fullness of the ego is *reason,* since we have just seen that the pure ego, or transcendental subjectivity, is identical with intentional constitution. But, once again, truth and reason are two ideal poles of possible consciousness; only the noesis, the effective *cogito,* insures the *de facto* (existential) actuality of consciousness. The *cogito* is what bears responsibility for the object and for the ego. Its history is what constitutes time itself, i.e., that well-known time consciousness (*Zeitbewusstsein*) in which the ego is concretely constituted. Thus, constitution of the object and constitution of the ego—or, strictly speaking, of the idea of the object and the idea of the ego—are necessarily correlative. When one has achieved its completion, the other has, too. The entelechy of the object implies and necessarily refers to the entelechy of the ego. This is another new way of expressing results already discovered: (1) to each being corresponds an ideally possible rational evidence (cf. *Ideas,* pp. 379 [333], 386 [340], 395 [349], 398 [351 f.]; *FTL,* p. 161 [144]; *EJ,* p. 20 [12]); (2) every being takes its sense and even its value from an originary givenness of which it is the index (cf. *Ideas,* §§ 55, 150; *CM,* §§ 21, 29; *FTL,* §§ 94, 97, 102, 104; *Crisis,* § 48). And the temporal structure of consciousness enables intentional analysis to ideally anticipate the absolute *cogito,* i.e., at the same time and correlatively the absolute noema coinciding with the fully intuitive object and the absolute noesis coinciding with the fully concrete and personal pure ego. In a word, analysis can anticipate the (one and infinite) consciousness defined by the adequation of an infinite reason and an infinite truth.

Thus the important problem of the originary constitution (*Ur-konstitution*) of the ego is resolved in principle (ideally). In

its particulars, this problem obviously presents the greatest difficulties. But in order to give it the evidence or rationality it requires, we must consider it in light of Husserlian exemplarism.
The ego lives: it is its own intentional life. Since this life is
infinite, it is originarily given only in its idea (in the mode of
the "and so forth"); and this idea is what rationally legitimizes
the apodictic positing of the ego's life. But let us not forget that
this life is really [*réellement*] lived by the ego. The pure ego is
therefore constituted in the real components of intentional experience, hylē and noesis. These are subject to the necessary
and universal form of time, which, being the form of the living
ego, constitutes the originary synthesis (*Ur-synthese*) of intentional experiences (*Ideas*, p. 334 [292]). Hence the constitution
of the ego will necessarily be historical, i.e., teleologically oriented
(*CM*, § 37); it will be intentional. But this must be understood
in two senses. Indeed, intentional experience is twofold: it is
the appearing of both the object and the ego. Constitution of the
object is therefore correlative with constitution of the ego. Parallelism is found here once again. The two constitutions correlated
here must not, however, be identified. This would be psychologism (the "easy way out"). The two constitutions are intentionally included in each other. There is therefore a properly
objectifying synthesis and another synthesis that is properly
constitutive of the subject. This second polarization of the lived
flow of consciousness is what intentionally unifies the noetic
experiences as experiences (*cogitationes*) of the same ego (*CM*,
p. 66 [100]). Thus, if the intentionality of this correlation is
carefully maintained, it can be said that the constitution of the
ego is the constitution of the object, in the same sense that we
can speak of Husserl's "Berkeleianism" (cf. above, p. 302). The
ego is constituted by being given a sense; this is the *Selbstbesinnung* of transcendental subjectivity. But this sense defines the
intentionality constitutive of the object, and it can only be noematic or objective. Intentional constitution of the object is thus
self-giving of sense on the part of the ego. Transcendental constitution of the object is transcendental self-consciousness.

　　Criticism of the object (i.e., of science) thus ends in constitution of the ego by itself. The object is criticized or clarified
when the noetic "how" of the intentional functions that constitute it is elucidated, when its sense is constitutively legitimized
(*FTL*, p. 10 [9]). But these functions are precisely those of the
concrete intentionality in which the ego lives (*CM*, § 30) and
constitutes its own sense (*Selbstbesinnung*). The ego, submitting

itself to criticism, constitutes its own sense (reflectively). This is an essential possibility in the nature of the ego.[91] To the extent that it discovers constitutively that its sense is intentionally the object, the ego constitutes itself by giving itself this sense. The pure ego is thus found to be pure relatedness to the object, and its constitutive elucidation by itself (*Selbstauslegung*) is equivalent to constitutive criticism of the object. Criticism must always be the phenomenological *Leistung* of self-explication on the part of a subjectivity reflecting on its intentional functions (*FTL*, p. 274 [242]). This constitutive self-reflection discovers that every objectivity belongs essentially to subjectivity as its proper sense and that the objectivity simply expresses the transcendental synthesis of the intentionality in which the ego is constituted by determination of its sense (*FTL*, p. 274 [242]). The phenomenology of the ego or phenomenology of reason is therefore equivalent to the phenomenology of the object. Phenomenology will be primarily a clarification of the transcendental ego. But the latter subsists only in the actual intentional experience. The phenomenology of the ego therefore includes the phenomenology of noetic experience. Similarly, noetic experience intentionally implies the noema, and the latter intentionally implies the object pure and simple (*Gegenstand schlechthin*). The phenomenology of the ego is therefore universal phenomenology in general. It is the science devoted to determining the intentional, transcendental, and originary constitution of every possible sense (*FTL*, §§ 103–4, esp. p. 274 [242]; *CM*, § 33).

But this presentation of phenomenology from the transcendental-phenomenological point of view is nothing but the terminus (telos) of logic. The transcendental reduction, which we are now completing, is in fact the critical return to the constitutive a prioris of logic or of science in general considered in one of its privileged examples, the science of the empirical natural object. Phenomenology is thus logic in its transcendental *en-tel-echeia;* it is transcendental logic. It is univocal, unique, intentional science. Hence it is science "at one go," since the three stages distinguished in the reduction (*cogitatum—cogito—ego*) are the result of analysis. In fact, once again what we have are three stages belonging to the same intentionality (*Verschiebung*

91. *FTL*, p. 273 (241). And always we are brought back to the object, since the "originales Selbst" of the ego is to be constitution (consciousness) of the object. *Selbstbesinnung* here corresponds in the order of phenomenological reality to the *Selbstnormierung* of phenomenology. Cf. *FTL*, p. 267 (236); and above, § 20.

der Intentionalität). The reduction is one and total. It is a single continuous dialectical movement which stops only in the ultimate thematization of transcendental subjectivity.

But even though intentional analysis so clearly manifests the correlation and phenomenological (intentional) equivalence between constitution of the object and constitution of the ego, it in no way depreciates the purely objective-logical analysis. We must therefore keep this notion that the ego = X, while keeping in mind that this ego can subsist only in its life as intentional *Leistung* (that this "faculty" can subsist only in its actual or potential operation). This is why the indeterminacy of the pure ego as X expresses the fact that the pure ego as such is a telos which is not yet reached or fully realized but which needs to be realized ad infinitum.

The ego is therefore the primordial fact, the *Urtatsache,* and the absolute transcendental foundation, but its determination remains an infinite task. The flow of experience is what must effectively realize this task, and the transcendental ego will be at the point of its constitutive fullness when the object is at the point of its intuitive fullness, i.e., when reason and truth are correlatively realized. The ego therefore needs to live in rational acts which affirm its constitutive autonomy and hence its freedom. In this sense *Ideen II* can speak of the ego as the subject of rational acts and as an absolutely free ego (cf. *Ideen II,* § 60). For the perfect rationality of the ego is manifested in its freedom; the pure ego is an ego of freedom.[92] Transcendental subjectivity as universally constituting can only be autonomous; and this autonomy, being originary, can only be absolute. The ego is the absolute beginning, to be sure, but it is action [*Leistung*] before everything and constitution of everything. Action is freedom, passivity is dependence (*Ideen II,* pp. 213 f.). If in the beginning is action, it must also be said that in the beginning is freedom (cf. *Crisis,* p. 156 [158]). It is unnecessary to emphasize the extraordinary echo this thesis finds in contemporary thought; we will have a few words to say about it in our "General Conclusion."

Obviously, we do not claim to have dealt with all the problems. We deliberately leave to one side the constitution of the empirical ego and that of the Other. These two problems are, moreover, interdependent. Constitution of the *Leib,* of the *corps*

92. *Ideen II,* p. 213. Here freedom is explicitly tied to *activity:* "freedom of operation" [*liberté d'efficience*].

propre, in Merleau-Ponty's words, is what enables me to go on to the constitution of the *corps propre* other than mine and thence to empathy (*Einfühlung*) with the Other as transcendental subjectivity. The paradox of the pure ego and the empirical ego thus continues in another paradox, that of the constitution of the Other as *constituting.* The Other, or *alter ego,* is also a constituting transcendental subjectivity. The Other is the only "object" other than the ego itself which is not a pure constituted. Hence it escapes me to some extent, and I escape myself insofar as the Other constitutes *me* in his own transcendental subjectivity and thus in a way diminishes my own autonomy. Between me and the Other, i.e., between the positing of my ego and that of the Other's ego, there is intercalated the constitutive analysis of the *corps propre,* with its organs, its senses, its kinestheses, its sensory fields. This is a very rich and complex domain, which Husserl, as usual, analyzes in all its details. It is the problem of the constitution of the sensible and spiritual world (problematic of *Ur-präsenz* and *Ap-präsenz*). We will not enter into these investigations. Despite their importance and interest, they would not bring us any new principle or element that would be useful in our present inquiry (cf. *FTL,* § 96; *CM,* §§ 42–43; *Crisis,* §§ 53–54; and esp. *Ideen II* in its entirety).

Let us simply make this observation: the solution in principle (ideal solution) of the consitution of the Other is quite simple, like the constitution of the ego. In fact, the phenomenology of reason is directed to eliciting the eidos of transcendental subjectivity, the idea of transcendental consciousness. This idea is obviously the result of an ideation, i.e., of the infinite variation of all *de facto* possible transcendental egos. Constitution of the *alter ego* as one of the possible egos is necessarily implied in this variation (*CM,* p. 84 [117 f.]). Thus the transcendental ego is in a universal way the structure of the universal eidos "ego in general," the universal a priori without which no transcendental ego (neither I nor the Other) would be conceivable (*CM,* pp. 71 f. [105 f.]).

GENERAL CONCLUSION

The Two Dimensions of
Intentionality

§ 54. *The idea-transcendental antinomy*

THE POINT OF DEPARTURE for phenomenological investigation is the immediate experience of history. The object of this experience is the fact, the fact in its history. As we will see, this is the fact in the process of its transcendental constitution. We consider this factical object in a completely general way; it is the fact in general, which includes in its generality every constituted objectivity, scientific theory as well as individual thing.

This fact can be examined from a twofold point of view; and the intentional analysis which undertakes to clarify it has, from the first, two dimensions, which for the moment we will call "progressive" and "retrogressive" (reflective). First, the fact can be considered as the (factical) example of the idea it strives to realize. Here intentional analysis discovers an ideal teleology which proves to be the mutual exemplarity of fact and idea. Second, the fact can be considered as the index of its subjective constitution, as the objective unity which refers to a constitutive subjective a priori.

Thus the fundamental idea appears that phenomenology is an original revival of the old problem of the one and the many, since in either case we have to do with the intentional relation between a unity and a multiplicity.

a) The fact anticipates in factical exemplary fashion the idea that it realizes. But by virtue of its very ideality, the idea infinitely exceeds the fact, which can be only partial in relation to it. Analysis therefore brings to light here the intentional unity of a multiplicity of facts which all strive to realize the same

[341]

idea. In other words, in the progressive dimension of analysis, the idea is revealed as anticipatively constituting itself in a multiplicity of real facts. The ideal reference of this multiplicity of factical examples—their unifying teleology, which is as such implied in their very sense—is explicated by intentional analysis, which elicits in itself that which is only pre-scribed in an anticipative manner in and through the factical examples. Consequently, the infinite manifold of the facts is ordered to an intentional unity of meaning which is constituted in it. This manifold assumes the specifically typical form of a history, which thus explicitly takes on the value of a *sense genesis*. The most striking example Husserl gives is that of phenomenology, which constitutes itself teleologically in the history of science in general.

b) The constituted object intentionally refers to the a priori of its constitution. By its very presence it necessarily implies the possibility of reactivating the system of intentionalities or transcendental evidences that governed its constitution. Every object must thus be capable of being intuitively legitimized, and this intuition is precisely the subjective a priori of constitution. But the object by itself is a stable ideality, an ideal identity transcending the process of its multiple constitution. Consequently, retrogressive analysis here goes from the intentional unity to the multiplicity of the constituting intentionality, which is simply the history of transcendental consciousness itself and of the evident steps it has had to set down (*leisten*) in order to constitute the object under consideration.

There is therefore on both sides an intentional ordering of a multiplicity to a unity, although the terms are considered in an inverse relation by an intentional analysis which itself goes through a course that is either progressive or retrogressive. Analysis therefore manifests two contrary dimensions. Historical experience, mere intuition under the reduction, gives us the fact in its development. Two questions, and only two, can be posed with regard to it: (1) Whence comes this development of the fact? and (2) Where does it go? On the one side, intentional analysis leads from the transcendent to the transcendental; on the other, it rises from the real [*réal*] fact to the idea. It seems, then, that the idea is "diametrically" opposite to the transcendental, as if it were a sort of "supertranscendent." The unity of intentional analysis seems to be broken. We must be able to show that, on the contrary, the idea is the transcendental itself and that progressive analysis and retrogressive analysis are identical. For this we will have to summarize the thrust of what we have covered up to now, which will enable us to formulate successively the necessary consequences of Husserl's doctrine at each of its stages.

§ 55. *Fact-idea exemplarity*

THE POINT OF DEPARTURE of the phenomenological advance is descriptive consideration of the development of science. We are in fact limited to this by submitting ourselves to the phenomenological attitude. But we can define this development only by its point of departure (*Ursprung,* transcendental consciousness) and its terminus (telos, idea). Are these elements— in particular the idea, since it is the first element we looked at —extrinsic to or immanent in the development?

It seems at first sight that analysis of the development leads us to infer a transcendence. This initial hypothesis is verified from two angles. On the one hand, it is established that science as progressive realization implies limits which determine and orient its strivings. On the other hand, science possesses a meaning, it is relation to a sense. By these two successive approaches we hit upon the terminus of the development and its sense-giving (*sinngebendes*) principle. The idea can thus be considered as telos and sense of the development, i.e., as transcending it. Thus we pass through a first stage, that of discovery of the idea.

But a second line of thought immediately asserts itself. It is from the fact that we set out to reach the idea, and the idea now turns out to be the norm of the factical development. Here there is reciprocity in two respects. (1) The fact makes it possible to know the idea (as the sign makes it possible to know the signified). In the genetic order of means of knowing, the fact leads to the idea. Conversely, the idea is what makes it possible to know the fact, since the idea is what gives the fact its intelligibility and its sense. (2) The fact makes it possible to determine the idea formally. There is a formal (univocal) continuity between them; if one grasps the fact, one can reach the idea by idealization (ideation). Conversely, the formal determination in itself of the idea is the norm (extrinsic formal determination) of the fact. Fact and idea mutually participate in each other. It will therefore be necessary to study this mutual exemplarity in the dialectic of the idea and the real.

But one of the dimensions of the dialectic between the idea and the real especially interests us. We sought the definition of the development. We established that development refers to the idea and that the idea refers to the fact. There must be a priority (an a priori) in this reciprocity. The idea is in fact the transcendental principle and hence the "first" in the constitutive sense. In this second movement of "redescent" toward the fact, then, it is reasonable that we should find definition of the development by the idea. This is an extrinsic definition, or rather a definition by extrinsic denomination, which indicates that the essential *quid* of the thing is not in the thing itself but outside it. But the determinate is what defines the less determinate or the indeterminate. If the idea is definition, it is act, whole, axiom— from which its own development derives as potency, part, "consequence." This is one aspect of the problem, the point of view of the value involved in the development, hence of the exemplarity of the idea in relation to the fact (development). The idea is value and, as such, determinate and "really real." But it is an ideal principle, a principle of measure, which is "extrapolated" from the development. The latter alone effectively exists; it is the existential milieu of history. The ideal actuality of the value idea is the counterpart of a radical potentiality of this same idea considered as existence. And from this second point of view the idea appears to us, correlatively, as possible, part, "imaginary." From this point of view it is only the ideal anticipation of the totality of the development.

Thus, if we take the first point of view, that of the value act (transcendental-phenomenological), the idea is entelechy, value, measure, norm; and as such it is transcendent to the development. If we take the second point of view, that of the existence act and hence of the exemplarity of the fact with respect to the idea (descriptive-phenomenological point of view), the idea is *dynamis*, anticipation, implication of the actual existent; and as such it is immanent in the development. The two points of view we distinguished are therefore in close connection. The telos that is reached is both transcendent and immanent. The transcendence is immanent, since it is an irreal transcendence; and the immanence is transcendent, since it is an intentional immanence.

§ 56. *Consequences of fact-idea exemplarity: the identity of being and becoming*

WE MUST ALWAYS RETURN to Husserl's fundamental affirmation: phenomenological method considers being in becoming. Knowledge, for example, is studied in its development and manifests itself as an operation or activity. But, like all activity, development is defined (partially) by its end. Husserl is therefore necessarily led to give a definition of science by the terminus or telos at which its concrete realization aims—a dynamic or "operational" definition, so to speak. This end is what gives a determinate and unitary consistency to the multiple successive phases of the cognitive operation.

Definition by the end. This may seem surprising. For the characteristic of definition is to determine what the thing is in its essence, in whatever brings it about that a certain thing is as it is in its own innermost nature, hence in its formality. But Husserl regards knowledge as inseparable from the development of its progressive realization. It would therefore be vain to seek to grasp it in the manner of the objective sciences, which use "fixed concepts." We must use intentional analysis, which gives us, not a fixed concept, but a "dynamic" intentional concept, thematizing an absence of limits in a process, in the eidetic form of the "and so forth." This method of investigation can obviously result only in a definition by the end (telos) and not in a definition by the form (essence, eidos). We are going in circles, then, unless it is admitted that the form is the end, that the eidos is the telos.

The dialectic between the idea and the real has taught us that the fact is extrinsically defined by the idea, since the fact does not possess its essence in itself but tends more or less adequately to realize its essence. This means, then, that the transcendence of the idea induces an operation of realization of which it is itself the terminus. Husserl repeatedly affirms that the idea is an end, an end idea (*Zweckidee, Zielidee; FTL,* pp. 26 [23], 28 [25], 75 [66], 272 [240] and passim). But the idea is precisely the essence of the fact (*das reine Wesen*) and, at the same time, the telos of its essential realization. The essence is both form and end of the fact. This form is necessarily immanent qua form, since form is immanent principle of determination; but it is necessarily transcendent qua end. It will therefore be an extrinsic form, i.e., a norm. In the case at hand, knowledge, in perpetual development, becomes more itself at each step. The closer it approaches its end idea, the more adequately it realizes its essence, i.e., that which brings it about that a science is formally a science. This extrinsic form or transcendent in-itself is thus the principle that makes it possible to measure the essential perfection of each stage of the development of knowledge. It is standard, value, and norm. This is precisely what we render with the word "exemplar": the telos conceived as both form (essence) and end can only be an exemplar. This exemplar is the "itself" of knowledge—its *Selbst*, as Husserl says.[1]

In this way we can understand the peculiar ambiguity of the idea, which is both intentional immanence and irreal transcendence. The idea is essence or form of the fact. The fact therefore participates in the idea; that is, the fact intrinsically possesses a participation in the idea. This is the immanence of the idea. But the fact itself is not its essence but only has it or participates in it. The in-itself or essential form of the fact is therefore external to the fact. The idea is therefore transcendent, and consequently it is the measure and a priori norm of the fact. This is a difficulty the ancients had already encountered. Plato spoke of the presence and the possession of the idea beside and by the thing. Aristotle showed that the one is both immanent in and transcendent to the many which it measures. Being measure, the one is transcendent; being first term of the multiple series,

1. Science in its ideal state of realization is completely itself (*selbst*). This expression is taken from the teleological description of perception of the object. Husserl shows in *EJ* how in the real [*réel*] process of experience the object is progressively determined to the point of reaching its "itself." The terminus at which the object is then given in itself, as it is in itself, "in the flesh," is obviously an ideal terminus. The object given in an originary manner is given "in der Fülle des Selbst" ("in the fullness of self-sameness"; *EJ*, p. 267 [321]). It is anticipated as such and constitutes an idea of reason (*EJ*, p. 287 [346]). "But the object itself, the original, is, on its side, . . . an *idea* . . ."; ("Der Gegenstand selbst aber, das Original, ist seinerseits . . . eine Idee"; *EJ*, p. 297 [358]). The same is true of the ideal object that is the *Sachverhalt* (*EJ*, pp. 244 [291], 284 [342], 287 f. [346]). We can see the latent idealism in the ostensibly realistic slogan "zu den Sachen selbst" ("to the things themselves!") which ties this imperative to rationality and hence to ideality. Cf. S. Bachelard, *A Study of Husserl's "Formal and Transcendental Logic,"* trans. Lester E. Embree (Evanston, Ill.: Northwestern University Press, 1968), p. xliii.

the one is immanent. The one both is and is not part of the many. In ideal anticipation we can conceive that the transcendence of the idea will be reduced, or rather that the immanence of the realization will absorb it. The definition of knowledge will no longer be an extrinsic definition (by participation) but intrinsic (by immanent determination). If, in the course of the development, the essence (idea) is a transcendent end and consequently an a priori norm of the development which tends toward it, then, at the (ideal) terminus of this development, it will have become an immanent end. Or, more exactly, since the idea is an end only because it is extrinsic formal determination, it will no longer be an end but solely an intrinsic formal determination. By definition, the movement will then be completed, the essence will be fully realized, the dialectic will be absorbed in identity. To identify end and form therefore necessarily amounts to conceiving an immanent finality, which is *provisionally* transcendence in the dialectic of development and hence provisionally exemplar and norm.[2]

Indeed, as we will see again, the significance of intentionality lies in reducing the duality of the two members of the fact-idea dialectic to identity. But this is to be taken in an ideal sense. This implies (1) that currently the essence-end is not fully realized (which immediate description already discloses) and (2) that it will never be realized, except ad infinitum. It remains the ideal, and therefore unrealized, limit of the process of

2. It should be noted that this identification holds true in the case of life. The living does indeed tend toward its fully developed state. The child, for example, tends toward the adult state, which normally realizes the essential virtualities of human nature. Here the end is immanent, since it is the fully realized essence. This is where we must seek the reason for the "biological tone" of certain philosophies. At the basis of such a philosophy will most often be found a conception of being on the model of the living organism, i.e., an identification of end and form. This is true of Bergsonism and of evolutionism in general, which is illustrated in recent times by Teilhard de Chardin. Husserl also permits a conception of the development of science as the development of a living adult or, better, of a living species. Just as the *germen* is perpetuated quasi-eternally and identically in various *somata*, the instinct that is the transcendental motive of genuine science is perpetuated omnitemporally and identically in the various generations of scientists. Biological dynamism is the ideal means of maintaining a univocal uniformity in a multiform movement and thereby showing that the terminus of this movement is an absolute identity. In this case finality becomes simply causality.

realization. It plays the role of end but is nevertheless not an end in the strict sense, since it does not terminate absolutely. It is an ideal end (*ideales Ziel*). It is a priori and originary; it is borne (realized) in the concrete historical development. The latter, taken in itself, anticipates it "really" ["*réalement*"] and thereby enables intentional analysis to elicit it ideally, according it the role of end and, most important, reestablishing it in its essential originariness. What can thus appear as end from the point of view of the current development is therefore in reality first, and absolutely first, on the level of ideality. This is the priority of the possible essence, the priority of the absolutely actual value idea. Far from pursuing an end, development realizes an idea; knowledge is motivated a priori and pre-scribed by the idea. It is measured by an exemplary principle which serves as a guiding thread, orienting it at each stage of its development and deciding its relative degree of perfection.

The teleology of knowledge therefore has no real terminus but rather an ideal terminus, which is the idealization of an infinite development (in the determinate and univocal form of the "and so forth"). "Ich kann mich aber überzeugen, dass keine Bestimmung die letzte ist, dass das wirklich Erfahrene noch immer, endlos, einen Horizont möglicher Erfahrung hat von Demselben" ("However, I can convince myself that no determination is the last, that what has already been experienced always still has, without limit, a horizon of possible experiences of the same" [*EJ*, p. 32 (27)]). No determination is definitive; this is the affirmation correlative with the idealization of the development. In fact, science is never terminated. It is realized asymptotically (which is a mathematical way of saying that it never reaches its end). Only the last determinations are valid. Science (and consequently knowledge) is infinite; it begins, it continues, but it has no end. The idea of science implies a beginning and a development (*Anfang und Fortgang*) only, an "order of cognitions, prior in themselves, related to others which are posterior in themselves" according to the two essential dimensions of time, the past and the future, which are intentionally tied together in the present moment. The idea (of science) implies a development (it is the ideation of the development in its totality) and as such specifies an order of the prior to the posterior, a dialectic of the *Ur-* to the *Nach-*, that is, the dialectic of participation between idea and fact (cf. *CM*, p. 12 [53]; *Crisis*, p. 339 [274]). The idea is the origin of a development which is the process of its own realization. It norms itself exemplarily; that is, it subsists in two modalities, one pure and ideal and the other "involved" [*engagée*] and empirical (cf. *Crisis*, p. 94 [97]). Realizing itself, it is found to be point of departure and point of arrival as well. This is the ultimate idealization of the empirical statement we made with regard to the successive stages of science: each is terminus and new point of departure. By idealizing this essential relativity, i.e., by seeing it apart from the time in which it is involved, by acting "as if" time were completed, we observe that the ideal point of departure and the ideal point of arrival coincide. In fact, though, we are in history; and what is one on the level of the ideal principle is, in history, marked off in successive stages. If the teleology is infinite, the progress of knowledge does not cease being an operation of approximation, and it never reaches its essence. The idealization of its development makes it possible to confer a certain unitary structure on it, but this idealization does not assign a real terminus to it. Thus, knowledge is necessarily development, its being is becoming. Universal knowledge is the operation of universal reason, and this reason manifests and reveals itself in the history of knowledge. But this is an infinite self-explication (*Selbstenthüllung*), in which the "itself" (*Selbst*) will never be reached.

> *Vernunft* ist das Spezifische des Menschen, als in personalen Aktivitäten und Habitualitäten lebenden Wesens. Dieses Leben ist als personales ein ständiges Werden in einer ständigen Intentionalität der Entwicklung. Das in diesem Leben Werdende ist die Person selbst. Ihr Sein ist immerfort Werden . . . (*Krisis*, p. 272).

> [*Reason* is the specific characteristic of man, as a being living in personal activities and habitualities. This life, as personal life, is a constant becoming through a constant intentionality of development. What becomes, in this life, is the person himself. His being is forever becoming; . . . (*Crisis*, p. 338).]

This important affirmation extends universally to everything, since transcendental subjectivity is universally constituting and sense-giving. Husserl does not fail to point this out: "Alles, was ist, ist, sofern es in infinitum wird und in das Kontinuum der entsprechenden Vergangenheiten verströmt" ("Everything that is, *is* so far as it *becomes in infinitum* and is *engulfed* in the continuum of the corresponding pasts").[3]

3. *EJ*, p. 386 (467). It will no doubt be said that in the passage quoted here Husserl is speaking of the constitution of an identical substrate, which could therefore play the role of an

The ultimate consequence of the identification of form and end is the identification of being and becoming. We thereby return to an infinite "Heraclitean" flux, and we undertake to escape from it by idealizing it. This is in fact the outcome of phenomenological method: it sets out from development or becoming; seeking to escape it, it conceives of finding a stable element by idealizing this becoming in its totality, and hence the method remains necessarily closed on itself. It defines the same by the same differently conceived.[4] This means that in the end it does not define, it describes. Just as development tends toward its telos and remains development ad infinitum by reason of the ideality of its telos, so the description which tends toward definition remains description pure and simple (*blosse*) in infinite becoming, since definition is the ideal telos of description. In this case, there are two possibilities. (1) Definition subsists as a "practical-logical" limit in the constant oscillations of linguistic meanings, a limit constituting a "normal" meaning which does not delimit the meaning proper but which at least enables us to orient ourselves practically in the judgments which depend on this meaning. Definition thus gives an average meaning, and it represents a *Kunstgriff*, a practical "artifice," designed to make possible the effective progress of knowledge (cf. *LI*, p. 498 [II/1, 301]). (2) Or else definition ends in a *petitio principii*: becoming is becoming. This amounts to conceiving the principle of identity as "$A = A$," which it is not (for, if it were, it would lose all value, save in a philosophy of a mathematical type) (cf. *FTL*, pp. 194 [172], 338–40, [296–98]).

From the point of view where we are now situated, it already appears that Husserl tends to emphasize the immanent character of the idea. The idea is absorbed in the fact, the totality of which is nothing but the idea itself. The fact is the idea realized, and the idea is the fact idealized. Unity is absorbed in multiplicity, in the multiple development which it norms a priori. The idea is thus a quantitative notion; this conclusion forces itself on us, since the idea is a negative infinite (a non-finite), the thematization of an absence of limit in a process. It is a whole to which

---

"essence which develops." It is not a question of an essence which develops, however, but rather of development which constitutes an essence (identical substrate). If we wish to continue qualifying the idea as a substrate, we must see in it an indeterminate X which is determined in development and which is constituted as an identical essence. As we know, this is one aspect of the idea.

4. These are always the two modes of "subsistence" of the idea.

something can always be added or, at least, a whole to which it can always be conceived (ideally) that something is added. The idea is the eidetic form of the "and so forth." Thus the doctrine of the one and the many, which the Greeks regarded as a qualitative doctrine par excellence, is quantified. In fact, it is difficult to conceive in its purity the qualitative mathematics of Plato, for example. The one and the many are more easily conceived quantitatively, whereas the ideal numbers were for Plato indivisible pure qualities. But, once quantified, the one and the many make possible the establishment of a dialectic ad infinitum. The one is the element, of course. But where is the element in pure quantity? Quantity is divisible ad infinitum. The one seems to dissolve into the many. All the same, a stable unity is needed in order to understand and define the many. In this case, the only means of thematizing the many, and of thematizing it as a unity, is to idealize it in its possible totality. And since this totality is negatively infinite (non-finite), the idea—the unity of the many—is an intentional or teleological unity whose "definition" is ideal. The process is without end in the strict sense; and just as the one dissolves into the many, so being is identified with becoming. The only *one* there is is therefore the infinite totality of becoming, i.e., the becoming itself (cf. above, p. 288).

§ 57. *Phenomenology as transcendental logic: constitutive exemplarism*

SCIENCE IS THUS DEFINED BY THE IDEA. The explication of this idea constitutes logic on its two levels, formal and transcendental. And just as the idea norms the process of its own realization, so logic norms science. The definition of phenomenology as logic will further confirm its exemplarist character. Logic is a normative science; it rules a priori over *de facto* science, being nothing but the eidos of the latter, the idea of its in-itself (*Selbst*). But just this normative character of logic seems to be denied by Husserl. Indeed, he strictly distinguishes formal logic from transcendental logic and refuses to define the first as purely normative. On the other hand, it seems difficult to attribute a normative character, at least in the usual sense of this word, to transcendental logic.

For Husserl, formal logic exercises a logical *function,* but it is not *essentially* normative. Essentially and in itself, logic is a theoretical science; indeed, it must be, since Husserl denies that formal logic is immediately the formal logic of possible truth. The latter form of formal logic is immediately normative, since it decides the truth value of logical configurations. If formal logic ends in this logical function, then, this assumes that of itself it consists in pure theoretical consideration of possible forms of predicative (or at least categorial) meanings given in the evidence of distinctness. In other words, the logic of possible truth assumes a theoretical nucleus which is factually realized in the pure morphology of meanings (*reine Formenlehre der Bedeutungen*) and the logic of pure consequence (*Konsequenzlogik*).

This distinction is not without difficulties. Husserl admits that the interest in the object (hence formal ontology and the logic of possible truth) is the sole logical interest strictly speaking. Nevertheless, nowhere does he deny that the morphology of meanings and the logic of consquence are logics. But the latter are concerned only with the pure meaning, in meaning qua meaning, and not immediately with meaning qua meaning of an object. So Husserl undertakes to justify the often affirmed parallel between formal logic and mathematical analysis, and he defines the pure formal logic of consequence as a mathematics of senses.

But even if pure formal logic is interested only in meaning qua meaning, it cannot absolutely ignore the important fact— and here intentionality reappears—that meaning is necessarily meaning of an object and that the reference to the object can be more or less indirect but cannot be absolutely eliminated. Insofar as formal logic concerns itself only with pure meanings, it necessarily also concerns itself with meaning qua meaning of an object. It is thus that the surpassing of formal logic in formal ontology is justified and that Husserlian formal logic is structured in two dimensions, one of which is pure apophantics and the other pure formal ontology. Each of these two logical disciplines manifests an originary mode of categorial givenness, the evidence of distinctness and the evidence of clarity, corresponding, respectively, to the primacy of the meaning as such, given confusedly in verbal articulations, and to the primacy of the categorial objectivity strictly speaking, i.e., the predicative formation of the primary objectivities of experience. Meaning and experience: the two dimensions of formal logic correspond to the two dimensions of intentionality, descriptive-phenomenological and transcendental-phenomenological. They are reciprocal, and they mutually imply each other to the precise degree that the meaning itself implies them both. In fact the judgment as such, or pure predicative meaning, is a categorial objectivity given evidently in the distinctness of its sense. It is therefore the proper theme of formal apophantics. But this categorial objectivity is the same as that constituted in the evidence of clarity. Only the mode of givenness differs; the categorial objectivity remains identical with itself, just as the idea is differentiated only by its specific mode of subsistence.

Formal logic therefore includes an objective dimension, and consequently it accedes to the normative function characteristic of traditional logic. Husserlian formal logic *is* not normative, then, but it *becomes* so functionally by reason of its intentionality to the object. And in fact formal logic exhibits the exemplarist structure in its internal organization. Each form of judgment, for example, refers to a proto-form; each presentation character or being character and each doxic mode refers to a primary character or mode which plays the role of measure and extrinsic definition of its own derivations. Just as the idea norms its own realization, the primary mode or primary character norms its own development in an exemplary manner. However, since formal logic is not essentially normative, it is not its own norm and it is not the last word of logic. The interest in the object is what will enable us to go beyond this first logical stage. For the interest in the object brings intentionality (i.e., transcendental constitution) into play. Each object is the index of its own constitution. It refers to a subjective a priori, i.e., ultimately to the transcendental ego itself, or at least to transcendental subjectivity, as we know. Consequently, formal ontology needs to legitimize its object. Even if this object is considered in its pure formality as object in general, it implies an intentional reference to an originary constitution. Intentional analysis in its reflective form will bring us from the fully formalized judgment of formal logic, bearing on objects which are likewise formalized, to a primary singular judgment of experience and then to experience. This originary basis of every theoretical configuration is the *Lebenswelt*, the world of lived experience. But we must proceed beyond this to constitutive evidence, to the *cogito*, the proper act of the transcendental ego. Once these various reductions are carried out, it is possible to formalize the results obtained and thereby elicit the eidos of transcendental constitution, the idea of reason or evidence. Formal ontology and formal logic in its entirety are thus surpassed in a transcendental logic which is precisely the phenomenology of transcendental subjectivity, first philosophy, formalized ultimately in eidetic phenomenology.

By bringing to light the excellent form of constitutive intentionality, namely, evidence or originary seeing, transcendental logic therefore manifests the ideal exemplar (the eidos) of all *de facto* constitution. This idea of transcendental constitution is explicated as reason, and its infinite correlate is truth. Here we have logical exemplarism, to be sure, but an exemplarism proper to transcendental logic. This is a constitutive exemplarism, since reason is the idea of all originary and evident constitution, the idea of the constitutive fullness of the ego to which the intuitive fullness of truth corresponds. Just as formal logic norms *de facto* science, transcendental logic norms formal logic, since it explicates the idea or telos of formal logic. It immediately appears that transcendental logic or phenomenology is therefore the ultimate norm of science insofar as logic is the idea of science. However, the normation on the part of formal logic is a "logical," static, analytic normation; the normation on the part of transcendental logic is a "phenomenological" or transcendental, dynamic, synthetic, constitutive normation. Let us add immediately that this latter is an ultimate normation, a teleological exemplarity, since it is infinite and ideal. Transcendental logic norms itself; phenomenology is to itself its own logic, it itself is its idea, it is its in-itself; it has realized its essence, since it is the entelechy of science in general. This is to be understood ideally, however, since phenomenology is the (infinite) idea of science. While formal logic has a normative *function,* then, transcendental logic is *essentially* normative. We must, moreover, take the first of these assertions in its full intentional sense. Formal logic is intentionally (functionally) normative because it implies an intentional reference to the transcendental logic that will clarify it.

Thus we find the shifting of intentionality once again. Logic is the idea of science, but this idea is a telos. The unique, genuine idea of science can be only transcendental logic or phenomenology, since this science alone is ultimate and absolute. Discovery of the idea of science is therefore a key part of transcendental logic; and since intentionality has several stages, it is right to delimit the formal level of logic before explicating the ultimate transcendental level. This does not mean that there is separation here; on the contrary, there is intentional continuity.

If the object in general needs to have its constitution justified by an intentional reflection on transcendental subjectivity, this is because only such a reflection can give it the evidence and intuitive originariness it requires. Evidence is thus nothing but the subjective a priori, the subjective form of the object in general. So, too, transcendental logic is the subjective a priori of formal logic. We must therefore conclude that transcendental logic is the evidence and infinite rational motivation of formal logic.

§ 58. *Consequences of constitutive exemplarism:* (a) *The idea is the transcendental*

BUT WE HAVE NOT RESOLVED the antinomy between the idea and the transcendental. On the contrary, we seem to be left with a dualist view, in which intentional analysis has two dimensions: one pressing on to the telos-idea, the other rising to the pure subject of constitution. In the relation between formal logic and transcendental logic, however, we have the means of overcoming this difficulty. This relation between the two forms of logic can in fact be seen in different ways. Husserl begins his investigations with a first phase in which he examines formal logic given in its historical facticity and submits it to a (progressive) intentional analysis designed to elicit its sense or idea. He explicates this idea by showing that transcendental logic is the necessary continuation of formal logic. In other words, from this first point of view he regards transcendental logic as the idea of formal logic, i.e., its ideal telos and transcendent essence. At this point the exemplarist structure finds application. Formal logic is the factical example which enables intentional analysis to anticipate the ideal exemplar, transcendental logic. However, even while explicating transcendental logic as the idea of formal logic, Husserl insists on the fact that transcendental logic is the subjective a priori from which this formal logic comes to be transcendentally constituted. Transcendental logic is the synthetic system of constituting intentionalities in which the various theoretical configurations of formal logic transcendentally "appear." In this sense we can maintain that transcendental logic is the evidence of formal logic. The idea of formal logic therefore coincides with its constitutive a priori. It must even be said that the idea of formal logic is nothing but its constitution, ideally completed and thematized in the form of rational evidence. We have here a universal assertion, one which is exemplary in the strongest sense of the word; for transcendental logic is the ideal thematization (eidetic phenomenology) of transcendental constitution or intentional consciousness in general, and what it formulates in its degree of "synthetic formality" is therefore valid for all *de facto* cases of constitution. In general, then, the idea is transcendental consciousness itself in its teleological form. It is the eidetic, exemplary thematization of the infinity of the constitutive evidence of the object in general. And in fact the idea of a certain objectivity is simply the ideal anticipation of its perfect constitution and originary givenness. Only the idea is evident and rational in phenomenology; the fact can only be inevident and irrational. At most it can be said that the fact is intentionally evident and rational to the degree that it participates in its idea and tries to realize it ad infinitum. Likewise, only phenomenology—indeed, only phenomenology formalized in eidetic phenomenology or constitutive exemplary logic—is evident, rational, and necessary.

This eidetic phenomenology is perfectly realized in *Formal and Transcendental Logic*. This logical work, *the* book of Husserl,[5] represents phenomenology in general, the intentional elucidation of evident and rational constitution in general. It has an eidetic character which specifies its subjective logical bearing. *Formal and Transcendental Logic* is indeed a subjective formal logic and therefore a transcendental logic, since the transcendental, being identical with the idea or the eidetic, is the formal, the constitutive formal, the motivating exemplary. Transcendental logic thus realizes this formal logic, this formal ontology "which relates to everything that exists in any sense: to what exists as transcendental subjectivity and to everything that becomes constituted in transcendental subjectivity" (*FTL*, p. 271 [239]). The formal in transcendental logic or eidetic phenomenology is conceived as the constitutive correlate of the formal of pure analytics (*FTL*, p. 212 [188]; cf. *CM*, § 36). It is *subjective form*, the constitutive correlate and transcendental motivation of *objective form*, and it defines the exemplarist character of transcendental logic. The exemplary is therefore constitutive.

In order to understand the import of this conclusion better, we can compare *Formal and Transcendental Logic* with the

5. S. Bachelard, *A Study of Husserl's "Formal and Transcendental Logic,"* p. xxx.

Crisis. The latter work realizes the phenomenology of objective science, hence *one* phenomenology, which by an intentional analysis grounds a certain ideal objectivity in transcendental subjectivity. Since logic is the science of the idea of science, *Formal and Transcendental Logic* therefore deals eidetically with what the *Crisis* exhibits factically. In fact, *Formal and Transcendental Logic* elicits the eidos of the line of advance followed by the *Crisis.* Rather than being *a* phenomenology or subjective material logic, *Formal and Transcendental Logic* is *the* phenomenology, the subjective formal logic. This is why eidetic phenomenology is transcendental logic.

Thus the idea is necessarily transcendental, progressive analysis and retrogressive analysis are identical, and the antinomy is overcome. The fact which is the factical example of the idea is by itself immediately the index of its own subjective constitution. The idea which is the ideal exemplar of the fact is also immediately its transcendental constitution, its rational evidence. Intentional analysis in its two phases always rises to the same transcendental foundation, consciousness. Only the mode of explication of this foundation varies. In one case it is grasped teleologically as ideal anticipation of the object in general; in the other it is grasped originarily as the ego in its pure function as transcendental subjectivity. Origin and telos therefore coincide in phenomenology. The idea is both point of departure and terminus, being both a priori norm and ideal end. This fundamental coincidence is the necessary consequence of phenomenological exemplarism, of the identification of the eidos-form and the telos-end in one and the same ideal exemplary norm. The accent can, of course, be placed differently to emphasize the originary or the teleological aspect. The fundamental reality is nevertheless identical. It is transcendental consciousness, constituting consciousness of the object—which, being the idea itself, the reason or a priori evidence of the object, is the synthetic norm of the object. The exemplarism we are finding in Husserl, which seems at first sight to be only objective-logical, extends to *transcendental subjectivism.* Transcendental subjectivity is subjective form, synthetic norm, constitutive exemplar of the object in general. This is the ultimate justification of the transcendental-logical character of eidetic phenomenology, the *idea of phenomenology.*

Intentional analysis thus reaches the unique principle, the sole absolute a priori. Let us note that it does so from a study of the object given in historical development. The two dimensions of analysis which we have distinguished up to now are both integral parts of one of the dimensions of intentionality. The empirically given fact is what enables analysis to rise either to the pure ego or to the eidos-telos, where it sees that these two dimensions are identified in the descriptive-phenomenological dimension of intentionality. The (transcendental-phenomenological) dimension represents constitutive intentionality in the direction from consciousness to object. Intentionality itself is therefore twofold. From the object to consciousness, the phenomenologist follows the descriptive-phenomenological way; from consciousness to the object, the phenomenologist follows the transcendental-phenomenological way. This duality is found again in transcendental logic, which is in turn formulated following the two intentional ways (*Formal and Transcendental Logic* and *Experience and Judgment*). To each dimension of intentionality, then, there corresponds a mode of intentional inquiry. However, one of these modes has a duality as well. The main point of the descriptive-phenomenological method is to take support in the originary experience of the fact. Depending on whether the phenomenologist sees in this experience the factical example of the idea or the index of its transcendental constitution, the descriptive-phenomenological way is progressive or retrogressive. And we have proof that this is really a matter of one and the same intentional dimension, since we have just shown that progressive analysis is identical with retrogressive analysis.

We must therefore draw a fundamental distinction between the two dimensions of intentional analysis (which are immediately based on the two dimensions of intentionality itself) and the two modes of descriptive-phenomenological intentional analysis (which are immediately based on the two functions which the fact given in historical experience can assume).

And if idea and transcendental can be identified, this is because Husserlian constitutive exemplarism has no metaphysics of the Platonic type. When the notion of exemplarism and mutual exemplarity is put into play, this is only the better to gain insight into the notion of intentionality and its two necessary dimensions. We could as well use the word "idealism" as "exemplarism," but it would be more equivocal.

Intentionality can now be defined in two ways. On the one hand, it can be defined as the reciprocal intentional teleology of fact and idea. Here the "logical," exemplary, normative aspect of the idea is emphasized. On the other hand, it can be defined as the correlation between consciousness and object (between noesis and noema), i.e., as transcendental constitution itself. These two formulas express the same reality under two aspects. The first applies more particularly to the descriptive-phenomeno-logical dimension of intentionality. Indeed, it is in this dimension that the words "example" and "exemplar" appear most often, as *Crisis* and *Formal and Transcendental Logic* testify. The second applies more particularly to the transcendental-phenomenologi-cal dimension. Likewise, if the following two formulas are not identical, they are at least equivalent.

It can be said that (1) the idea is the exemplar, the norm and essential subjective form of the fact, and (2) the transcendental subject is the evidence and the reason of the object. But both the idea and the transcendental subject represent the essential possibility or teleological actuality of the fact (or of the object). The exemplar is constitutive, the form is subjective, and reason is synthetic normation. In a word, then, the *transcendental subject* is the *idea* of the *object in general*. In this assertion the subjective formality of evidence in general is also expressed and hence the constitutive exemplarity of the ego as the teleological reference of a constituting multiplicity to an intentional unity. The object, since it is the sense of consciousness, is the measure and ideal end of constituting intentionality, the exemplary unity of its multiplicity. We do find mutual exemplarity again here, but it is the exemplarity between consciousness and the object. This exemplarity can obviously be maintained only within the framework of a transcendental logic conceived as eidetic phenomenology. It expresses the fundamental phenomenological reciprocity, according to which intentional constitution of the object is intentionally equivalent to self-constitution of the sense of subjectivity in transcendental consciousness.

§ 59. *Consequences of constitutive exemplarism:* (b) *Identity of the descriptive-phenomenological point of view and the transcendental-phenomenological point of view; the question of phenomenological realism and idealism*

However, once again we come across a duality. One last effort will enable us to go beyond it. As a matter of fact, the descriptive-phenomenological point of view will in a way absorb the transcendental-phenomenological point of view, from which the idea is seen as constituted in its own factical realization.

This is where the troublesome question of the realism or idealism of Husserlian phenomenology arises and is resolved. Does the idea constitute the fact in an absolutely preeminent way, or does the fact preeminently motivate the idea? Where is the definitive priority? But is it absolutely necessary to seek a priority on the part of either the idea or its realization? Husserl affirms both the one and the other. And he insists so strongly on the reciprocity of the two points of view that it must be asked whether there is truly an order of precedence between them. To affirm the priority of the idea exclusively would be to return to a Kantian conception of consciousness, an empty and purely ideal consciousness which is abstract and therefore atemporal. Husserl challenges this conception. For him, consciousness is a concrete subjectivity, replete with sense, living—a temporal flow of consciousness rather than an empty a priori principle. But, on the other hand, to insist solely on the "realism" of this flow would equally falsify Husserl's thought by inclining it toward a sort of subjectivist empiricism, which he rejects just as vigorously.

We must get away from this alternative. The old quarrel between realism and idealism can be held to be liquidated as a false problem in Husserlian phenomenology, thanks to the notion of the constitution of the idea in its realization. The ambition of phenomenology is to be beyond this alternative, which still troubles so many minds. Is it a realism or an idealism that can maintain that the idea is realized to the same extent that the real is idealized, to the point that idea and real are in the end identified? Idea and fact are simultaneous and are constitutively implied in each other. The two dimensions of intentionality should not lead us to make an arbitrary choice between fact and idea. Fact and idea are reciprocal; they participate in the same dialectical unity and hence in the same "real" identity. The transcendental-phenomenological order is kept in its priority, but it manifests itself only in the descriptive-phenomenological order of factical realization. The idea would remain forever empty, sterile, and unknown if it did not motivate a process of realization which enables intentional analysis to rediscover it (*Nachverstehen*). It is in this process of realization that the idea manifests itself (*Kundgabe*) and finds its appropriate expression or "language." The two orders of priority are there-fore indispensable to each other, since neither could subsist without the other. This is the mutual exemplarity of fact and idea: on the one hand the priority of the fact with respect to the idea, and on the other hand the priority of the idea with respect to the fact. Furthermore, the two priorities respectively ground the constitutive character of the fact and the idea. The development of the fact constitutes the idea anticipatively-teleologically, and the idea constitutes the fact normatively-transcendentally. But the idea in general is a transcendental motive that is not yet clarified. It is clarified either by and in the concrete evolution of history or by an intentional analysis which, on the basis of a portion of this evolution, anticipates it ideally in its totality. If there is teleology, then, the phenome-nologist can finally decide the direction of this teleology only when the fact has reached its full state of completion. The idea can be "inferred" from the present fact but will be fully moti-vated by it only at the end of its development. (This is a figure of speech, since the end of the fact's development is precisely the idea.) The process of realization thus reveals the idea to itself, and it therefore reveals reason itself. The idea, implicitly constituted in and by transcendental consciousness, is fulfilled and made explicit by the fact itself.[6]

If it is said that the idea is a priori, this point must be made clear. "A priori" can be understood here in either a historical sense or an ideal sense. The idea of knowledge, for example, historically precedes the effective development of science in the same way that the first scientific step precedes the further steps. But it is in this first step, which is the germ of scientific or philosophical resolution, that the idea of science is implicitly constituted. This is a constitution of the idea by concrete realiza-tion, constitution in the strict sense, but anonymously exercised and not explicated by history. Only intentional analysis can elicit the idea as a separate a priori. It alone enables us to explicate the constitutive exemplarity (synthetic normation)

6. *Crisis*, p. 338 (273). This is why Husserlian exemplarism is reciprocal; the fact constitutes the idea as the idea constitutes the fact. Platonic exemplarism also has two dimensions. But for Plato, one dimension is absolute; this is the dimension of participation, which grounds the intelligibility of the thing in the idea. The other dimension is only the way of access to the ideas for human in-telligence.

exercised by the idea. In itself, the idea subsists in its realization,[7] inseparably from the concrete act of norming its own development in an exemplary manner. But this development is the idea's own realization; the idea that is realized in the factical development is constituted in and by it. A minimum of realization is of course necessary before intentional analysis can explicitly elicit the idea. The farther advanced the realization and the more developed the human knowledge interest, the more trustworthy is the motivation of the idea, the more weight and compelling force it has (cf. *Ideen II*, p. 45). Theoretically, the first act of knowledge provoked by the first scientific wonder implies the idea of science; but this idea is found in such an embryonic state that it is most difficult to discern it in its ideal purity. A series of successive "gropings" is necessary in order little by little to specify this guiding idea. And just because the idea they imply is very confused, these gropings may be checks as well as successes. It clearly follows from this that only the end of the process of realization—once the possibilities of error, of deviations and inhibitions of the cognitive tendency, are exhausted—will manifest this idea with vividness and evidence (*Einsichtigkeit*)—an idea that has been latent within this process since its origin. In particular, only the end will show whether this idea is truly the absolute it claims to be.[8]

Thus we see that the simultaneity between the idea's constitution and its realization puts us in a position to assert the a priori status of the idea. Effective realization of the idea retraces the constitution of the idea, the infinite transcendental motive to which it will never be perfectly adequate. And the more the realization tends to its perfection, the more the idea manifests its a priori character, i.e., its transcendence. Thus, in a very evocative way, we see transcendence constituted in im-

7. In this sense, realization is a moment of the idea, whereas intentional analysis enables us to elicit the idea as a "separable part" (*Stück*) of the development. Cf. above, § 12.

8. In fact, all possibilities of error, etc., need not be exhausted. The progressive realization of the idea allows us to become more clearly aware of it (in this sense, history is a true *Klärung*), so that the movement of approximation is accelerated and the tendency of knowledge is directed in a more and more linear manner toward its telos. The process of realization grows in approximation to the idea in a quasi-geometrical progression, which the word "asymptotic" renders quite well. Cf. *Crisis*, pp. 15 f. (13 f.), 72 f. (74). It would be appropriate here to exhibit the similarities between Husserl's intentional dialectic and Marx's historical dialectic.

manence. This transcendence is irreally included in the immanence of the realization; it is a transcendence of irreal inclusion
(*Transzendenz irreellen Beschlossenseins*), in the excellent
words of the *Cartesian Meditations*. And since the realization is
necessarily historical, history itself is therefore transcendental
constitution in that it is infinite teleology unitarily thematized
as idea. Again we come across this notion of infinite development, which is simply pure intentional operation (*Leistung*).
In the beginning is action; "Am Anfang ist die Tat." Husserl
paraphrases the cry of Faust, and thereby Saint John's "In the
beginning was the Word." [9] *At the end is action,* since no determination is ultimate, i.e., since there is no end to the process of
determination.

Having been formulated in terms of exemplarism, the results
of these last reflections can be formulated again in intentional
terms strictly speaking. In fact, the pair "fact-idea" coincides
with the pair "object-consciousness." The realization of the idea
is a *Leistung* of consciousness, and the transcendence of the
idea is an immanent (intentional) transcendence of consciousness or transcendental subjectivity. Therefore, just as the mutual
exemplarity of fact and idea is absorbed in a dialectical unity,
the two dimensions of the correlation between noesis and
noema—consciousness-object and object-consciousness—are
identified. In this way the identity of the two phenomenological
points of view, descriptive and transcendental, can be established in express terms of intentional *consciousness*.

For constitution of the object is precisely self-constitution
of the transcendental subject (transcendental consciousness);
Sinngebung is a *Besinnung*. The object is defined by Husserl as
the sense of consciousness, as that toward which the immanent
meanings of consciousness tend. Constitution of the object
therefore necessarily coincides with the originary self-giving of
sense on the part of transcendental subjectivity. In constituting
the object, subjectivity gives itself its sense and therefore constitutes itself. The transcendental reduction thus on the one
hand leads the constitutive investigation of sense-giving (*Besinnung*) to an absolute presupposition which gives its sense to
itself (*Selbstbesinnung*), and on the other hand it leads to a
subject which is a norm in itself, an intentional (infinite synthetic) norm, an a priori self-consciousness (*Selbstnormierung*).

9. *Crisis*, p. 156 (158). [The standard English translation of
Husserl (and Faust) here is "In the beginning is the deed."—TRANS.]

The reduction appears in two fundamental modes. One is expressed in terms of consciousness and manifests the constitution of every objectivity in transcendental subjectivity. The other is ideal or eidetic; it is expressed in terms of logic and manifests the constitutive a priori normation of every objectivity by transcendental subjectivity. But either way the two dimensions of intentionality are identified. We have just seen this for the pair "idea-fact," and now we can say it for the pair "consciousness-object." Transcendental self-consciousness is the terminus of the reflective (descriptive-phenomenological) advance, which grounds the sense of the object in transcendental subjectivity; and transcendental constitution of the object is the terminus of the transcendental-phenomenological dimension. If the two intentional dimensions are identical, their termini intentionally coincide. And so the consciousness-object antinomy—another, more classic aspect of the opposition between idealism and realism—is resolved. Must knowledge be given precedence over being, or being over knowledge? Is being the measure of knowledge, or is knowledge the measure of being? This opposition is too coarse and simplistic. There is a middle way, that of intentionality, which shows the simultaneity and necessary correlation between the act of knowledge and the object in the constitution of the ideal objectivity of meaning (cf. above, § 22). It is no longer necessary to choose between the act of knowledge (idealism) and the thing (realism).[10] Since the thing *is* for us only in originary experience, we must take both the one and the other. This is the (synthetic) position of phenomenology.

These last considerations indicate a *tendency* of phenomenology, but this tendency is already perfectly indicated in Husserl's thought. It is not simply a tendency the historian discovers in Husserl's work; it is an intentionality strictly speaking, one that is essential to this work. The identity of fact and idea and the coincidence between transcendental constitution of the object and transcendental self-consciousness are in themselves already teloi of an infinite intentionality. Husserl himself suggests this by the emphasis he places on the descriptive-phenomenological dimension. So we should not be surprised if Husserl's avowed disciples develop this aspect of intentionality especially. It seems that the descriptive-phenomenological point of view (description of teleology) prevails now and that consti-

10. Cf. J.-P. Sartre, *Situations*, I, p. 32: "Consciousness and the world are given at a single stroke." [This is contained in the article mentioned above, p. 3, n. 1.—TRANS.]

tution of the idea is purely and simply left to this teleology itself, which is concretely realized by history or development in general. Intentional analysis thus seems to be ignored, and contemporary phenomenology gradually abandons Husserl's affirmation of the transcendence of the idea.

Three examples from the domain of ethics and aesthetics will help us make this continuation of Husserlian phenomenology understood.

§ 60. *Contemporary perspectives*

JUST AS INTENTIONALITY enables us to overcome the theoretical opposition between idealism and realism, so it enables us to get beyond the opposition between the "realist" ethics of happiness and the "idealist" ethics of duty.[11] Here, too, phenomenology refuses to accept the alternative. For Merleau-Ponty, for example, human operation is essentially characterized by its freedom or spontaneity. Nothing, therefore, determines it a priori—neither moral finality or moral exemplarity, neither the good nor moral law. This does not amount to giving human operation over to arbitrariness or chance. It is teleologically oriented and motivated. For from the mere fact that it *is*— however little else it may be—human operation has a direction; it is an *existential project*. But as such it denies any other project, any intellectual project, for example, which would be an a priori presupposition of action. Intentional analysis can of course elicit this existential project and posit it in itself, in which case the project can take on the appearance of an a priori. But this amounts to admitting that it has no value in itself but only in its realization and that its entire value is its being lived. Intentionality is what grounds this simultaneity, this absence of "real" [*réel*] a prioris, or, in the present case, this absence of moral ends or laws—intentionality being *to* its object or *with* it (*Mit-sein*) rather than norming or orienting it *von oben her*, as an a priori. Merleau-Ponty therefore rejects any predetermination of human action; if it is to be free, how can it be

11. This shows that intentionality is not a structure of consciousness limited to the theoretical domain alone but that it extends universally to every *Leistung*, both theoretical and practical. In fact, intentionality is not differentiated as theoretical, ethical, and aesthetic; cf. *Crisis*, p. 341 (275).

determined? He excludes all real or ideal finality under the general heading of "intellectual projects" and wants to take into consideration only the "existential project, which is the polarization of a life towards a goal which is both determinate and indeterminate, which, to the person concerned, is entirely unrepresented, and which is recognized only on being attained." [12]

Is this anything else than what Husserl says when he asserts that only the fulfillment of the teleological development enables us to decide ultimately and absolutely whether the telos (which seems to be pursued and which intentional analysis has ideated) is a genuine transcendental motive? (Cf. *Crisis*, § 6 and passim.)

Dufrenne's aesthetics reproduces the same structure of thought, at least with regard to artistic creation and execution.[13] The telos of artistic operation is the work, and the work is what gives the process of creation its sense, its direction. The dynamism of creation is not that of the artist who wills the work, however, but that of the work itself, which, needing to be realized, wills itself through the artist. At the outset the work is mere inexistent exigency, aesthetic creation being creation *ex nihilo,* and at the end of the creative activity it is concrete existence. Consequently, creation is the deed, not of the artist, but of the work itself, or at least of the inspiration which teleologically results in the work. The artist himself does not know what the outcome of his activity will be. He will know this only when the work is completed and finally brought into existence. In other words, like man in Merleau-Ponty's moral act, the artist does not know the terminus of his undertaking; only the development will reveal it to him. In this sense the telos is both determinate—since it is the end of the creative activity (the activity necessarily pre-scribing in itself an end to be attained) —and indeterminate—since it is not known to the artist. Dufrenne therefore denies the presence of a guiding idea in the

12. *The Phenomenology of Perception,* trans. Colin Smith (New York: Humanities Press, 1962), p. 446. Clearly, moral activity under these conditions no longer implies choice, since deliberation is excluded (*ibid.,* p. 500). How can one deliberate concerning a proposed human act if there is no representation of the end to be attained prior to reaching this end? We should show here how this conception of the human moral act results from the transposition of an aesthetic way of thinking into the ethical domain (cf. below).

13. *The Phenomenology of Aesthetic Experience,* trans. Edward S. Casey *et al.* (Evanston, Ill.: Northwestern University Press, 1973), Part I, "Phenomenology of the Aesthetic Object," pp. 30 ff.

work, or at least in the creative operation. He rejects this idea, just as Merleau-Ponty rejects any intellectual project in human activity.[14] In this sense the artist only sustains an artistic inspiration of which he is not master and which draws him along fatally in a process of creation (whence the classic theme of the bewitched artist). The work needs to be realized and therefore requires that the artist be reduced to a mere instrumental function. Dufrenne does not, of course, deny that creative operation is conscious. But basically he believes that everything happens *as if* it were unconscious, as if it were simply a teleology of the work itself. Like Merleau-Ponty's moral act, artistic activity therefore excludes choice. The critical function which choice performs is ascribed to the series of sketches necessary to the creation of the work, just as Husserl regards history as having a critical function with respect to the transcendental motive that it sustains and realizes. Even though the work is mere exigency of realization, the process of creation does not lead necessarily and immediately to the completed work. Certain imperfect forms must be eliminated before the ultimate and perfect form is reached. The choice that criticizes the inspiration eliminates certain of these forms as possible; the imperfect sketches permit elimination of certain of these forms as realized. What warns the artist that a certain sketch is not yet the work is the consciousness of inadequacy it provokes, a consciousness exactly like the "consciousness of remainder" we encountered above (cf. § 12). This is in a way an "unconscious" consciousness, since the work is only possible and is never anticipated— even imperfectly—in the form of a guiding idea.

Merleau-Ponty and Dufrenne represent the same philosophical position, one in ethics and the other in aesthetics. By insisting on the fact that human *operation* is essentially free, these writers come to suppress the freedom of *man*. Man thus becomes the bearer of a universal intentional teleology, just as scientists are bearers of the universal scientific knowledge interest which extends beyond each of them. This freedom is a curious freedom, one that hypostatizes human operation while preventing man from being truly responsible for it. I am not responsible for a work of which I am only the instrument.

14. This idea would be an imaginary aesthetic object (Dufrenne, p. 31), which corroborates the position we expressed in § 11, above, that only the descriptive-phenomenological point of view (that of phenomenological "realism") allows us to hold that the idea is imaginary.

Dufrenne touches on important truths, however, and it would be possible to correct his position by applying the exemplarist structure we have discovered in phenomenology.

There is surely a representation prior to the work. This idea is potential as to existence, since it represents the work as possible. But it is also potential as to determination, and here we must relax the framework of the two dimensions of intentionality, which is too rigid in the case at hand. From the descriptive-phenomenological point of view, the artist's idea is clearly potential, since it is the work as possible. But it must be added that the artist's idea is not in act from the transcendental-phenomenological point of view either, i.e., it is not a value act. We must agree with Dufrenne that the artist fully knows the end (the terminus) of his work only at the moment when it is completed, since the artist is an artist only by his act.[15] But the fact that he fully knows the end of his work only when it is completed and perfect does not mean that he has no representation of it at all, however imperfect. The artist's idea is potential in two respects: as to the existence of the work it pre-scribes and as to its exemplary determination. If we undertake to transpose the intentional schema into creative operation, then, this schema must indeed be modified to some extent but not transformed to the point of denying even the presence of the idea.[16]

The examples of Merleau-Ponty and Dufrenne show the

15. Cf. Dufrenne, p. 35.
16. The case of the artist's creative activity is the one case in which it is legitimate to claim that the telos is determined in its absolute validity as telos only at the terminus of the teleology. (The moral intention, on the contrary, allows us to anticipate the telos of ethical operation in its absoluteness without living it concretely and in evidence.) The idea is potential even as to its exemplary determination, and this implies that the process of creation in a way clarifies the idea and that the idea will be fully idea at the moment when it is fully a work. It is in the process of artistic creation that this identification of act and idea—from both the descriptive and the transcendental points of view—is best confirmed. (An identification that is necessary in principle—"aus prinzipieller Notwendigkeit," as Husserl might say.) A most interesting horizon opens up to us after these reflections. It would be useful to show how Husserlian phenomenology possesses an "aesthetic" structure precisely insofar as it is exemplarist. And Dufrenne, who thinks he is applying a theoretical method of investigation to a particular domain, only brings the phenomenological method to its native domain—whence the very pertinent character of his work.

extent to which the phenomenological school following Husserl shows itself to be sympathetic to the descriptive-phenomenological point of view of intentionality. This is an ultimate form of the refusal to Platonize, the refusal to admit the reality of metaphysical ideas. From this point of view, ideas are on this side of the real [*en-deça du réel*], and only the reality of the world immediately imposes itself. Whence the "realism" of contemporary phenomenology. It moves solely on the level of the existence act. Existence precedes essence, and this "preceding" implies a veritable devaluation of essence. Existence constitutes essence; and, since there are no universal essences, there is in practice only *existence which becomes*.

We keep coming back to this fundamental conclusion: nothing is foreign to becoming; everything, insofar as it *is*, is becoming. For form and end are identical. The transcendence that "emerges" from the immanence of the process of realization proves to be the end of this process, an ideal and a priori end. Each stage of science finalizes itself by constitutively assigning itself its intentional telos, by more nearly determining the end idea that motivates and directs it a priori. It can therefore be said in general that the process of realization of the idea finalizes itself; it is to itself its own end, as long as it determines and constitutes its end idea. Becoming or development finalizes itself. It has no other end than itself. This ties in with some results we obtained above: (1) development is infinite, (2) the idea is the idealization of the total development, and (3) development is defined by itself. These results gave us the formal (*wesensmässig*) aspect of the development, while here we have its final (teleological) aspect; and, as we know, these two aspects coincide in identity. So in the end we come back to the same result. Phenomenological exemplarism thus leads necessarily to unity.

Finally, let us consider the Sartrean transposition of Husserl's phenomenology. It is perhaps more faithful than the two examples discussed above, although it too exaggerates the descriptive-phenomenological dimension. Here too we find—but in an original form—the primacy of motivating subjectivity or freedom, the (teleological) tendency of subjectivity to explicate itself in historical development. That is, we find the progressive emergence of freedom in its exercise of being (existence), the *processus ad infinitum* of realization, i.e., the infinite transcendence of the freedom which pursues itself. Alongside these common notes, however, we also find some specifically Sartrean characteristics. A wind of harsh lucidity blows through this work, refusing all euphoric satisfaction—something which cannot always be claimed for Husserl's work.

Now, what does the descriptive experience of man yield? Does it immediately reveal the essence of man to us as a necessary a priori? No, it does not; instead it gives only man's becoming or development, his flowing realization, his life or exercise of existence. This flowing reality cannot be defined by a concept delimiting an essence. In conformity with phenomenological doctrine, this becoming is a subjective *Leistung* which as such must have its roots in a constituting subjectivity. If what appears of man is his human operation and hence his active existence, this acting must be rooted in a subjectivity. This subjectivity is grasped as being essentially freedom, since in the *cogito* in which it expresses itself it grasps itself with no intermediary and therefore with no a priori. It grasps only itself as living source of spontaneity, pure act, free existence. All human operation is consequently suspended in this fundamental evidence, whose practical aspect appears immediately: concrete immediacy of the free and autonomous ego. The phenomenological principle of the absolute primacy of subjectivity is preserved in a purely practical mode. Moreover, the transcendental point of view will immediately be absorbed in the descriptive point of view. Subjectivity or freedom is no more separable from free action than transcendental consciousness is separable from the flow of its experiences. It is necessarily committed [*engagée*], and it is determined and defined in this commitment. This is a transposition of the simultaneity between constitution and realization of the idea. Freedom *is* only insofar as it is exercised; it is never isolated [*degagée*] from its exercise. Subjectivity will never be isolated from its existence. There is no essence independent of existence. On the contrary, the very essence of man is to exist, and for this very reason no essence is a priori there (none precedes it) to orient this exercise of being. Existence will be essentially freedom. Man therefore exists before being thus or so. But what determines what he wants to be except himself—that is, except his freedom? Existence is therefore what determines the essence of man. "Existence precedes essence": even this is a truly Husserlian assertion, insofar as phenomenology reduces the duality of the dimensions of intentionality to a single descriptive dimension (or, more precisely, identifies the two dimensions). Existence pre-scribes essence just as development pre-scribes the idea. Since the development or becoming of this existence is the emergence of freedom, man becomes what he wants to be. He freely creates himself, he is to himself his own measure, just as phenomenology is to itself its own logic and just as transcendental subjectivity is the measure of every constituted objectivity. Man is "his own artist," and his moral acting thus takes on an aesthetic and exemplary mode.

As a matter of fact, Sartre does not take will to be conscious decision any more than Merleau-Ponty or Dufrenne, since in the strict sense this would be to give the act a prior intention. Man's freedom is not to will itself something; it is to exist purely and simply, with no predetermination by any a priori norms handed down by a god or by a social tradition. It is a state of essential indifference, a pure exercise and hence a sheer gratuitous existing. Man's freedom is this very exercise, this pure existing, which is not necessarily reflective. Freedom is lived, it is life. Man is his life, and this is why death seems supremely absurd to him. As such, man is alone, having neither behind nor before him justifications or excuses in the form of values given as such. His only value is himself, his own humanity, which is not that of others. Since he is nothing but a sheer existing, man has no nature in common with others.[17] In other words, he is to himself his own end (which connects with our observations on life and immanent finality). From this it further follows that everything man does is within the immediate dominion of his responsibility; he is fully responsible for his existence. What he is in the course of time, he is by himself. His principal duty—and this is the only "categorical imperative" of Sartrean ethics—is therefore to preserve this sovereign freedom intact, not to let it be contaminated by prejudices or by external circumstances. Only on this condition (which is obviously impossible to realize) can he say that his action is autonomous, that his existence is authentic, that his freedom is objectified or constituted at the very moment when it effectively realizes itself. But this freedom is not exhausted in a single act. Human existence comprises a certain duration. Each act is inscribed in time; it is the result of

17. Nor, consequently, a communicable nature. The human race is condemned, and anti-intellectual practices are philosophically justified. This is exhibited in some of Sartre's novels, such as *The Age of Reason*. The fruition of love and the fecundity peculiar to it obviously destroy the gratuitous character of this particular mode of human action, and they therefore destroy the sovereign freedom of man.

preceding acts and the motivation of subsequent acts. (We are familiar with this relativity, having encountered it in the case of the dialectic of science.) In other words, freedom is an infinite tendency to realize itself, a tendency which is concretized *hic et nunc* and is therefore necessarily partially realized. In this sense, man as a sheer existing needs to exist again and again. He throws himself into the future and unceasingly anticipates; he is a project. This is all the more true because man, having no essence which would dictate the modality of his existence to him a priori, is *condemned* to be free. If he wants to be anything at all, man is condemned to exist and to invent himself unceasingly. Just as the artist is condemned to create if he wants to be an artist, man must exist if he wants to be man. Insofar as he is thrown into the world in which he exists, he is necessarily free. His being is freedom.

Here it will be found that the parallel with phenomenology is no longer warranted. Phenomenology inscribes in development a sort of necessity to realize the idea. Despite certain always possible deviations, this necessity (obscure motivation) does not fail to reach its terminus. But it must be noted that the identification of being and becoming (of form and end) allows us to affirm pure necessity (absolute determinism) and pure freedom (to the point of arbitrariness) as equivalents. In that case there is no need to admit one rather than the other. Without a human nature, it amounts to the same thing to say that human operation is gratuitous or that it is determined; without the freely voluntary and reflected act of the artist, it amounts to the same thing to say that aesthetic creation is the necessary result of aesthetic exigency or that it is the product of chance.[18] Man's freedom is in fact a necessity resulting from the appearance of man in the world. Being "born into the world," which, according to Merleau-Ponty, is the principal characteristic of freedom, is at the same time the most radical negation of freedom. The man who is condemned to be free thereby denies his own freedom, or at least denies that his freedom is absolute. But freedom is or is not; it cannot be relative. Sartre's freedom cannot remain so absolute when in fact it takes derived forms. It will reside, for example, in the subjective attitude I can take with respect to a certain fact which is not under my jurisdiction, a certain fact beyond my power, and it will reside primarily in the attitude I can take toward my "appearing in the world."

18. Dufrenne, p. 35.

Thus we have here, in a general way, a parallel with the motivation of the idea by its realization. Just as each stage of realization of science further determines its end idea and thus tends toward it by anticipating it, so each of man's free acts of existing is a project toward a further existing. The project is thus a free act of existing which anticipates another act of existing. Man subjectively lives his tendency of absolute freedom, concretely limited for the moment by this or that project. From project to project, man exercises his existence and therefore makes his freedom emerge and realizes himself. Man constitutes his essence by exercising his existence. This is the same conclusion we reached in the case of the Husserlian idea, which is constituted by being realized in development. Freedom is nothing apart from commitment in action. It needs to emerge fully in this action. The act of existing is therefore finalized only by freedom itself. Freedom aims only at freedom, and hence it aims at the essence of man as its end. It is a development finalizing and defining itself. Here, too, the form is the end—an immanent end, since existence is life. Freedom is therefore the definition of man; it is his *essence*, an essence which is a *creation* of the exercise of his existence and which is consequently the *end* of this free creation. It is an indeterminacy determining itself; and in this determining, it is seeking only its own fullness, the state in which it will most be itself (*Selbst*). But there is no terminus to this process. Becoming or development which finalizes itself needs to be pursued indefinitely.

Death, then, is the ultimate defeat. The will that seeks itself, the existence that pursues itself, the freedom that projects itself ad infinitum in order to realize itself fully, are radically thwarted by this death—which, being the negation of man, becomes absurdity.[19] Death thus takes its place among the philosophical concerns of our time, manifesting the stoic complexion that existentialism has, over and above its very distinct voluntarism. Death again becomes the enigma of enigmas, and this is a healthy sign in a thought that departs with difficulty from an idealist climate. If love is suppressed by identifying end and form, as it is by idealism in all its forms, then the "limit experience" of death is all that is left to guarantee a philosophical sense of the real and the true—a negative guarantee, but one which is all the more tangible and "absolute" for us.

19. Notice that death, even though it may seem to be an absurdity, saves us from another absurdity, that of infinite becoming—which could not fail to bring despair with it.

Bibliography

[This bibliography differs from that in the original work in the following ways: (1) In part (*a*) I have added in brackets publication data for German editions of Husserl's works which have appeared subsequent to the original publication of the present work. (2) In part (*b*) I have listed English translations of those of Husserl's works to which the author explicitly refers in the text, as well as the French translation of *Ideen I*, which contains extensive translator's footnotes. (3) In parts (*c*) and (*d*) English translations of philosophical works are listed wherever possible rather than the originals or French translations which the author cites.

In addition, I have added a fifth part to the bibliography consisting of a list of publications by Professor de Muralt.—TRANS.]

(*a*) WORKS OF EDMUND HUSSERL

Cartesianische Meditationen. The Hague: Martinus Nijhoff, 1950.

Erfahrung und Urteil. Hamburg: Claassen Verlag, 1954. [A fourth edition of *Erfahrung und Urteil* has been published by Felix Meiner Verlag of Hamburg. This excellent volume, prepared by Ludwig Landgrebe, contains an Afterword by Lothar Eley as well as an index.]

Ideen zu einer reinen Phänomenologie und phänomenologischen Philosophie. Vol. I: *Allgemeine Einführung in die reine Phänomenologie.* The Hague: Martinus Nijhoff, 1950. Vol. II:

Phänomenologische Untersuchungen zur Konstitution. The Hague: Martinus Nijhoff, 1952. Vol. III: *Die Phänomenologie und die Fundamente der Wissenschaften.* The Hague: Martinus Nijhoff, 1952.

Die Krisis der europäischen Wissenschaften und die transzendentale Phänomenologie. The Hague: Martinus Nijhoff, 1954.

Logische Untersuchungen. 2 vols. Fourth edition. Tübingen: Max Niemeyer Verlag, 1928.

Pariser Vorträge. The Hague: Martinus Nijhoff, 1950.

Philosophie der Arithmetik. Halle: C. Pfeffer, 1891. [Also published in the *Husserliana* series. The Hague: Martinus Nijhoff, 1970].

"Philosophie als strenge Wissenschaft." *Logos,* I (1911), 289–341. [Also published in book form, with helpful additional material by Wilhelm Szilasi. Frankfurt am Main: Vittorio Klostermann, 1965.]

(b) TRANSLATIONS OF HUSSERL'S WORKS

Cartesian Meditations: An Introduction to Phenomenology. Translated by Dorion Cairns. The Hague: Martinus Nijhoff, 1960.

The Crisis of European Sciences and Transcendental Phenomenology: An Introduction to Phenomenological Philosophy. Translated, with an Introduction, by David Carr. Evanston, Ill.: Northwestern University Press, 1970.

Experience and Judgment. Translated by James Spencer Churchill and Karl Ameriks, with a Foreword by Ludwig Landgrebe and an Afterword by Lothar Eley. Evanston, Ill.: Northwestern University Press, 1973.

Formal and Transcendental Logic. Translated by Dorion Cairns. The Hague: Martinus Nijhoff, 1969.

Ideas: General Introduction to Pure Phenomenology. Translated by W. R. Boyce Gibson. New York: Humanities Press, 1931.

Idées directrices pour une phénoménologie. Translated by Paul Ricoeur. Paris: Gallimard, 1950.

Logical Investigations. Translated, with an Introduction, by J. N. Findlay, 2 vols. New York: Humanities Press, 1970.

(c) Philosophical Works

Aristotle. *Categories, On Interpretation, Metaphysics.* In *The Basic Works of Aristotle,* edited by Richard McKeon, pp. 3–37, 38–61, 689–926. New York: Random House, 1941.

Descartes, René. *Rules for the Direction of the Mind, Meditations on First Philosophy, The Principles of Philosophy.* In *Philosophical Works of Descartes,* translated by E. S. Haldane and G. R. T. Ross, pp. 1–77, 131–99, 201–302. London: Cambridge University Press, 1911.

Dufrenne, Mikel. *The Phenomenology of Aesthetic Experience.* Translated by Edward S. Casey *et al.* With an Introduction by Edward S. Casey. Evanston, Ill.: Northwestern University Press, 1973.

Heidegger, Martin. *Introduction to Metaphysics.* Translated by Ralph Manheim. New York: Doubleday, 1961.

———. *Kant and the Problem of Metaphysics.* Translated by James S. Churchill. Bloomington: Indiana University Press, 1962.

———. *What Is Called Thinking?* Translated by Fred D. Wieck and J. Glenn Gray. With an Introduction by J. Glenn Gray. New York: Harper & Row, 1968.

———. "What Is Metaphysics?" In *Existence and Being,* edited by Werner Brock, pp. 325–61. Chicago. Henry Regnery, 1949.

Kant, Immanuel. *Critique of Pure Reason.* Translated by Norman Kemp Smith. London: Macmillan, 1929.

Merleau-Ponty, Maurice. *In Praise of Philosophy.* Translated by John Wild and James M. Edie. Evanston, Ill.: Northwestern University Press, 1963.

———. *Phenomenology of Perception.* Translated by Colin Smith. New York: Humanities Press, 1962.

———. *Sense and Non-sense.* Translated, with an Introduction, by Hubert L. Dreyfus and Patricia Allen Dreyfus. Evanston, Ill.: Northwestern University Press, 1964.

Plato. *Parmenides, Sophist, Statesman, Republic.* In *The Collected Dialogues of Plato,* edited by Edith Hamilton and Huntington Cairns, pp. 920–56, 957–1017, 1018–85, 575–844. New York: Random House, 1961.

Sartre, Jean-Paul. *Being and Nothingness: An Essay on Phenomenological Ontology.* Translated, with an Introduction, by Hazel Barnes. New York: Philosophical Library, 1956.

————. *Imagination: A Psychological Critique*. Translated, with an Introduction, by Forrest Williams. Ann Arbor: University of Michigan Press, 1962.

————. *The Psychology of Imagination*. Translated by Bernard Frechtman. London: Rider, 1949.

————. *Situations*, Vol. I. Paris: Gallimard, 1947.

Spinoza, Benedict. *On the Improvement of the Understanding, The Ethics*. In *The Chief Works of Benedict de Spinoza*, translated, with an Introduction, by R. H. M. Elwes, Vol. II, pp. 1–41, 43–271. London: George Bell & Sons, 1883.

(d) Works Consulted: Historical and
Doctrinal Studies and Commentaries

Bachelard, Suzanne. *A Study of Husserl's "Formal and Transcendental Logic."* Translated by Lester E. Embree. Evanston, Ill.: Northwestern University Press, 1968.

Berger, Gaston. *The "Cogito" in Husserl's Philosophy*. Translated by Kathleen McLaughlin. With an Introduction by James M. Edie. Evanston, Ill.: Northwestern University Press, 1972.

————. "Les Thèmes principaux de la phénoménologie de Husserl." *Revue de métaphysique et de morale*, XLIX (1944), 22–43.

Brentano, Franz. *Psychologie vom empirischen Standpunkt*. Leipzig: Duncker & Humblot, 1874.

Brochard, Victor. *Etudes de philosophie ancienne et de philosophie moderne*. Paris: Vrin, 1926.

Brunner, Fernand. *Science et réalité*. Paris: Aubier, 1954.

Fink, Eugen. "The Phenomenological Philosophy of Edmund Husserl and Contemporary Criticism." In *The Phenomenology of Husserl: Selected Critical Readings*, edited, translated, and with an Introduction by R. O. Elveton, pp. 73–147. Chicago: Quadrangle Books, 1970.

————. "Das Problem der Phänomenologie Edmund Husserls." *Revue Internationale de philosophie*, I (1938–39), 226–70.

————. "Vergegenwärtigung und Bild." *Jahrbuch für Philosophie und phänomenologische Forschung*, Vol. XI (1930).

Gilson, Lucie. *Méthode et métaphysique selon Franz Brentano*. Paris: Vrin, 1955.

————. *La Psychologie descriptive selon Franz Brentano*. Paris: Vrin, 1955.

Gurwitsch, Aron. "Philosophical Presuppositions of Logic." In

Aron Gurwitsch, *Studies in Phenomenology and Psychology*, pp. 350–58. Evanston, Ill.: Northwestern University Press, 1966.

Gurvitch, Georges. *Les Tendances actuelles de la philosophie allemande*. Paris: Vrin, 1930.

Laporte, Jean. *Le Problème de l'abstraction*. Paris: Alcan, 1940.

———. *Le Rationalisme de Descartes*. Paris: Presses Universitaires de France, 1950.

Lauer, Quentin. *Phénoménologie de Husserl*. Paris: Presses Universitaires de France, 1955.

Levinas, Emmanuel. *De l'existence à l'existant*. Paris: Fontaine, 1947.

———. *En découvrant l'existence avec Husserl et Heidegger*. Paris: J. Vrin, 1949.

———. *The Theory of Intuition in Husserl's Phenomenology*. Translated by André Orianne. Evanston, Ill.: Northwestern University Press, 1973.

Mieville, Henri-Louis. "Le Cogito dans la phénoménologie de Husserl et le Cogito de Descartes." *Jahrbuch der Schweizerischen Philosophischen Gesellschaft*, I (1941), 1–19.

Ricoeur, Paul. "Husserl and the Sense of History." In Paul Ricoeur, *Husserl: An Analysis of His Phenomenology*. Translated by Edward G. Ballard and Lester E. Embree, pp. 143–74. Evanston, Ill.: Northwestern University Press, 1967.

———. "Husserl's *Ideas II*: Analyses and Problems." In *Husserl: An Analysis of His Phenomenology*, pp. 35–81.

———. *Philosophie de la volonté*. Paris: Aubier, 1949.

Rodier, E. *Etudes de philosophie grecque*. Paris: Vrin, 1926.

Schmalenbach, Hermann. *Geist und Sein*. Basel: Verlag Haus zum Falken, 1939.

Thévenaz, Pierre. *L'Homme et sa raison*. Neuchâtel: La Baconnière, 1957. (Three studies from this work appear in the following collection: *What Is Phenomenology?* Edited, with an Introduction, by James M. Edie. Chicago: Quadrangle Books, 1962.)

———. "La Philosophie sans absolu." *Revue d'histoire et de philosophie religieuses*, 1954, no. 2.

Tran-Duc-Thao. *Phénoménologie et matérialisme dialectique*. Paris: Editions Minh-Tân, 1951.

———. "Les Origines de la réduction phénoménologique." *Deucalion*, Vol. III (1950).

Vaihinger, Hans. *Kommentar zu Kants "Kritik der reinen Vernunft."* 2 vols. 2d ed. Stuttgart: Spemann Verlag, 1922.

————. *Die Philosophie des Als-ob.* Berlin: Reuther & Reichhard, 1911.

Van Breda, Henri, ed. *Problèmes actuels de la phénoménologie.* Brussels: Desclée de Brouwer, 1952.

————. "Réduction et authenticité d'après Husserl." *Revue de métaphysique et de morale,* LVI (1951), 4–5.

Waelhens, Alphonse de. *Une Philosophie de l'ambiguïté: L'Existentialisme de Merleau-Ponty.* Louvain: Publications Universitaires, 1951.

————. "Descartes et la pensée phénoménologique." *Revue néoscolastique de philosophie,* XLI (1938).

————. "Husserl et la phénoménologie." *Critique,* LV (1951), 1044–57.

————. *Phénoménologie et vérité: Evolution de l'idée de vérité chez Husserl et Heidegger.* Paris: Presses Universitaires de France, 1953.

Wahl, Jean. "Note sur la première partie de *Erfahrung und Urteil* de Husserl." *Revue de métaphysique et de morale,* LVI (1951), 6–34.

(e) Publications of André de Muralt

BOOKS

La Conscience transcendantale dans le criticisme kantien: Essai sur l'unité d'aperception. Paris: Aubier, 1958.

L'Idée de la phénoménologie: L'Exemplarisme husserlien. Paris: Presses Universitaires de France, 1958.

Philosophes en Suisse française. Neuchâtel: La Baconnière, 1966.

Die Einheit der heutigen Philosophie. Einsiedeln: Johannes-Verlag, 1966.

ARTICLES

"Logique transcendantale et phénoménologie eidétique." *Studia philosophica,* XVII (1957), 140–49.

"De la participation dans le *Sophiste* de Platon." *Studia philosophica,* XVII (1957), 101–20.

"Les Deux dimensions de l'intentionnalité husserlienne." *Revue de théologie et de philosophie,* VIII (1958), 188–202.

"Les Deux voies de la philosophie aristotélicienne." *Etudes de lettres*, Vol. IV (1958).

"La Solution husserlienne au débat entre le réalisme et l'idéalisme." *Revue philosophique*, CXLIX (1959), 545–52.

"L'Elaboration husserlienne de la notion d'intentionnalité: Esquisse d'une confrontation de la phénoménologie avec ses origines scolastiques." *Revue de théologie et de philosophie*, X (1960), 265–84.

"Adéquation et intentions secondes: Essai de confrontation de la phénoménologie husserlienne et de la philosophie thomiste sur le point du jugement." *Studia philosophica*, XX (1960), 88–114.

"Réalité, conscience, langage." *Studia philosophica*, XX (1960), 132–53.

"Prudence, art, logique: Situation de la logique parmi les activités humaines en perspective aristotélicienne." *Studia philosophica*, XXI (1961), 157–86.

"Parole et tradition." In *Dauer im Wandel*. Munich: Callwey, 1961.

"Le Fondement d'intelligibilité de la logique: Etude critique sur la situation de la logique formelle mathématique par rapport à la psychologie génétique et à la philosophie dans la pensée de J.-B. Grize envisagée comparativement aux conceptions aristotélicienne et moderne de la logique." *Studia philosophica*, XXII (1962), 83–103.

"La Genèse de la métaphysique. La primauté de l'être en perspective aristotélicienne." *Revue de théologie et de philosophie*, Vol. XIII (1963).

"Comment dire l'être? Le Problème de l'être et de ses significations chez Aristote." *Studia philosophica*, XXIII (1963), 109–62.

"Le Sens de la phénoménologie husserlienne." In Spanish translation: *Cuadernos filosoficos*. 1964.

"Die Einheit der gegenwärtigen Philosophie." *Kant-Studien*, Vol. LVII (1965).

"L'Unité de la philosophie contemporaine." Series of articles in *Gazette littéraire de Lausanne*, autumn, 1964.

"Epochē—Malin génie—Théologie de la toute-puissance divine. Le Concept objectif sans objet. Recherche d'une structure de pensée." *Studia philosophica*, XXVI (1966), 159–91.

"Analogie et négation dans la théologie aristotélicienne." In *Le Langage: Actes du 13ᵉ Congrès des sociétés de philosophie de langue française*. Neuchâtel: La Baconnière, 1966.

"Révélation et langage." *La Table Ronde,* no. 250 (1968), 69–82.

"Anarchie: Réflexion sur le radicalisme contemporain." *La Table Ronde,* no. 251/2 (1968–69).

"Signification et portée de la pensée de Jean Duns Scot: Introduction, traduction et commentaire à la distinction 17 de l'Opus oxoniense II." *Studia philosophica,* Vol. XXIX (1969).

"La Théologie de la mort de Dieu." *Gazette de Lausanne,* December 19, 1970.

"Bref tableau de la pensée philosophique et théologique de l'Espagne du XVI⁰ et du XVII⁰ siècle." *Studia philosophica,* XXXIII (1973), 172–84.

Analytical Index

This index has three goals: (1) to define the fundamental concepts of Husserlian phenomenology; (2) to order these concepts in relation to one another, specifically from the exemplarist point of view defended in this work; (3) to indicate the places in this work where they are discussed. Asterisks within an entry mark words or phrases for which there is a pertinent separate entry. The most important discussions of a concept are indicated by italic numerals.

Absolute distinction between sense and object: 17–18, 172–73, 192; assumes two operations of reason,* pure and applied, 57; corresponds to the distinction between the actual and the idea, 57; between reality (*Wirklichkeit*) and quasi-reality (*Wirklichkeit-als-ob*, *Quasi-wirklichkeit*) (*see* Phenomenological fiction), 57; between *Objektivität* and *Gegenständlichkeit*, 121–25; and between being as consciousness (*see* Meaning) and being as thing, 127; grounds the distinction between the logic of consequence* and the logic of noncontradiction,* 171; and neutralization,* 272, 272n

Abstract, the (*Abstrakt*): partial, 63

Act and potency (*energeia, entelecheia; dynamis*): the idea* subsists in two modes, actual and potential, 18; the actual is defined* by the possible, *46;* the actual pre-scribes* and motivates* the possible, 47–48; the dialectic of act and potency is reversed by Husserl, 48–49, 67; the act in the classical sense determines a real finality, the idea* (the Husserlian possible) determines an ideal finality, *49;* intentional analysis* elicits act from potency, 101; the evidence of distinctness* of the judgment is the potency of which the evidence of clarity* is the act, 178; the experience* [*vécu*] passes from potency to act, 290. *See also* Noetic act; Value act and existence act

Adequation (*Adäquation*): is the second (critical) concept of evidence,* *196–97;* possibility of adequation of the judgment, 220–

Character (*Charakter*): character of the judgment* (*see* Quality), 217*n;* positional objective characters of the noema,* 268–69; based on the sense of the noema, 269; originary character, 270; the neutrality* character gives the noema in its pure sense, 271–72; characters of the noesis,* 291–99; belief characters of the noesis (*see* Doxa), 293–94

Claim (*Prätention*): the consciousness of remainder* constitutive of the partial character of the successive stages of the development of science corresponds to a claim, 64–66; the judgment as intended = truth claim, 196

Clarification (*Klärung*): as intentional analysis* of the idea* and criticism of genuineness,* 12–13; as passage from the evidence of distinctness* to the evidence of clarity* of the judgment, *178;* is the operation of constitutive evidence,* 227; clarification of the judgment by reduction* to experience, 230

Clarity of anticipation (*Klarheit der Antizipation*): is evidence* of the idea* as "simulated" possible, 55; is a prefiguration (*Vorverbildlichung**) of the idea, 55; evidence of the anticipated clarity* of the judgment (*see* Evidence of distinctness), 177–78. *See also* Fullness of clarity

Cogitatum: appears as index* of the *cogito** (descriptive-phenomenological point of view), 256, 259; as telos* of the *cogito* (transcendental-phenomenological point of view), 258–59; is the objective pole* of all intentionality,* 259

Cogito, cogitatio: the presently actual *cogito* cannot be grasped immediately, 250, 287, 288; as constitutive and sense-giving act, it guarantees the actuality of intentionality,* 259, 283; = infinite transcendental constitution* (*see* Idea), 283; is the only phenomenological absolute, the life of the ego,* 285, 287, 299–300, 329; performs the intentional function* of the ego and insures transcendental motivation,* 306; = evidence* in general, the theme of eidetic phenomenology,* 321–22; constitutes the ego and the object,* 332–33; constitutes time,* 333

Concrete, the (*Konkret*): total, 63; ideal, 66–67; only intentionality* is concrete, 284–85

Consciousness (*Bewusstsein*): as residuum or transcendental "nothing," 255–56; = actual life of the ego,* 286–87; the unmodified consciousness intentionally includes the modified consciousness, 291–92, 293–94; can only be intentional, 300; its originary form is synthesis* (*see* Evidence), 311; is doubly polarized, 325; is one and infinite: adequation of infinite reason* and infinite truth,* *333;* transcendental self-consciousness is transcendental constitution of the object, 363–64. *See also* Transparency of consciousness

Consciousness of remainder (*Überschuss-, Plus-Bewusstsein*): as constitutive evidence of the independent part,* 63

Consistency (*Konsequenz*): with other judgments is purely analytic (*see* Syllogistics), in the simple judgment is objective noncontradiction, 180–81. *See also* Formal logic of consequence

Constitution. *See* Originary constitution of the ego; Transcendental constitution

Constitution of the alter ego: is implied in the ideation* of the ego* in general, 336–37

Contemplation in Husserl: is without love (without alienation), 264–65; aesthetic contemplation and neutralization,* 273n; is a disinterested viewing (*see* Epochē), 265

Content (*Inhalt, Materie*): distinction between content of the judgment,* judgment as such, and quality,* 216–17, 217n; the content of the judgment is its sense* (*see* Matter), 216; content of the noema* (*see* Sense), 274–78; real and intentional content of the experience* [*vécu*], 299–300

Correlation. *See* Intentional correlation

Counter-sense. *See* Non-sense

Crisis of European Sciences and Transcendental Phenomenology, The: its continuity with *Logical Investigations*, 20; its continuity with *Ideas*, 26n; is in the same phenomenological dimension as *Formal and Transcendental Logic* but studies a particular case, 236–37, 246, 258–59, 356–57, 359; presents a continuous reductive procedure, 256–57

Decidability (*Entscheidbarkeit*): the decidability of the judgment is the ideal anticipation of its effective adequation, 226

Deductive science (*deduktive Wissenschaft*): represents an ideal of analytical truth of pure consequence, 72; and an ideal of perfect homogeneity, 73; explicates the consequences included a priori in the principle, from the point of view of intelligibility, 74–75; nomological* science is defined as deductive science, 98–99; the deductive ideal is not valid for phenomenology, 74n, 75–76

Definite multiplicity (*definite Mannigfaltigkeit*): is determined by a system of mathematical axioms, 71; the development of science defined by the idea* is analogous to a multiplicity defined by an eidetic axiom, 72. *See also* Deductive science

Definition (*Definition*): as determination of the essence, = telos of description,* 45; phenomenology defines by the telos, i.e., by the idea,* 45–46, 345; and defines the actual by the possible, 46–47; is potential with respect to description.* 45–46; the infiniteness of development entails the definiteness of the idea,* 69–70

Demonstrative inference (*Begreiflichmachen durch Schlüsse*): is forcefully rejected by Husserl (*see* Intuition), 83n, 242–43

Derivation (*Abwandlung, Ableitung*): is the mode of subsumption of species under genus,* 147–48

Merleau-Ponty, M., 65n, 126n, 127, 226, 337, 365–72

Method: our method explicates the pure sense of phenomenology by intentional analysis and ends with the idea of phenomenology, 6–8, *357–58*, 363; exemplarist method of phenomenology, 22–28; phenomenological method is twofold, deductive method is univocal, 75–76; phenomenological method remains within development, 350

Modalization (*Modalisierung*): is the mode of "subsumption" of species under a genus,* 147–49

Mode (*Modus*): every mode can become originary (*see* Originary form), *148–49*, 195, 270n, 294–95, 296

Morphology of meanings (*reine Formenlehre der Bedeutungen*): establishes the universal condition of the judgment's unity of sense, *143–44;* admits counter-sense but excludes non-sense,* 142–43, 165; its laws are not genuinely logical, *144–45*, 152, 154; is a pure a priori grammar, 145; determines the originary form of the meaningful judgment and the total system of possible meaningful judgments, 132–33, *143–44*, 146–52; constitutes a definite multiplicity,* 149–50; is surpassed in transcendental logic* by means of the concept of operation, 152; cannot disregard the evidence of distinctness, 165–66

Motivation, motive (*Motivation, Motiv*): = transcendental constitution, evidence,* 310–11; idea* = motive of realization, 16, 42, *316–17;* realization = motive of the idea, 19; sign = motive of the signified, 19; the possible (idea) motivates the actual, *46–47;* theory of truth = motive of realization more than a doctrine, 198; motive of logic = interest in the object (*see* Philosophy), 206; the reduction* is a motivation, 229, 231; is insured by the *cogito*,* 307; has two directions corresponding to the two dimensions* of intentionality, 48–49, 52n, 224–25

Multiplicity. *See* Definite multiplicity

Mutual exemplarity: mutual motivation* of idea and realization, 16, 19; mutual motivation of ideal science and real science, 22; mutual motivation of the idea and the real in general, 23–24, *341–42;* the idea is realized and the real idealized, 25; in Plato* and Husserl, *38–43;* expresses the two dimensions of intentionality, *104;* resolves the infinite regress of the search for the foundation, *110–11;* as originary reciprocity of the two evidences of the judgment, 200; is verified only in an eidetic phenomenology,* *359.* *See also* Two dimensions of intentionality

Nach-verstehen, reflective analysis: is a mode of intentional analysis* in the descriptive-phenomenological dimension, 34n, 161–62; is a second understanding,* fulfillment of the verbal anticipation of the judgment, 159; is the originary mode of judication from the descriptive-phenomenological point of view, 160–62; reflective analysis is the more natural procedure, 161; as intentional analy-

Originary constitution of the ego (*Urkonstitution des Ichs*): by the *cogito*,* *333–36;* = intentional constitution of the object, *334;* is both historical and intentional, 334

Originary form (*ursprüngliche Form, Urform*): there is only one originary form, 146n, 148–49; each modified form is in turn an originary form (*see Processus ad infinitum*), *148,* 195, 270n, 294, 296; subjective originary form is explicated by transcendental logic,* 236; the mode is intentionally included in the originary form, *291–92,* 294

Parallelism (*Parallelismus*): an inadequate expression for intentional correlation,* 286, 291, 307, 327, 329

Part (*Teil*): the part really anticipates the whole, 61; independent part (*Stück*) and dependent part (*Moment*), 62–64; the part is abstract, 63; is concrete, 67

Participation (*Methexis*): in the dialectic* of being and having, 25, *30–32;* is partial possession of idea by fact, 18; entails substitution of definition by an exemplary extrinsic form for definition by an immanent form, *30–31;* constructive participation (normation*), 33, 37; continuity between idea and fact is more complete in Husserl's notion of participation than in Plato's, *37–38*

Perception (*Wahrnehmung*): as experience, is the evidence* proper to logic from the transcendental-phenomenological point of view, 117–18; as infinite noesis, 287–90; as actual and originary noesis of the ego,* *291–92;* is the only presentation, 292; intentionally includes its modes, 292; is the originary positing (*Setzung*) on the part of consciousness, 297; is the only experience* whose hylē* is itself noesis,* 298; is originary evidence of the empirical object, 308, *313, 321–23;* as originary mode of consciousness (*see Idea*), 295, 313–14; privilege of perception, *313–14;* distinction between immanent and transcendent perception, *317–18*

Phenomenological fiction (*phänomenologische Fiktion*), the "as if" (*Als-ob*): intentional analysis* takes the mode of the "as if" (*Als-ob*) from the descriptive-phenomenological point of view, 54–56; idea = "as if" reality, 54; idea = imaginary (fictional) irreality (*see* Imagination), 55; idea = quasi-reality, 57; fiction is not arbitrary (*see* Possible), 58; makes possible a practical equivalence* between the partial realization of the idea and the idea itself, *58–60;* in neutralization,* 273

Phenomenology (*Phänomenologie*): is structured by the two dimensions of intentionality, 5; is constituted in the idea of science in general, 342; begins with a study of language,* 20; crux of phenomenology: idea* = function* of unity, i.e., pre-scribing norm,* 26–27, 38, 23–24; phenomenology is the end idea and infinite task of scientific development in general, 28; is at the beginning of beginnings, 28, 249–50; as philosophy of participation,* is a philosophy of having, 31; is a Platonism reduced to its pure sense, 41–43, 104; cannot be a deductive science,* 73–76, 74n; is meant to be simply an intuition of essences, 76; must therefore be eidetic, 76; is the only subjective science of the subjective (by contrast with psychology*), 96, 248; is the telos of prior transcendental philosophies and of the logical interest of the ancient philosophers, *101;* as phenomenology of science, is also phenomenology of logic, 102–5; is first philosophy, since it is constitutive phenomenology of being, 107–8; is synthetically normative, 286; is a concrete logic, 112; is self-normative (*Selbstnormierung*), 109, 334–35, *354, 363;* phenomenology of the object = phenomenology of the ego,* *334–36;* is a revival of the problem of the one* and the many, *341*

Phenomenology of reason, eidetic phenomenology: its object is evidence,* value, lawfulness* of every objectivity,* *308;* eidetic phenomenology culminates in the phenomenology of reason,* of ideal and exemplary consciousness, *319;* = phenomenology of evidence in general, *321;* = transcendental logic,* *335;* eidetic phenomenology: science of the form of all constitution = transcendental logic, 323–24, 351–55; is evident, rational, and necessary, *356;* as phenomenology of the ego* = phenomenology in general, *334–35*

Phenomenon. *See* Transcendental phenomenon

Philosophy: for Husserl, philosophy is at once logical, critical, and constitutive, *104, 106–7;* phenomenology is philosophy insofar as it platonizes, *104;* logic becomes a transcendental philosophy of being, *106;* the interest in the object is philosophical, *184;* philosophy *von oben her:* a priori dogmatism, 82–83

Plato, 24n, 68n, 79, 121n, 224n, 346; nonbeing in Plato = being other, 18–19; Husserlian Platonism, 35–43; Husserlian Platonism makes it possible to disprove psychologistic empiricism* and to affirm the theory of transcendental constitution,* 41–43; Husserl intentionally realizes Plato's logical ideal, 92–93

Point of view (*Standpunkt*): two senses of this notion, 251–52; the *Lebenswelt* gets beyond every point of view, 249

Pole (*Pol*): object pole and subject pole, 325

Positionality, positing (*Positionalität, Setzung*): the idea as anticipated possible is quasi-positional (*see* Phenomenological fiction), 55–56; the meaning* has a positional evidence, 195; positing = originary doxa,* 296

Possible experience (*mögliche Erfahrung*): intentional analysis* of the potential idea* implied in the actual remains within possible experience, 25

Potency. *See* Act and potency

Potential, possible (*potential, möglich*): the possible defines the actual, 46; motivated possibility and empty possibility, 47–49; the possible = the idea,* 48; the possible idea motivated by the real, 56–58; formal logic = possible science, 98

(*quomodo*) of the object, 282–83, *308;* the subjective "how" is the appearing* of the object, 285

Real and ideal (fact and eidos): the real and the ideal are mutually implied, 18; the dialectic of fact and eidos epitomizes the two pairs of points of view formulated in the present work: transcendental- and descriptive-phenomenological, and value-act and existence-act, *52–53*

Realism and idealism: phenomenology gets beyond this antithesis by the doctrine of meaning,* *119–20, 123;* by the notion of the idea,* *360–64;* phenomenology is able to do this because the two dimensions* of intentionality are identified, *363;* getting beyond this antithesis in ethics (Merleau-Ponty*), *365–69;* in aesthetics (Dufrenne*), *366–69;* in Sartre's thought, *369–73*

Reason, rationality (*Vernunft, Vernünftlichkeit, Rationalität*): is the ideal thematization of intentionality,* 8; the world is intentionally rational in its totality, 240, 245–46; rationality is a character of the noesis* resulting from fulfillment of the intention, 310; for each object there is a possible reason, *315, 342;* rational consciousness = exemplary idea, infinitely realizable intentional norm, *316;* rational consciousness = infinite transcendental constitution thematized as idea,* 354; rational consciousness = idea of intentionality, *319–20;* rational consciousness = subjective form of the object = ego,* *332;* reason is thematized by eidetic phenomenology,* *319*

Recollection. *See* Memory

Reduction (*Reduktion*): distinction between phenomenological reduction (= epochē*) and transcendental reduction (intentional analysis*), *235;* the transcendental reduction is the consequence of the epochē,* 251; the phenomenological reduction is carried out by language,* *128;* the transcendental reduction of the judgment to experience,* *229–35;* = clarification* or motivation,* 230, 231, 246; = sense-giving, 246; the reduction follows a course the reverse of formalization,* *140, 230;* is a process of radicalization, 232, 252; = a turning to nonpredicative evidence, 233; reduction of objective science to the *Lebenswelt*,* *244–46;* the reduction is intentional analysis (descriptive-phenomenological point of view), 254; has two modes corresponding to the two dimensions* of intentionality, *254–59;* in *Crisis*,* proceeds from *cogitatum** to ego,* 259; is one and universal, 260; has an eidetic value, 262n; its first stage, *259–80;* its second stage, *280–324;* its third stage, *324–37;* the reduction is completed with the phenomenology of the ego,* *335–36*

Reflective awareness (*prise de conscience, Besinnung*): = clarification,* *12–13;* = criticism of genuineness, 13; *Besinnung = Sinngebung, 363*

Richtung: a descriptive word for intentionality, *12n*

Ricoeur, P., 55, 256n, 269n